The Triumph the Country

To the memory of
my mother and father

The Triumph of the Country

The Rural Community in Nineteenth-century Jersey

By

John D. Kelleher

in association with

Société Jersiaise

British Library Cataloguing-in-Publication Data.

A catalogue record for this book is available from the British Library.

First published in Great Britain in 1994

ISBN 0-9518162-4-1

Published in Jersey, Channel Islands, by

J.A.B. Publishing

Les Ormes

Ville Au Bas

St Ouen

Jersey C.I.

in association with

Société Jersiaise

Contents

Maps and Figures

Acknowledgements

In a study of this size, many debts are incurred. I have received a great deal of help and support from a large number of people and I would like to take this opportunity to thank them all.

My principal academic debt it to my supervisor, Dr Robin Okey, of the History Department at the University of Warwick. I owe him thanks for his patience, advice, criticism and, most of all, his belief in the project. Without his dedication, researching and writing this work would have been a much less rewarding experience. I also wish to thank Dr Bernard Capp for his advice at certain critical stages during the writing up of this work.

Financially I received support from many quarters. Many individuals and institutions put their faith in me and I hope I have borne that out. I would like to thank: Robert Parker, G.P.E Howard, Dr H. Thurston, Richard Falle, Cath and Graham Vint, the De Lancey and De La Hanty Foundation, the Tison Trust, the W.O. Street Charitable Trust and A.P. Langlois and Sons.

For the people who gave me physical support, I reserve a special thanks. Such support ranged from helping to transcribe census data from various microfilm archives to searching through obscure periodicals, following up a lead. I would particularly like to thank Cathy Kelleher, Chris Kelleher, Anne Machon, Nick Le Cornu, Philip Stevens and Ian Monins in this regard. Cathy deserves a special thanks for her help at the printing stage.

John Kelleher

St. Helier

Jersey

November 1994

PRINTED IN GUERNSEY BY NORPRINT 1990 LTD.

Foreword

When the Board of Governors of the *The De Lancey & De La Hanty Foundation Limited* decided financially to enable Mr. Kelleher to start a comprehensive research into the history of the rural community of Jersey, they had in mind a study accessible to all those who are interested in the history and culture of the island.

I think it appropriate to remember the benefactor of the Foundation, the late Baron Cornelius Ver Heyden de Lancey, a man with an extraordinarily strong personality and vision, whose life was as eventful as it was active. During his life he was accomplished in at least five professions, learned to speak four foreign languages and collected a formidable knowledge and experience in art and history.

He was born in the Netherlands on 18 July 1889 as the eldest son of a Dutch general practitioner, but left the Netherlands after he finished High School. De Lancey then went to the United States to study dentistry and subsequently left for the United Kingdom where he practised as a dentist. During the First World War he earned a reputation as a skilful jaw surgeon in a London Hospital where he treated soldiers who had been inflicted with jaw injuries on the battlefield. However, while still a dentist he utilised his considerable energy by studying medicine and law, qualifying in both.

When the war was over, and he had acquired British citizenship, he left England to take over two dental practices, in Rome and Florence, where he stayed for about ten years. During this time he learned to speak Italian, enjoyed Italian art and even worked as an art critic.

De Lancey subsequently went to Monaco where he worked on publications in the fields of art and genealogy. It was in this period of his life he obtained a precious collection of historical documents, particularly out of the Napoleonic era, and acquired a profound knowledge of the history and background of French noble families.

After he returned to the United Kingdom, shortly before the outbreak of the Second World War, he was appointed a member of a team charged with preparing convalescent centres in the Channel Islands for wounded military personnel. Thus he made acquaintance with Jersey, where he stayed on as a doctor after the dramatic events of the Spring of 1940 when German occupation of the Channel Islands began and he shared the fate of the Jersey people.

After the war he became an Advocate of the Royal Court, worked as a dentist and also aquired a fortune through skillful dealing on the Stock Exchange. He decided to spend his wealth not for his own pleasure but on the promotion of art, academic teaching and research by means of subsidies, scholarships and awards. To make this possible he established *The De Lancey & De La Hanty Foundation Limited* in December 1970.

He died at the age of 95, on his birthday, leaving a widow, who died in September, 1993 at the age of 104, being the oldest resident of Jersey.

He was attached to Jersey and would have applauded the contribution by a young Jersey advocate to the spreading of knowledge about this prosperous and beautiful island where de Lancey spent the happiest years of his long and eventful life.

Few people are aware of Jersey's rural background or its long and fascinating history. Mr Kelleher's interesting description of an important aspect of Jersey's social past is a substantial contribution to the knowledge of the island and merits a vast circle of readers. The Governors of the Foundation are glad this publication has been made possible through the cooperation of the *Société Jersiaise* and the mediation of Mr John Appleby, who is a member of the Société and a governor of the *De Lancey & De La Hanty Foundation Limited.*

R.P.H. Ritter

Chairman

The De Lancey & De La Hanty

Foundation Limited.

November 1994

Preface

This study is in many ways a pioneering work as the range and sources uncovered and the facilitation of access to them will prove a useful precedent for the study of nineteenth-century Jersey. The modern history of Jersey has received relatively little serious academic attention, particularly in the social and political spheres. Balleine's *History of Jersey*, the only substantial general text on the Island's past, reflects this state of affairs in its two chapter treatment of the nineteenth century as opposed to the six chapters on the English Civil War. One aim of the present work it to go some way to restoring the balance.

The choice of subject for this book was determined by several factors. Preliminary research confirmed the impression that the nineteenth century stood out from previous centuries as a period of momentous change. Here were the various elements - economic expansion, immigration, anglicisation - which together provided much of the foundation to modern Jersey. The period offered to provide an explanation of how and why a previously little-known Island, with a small population who were French in all but political affiliation, was opened up to large-scale immigration and developments which transformed it into a bustling trading enterprise of English speakers. Given the potential of the period to elucidate these changes, the choice of the rural community as the viewpoint from which to assess their impact appeared logical. Where better to assess the impact of change on local life and institutions than through the experiences of the traditional country folk?

The study of Jersey history creates certain problems for the historian. Jersey has no public record office. Historical sources are scattered amongst a large number of collections, ranging from those held in States' departments to those belonging to private individuals. The one central location of any size is the Société Jersiaise, a private society established in 1873 which has become the repository for a large amount of important material. Generally speaking, however, and this includes the Société, the holders of sources are unprepared for the intrusion of the historian. Access, more often than not, requires a series of letters, references and special arrangements. On site, one is faced with material which is not indexed and often kept without care. On the latter point, reference must be made to the Methodist archive where the careless treatment of material has resulted in a great loss to local heritage.

That said, the process of discovery is its own reward and the research for this work has proved most fruitful. The study centres on the nineteenth century in a broad way as much of the historical landscape for this period was uncharted. The importance of the newspapers cannot be over-stressed. It is the newspapers which enabled a framework of study to evolve, pinpointed crucial happenings and led to a host of further sources. Jersey's first newspaper, *Le Magasin de L'ile*, was established in 1784. During the course of the nineteenth century the Island was home to a total of at least 17 newspapers, although the majority were shortlived. Research concentrated on the papers which were representative of the two main elements in Jersey society in the period. The *British Press* (established 1822, but not available until 1832) and the *Jersey Times* (established 1832) and their amalgamated form - *British Press and Jersey Times*. From 1848, the paper spoke for the main body of English immigrants and urban interests generally. Among the French language papers, partisan and thoroughly representative of native, above all, rural interests was the *Chronique de Jersey* (1814-1929) and to a lesser extent, the *Constitutionnel* were widely used, particularly because of their affiliations to local party politics.

It is worthwhile making a brief historiographical note, enabling the contribution of this work to be placed in context. The study of Jersey history has received much local attention, but far less academic study. Local study has stemmed from two sources, the longer tradition of interest in the Island because of its unique combination of Norman laws, traditions and religion with loyalty to the English Crown and the more recent works which result from the establishment of the Société Jersiaise in 1873 and the linking of local study with the need to establish a Jersey identity.

The starting point for study of the Island must be in the seventeenth century with the completion of three works on the Island: Jean Poingdestre, *Caesarea or a Discourse on the Island of Jersey* (not officially published until 1889); Philippe Dumaresq, *A Survey of the Island of Jersey* (London 1685); and Philippe Falle, *An Account of the Island of Jersey* (London 1694). Falle's was by far the most comprehensive work but he acknowledged that he took from the two studies. All three were essentially contemporary accounts with some historical basis, and provide important material on, among other things, enclosure. All three authors were leading members of the small local intelligentsia and their works were written in English.

Falle revealed his purposes for compiling the work as the need to inform England of Jersey's existence: "We were as great strangers as if these Islands had been by some degrees beyond the line. Then it was that honest zeal for my country suggested the thought of doing something that might remove prejudice and rectify misapprehensions" (*An Account*). That which all three works revealed historically was simplistic but reflected how members of the Royal Court and the States were aware of the Royal Charters and Papal Bulls of Neutrality which defined Jersey's identity and allegiance.

The latter point was taken up by the works of Philippe Le Geyt (1635-1716) the great legal historian of Jersey, whose *Privilèges, Lois et Coutumes de l'Ile de Jersey et Règlements*

Politiques is greatly respected to this day. Ironically, the next substantial works on constitutional history came from the pen of the most renowned and locally disliked political agitator, A.J. Le Cras. All his works for instance, *The Origin and Power of the States* (Jersey 1855), *Jersey, its Constitution and Laws* (1858) took a decided political stance, aimed at proving that Jersey's right to govern itself was based on fraud and usurpation. If his intentions were suspect, his industriousness and output were prolific and his scholarship was often overshadowed by his personality and journalistic style, something which no doubt resulted in an avoidance of his work.

By the nineteenth century the contemporary account, with brief concession to any serious history, became commonplace as writers flocked to an Island which was clearly arousing interest abroad, particularly on the English mainland. The better works in this mould derived from those Englishmen who spent some considerable time in the Island, notably H.D. Inglis, *The Channel Islands* (London 1834) and Ansted and Latham's, *The Channel Islands* (London 1862). A host of travel writers devoted much paper, but little thought, to the Island. The economic theorists who visited Jersey, and we shall come across them in the text, were concerned essentially with matters of land tenure and peasant prosperity, again a purpose more contemporary than historic.

The establishment of the Société Jersiaise in 1873 with the stated aim of studying the language, institutions and history of the Island resulted in a large collection of local documents and an annual periodical which to this day remains the only major historical forum on Jersey's past. Articles range from a small number of academic treatments of particular issues to more localised studies of particular buildings, phenomenon and genealogy.

Jersey has received its most serious academic attention this century. The early medieval scholar John Le Patourel, himself a Guernseyman, extended his studies to include major research on the Channel Islands, particularly in his, *The Medieval Administration of the Channel Islands 1199-1399* (London 1937). A.J. Eagleston's, *The Channel Islands Under Tudor Government* 1485-1642 (Cambridge 1949) gave the Tudor period in the Islands its first and, as yet, only treatment. This was followed by G.F.B. de Gruchy's more specific *Medieval Land Tenures in Jersey* (Jersey 1957), a work subsequently criticised on matters of detail, but still most informative.

In the last two decades more modern history has received its first academic treatment with two doctoral theses and a States sponsored maritime project. R.G. Le Herissier's thesis, published as *The Development of the Government of Jersey 1771-1972* (Jersey 1974), is essentially a legislative study of Jersey's move to an ever greater degree of independence and political development. R.E. Ommer's thesis, 'From Outpost to Outport: the Jersey Merchant

Triangle in the Nineteenth Century' (McGill University 1979) studies the great Jersey merchant houses at the codfisheries of Newfoundland. This had been recently augmented by, A.G. Jamieson (Ed.), *A People of the Sea: The Maritime History of the Channel Islands* (London 1986), a large scale overview of Channel Islanders and their relationship with the sea.

The 'Rural Community in Nineteenth-century Jersey' takes its place in the historiographical framework as outlined above. It is hoped that these few pages provide a useful, if general, preface to that which follows.

Section 1

The Roots of Nineteenth-century Jersey

Chapter 1

Institutions and Settlement

The Channel Islands are situated in what might be called the Western English Channel, sometimes referred to as the St.Malo bight (see Figure 1.). To the north lies the South-west peninsula of England, over eighty miles away from Alderney, the most northern Isle. To the south and east lie Brittany and the western part of Normandy, at its closest only fifteen miles away from Jersey. They are Islands as a result of the Hercynian mountain building period, which in a united Armorica also created the hills of Brittany and the now eroded moors of Devon and Cornwall.

Armorica sprawled across the Southern Channel and is responsible for similarities still evident today, ranging from geology to ancient dialect, from landscape to defiant regional independence. For the now physically separated Channel Islands the shared geological past has helped shape a situation expressed on many levels, whereby they combine social, cultural, religious and traditional elements from both sides of the Channel.

Jersey is the most southerly Island in the group, comprising an area of forty-five square miles. The total land mass of the Islands is only seventy-five square miles. Despite this the Islands have always held large populations, the present Jersey population being just over eighty-four thousand (1991), compared with fifty thousand in 1851. Jersey slopes south-wards and in general terms is composed of a large area of plateau in the north and north west, open sand dunes in the west and gently sloping lowlands in the south and south-east. The major valleys slope from north to south and effectively dissect the Island, making movement in an easterly or westerly direction difficult and slow unless by the northern plateau. The land reaches a height of 450 feet in only a few places. The soil is generally fertile, though deficient in lime and phosphorous. Rainfall is well distributed throughout the year. The more southerly clime and the nature of the relief results in a climate generally more moderate and more equitable than that of southern England. [1]

The Political Relationship with England

"Jersey is neither a colony nor a conquest, but a peculiar and immediate dependency of the Crown". [2] So wrote Joshua Le Bailli in 1860, on behalf of the Jersey Chamber of Commerce, in one of the Island's many representations to the English Crown. It is a most succinct description of the relationship between the United Kingdom and the Channel Islands in which is summated the whole Channel Island experience since the eleventh century.

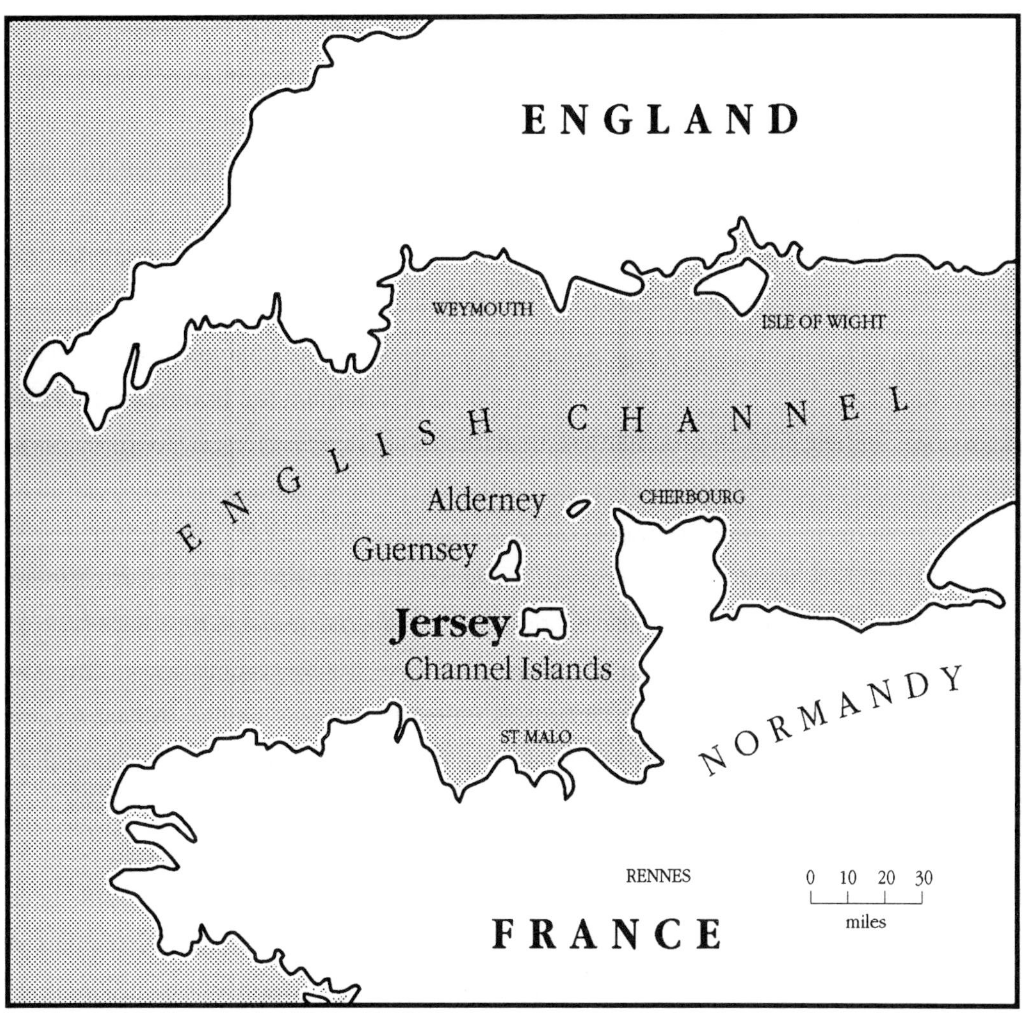

FIGURE 1. *Jersey and the Channel Islands in relation to England and France*

In 933 the Channel Islands were annexed to Normandy and became a part of the Duchy of Normandy. In 1066 William, Duke of Normandy, was crowned King of England and initiated the combined rôle of sovereign of England and Duke of Normandy which survives to this day in the present monarch of England. In 1204 the English Crown lost all its lands in Normandy, with the exception of the Channel Islands. These off-shore remnants of once held Norman lands were not integrated into England. Instead, on account of their loyalty and usefulness to the English Crown, the Islands developed a special relationship with their feudal duke, which at its fullest was and still is tantamount to semi-independence.

As a result of the separation of 1204 the Channel Islands found themselves in a rather anomalous position. Their strategic significance, as English outposts lying just off the French coast in what was to prove over six centuries of Anglo-French hostilities, lasting until the beginning of the nineteenth century, enabled a degree of autonomy and independence which such small entities could never otherwise have envisaged. Retention of loyalty was a major objective for successive English monarchs and in return the Islands were granted certain immunities and liberties. These privileges enabled the Islands to continue and develop as the Norman Isles that had entered history under William, preserving their language, their law and their ecclesiastical organisation. It also enabled them to develop the institutions of self-government. [3]

Parliament has never been the constitutional link between the Channel Islands and the United Kingdom. That link has always been channelled through the Sovereign. In 1765, Blackstone defined the position in his Commentaries: "The Islands of Jersey, Guernsey, Sark, Alderney and their appendages, were parcel of the Duchy of Normandy and were united to the Crown of England by the first princes of the Norman line. They are governed by their own laws, which are for the most part the ducal customs of Normandy, being collected in an ancient book of very great authority entitled *Le Grand Coustumier.* The King's writ or process from the courts of Westminster is there of no force, but his commission is. They are not bound by common Acts of our Parliament unless particularly named. All causes are originally determined by their own Officers, the Bailiff and Jurats of the Islands, but an appeal lies from them to the King in Council, in the last resort". [4]

The monarchical link, as opposed to the parliamentary link, was crucial to a political development which was basically independent from that of the English state and the later United Kingdom. In the medieval period it was quite natural that the English government should treat the Islands as a possession of the King, separate and distinct from his kingdom of England. The subsequent development of the Channel Islands has been in the context of this relationship. [5] Even when, in the nineteenth century, certain spheres at Westminster began to view the Islands as parasitic and as a burden, the relationship with the Crown remained paramount and provided a significant check on parliamentary attempts to intervene.

Up until the nineteenth century Jersey, and the Channel Islands in general, exploited their constitutional position without much opposition from the United Kingdom. In effect this position enabled freedom from the harsher aspects of Westminster legislation alongside inclusion in the metropole's more favourable economic policies, notably those that were protectionist.

From the United Kingdom's point of view the Channel Islands were also there to be exploited in a strategic sense. Yet, this exploitation was for the most part passive, in that the Islands were defended as potentially useful Crown possessions, as opposed to being used as springboards for aggressive action. In the thirteenth century, they had proved valuable as a legal basis to argue for the return of the rest of the French lands, as well as a conveniently sited port for ships transporting wine from Gascony. [6] By the French Wars the Islands were again proving themselves advantageous with their fleet of Privateers, whilst Jersey was the control point for the British spy network in revolutionary France. [7]

Command of the sea around the Islands was the key to both defence and attack for the English and French alike. Once England finally secured that command, in the wake of the defeat of France in 1815, the Channel Islands ceased to be of major strategic importance. With the exception of a French naval build-up in the 1830s and 1840s, and the corresponding response of the English with a further fortifying of the Islands, centuries of Anglo-French animosity were coming to an end. After the Franco/Prussian conflict of 1870/1 British maritime strategy shifted its emphasis away from the Channel to the North Sea, and the strategic significance of the Channel Islands was virtually at an end. [8]

This decline in strategic significance was of fundamental importance to the Channel Islands. In the wake of the Napoleonic Wars Britain needed to reduce its forces and keep down defence spending. The cost of defending the Channel Islands in wartime was £500,000 per annum, but, because of their isolated position, was equally high in peacetime. As the free trader J.R. McCulloch pointed out, in 1837,"the advantages derived from their possession seem neither very obvious nor very material". [9] Nonetheless, the Islands had allies too. R. Montgomery Martin, writing in 1835, pointed out how the Channel Islands' "attachment to England ...deserves the marked gratitude of all who desire the perpetuity of our Islandic Empire". [10] The Duke of Wellington provided the greatest accolade for the Islands in his 1845 *Memorandum on the Defence of the United Kingdom*, a pamphlet which extolled their value as strategic locations populated with loyal subjects. [11]

The evolution of a constitutional monarchy brought further problems for the Channel Islands. As Crown property the Islands were originally outside the ambit of Parliamentary control. In its capacity as feudal lord the Crown administered the affairs of the Islands via Orders in Council. All local legislation had to be ratified by the Crown, acting through the Privy Council. Parliamentary legislation applicable to Jersey used the same medium and had for centuries been forwarded to the local authorities only after due registration in the form of Orders in Council. This was the accepted procedure and Parliament's involvement in the process suggests a degree of agreement on its part. By the nineteenth century such a Crown-based relationship appeared something of an anomaly within the British Parliamentary system. To argue that sovereignty remained vested solely in the Crown totally ignored the shift of power that had occurred from Monarch to Parliament prior to this period. [12]

By the beginning of the nineteenth century Jersey had achieved a high degree of self-government. The Crown was still effectively in control, but delegation enabled the local legislature, the States (Les États), to exercise a greater share of power in initiating legislation and finance, subject to final ratification.

The States were composed of both elected members and Crown appointees. Each parish was represented by its municipal head, the Connétable, who combined his rôle of parish administrator with membership of the legislature. Twelve Jurats or 'popular law finders' were elected for life on an Island-wide franchise and sat both in the Royal Court and the States; they were to be the target for most criticism by reformist groups during the period covered by this book. The Island's Rectors, appointed by the Crown, likewise sat in the legislature. The Bailiff, the chief magistrate and effective civil head of the Island, also a Crown appointee, presided over the States.

It is not proposed to deal here with the development of government separately in the nineteenth century, because this was closely tied in with the response of Jersey to the various internal and external pressures that the Island faced during this period. It is relevant, however, to note that Jersey's powers of government had evolved within a process of extracting privileges from the Crown. The constitution was essentially a home-made one. Local efforts were exerted in preserving and developing the Island's independence and advantages. Not surprisingly, the Islands viewed the relationship with the Crown in self-interested fashion, yet loyalty to the Crown was never in question. In nineteenth-century Jersey there was always a fine balance between deference to the sovereignty of the Crown and attachment to local independence and self-government.

The Influence of Feudalism

The fief was of fundamental importance to the internal structure of Jersey. Along with the parish, in both its civil and ecclesiastical mould, the fief provided the basic framework for rural life. Fief and parish were the major units of cohesion and identity in a society whose inherent dislike for centralisation could be observed in its dispersed settlement pattern.

Of the two structures, more is known about the origins of the fiefs but, even then, little is certain prior to the twelfth century. The earliest documents available show Jersey as thoroughly feudalised, with the majority of the population being tenants holding land from seigneurs in five whole parishes and the best part of the remaining seven. [13] Among the earliest of documents available on the Channel Islands is one dated between 1022 and 1027 showing Duke Robert of Normandy (1027-35), and possibly his predecessor, in direct possession of a large part of Jersey. The Church too had extensive rights in the Channel Islands. Although the area would have been relatively unimportant to the Duchy of

Normandy it was clearly exploited and Island land included among the rewards given by the Duke to his military aristocracy. Thus the fief of St Ouen, the largest and most important in Jersey, was at some time prior to 1135 given to the de Carteret family who held extensive lands in Carteret, and who, after King John's loss of Normandy in 1204, decided to settle in Jersey. [14]

Between the twelfth and twentieth centuries 245 fiefs are said to have existed in Jersey, though not all simultaneously. In size they ranged from the minute, such as the Fief de Burrier in St Martin, to the largest, that of St Ouen. The Church lands were confiscated by the Crown during the Reformation and much of them rented out on perpetual leases. By the nineteenth century, residual feudal powers covered the whole Island to varying degrees. It is difficult to ascertain the exact number of operative fiefs at this period, but judging by the records of the larger fiefs such as Samarès, St Ouen and Rozel, all of which had swallowed up a host of smaller fiefs, and the continued existence of the office of Crown Receiver, the Island remained thoroughly feudalised in its pattern of land tenure. [15]

Jersey's feudal experience began with Normandy's and remained remarkably similar to it. This is not surprising in an Island which was typically Norman in its customary law, institutions, language and traditions. Yet, even prior to King John, there were many variations, no doubt facilitated by the Island's physical separation and relative insignificance and accentuated by its isolation after 1204. The dues, services and rents owed in Jersey were extensive, in some cases onerous, but no one fief included them all and many included only a few. Serfdom was unknown in the twelfth and thirteenth centuries and there is nothing to suggest an earlier existence. Compared with Normandy the conditions of tenure endured by the peasantry were favourable, rents as opposed to services being the important part of the feudal relationship. [16]

The Jersey peasantry appear to have preserved a degree of freedom lost elsewhere. The reasons for this have not been examined by local historians but probably lie in the relative insignificance of the Island in the Duchy and its isolation after 1204. However, if these factors lay behind a comparatively tolerable feudalism they also ensured its continued existence well into the nineteenth century. Whilst certain aspects of the feudal relationship proved onerous enough to result in isolated outbursts against it, the whole system does not appear to have been so oppressive as to have resulted in a united effort by the peasantry to overthrow it.

Historically, certain aspects of the feudal relationship aroused tenant reaction. The demanding of what were considered onerous or unreasonable dues or services, notably those to do with inheritance and change of ownership, like the 'année de succession' and 'aveux', resulted in opposition. In the sixteenth and seventeenth centuries, for instance, the seigneurs of the three major fiefs (St. Ouen, Rozel and Samarès) made what the tenants considered unfounded claims for labour services on land and were successfully thwarted.[17]

Seigneurialism, and we use the term in Cobban's sense to denote a commercialised form of the original feudal relationship, was in 1800 still very much a reality for the Jersey population. [18] Whilst many of the rents and dues owed had decreased in relative value because of inflation, many tenants still had to part with a share of their produce and income. The 'champart' (the seigneur's right to every twelfth sheaf of corn or bundle of flax remained, although the advent of new crops such as the potato lessened the burden, because they were not liable. A variety of tithes were still owed to the seigneur, the parish clergyman and the Crown. Payment in kind was still common. The Fief de la Fosse in St Helier, for instance, had seigneurial dues of 32 capons, 24 hens, 112 eggs, six poulets, five crowns, two chicks, two geese, three 'mailles' (copper coins) and six quarters of vraic ash still owed upon it as late as 1868. [19] 'Aveu', a statement as to the extent of land held by each tenant, was demanded almost universally and generally linked to a change of seigneur. The Fief de Nobretez in St Peter held court sittings specifically for the making of aveux twenty-five times between 1748 and 1792. [20]

Feudal courts were sitting regularly in the eighteenth century to administer the affairs and crises of their own domains. Since they had little real power, recourse to the Royal Court, the supreme judicial body in the Island, was often necessary. The offences were often trivial infringements such as misuse of the commune and default in the payment of rents and fines. Tenants themselves continued to bring cases against both the seigneur and other tenants. Of eleven sittings of the court of the Fief de Nobretez between 1748 and 1801, that is sittings not specifically for the making of aveux, two concerned tenant complaints about other tenants, five were actions by the seigneur for infringements and four his claiming of certain rights, such as the use of the property of two tenants who were 'en décret' or bankrupt. [21]

The seventeenth and eighteenth centuries, as yet little studied by historians, may hold some keys to the nineteenth century attitude to the feudal burden. In the 1730s, sporadic violence against the collectors of Crown tithes, particularly in St Ouen, St Brelade and Trinity, and a march on the Town of St Helier showed how potent an issue seigneurial rights were throughout the Island. The popular nature of the outbursts was reflected in the refusal by a majority of the Jurats to punish those responsible and resulted in a severe warning from the Privy Council. [22] What was sporadic in the 1730s became an organised revolt in 1769, culminating in the temporary seizure of the Royal Court by an angry mob and the demand for reform. The outburst was centred on a political feud between the Royal Court and the States, a dispute resolved to some extent by the Code of 1771: the Crown's attempt to separate the judiciary from the legislature. [23] Personal animosity between the Island's leading statesmen and a popular dislike for what was felt to be a dictatorship by the Bailiff, Charles Lemprière, provided the long term causes, but the spark came from an urban reaction to a corn shortage. The whole affair acquired an overtly anti-seigneurial character. [24]

The Jurat and diarist, Daniel Messervy, numbered the rioters of 1769 as at least 300. They were composed mainly of artisans and labourers, and came from all over the Island. The riot was organised, although the only conspirator to step out of the shadows was Thomas Gruchy, a moderately well-off farmer, Captain in the Jersey Militia and churchwarden of his parish. Gruchy's status suggests that this outburst was no revolt of the masses, rather a calculated attack on Royal Court dominance. This aim was reflected in a successful Island-wide petition to the Privy Council, which demanded an investigation into local grievances. [25]

Some limited reform was achieved at the Crown's instigation. This included a prohibition on the farming-out of Crown revenues, which at least ensured a more uniform and fair collection of tithes, and a codification of local law. The more radical demands for an end to seigneurial rights, particularly the champart and the année de succession (the seigneur's right to the property of a tenant dying without lineal heirs), were ignored. The issue became lost in the general state of emergency that resulted from the threat of French hostilities and the invasion of Jersey in 1781 by a French force led by Baron de Rullecourt. [26] Anti-seigneurial attitudes remained, and on the eve of the French Revolution became apparent in certain areas of the Island. In the parish of St Ouen in 1785 an anti-seigneurial document was written into the Parish Assembly minutes. It contained thirty-six articles and was said to represent the wishes of the leading men of the parish. Among the wide ranging demands for reform were several which were targeted at feudalism, including the abolition of services, a clarification of the *année de succession* and an end to the seizure of goods following bankruptcy. Article 22 demanded a clarification of all seigneurial rights, so as to put an end to abuse by the seigneurs. [27]

The St Ouen's articles were paralleled in the parishes of St John and St Helier, and by an article in *Le Gazette de L'Ile de Jersey*, the only Island newspaper of the time. [28] In the latter, the recent feudal past was presented as a period of "prétendus droits", which would come to be known "sous leurs véritables titres d'usurpations ou de vols commis par les propriétaires de fiefs sur leurs vassaux". [29] In immediate terms, as after the 1769 riot, such demands did little to effect change in seigneurial rights, but they did form the basis for a more sustained struggle in the nineteenth century. [30]

It is one of the peculiar aspects of Jersey society that, in spite of its thoroughly feudalised nature from at least the eleventh century, the basic feudal division, the fief, has played a minimal organisational rôle for the rural population. There is no physical correlation at all between the lay-out of fief and parish. Only among the larger fiefs, particularly that of St

Ouen, is the parish sufficiently dominated by a single manor for the scene to resemble the typical set-up of feudal England or Normandy. In fact, it is only in the parishes of St Ouen and Trinity that there is any obvious relationship between the siting of manor, parish church and settlement.[31] The fief initially possessed some potential as a primary social unit. In the medieval period it was the unit for agricultural production, while the feudal court provided a further focal point for tenants. But the fact that the peasantry were not coerced into living around the manor house, and were, instead, free to live anywhere on the fief, weakened the feudal structure as a social unit. Moreover, in an Island where the geographical layout of fief and parish showed no correlation, the feudal era already provided rival frameworks of existence, the one economic and judicial, the other religious, political, social and educational. The enclosure of the land in the late sixteenth century shifted the centre of economic production from the manor to the individual household. Sheer practicality determined the utilisation of the parish for a variety of purposes, including the collection of all tithes for both the Crown and the Church, and the provision of information for the King's surveys or 'extentes' of his domain, as in 1331.[32] It is indicative of the differing fortunes of the feudal and municipal organisations that by 1771 the supervision of the feudal 'banon', the practice of releasing livestock to wander freely after harvest, was performed by parish officers.[33]

The Parish

The remarkable uniformity of the twelve parishes of Jersey provided them with an obvious advantage over the haphazard sprawl of fiefs. It has been suggested that this uniformity (which may be observed in Figure 2) is a result of a common design dating from the reorganisation of the Diocese of Coutances, of which Jersey was a part, following the Viking devastations of the tenth century.[34] Church design, parish name and general appearance reflect a similarity which has remained through the centuries. Thus additions to the parish, mainly structural as in the case of Church extensions, Militia sheds and parish halls, not surprisingly in so small an island, perpetuate this identity. This blueprint for the Island divided into parishes drew from the already existing collection of early Christian buildings and favoured saints, but in its modern manifestation was essentially a reorganisation under Archbishop Geoffrey de Montbrai in the twelfth century, a part of a wider programme in the Duchy of Normandy to repair the devastation of the Vikings. Uniformity facilitated exploitation and control. Evidence on the process of reorganisation is scarce, but it has been shown that prior to 1150 the parochial pattern was far less uniform than it was following de Montbrai's work.[35] The churches had been in existence before this date, with at least seven in private hands which were handed over to the church some time in the period. All that is known is that the pattern that emerged paid little heed to the boundaries of fiefs, and even less to geographical factors, such as potential sites for population. Thus the sheltered anchorages of Gorey and St Aubin were ignored as potential parish centres. [36]

It is from this period of reorganisation in the twelfth century that we can trace the development of the parish in both its civil and ecclesiastical mould. In the first instance, it was a unit of ecclesiastical organisation but, unlike France where it remained confined to this rôle, in Jersey it became also a unit of civil and military administration. A parish was the area of jurisdiction for the rector, the chief ecclesiastical officer, appointed initially by the holders of the advowsons, various Norman monasteries, and after their confiscation, by the Crown.[37] The utility of the parish as a unit for administration, organisation and, at times, coercion, resulted in its exploitation early on as an important unit of secular administration.

Despite the fact that the medieval period is the area of Jersey history that has received most serious academic attention, there is little evidence as to the origins of the parish civil. From early on it is known that the 'eyre' (circuit court) used the parish to provide a jury of presentment, whilst as we have seen the 'extentes' of the Channel Islands in 1331 were drawn up on a parish basis. [38] Likewise, by the thirteenth century the parish as a unit was considered to be representative enough to be considered a community and an entity in law. This is shown by the fact that justices could punish whole parishes for infringements. [39] In Latin documents the term 'villa' was applied to the parish, and, on rarer occasions, it is referred to as 'the field of the parish' ('campo parochie'). [40] As an illustration of the reality of the parish as a unit in the popular mind, we have the ancient practice of the 'ouie de paroisse', recognised in law as the recording of contracts, court decisions and legislation within the communal memory, literally in the 'hearing of the parish'. [41]

The utility of the parish as a unit of organisation and identification was realised by the military at least as early as 1545, when the States ordered that the Island be divided into districts for defensive purposes. This division was made on a parish basis, with a captain appointed to each district. [42] This marked the beginning of a long relationship between parish and military organisation. Early archery ranges, generally located near the Church and known as 'Les Buttes', as in St Mary and St Martin; the siting of arsenals, originally in a section of the Church; and parade grounds which by 1806 had become drill sheds, sited at the parish centre and in the event of invasion to be used as command posts; all evidence to the use of the parish centre as both a training and storage area for the military. [43] It is also likely that the names of the parish officers, Connétable, Centenier and Vingtenier, are military in their origins, relating to units of militia organisation mentioned in a document of 1337 ('in millenis, centenis et vintenis'). [44]

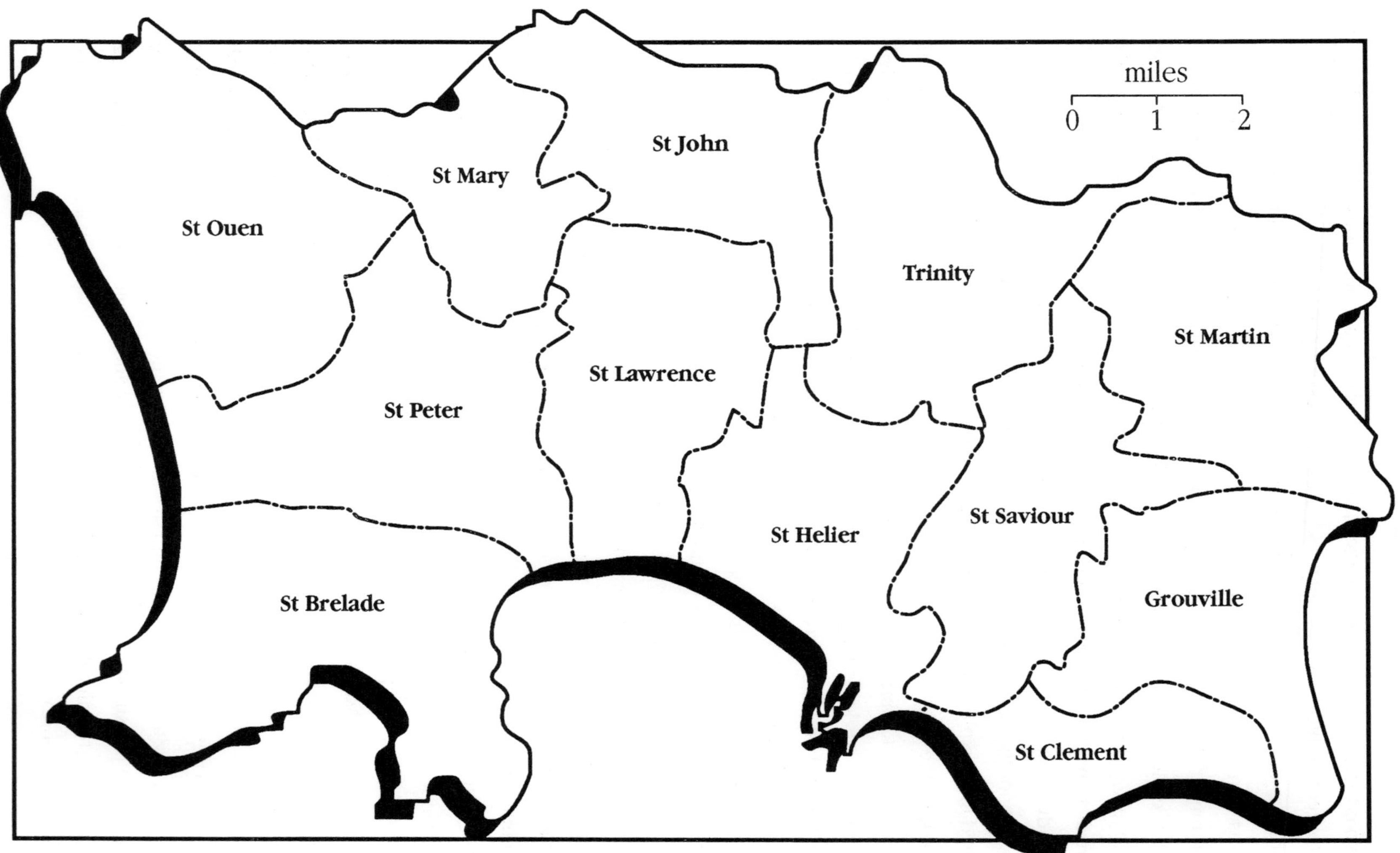

FIGURE 2. *A Map of the twelve Parishes of Jersey*

As one further illustration of both the usefulness and endurance of the parish as a social unit, it must be noted that there is nothing to suggest that any of the urban areas of Jersey were ever administered on a footing any different from that of the surroundingcountryside. The towns of St Helier, St Aubin and Gorey were administered by the parish within which they fell and, in feudal terms, were divided among the various fiefs of their area. [45] By the nineteenth century, many reformists, the majority of whom were town-based, fighting what they perceived as power vested in the land, found this situation difficult to come to terms with. St Helier, predominantly urban and by far the wealthiest parish of that century, was administered as just another parish.

With the parish regarded as a community and as an entity in law from at least the thirteenth century, the extension of limited powers of municipal government to the wealthiest members of a parish was natural. Parishioners were divided into two classes, a separation which marked the divide between power and subordination. A document of the early thirteenth century shows the people of St John and St Clement divided into 'capitales parochiani' and 'parvuli' for the purpose of assessing burial fees, the latter group representing the poorer members of the parish and paying a reduced sum. [46] The former group became the 'principaux', those landowners wealthy enough to be rated above an annually fixed sum. These principaux were eligible to rule their parish.

The actual composition and number of the 'principaux' was determined by the level of rate raised in each parish. Many parishioners paid rates, but only a select number of property owners, who were also heads of the household, were rated high enough to become principaux. These principaux made up the Parish Assembly, the ruling body of the parish, which set the rate and determined eligibility to vote in elections and internal affairs. The number rated was purely arbitrary and depended on the funds required by the parish, as well as political considerations. Since those who assessed the rate were those who had to contribute to it, it was in their interest to keep rates at a minimum. For a parish oligarchy keen to remain in power, the ability to regulate those who were rated and those who could vote was a distinct advantage.

Those who ruled the parish in an official capacity did so within a framework of administration that had developed alongside the two main arms of medieval administration, the King's ministers and the feudal officials appointed by individual fiefs. Parish concerns were dealt with on a daily basis by the honorary system, officers elected by the principaux, who served in an unpaid and part-time capacity. The chief civil officer of the parish was the Connétable. His rôles were multiple: he was in turn the civil head of the parish, the president of its assembly, controller of parish moneys, head of the parish police, custodian of parish records, executive officer charged with law enforcement, president of the 'enditement' or petty jury in criminal cases, collector of rates and finally, representative in law of the parish, to sue and defend on its behalf, and in the case of the Connétable of Trinity in 1854, be gaoled on behalf of the parish. [47]

The historian Thomas Dicey, writing in 1751, recorded the rôle of the captain of the parish: "The Constable when required, is to make them search for stolen goods; to take account of all strangers that come; and to see them lodged. ...He is to visit all taverns, and taste the wine, cider or beer, which if he judge not be good and wholesome drink, he is to see it destroyed: ...He is to take care that none go wandering about begging; and when he finds any such, if stranger, he is to send them out of the Island by the first ship; if inhabitants, they are to be put to work upon the parish account". [48]

Though incomplete, Dicey's assertions about the rôle of the Connétable reflected practical reality. The Connétable worked within a broad and ill-defined framework and acted on the traditional precepts of the customary law, except in areas specifically legislated upon by the States or directed by the Parish Assembly. Discretion was the fundamental basis for the rôle of Connétable, which naturally enough opened itself to much criticism for partisanship, particularly over the policing function. John Le Couteur, elected Connétable of St Brelade in 1826, was warned by his friend, the Bailiff of Jersey, "...that as Constable I need not interfere in any private grievances. Public wrongs were all that a Constable had to notice".[49] Nonetheless, and surprisingly for Le Couteur who was a leading anglophile and reformist, he did interfere in private grievances and settled them in the traditional manner without recourse to the law. [50]

The exact origins of the rôle of Connétable are uncertain, but it is likely to have been military and the earliest explicit mention of the office is in 1462. [51] There is no exact parallel with the office in either England or Normandy, although François Victor Hugo, the son of the poet, was certain that whilst "le bailli est normand, le jury est normand, le vicomte est normand, la coutume est normande. Le Connétable est anglais". [52] In some respects the Connétable might be considered a more powerful version of the English mayor. This power was realised in his capacity as head of the Parish Assembly in all but ecclesiastical spheres where the Rector presided, as head of the police force, and in his rôle as ex officio member of the Island legislature.

The Connétable was supported in his various rôles by a number of subordinates. Chief among this group was the Centenier, primarily a police officer but able to fulfil the rôle of Connétable should the need arise. Originally each parish had one Centenier, but this changed to a number varying from two to six depending on the population of the parish, seniority being then expressed by the appointment of a Chef de Police. The office dates back to as early as 1502. [53] The parish treasurers, the Procureurs du Bien Publique, date back to

1434. The Vingteniers, so called because each administered a vingtaine, a fiscal division of the parish, can be dated back in their fiscal function to 1462.[54] The Vingtenier's rôle was that of collector of rates, fines and defaults. Each vingtaine also had two Inspecteurs des Chemins who ensured that each parishioner fulfilled his corvée: a duty to repair the parish roads which ranged from six days labour in a year, the basic requirement, to the provision of cartage of road materials demanded of landowners and those in possession of a horse.[55]

The second head of the parish was the rector, whose power over the parish was restricted in theory to spiritual matters and presidency of the Assembly in matters concerning the Church or the poor. Rectors were not elected by parishioners, originally being appointed by the continental religious bodies who held the advowsons and, following their alienation, by the Crown. The general requirement of a rector, though not always observed, was that he be local and in possession of a degree. Rectors, like the Connétables, also sat in the States, but not as a representative or delegate of their parish, rather, it has been suggested, on account of their learning.[56] In their parish duties they were aided by two elected Surveillants (Churchwardens).

In practice the parish rector found himself in a powerful position. As in so many spheres of Jersey life this was, in part, the result of the semi-independent position in which Jersey found itself vis-à-vis the English Crown. This state of semi-independence was enhanced by the fact that, after the separation of 1204, the Church remained within the Norman diocese of Coutances.

When the Reformation arrived in Jersey it came from France. Because of the Island's unique circumstances, the English Crown showed itself willing to tolerate Calvinism as opposed to uniformity with the Church of England. This toleration was all the more marked since the Channel Islands were by this time incorporated into the diocese of Winchester, Henry VII having bribed Pope Alexander Borgia to this end in 1496.[57] Calvinism was officially ousted in 1620, when Jersey was brought within the Anglican Church, but its influence was to stretch well into the nineteenth century, lending Jersey religion an individuality perpetuated by basic differences from the English mainland, particularly in the French language. At full strength at the end of the sixteenth century, the Calvinist Church, with its strong organisation, played a major rôle in what were formative years for the legislature.[58] On a separate level the Presbyterian form of government utilised and reinforced the parish as the major communal unit to ensure discipline and control among its congregation. In a faith which paid strict attention to spiritual, moral and social discipline the distinction between religious and secular became blurred and, with the support of the State, the Church extended its jurisdiction to all areas of private and public life.[59]

In 1623 James 1, in response to bitter civil and ecclesiastical disputes over such jurisdictions, gave the Ecclesiastical Court in Jersey its own constitution. This constitution afforded the Church competence over ecclesiastical matters like divine service and the dissolution of marriages, as well as over probate of wills. [60] The Church was likewise given a Dean who, due to the Bishop of Winchester having only appellate jurisdiction over the Islands, became effectively Bishop of Jersey. [61] Nonetheless, at Island level James' definition of the Church's rôle amounted to a curtailment in the secular sphere. No such distinction between the limits of civil and ecclesiastical power was made at parish level, allowing a Church which, though outwardly Anglican, remained Calvinist at heart and able to exercise much power. [62]

One office remains to be noted, that of the Jurats or popular law finders. These honorary judges, interpreters of the customary law, were instituted sometime between 1204 and 1215 in the reign of King John and sat in both the Royal Court and the States. [63] The Island had twelve Jurats, popularly elected by the parish principaux. Jurats had automatic membership of the Parish Assembly of the parish in which they lived, though it is likely that the majority of them would have qualified by virtue of property owned anyway. It was not unusual for Connétables to go on to become Jurats. It is unfortunate that there is little known about the early rôle of the Jurat in the parish and the Island as a whole. If the late eighteenth and nineteenth centuries can be seen as indicative, the Jurats' spheres of influence in both the judiciary and the legislature made them an extremely powerful body. Much of the ill-feeling expressed in the riots of 1769 derived from their power in the Royal Court and a belief that they were too old and infirm for the job. [64] The separation of powers directed by the Privy Council in 1771 was an attempt to curb this oligarchy. We shall deal with this at a later stage.

Settlement

Nineteenth century Jersey was essentially a land of small closes, enclosed by huge earth banks or, particularly in the west of the Island, by substantial stone walls. The people of Jersey showed no tendency towards communal living or centralised settlement and, with the exception of the only major urban area, the town of St Helier, habitation was dispersed. This complex of irregular closes and scattered settlement was dissected by a network of nearly three hundred miles of lanes, the majority of which were narrow, deep and often impassable.

The Richmond Map of 1795 is the most useful guide to the landscape of early nineteenth century Jersey. As Figure 3 illustrates, the Jersey landscape is one of numerous small closes, which have a tendency to be oblong in shape and are evidence of a great carving up of the land. The land would appear to be excessively subdivided. The only area of the Island unenclosed and left in the feudal pattern of cultivated strips is Les Quennevais in the west of the Island (St. Peter and St Brelade), a comparatively large land mass composed of sand dunes. The map also shows a population dispersed throughout the countryside. Even around the churches, the traditional parish centres, the houses are no denser than elsewhere.[65] W.T. Money, a traveller who visited Jersey in 1798, described the parish centre of St John "as a small village with a neat church and two taverns". [66] An estimate taken from the Godfray Map of 1849 shows that St John's village was composed of, at most, ten dwellings. As Figure 2. shows, these dwellings are dispersed properties on their own small estates. Similarly, St Ouen's parish centre was described thus in 1847: "autour de l'église sont rangées une demi-douzaine de maisons assez-tristes, chétif village". [67]

Small clusters of houses or hamlets are present on the Richmond Map. These isolated examples of centralised settlement are better explained on the Godfray Map, where they are described as 'villes' or 'bourgs', and often followed by a local surname e.g., Ville ès Normans, ès Brée, ès Nouaux. [68] These are very likely to have originated as extensions of the chief residence of a family, children building on family property. It would be too much to see in this a tendency towards communal living.

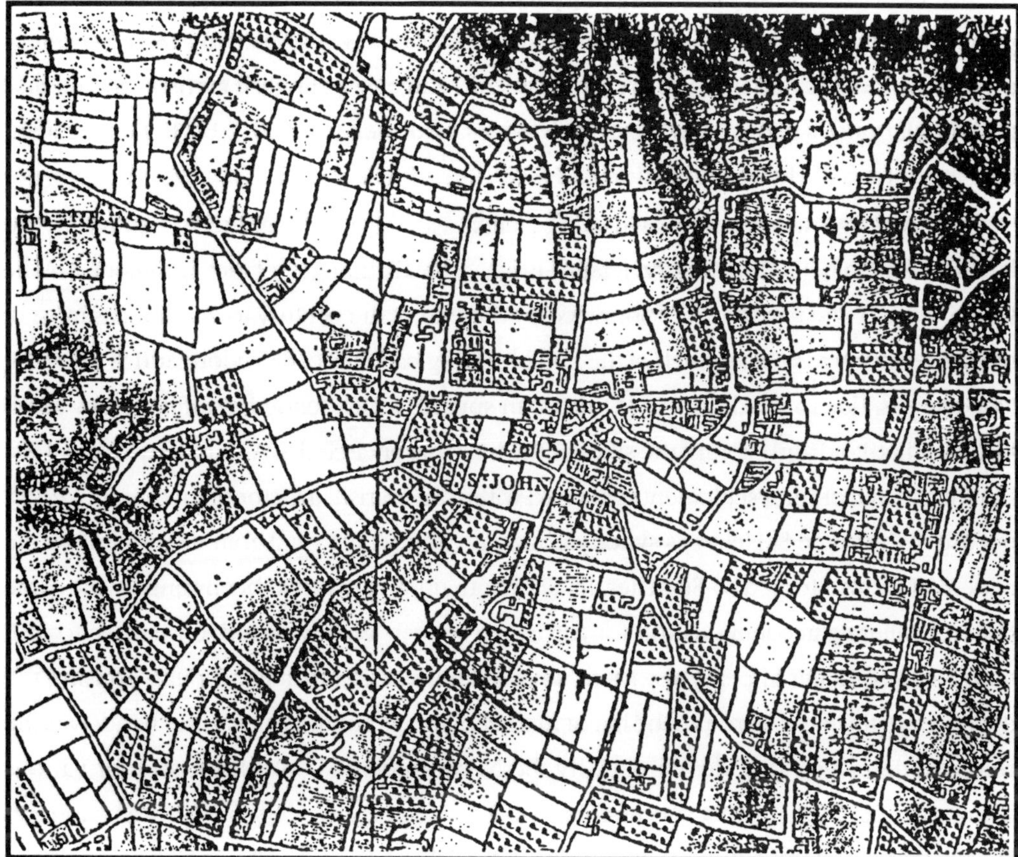

FIGURE 3. *The Parish of St John in 1795: Extract from the Richmond Map.*

Settlement in Jersey avoided the open plateau, probably because of the strong winds, and the valley bottom. In this respect, the population was aided by the abundance of springs, the popularity of the term 'Fontaines' as a house name providing evidence of this. By building a dwelling in one of the many 'valletes' (off-shoots of the major valleys) the need for both water and shelter could be satisfied easily. The majority of houses faced south, even if it meant the approach to the building was from the back. The more substantial dwellings were often approached by a long narrow avenue, known as 'une chasse', although many places have the house bordering the roadside. Shaw-Lefevre, an economic theorist writing in 1879, noted that "What most strikes a visitor to the Islands is the manner in which their population is housed. In Jersey, small but most comfortable farmhouses are spread over the whole country, at short distances from one another....There are few cottages in the ordinary acceptance of the term, or that remind one of those so common in rural England". [69]

Urban areas on the Richmond Map are situated in the parishes of St Helier and St Brelade. In 1787, when the survey was actually recorded, both areas were roughly equal in size and, relative to the population, small. The census of 1788 put the population of Jersey at near twenty thousand, with the urban population of St Helier numbering 3,600; the total population of the parish including its significant rural area was 4,000. [70] By 1806, St Helier's population, augmented by 1,800 French aristocrat refugees, an English garrison and English and Irish labourers involved in erecting defences, had risen to 6,500. [71] By 1841 the census accounted for a St Helier population of 24,000. [72]

The rapid growth of the Town of St Helier was the most significant change in the landscape in nineteenth-century Jersey. From a small triangle of development on the southern tip of the parish, it had sprawled by the end of the century to encompass most of its own territory, as well as much of the neighbouring parishes of St Saviour and St Clement. Nonetheless, due to the direction of the urban spread, which tended to infill the low semi-saucer of flat-land and capture the sides of the hills that encircled St Aubin's bay, a small but significant area of rural settlement remained within the parish, a factor often overlooked by the use of the name St Helier as synonymous with 'The Town'. St Aubin did not follow the pattern of growth forged by St Helier. In 1776 both urban areas had been roughly the same size; the billeting accommodation for garrison troops in both was said to be three to four hundred. [73] St Helier appears always to have been the administrative capital, housing the Royal Court, the legislature and the major market place. St Aubin, on the other hand, was the centre of the overseas trade, particularly the Newfoundland cod-fishery, and for various periods the base for a highly successful privateering enterprise. [74] Its growth was based on the fact that it was the only port of any size in the Island. Surprisingly, St Helier possessed only a small harbour until about 1840, when a massive harbour development allowed the displacement of St Aubin in this sphere. [75] The St Helier harbour project reflected the ascendancy of that town in the early nineteenth century, a rise related to population expansion, an increase in importance for the insular legislature and, in the longer term, a shift in the economic base of the Island away from overseas trade and shipping towards agriculture and tourism. It is highly significant that by 1850, of the two largest of St Aubin's merchant houses, Janvrin's ceased business and Robin moved to St Helier. [76]

With the exception of St Anne in Alderney, there is no centralised village settlement in the Channel Islands, and no evidence to suggest that one existed in recent historical times. The town of St Helier was no more such a settlement than anywhere else in the Island. As we have seen, the urban area of St Helier was situated on the extreme southern tip of the parish of the same name, backing on to the south coast. Its site was one of sand dunes and marsh, in contrast to the highly fertile arable land elsewhere in St Helier. St Anne in Alderney, by comparison, is a nucleated settlement surrounded by an agricultural area known as Les Blayes. The tradition has been that farms are situated in the village with the adjoining lands worked from this base. [77]

Explanations for this absence of nucleated settlement include: defence considerations, the feudal experience and, closely linked to the latter, the psychological outlook of the peasantry and their traditional individualism. One of the better theories put forward by a local scholar in this vein is that of G.F.B. de Gruchy and is based on the Islands' needs for defence. Jersey and Guernsey, the largest islands, had no need for such a settlement on the grounds of defence because they were defended by a ring of high and dangerous cliffs and, more importantly, by large populations. Alderney, on the other hand, is not only the closest Island to France but has physically the landscape most open to attack. The theory is based primarily on a letter written by the Warden of the Isles, Jean de Roches, in 1328, who pointed out that Alderney, unable to defend itself in a similar manner to the other islands, was raided continually by the French. A compact and defendable village was the only means to survive, aided by the fact that a long siege was unlikely due to English supremacy at sea. [78]

De Gruchy's theory is a useful starting point for an analysis of the origins of the settlement pattern. The location of settlement, to an extent, supports the defence theory, and it is indeed rare to find a pre-eighteenth-century Jersey house located within sight of the coast. However, the theory only explains partially the absence of centralised settlement. The Jersey people have never shown any inclination towards centralisation. Few old houses are sited near the parish churches, the traditional heart of the community. More surprising, considering that the agricultural scheme in the feudal period was based on the fief and not on the parish, there was no more a tendency to settle around the manor house than around the church. This is illustrated by the re-settlement of Sark by tenants of the fief of St Ouen, following its depopulation by the French in the Elizabethan period. The tenants made no attempt to build a village, preferring instead the decentralised pattern of their own Island.[79]

Architecture in early nineteenth century Jersey was remarkably uniform in style and size. The rapid growth of St Helier, particularly due to the influx of a wealthy English population, many of whom were half-pay officers returning from the French Wars, resulted in a divergence of building styles between town and country. It is reflective of the rather peculiar position of the French refugees in the Revolutionary and Napoleonic period that, in spite of their large number, their social status (most of them were aristocrats) and their long residence, they had no obvious influence on the architectural appearance of the town.[80] After 1815 the impact of the new immigrant population could be observed in the development of Regency residences, in the shape of terraces, crescents and villas.

Earlier town dwellings were, like their rural counterparts, substantial dwellings of stone in a farm-house style.[81] This uniformity of style and size was, in the first instance, dictated by the building materials obtainable locally, namely granite, and the absence of timber. In the latter case, this meant an absence of the Elizabethan frame-house. Lime was also absent as a raw material in the Island so this often meant houses were ill-glued together. Similarly, they were usually built 'sur l'herbe', that is without foundations.[82] The Reverend John Skinner described the countryside on his visit to the Island in 1827, claiming its similarity with "Somersetshire in its waving slopes, rich pastures, Corn fields and Orchards, comfortable residences, neat hedgerows and Bartons. All the houses are built of stone, having sached windows: not a casement is to be seen: they are for the most part neatly thatched, and rising to the height of two stories, with garrets in the roof...in several of the larger houses, the Norman doorway and loftier archway, opening into the Farm Yards, was preserved".[83] In similar fashion, the agriculturist William Bear described what he saw as the average country household in the 1880s, claiming nothing "strikes the visitor familiar with the rural districts of England so forcibly as the wonderfully prosperous aspect of the dwellings of the people. There are scarcely any cottages in Jersey, for the smallest of the farmers. as a rule, live in comfortable granite houses, with well-kept flower and vegetable gardens attached to them".[84]

One of the more peculiar aspects of the Jersey historical landscape is the absence of labourers' cottages. The argument was often put forward by nineteenth century commentators that this absence was explained by the lack of a significant labouring class.[85] Certainly, Jersey possessed no agricultural labourers' cottages of the type found in England. At Trinity Manor in 1851 the four lodges that guarded the entrances to the seigneurie were occupied by farm staff, but this was a rare case of accommodation provided specifically for labourers.[86] As we shall see at a later stage in this book, however, contrary to what commentators suggested, the country population did include a large number of labourers, many employed in quarrying and artisanal trades, as well as in agriculture. Census material reveals that the labouring class often had separate dwellings, but equally often lived within parts of larger dwellings, in many cases next door to their employer.

On the Richmond Map of 1795 the only buildings that stand out, excepting churches and fortifications, are the manor houses. This is particularly the case with seigneuries on the more important fiefs of St Ouen, Rozel and Samarès, although many others are recognisable by their size. [87] This was substantiated by Quayle, researching the island on behalf of the British Board of Agriculture in 1815: "The country residences of the Jersey gentry are substantial and roomy. Some few houses, in particular the Manoir de St Ouen...bear a strong resemblance to French chateaux; but the greater number, those particularly erected in the neighbourhood of the principal town, following English models, stand in well chosen situations". [88] The homes of the gentry were often under renovation and, by the nineteenth century, seigneuries were tending to lose their traditional farm buildings. St Ouen's Manor, for instance, lost its extensive farm buildings in a late nineteenth century reconstruction, which was one in a long line of many. [89]

During the course of the nineteenth century the seigneurial monopoly over substantial dwellings was undermined by the influx of wealthy immigrants who, if English, and the vast majority were, could purchase property in the Island. To this section of the population must be attributed the magnificent Georgian and Regency terraces, crescents and villas of St Helier and its adjoining parishes of St Saviour, St Clement and St Lawrence. The majority were satisfied to remain in the urban areas, but some moved out into rural Jersey and found themselves or built suitable accommodation. These people were few in number. In St John, for instance, the English population amounted to only 50 out of a total parish of 2,005 in 1851 and only two of them classed themselves as having independent means or professional status. St Saviour, on the other hand, which was partially urbanised by 1851 had 800 English residents out of a total 3,406, with 143 classing themselves among the wealthier section of the population. [90]

Among the vast bulk of the rural population the architectural design of a basic symmetrical pattern of dwelling house and courtyard dominated, as it had in the preceding two centuries. [91] "The most usual plan", explained C.P. Le Cornu, a local farmer and seigneur, "is for the dwelling-house to border upon the roadside, with only a small garden or yard intervening. If it be a garden, it is laid out with flowers and vegetables: if a yard, it is kept gravelled and clean, and through it is a path which leads to the principal entrance... The interior contains on the ground floor, two kitchens, one parlour, and a room appropriated for the dairy: on the upper floor are four bedrooms... The bake-house is a small room, containing a bread oven, and a copper for boiling or steaming roots; this room is also frequently used as a washhouse. The horse and cow stables are inelegant, but paved and divided into stalls". [92] This remained very much the pattern for nineteenth-century rural dwellings, including those newly built or restored which added the trappings and the designs popular in England at the time.

Dissecting this landscape of small closes and substantial dwellings was an intricate network of roads and lanes. Many of these routes belonged to private estates and, during the course of the nineteenth century, were handed over to the parish authorities for public use and upkeep. Early nineteenth-century writers were unanimous in their criticism of the communication system. "The roads of this island are, in general, very bad and sunk so low that they act as drains to the adjoining fields, and in the winter are nearly impassable". [93] These comments by a traveller in 1808 were matched by those of Quayle in 1815, who wrote "The ancient communications in the island under the name of roads are numerous; but narrow, winding, and, in consequence of frequently branching off and crossing each other, very intricate. They are sunk below the level of the land, flanked each side by the enormous mounds usual in the island, which are crowded with trees over-canopying the road, and, in a rainy season, rendering it a real gutter... To express anything very old, a Jerseyman says 'Vieux comme les Quémins'". Furthermore, "Two carts meeting each other on the 'chemin du roi', could not pass; one or the other must back till it reached the nearest field, gateway, or some other recess, to which it might retreat, during the passage of the other. To this little circumstance in their internal economy, and the disputes which it engendered, may perhaps in part be attributed the remarkable proficience of the Jersey populace in swearing". [94]

Modernisation of the antiquated road system was forced upon the Island by the perceived necessities of war. This took place under General Don, Lieutenant-Governor of Jersey 1806-1814, who was convinced that modernised communications would enable a better defence of the Island, as the existing road system precluded the rapid movement of artillery. Ironically, much of the opposition to his plans came from local people, who were convinced that the deep and impassable lanes were Jersey's best defence from an invader. A parish rector is claimed to have preached that 'The broad road leadeth to destruction'. [95] Clearly, a new road system was bound to incur problems. By its very nature, it involved expense and interference with private property, but a further complication was that it was being imposed by the military commander of the Island and a chief representative of the Crown. The parishes were not keen on having their municipal power overridden. The St Helier Parish Assembly went so far as to forbid the completion of the Trinity main road inside its bounds. [96]

Under General Don, eighteen roads were constructed throughout the Island, providing a basic framework which linked all the minor complexes of lanes. Don's most acclaimed success was the building of a road linking the towns of St Helier and St Aubin, which, despite being located in the same bay, had previously been joined only by crossing the sands at low tide. He also set the trend for infrastructural development throughout the century, undertaken jointly by the States and the parishes, with the former providing the necessary finance.

The wider implications of the new network of roads are not difficult to assess. Movement was generally facilitated throughout the Island, particularly between St Helier and the outer extremities. Previous to the improvements, the antiquated road system had apparently not deterred the country folk from coming into the Town to market their produce, but after 1810 greater interchange was possible on more than an economic level. Certainly, greater bulk loads of produce could now be transported and this was to have major implications for the potato industry, but perhaps more important was the ability to visit St Helier on a regular basis. Such ease of communication must have been of benefit to the members of Town-based societies, such as the Royal Jersey Agriculture and Horticulture Society, and to municipal heads whose office required time to be spent in the Town.

This greater interchange between town and country was further accelerated with the establishment of the railway in 1870. When completed, the railway linked St Helier with both the western extremity of the Island, at La Corbière, and the eastern coast as far as Gorey Village. [97] Add to this regular parish communications "by omnibus, established in very basic form as early as 1788, and Jersey was, by the end of the nineteenth century, if not earlier, completely opened up. It may seem an misnomer to talk about the opening up of an Island which is so small but it must be borne in mind that Jersey's landscape was, as we have seen, extremely broken up, the predominance of south sloping valleys making movement from east to west extremely onerous. It was to be of fundamental importance to the local economy that the facilitation of greater intercourse between town and country took place simultaneously with the opening up of the Island to the outside world and, in particular, to the English mainland.

The dissected countryside around which the new road network was forced to wind its way was surrounded on all sides by man-made earth, or occasionally stone, mounds, called 'Fosses'. These hedges were substantial, both in height and width. "One is not to imagine," claimed Philippe Falle, writing in the late seventeenth century, "such low Fences here as in England, but great Bulwarks of Earth...raised, with much Labour and Expense, six and eight foot high, sometimes more, answerably thick and solid, planted with Quickset or Timber trees, many of them faced with stone to a competent height, as you see the outside of a Rampart in Fortification..". [98] Quayle described the scene in 1815: No country is more strongly enclosed than Jersey: from the minute sub-division of property, the diminutive size, and irregular form of the fields, together with the frequent intersection of narrow roads branching out in every direction, the fences are multiplied; but they are still more remarkable for their solidity. Mounds of earth, 12 feet wide at their seat, are elevated o the height of six or eight feet, sometimes even higher, and crowned with timber trees and pollards, growing thickly in rows".[99]

The choice of material for these hedges was probably dictated by availability and cost. Stone, in the form of granite, was available as a building material but little used in the construction of hedges, except for occasional facings and, even then, probably only as a later reinforcement. Only in St Ouen was there any great number of walls as opposed to hedges, and this was no doubt dictated by the sandy constitution of the soil.

The substantial nature of Jersey's enclosures derived from the need to protect the apple trees that had become so popular as a cash crop from the mid-seventeenth century onwards. This protection was crucial in the delicate blossom stage. The hedges were further fortified with the planting of trees, usually elms, along the top.

By the nineteenth century these enclosures had become the very basis of the broken-up countryside, interspersed by deep lanes overshadowed by trees. This landscape made an aggrandisement of holdings and large scale farms virtually impossible because of the major restructuring which would have been required. What finally ruled out such a process was the practice of inheritance.

In Jersey, inheritance was a form of limited primogeniture, a general sharing between the children but with an obvious bias towards the eldest. Almost as a reflection of the peculiar position of the Island between England and Normandy, the system of inheritance followed a mean between the primogeniture of the English mainland and the gavelkind of the French. It was the subject of most dispute between the numerous social theorists who visited the Island, keen to draw parallels with Ireland and elsewhere and to analyse the implications of such a practice for land tenure and progressive agriculture.

The Jersey 'partage' was based on the customary law and received no effective statutory basis until the late nineteenth century.[100] Property could not be devised at will, a situation only partially remedied in 1851 after pressure from reform groups and, even then, applicable only to non-inherited property.[101] The eldest son was entitled to the family property and to a larger share of the land, the rest being divided between the other sons. The widow was entitled to a third of everything during her lifetime.

From the point of view of the landscape, the inheritance system would appear to have strengthened its broken-up nature and perpetuated the small closes. It is, however, far harder to gauge whether historically there was any tendency towards increased fragmentation. As early as 1635, that is soon after enclosure, an Order in Council enabled the population to entail property upon a single line of succession.[102] It was a response to the fear of excessive fragmentation: "Gavelkind.... destroys many an inheritance, by mincing it into several parcels; which peradventure in the next generation shall be divided again into still lesser portions, and so on, till an Estate is reduced to almost nothing".[103] However, there is nothing to suggest that the Order in Council was ever followed because, by the nineteenth century, certain reform groups were fighting for the very same thing; "The effect of the insular tenures for so many generations, having necessarily been to produce a minute division of property, the same cause constantly operating may be expected, if not to reduce their size still more, at least to prevent the accumulation and the continuance of any considerable landed property in one family".[104]

The changing landscape of the nineteenth century will be dealt with in some detail at a later stage in this book. But it should be noted that, faced with such an intractable landscape and rigid inheritance practices, the Jersey countryside was not to change significantly in the nineteenth century. It remained a land of small closes, enclosed by large hedges and broken up by a network of small and winding lanes which, following General Don's initiative, were gradually modernised throughout the period. Settlement remained generally dispersed, the exception being isolated ribbon developments, generally along major highways. Areas such as Sion in St John, Le Carrefour Selous in St Lawrence, and Victoria Village on the border of St Saviour and Trinity, grew out of their location as half-way points along major routes. During the course of the nineteenth century, these developments came to resemble alternative parish centres with Nonconformist chapels, shops, schools and the obligatory tavern. Nonetheless, the French agriculturist Galichet, could still comment in 1912 on the decentralised pattern of the Jersey landscape, and note how parish centres consisted of little more than church, school, hall and hotel.[105]

Chapter 2

Economic and Social Life

Jersey is a small island and historically has lacked economic resources, both human and natural. A small economic base meant an inability to sustain an expanding population and, as has been suggested, the likely outcome would have been an Island subjected to a cycle of high population growth followed by large-scale emigration. [1] Nonetheless, Jersey showed itself capable of escaping this potential predicament. As in the sphere of internal government, the answer to the Island's small size and relative insignificance lay in its geographical location and in its political position after 1204. [2]

Jersey's economic development reveals two sectors: the domestic, where the land provided the only viable resource, and the external, which rested on an ability to extend the economic base and exploit exogenous resources. In the first case, internal development remained on a self-sufficiency footing until it was realised that specialised cash-crop production of an exportable commodity, cider, could yield significant returns. Domestically such a development exploited Jersey's southerly location and mild climate, and was ideally suited to a land of small proprietors. In the second case, external development rested on Jersey's prime trading location in the Channel. In both instances, islanders exploited Jersey's peculiar political position, maintaining a near unbroken record of inclusion in favourable and avoidance of unfavourable Parliamentary legislation well into the nineteenth century.

Enclosure and Internal Development

Until the sixteenth century, Jersey's economy remained firmly based in the feudal open-field agriculture, with the exception of communal cropping patterns which were no longer so rigidly enforced. Cultivation was essentially for self-sufficiency entailing a variety of dairy produce, meat, vegetables and fish. The surplus of the main crop of wheat was exported and bartered with Spanish merchants in St Malo. [3] Enclosure had made no great progress, although isolated examples had taken place as early as 1215. [4]

In the course of the sixteenth century Jersey underwent a great transformation. By 1629, Heylin, a visitor to the Island, could describe the Island as "very much of small inclosures".[5] Heylin was not alone in his observations. Edward Cotes described Jersey, and nearby Guernsey, in 1656, as consisting "very much of small Inclosures, every man in each of them, having somewhat to live on his own. Only the difference is, that here mounds are made with ditches and banks of earth cast up, well fenced and planted with several sorts of apples, out of which they make a pleasing kind of cider, which is their ordinary drink". [6] The local historian Poingdestre, writing in 1682, stated that the Island "lay heretofor, about a hundred years since, almost open, with fewe Inclosures in it and, very fewe Orchards". [7] Philip Falle, a local Rector writing in 1734, similarly dated enclosure to a hundred and fifty years previous.[8]

The onus for enclosure came from the peasantry themselves and although, technically, seigneurial permission was necessary, no evidence of this has been found. [9] The main reason for enclosure was the realisation of the profits available from cider manufacture, an industry that was buoyant enough to enable a move from near self-sufficiency to cash-crop agriculture. Contemporary accounts give some indication as to the reasons for this sudden transformation, most of them bemoaning the decline in grain crop production. Falle's censure is explicit: "I might have named another great Obstruction to Tillage, but such as can hardly now be removed. 'Tis the prodigious Augmentation of Inclosures (about 150 Years ago the island lay pretty much open, but when the Humour of planting seized our People they fell to inclosing for Shelter and Security to their Fruit) Fences, Hedgerows, and highways....which waste a great deal of good Land that might be turned to better Account".[10]

By 1795, 20 per cent of all the land in Jersey was under orchard. In the parish of St Saviour the figure was 36 per cent. [11] Every farmhouse had its own granite apple crusher and cider press. In 1734 Falle had claimed that a veritable "sea of cider" was produced, with 24,000 hogshead every year. [12] By 1810, the eminent local expert on cider, the Reverend Francois Le Couteur, claimed the number of orchards had increased by half since the time of Falle's writing. [13]

The move to cider cultivation and the subsequent decline in grain production was related to further upheaval in Jersey society. The attractions of the sea and of locally based knitting manufacturing had drawn many away from the land. Cause and effect remain entwined, but by the seventeenth century the Jersey economy had shifted from a primarily land-based, labour intensive self-sufficiency to a cash based mixed economy of cider production, manufacture and commerce.

Like cider, which had been drunk in Jersey from at least the fifteenth century, knitting manufacture had a long history in the Island. [15] In 1586 a visitor to the Island noted that "The women make a very gainful trade by knitting of hose which we call Jersey stocks". [16] Men also took up the profitable trade, so much so that the States felt obliged to ensure continued cultivation of the land and banned knitting during harvest and vraicing (the collection of seaweed for fertiliser) in 1608. [17] Likewise, the States felt it necessary to ensure quality manufacture and in 1617 official stocking inspectors were appointed to that end. [18] The numbers involved were large, Poingdestre claiming in 1682 that "The greatest part of the inhabitants are knitters. There be many houses where man, wife and children, beginning at the age of 5 or 6, have no other employment, and may be said to make every one a pair of stockings each week; which must according to my account come to more than 10,000 pairs weekly".[19] The finished articles were taken to market on Saturdays to be sold to merchants, who then exported them to as far away as Spain and America.

Whether or not knitting merchants acted as 'putters out' is unclear, but the importance of the knitting industry to the rural community was that it involved them in markets beyond their own small base. Its popularity, alongside an increased interest in commerce and navigation, was considered detrimental to the well being of the land by contemporary writers. Dumaresq complained that Jersey owned "forty vessels with topsails and decks, beside many smaller craft", whereas twenty would suffice.[20] Regardless of such complaints, the taste for international markets, which was to be so evident in the nineteenth century, was established by these early excursions into trade.

The External Development of the Economy

The upheaval in the seventeenth century Jersey economy, brought on by enclosure, cider cultivation and the knitting industry, involved a dramatic extension to the external economic base, as well as an internal restructuring. Prior to the sixteenth century perpetual Anglo/French hostilities had precluded anything other than a minor involvement with the sea for Channel Islanders. In the sixteenth century they joined the British and French expansion to the cod fisheries of Newfoundland and became a part of the general European maritime expansion. More importantly, the peculiar relationship with the English mainland enabled a share in the British rise as a maritime power.[21]

In 1394 Richard II had granted a Charter which stated that the people of the Channel Islands were not to be treated as foreigners and were to be exempted from duties and taxes in English towns and ports. This was subsequently confirmed by successive monarchs, notably Edward IV who, in 1468, extended the privileges to include "other possessions beyond the seas".[22] In 1716 Parliament reassured the Islands that, despite certain constitutional changes, it would retain the previous position of "encouraging the said Inhabitants to continue that steady and firm Loyalty to the Crown of Great Britain, which they have formerly and constantly shewn to the Crown", and that they should continue to be able to "Import into any Lawful Port of Great Britain, any Goods, Wares, and the Merchandises of the Growth, Produce and Manufacture of the Islands, or either of them, without paying Customs, Subsidies or Duties".[23]

It was to be the cod trade and the connected international carrying trade that utilised these privileges to the greatest extent, particularly in its peak period, commencing in the late eighteenth century. Jersey maritime development depended on external forces and remained within the framework created by the great powers, particularly England and France.

With the possible exception of the innovative cod trade, Jersey's overseas business involved a trading on the margins of developments which were not of its making. As an insignificant dot in the English Channel, Jersey could not hope to be a great economic initiator. However, the Island continually showed itself quick to respond to changes in the world around it. Thus, the advent of the Second Hundred Years War (1689-1815) saw Jersey respond with a fleet of privateers; and William III's ending of two centuries of papal sanctioned neutrality in time of war (the Bull of 1484) gave Jersey the opportunity to establish a flourishing smuggling trade.

The Impact of the Napoleonic Wars

The Napoleonic Wars did not provide a revolutionary departure for the economy, rather a continuation of pre-1793 trends with an adjustment to the needs of war. The Island was once again an outpost, significantly augmented by French refugees from the Revolution, a British garrison and a naval squadron. Jersey agriculture, dominated by cider cultivation, found itself with a large confined market of consumers and responded with a marketable surplus, though not to the detriment of its export trade. The potential of the potato as a cash-crop was also discovered. In the merchant sphere, Jerseymen responded to the war in time-honoured fashion, becoming either privateers or armed merchant men. The overseas trade, its former markets in the Mediterranean and Iberia intermittently closed, turned to new areas in Latin America and the Caribbean. The Napoleonic seige was to prove a boom time for an Island with an entrepreneurial spirit.

By the end of the eighteenth century, however, little had changed in the basic spheres of the economy since the upheavals of two .hundred years earlier. The only exception to this pattern was the knitting industry which received its death blow sometime after 1750, probably because of changing market demands. This resulted in a decline in the number of sheep in the Island, previously not particularly popular among agriculturists but useful for their wool. [24] In 1851 the *Jersey Times* made mention of the former industry, referring to the few remaining one-time knitters, including "four venerable women residing in a house near Mont Mado; all in their seventies". [25] In its place came a smaller demand for footwear from the carrying trade and a nineteenth century brick manufacturing industry, but nothing ever as prolific as the knitting industry in its heyday.

Cider apple cultivation remained the major industry of the Island. Thus, according to James Playfair, writing home in 1781, whilst "There is nothing of what may be called agriculture carried on here," nonetheless, "More than one fourth of the inclosures of the island are planted with apple trees under which cows feed". [26] The two elements of the agricultural industry that were to dominate the nineteenth century, the Jersey cow and the potato, were present by 1800, albeit only in a minor way. Cattle rearing had already become important, and although the animals of this period were to be later considered ill-shaped and ill-bred, some export had taken place. Indeed, the breed was considered worth protecting and in 1786 the import of other breeds was banned; beef for local consumption appears to have been tacitly excluded from the ban.[27] Potatoes were introduced some time in the 1740s, but traditional prejudices and the preference for the parsnip meant that it remained unpopular until the end of the eighteenth century.[28]

Napoleonic Jersey was predominantly agricultural. An interpretation of the Richmond Map of 1795 reveals that 80 per cent of the whole Island was enclosed, only the sandy areas in the western parishes of St Brelade and St Ouen remaining significantly open with 63 per cent and 44 per cent respectively of their land mass unenclosed.[29] Orchard land accounts for some 15 per cent of the total land area, denser in the east and widely distributed on the plateau. Even by 1840, when the potato had overtaken orchard cultivation as the most popular crop, John Le Couteur, who lived in St Brelade, could claim that "the farmers of the eastern district are Ciderists, and ours generally corn growers".[30] St Saviour was the parish with the most land devoted to orchard at 36 per cent, St Ouen with the least at 3 per cent. At the beginning of the French Wars, then, over seven square miles of Jersey land was devoted to a specialised cash crop.[31]

In 1801 concern over the price of provisions, particularly grain, resulted in a call from the British Parliament for acreage returns throughout the land.[32] The Channel Islands were included and in the replies to the request of the Diocese of Winchester we are provided with a further statistical guide to the Island during the Wars, although only six of the twelve returns appear to have survived.[33] The returns show that 24 per cent of the total land area was in tillage and that 78 per cent of this was in cereals, particularly barley, 8 per cent in potatoes and 9 per cent in peas and beans.[34] In 1815 Quayle reported in his agricultural survey that one quarter of the Island was under the plough, a figure which is consistent with the 1801 figures.[35]

The statistics reveal much about both the situation during the war period and the preceding century. Enclosure, as we have seen, was unpopular among certain writers during the seventeenth and eighteenth centuries. It was claimed by Heylin in 1656 that the shift to cider cultivation had resulted in a deficiency in the amount of corn grown.[36] In the eighteenth century, corn shortages were a source of much criticism and complaint. In 1709 'The Groans of the Inhabitants of Jersey' had bemoaned the diminution in grain production and pointed out its effects on the poor.[37] In 1769, as we have already noted, the riot which broke out in St Helier was sparked off by the high price of corn in the market-place.[38]

A paper in the La Hague documents dated 1800, and possibly connected with the returns of 1801, contains various calculations regarding the grain situation. It suggests that nearly twelve thousand vergées (2 ¼ vergées equals 1 acre) of grain were under cultivation in the Island, a figure compatible with the estimate for the six parishes in 1801 which gave a total of 6,327 vergées. Furthermore, the paper calculates that the Island was producing over 300,000 cabots a year for an estimated local demand of no more than 280,000 cabots, on the assumption that a man would eat ten cabots in a year (a cabot weighed 40lbs.).[39] Available statistics clearly demonstrate, therefore, that the shortage of grain in the eighteenth century (and this had been foremost in the minds of the rioters of 1769) was caused by the export of local produce.[40] Jersey agriculture in the eighteenth century was already a commercial affair.

The agriculturists' demand for the export of marketable produce at all costs, even to the detriment of the local population, was curbed somewhat by the demands of the near siege conditions of the Napoleonic Wars. Export did not cease entirely, but selling in a local market place where demand was high and competition, with the possible exception of some imports, almost zero, no doubt satisfied local farmers. In fact, the only time grain appears to have declined in tillage was during the war period when an alternative profit maker had been discovered. Quayle reported, on the authority of the King's Receiver in the Island, that between 1778 and 1815 the quantity of grain grown had diminished by one third.[41] The reasons given were a further increase in orchards and, more significantly for the nineteenth century, the increasing popularity of the potato and livestock rearing. It was thus in the war period, with the French suppliers cut-off, that production for the local market brought the potential of the potato and the Jersey cow to the attention of Island agriculturists.

Local agriculturists were quick to react to changed circumstances. This much was noted by the Reverend François Le Breton, Rector of St Saviour, in his reply to Lord Pelham's 1801 enquiry. The entrepreneurial spirit was evident, he claimed, in both livestock rearing and crop production, no more so than with potatoes: "as yet, being a new culture, before the news of peace (in 1801/2) the potatoes sold for 15 pence for a measure weighing 40lbs the wheat being then ten shillings per bushel winchester, so that a field of potatoes was worth three times as much, as it would have produced in best wheat".[42] The crop had only arrived in the Island in the 1770s, but already by 1812 it was necessary for a States Ordinance to forbid export on the grounds of local need.[43]

The crop was exported from as early as 1803, probably to England where market prices were high, and between that date and 1812 export averaged 962 tons a year.[44] Cider was also exported, as it had been throughout the preceding century, although export appears to have fluctuated considerably. The cider export figures are unreliable, François Le Couteur claiming 3,227 hogsheads for 1805, .Quayle only 717. [45] The average number of dairy cattle exported for the same period, according to Quayle alone, was 610. [46]

It is unlikely that the Island was totally self-sufficient. Jersey had not been so from at least the period of enclosure and, whilst statistical breakdowns show that consumable staples such as wheat, barley, potatoes, peas, beans and parsnips were being produced, it is not known if extra food was imported. Beef had previously been imported, but whether this continued during the Wars is unclear. [47] It is likely that local cows, although reared as dairy animals, were used for meat. [48] Despite the desire for profit some sacrifice had to be made. As the Reverend Le Breton noted, much of St Saviour was under grass in order that the great number of army saddle and draught horses in the town might be fed; hay sold for only two thirds of the price that could be obtained for wheat. [49]

Consumer prices in the market were artificially high for the war period. In his general survey of the Island, William Plees pointed to a rise in every quarter because of the huge demand; even Torbay fisherman found it worthwhile to sell their catch in the Island. [50] Nonetheless, as Stead pointed out in 1809, the cost of living was still considerably lower than in England and the large population (22,855 according to Don's 1806 Census) combined with the commercial benefits of war resulted in an abundance of capital. [51] Quayle reiterated the point, claiming that "A state of warfare, destructive as it is to the industry of other countries, even though they are not its immediate seat, brings perhaps on the whole to Jersey, considerable local advantage. The pay of an augmented garrison circulates in this island, as well as that of numerous artizans... [engaged in building fortifications, such as Fort Regent]; many of whom earn high wages, and economise small part of them". [52] The balance of trade, claimed Stead, was £58,317 in Jersey's favour, with imports from Britain amounting to £1,200 and from abroad £21,616. [53]

The value of exports to England in 1809 was claimed to be in the region of £91,936 and the major portion of this was probably re-exports. [54] An extensive commercial infrastructure had existed prior to 1793 and certain sections of the merchants continued to thrive. As had been the practice in former conflicts, many merchants obtained letters of marque and turned to privateering, although in this conflict many more of them became armed merchantmen, thus ,enabling a continuation of trade. [55] Trade routes were disrupted, especially the cod trade whose markets in the Mediterranean and Iberia were variously closed. Nonetheless, new markets for dried cod and European wines were sought and found in Latin America and the Caribbean, a change that would have some bearing on the development of the carrying trade in the post-war period. [56] After nearly two centuries of relative continuity in the economic sphere following in the wake of the enclosure movement, the Napoleonic Wars showed the Island's potential to thrive economically even under near siege conditions. It was a period in which the economy was to become subtly realigned towards its nineteenth century norms. This was particularly the case with agriculture, with a large enclosed market revealing the potential of the potato as a cash crop.

The Social Structure

The idealised representation of Jersey as a land of small peasant proprietors, content with simplicity and self-sufficiency, can be traced back at least to the seventeenth century. In 1694 Philip Falle described himself as descending from an ancient agricultural family who "belonged to that happy class of substantial freeholders, who are not sufficiently elevated to excite envy, but who enjoy enough of the necessaries, and even comforts of life, to be independent, and to preserve their integrity unsullied by the temptations of avarice or úambition". [57] The picture of rustic contentment and equality continued into the nineteenth century, perpetuated by the majority of writers and commentators, both locals and outsiders.[58] It was an image which borrowed much from the equally idealised English recall of the class of yeoman proprietors. It contained an element of truth, particularly as regards a substantial body of landowners, but it simplified a complex social structure, and one that became all the more complex as the century progressed.

In 1851, out of a population of 57,155, 34.3 per cent of those active in the economy classed themselves as labourers. Artisans (31.6 per cent) and farmers (10.3 per cent), account for a middle section of 41.9 per cent, whilst those individuals who listed themselves as professional or managerial make up 5.6 per cent. Those of independent wealth, living off unearned income, represent a further 18.2 per cent. [59] The Census of 1851 is the first statistical digest detailed enough to allow such a breakdown. It is a simplified and arbitrary breakdown and blurred in certain areas, particularly the middle grouping where differentiation between affluent and poor is not possible. Nonetheless, it provides the most comprehensive breakdown available.

The Census provides a breakdown of social structure by occupation, but in the nineteenth century this structure can be more usefully seen in terms of the ownership of land. Status was determined by the relationship of the individual to the land he lived on. This determinant is reflected in the Island power base, which by the middle of the century was not a fair representation of the wealth in the Island. The nineteenth century in Jersey was not quite an 'age of capital', as the problems that successful merchants and wealthy English incomers had in finding access to political power were to show.

In terms of social analysis, the only practical index to the land and those who owned it is provided by the rate lists, which by their arbitrary and irregular nature give at best a rough guide to the wealthiest in each parish. The rates were a levy on real and personal property, but their assessment relied on the whims and political requirements of the parish oligarchy. Yet, despite the unreliable nature of the system which taxed the supposed value of real property and proved incapable of making a fair assessment of personal wealth, there was in every rate list a body of parishioners who stood out clearly as the wealthiest in the parish.[60]

In rural Jersey the seigneurs were the greatest landowners. In 1823 the parish of Trinity rated the Seigneur of Trinity Manor, Captain de Carteret, at 160 Quarters. Out of the 357 household heads rated, the closest four to de Carteret were rated at 15 Quarters. The total rate for the parish amounted to 1,225 Quarters, meaning that the Seigneur paid 14 per cent of the total.[61] In St Clement, the Seigneur of Samarès paid one fifth of the rates for the whole parish.[62] Only St Mary, among the eleven rural parishes, was not dominated by a seigneurie; instead its rate lists were headed by the Arthur family, landowners who provided four of the top ten rate payers for 1858.[63]

The only significant challenge to seigneurial control of the Island's landed wealth came from urban dwellers. In St Helier, even though the larger fiefs of Mélèches and Colette des Augrès owned much of the land, including the increasingly fashionable living areas in and around the Town hills and the Town centre in the Canton du Haut de laVingtaine de la Ville, the seigneurs found themselves sharing the top section of the rate list with merchant families, such as the Janvrins and the Fiotts, and property speculators like Robert Brown and Nathaniel Westaway.[64]

The exact extent of the fortunes of these wealthier parishioners is difficult to assess. Inglis, an English resident who spent some time in Jersey in the 1830s, observed that "there are not in Jersey, a great many wealthy people, as that term would be understood in England. Fortunes, generally speaking are moderate. ...I believe I may safely say, that no one in Jersey, spends £1200 per annum; and that, with two or three exceptions, £800 per annum, is the extent of Island expenditure".[65] Nonetheless, land was a valuable commodity in a small Island with a high population, particularly with a significant cash crop agriculture. Seigneurs themselves had difficulty ascertaining the extent of their own lands, hence the emphasis on *aveux*(see above, Chapter 1), and if the manor remained within the family the historian faces equal difficulty. When Trinity Manor was sold in 1909 the lands were said to extend to 270 vergées, probably making the manor of the 1820s the largest single holding in the Island.[66] Add to this Philip de Carteret's investment in rentes or mortgages and the potential of his rights as Lord of Trinity, such as the mills and the *année de succession*, and we are near to assessing his fortune, although his capital investments are unknown. His farm diary for the period 1820/21, however, shows the capacity to inject funds into modernising the enterprise, including the making of trips to England to purchase machinery and pedigree stock.[67] Clearly, in Jersey terms at least, he was a wealthy man.

Fiefs were worthwhile investments, as the accumulation of François Godfray, one of Jersey's leading advocates (the Jersey equivalent of the English barrister) in the nineteenth century, shows. Godfray's tally of seigneuries amounted to seventeen, and included some of the major ones such as Mélèches, and three of the four branches of the divided Seigneurie de St Ouen. [68] Business investment was also an option, particularly popular among merchants, who were responsible for the large department stores of de Gruchy and Le Gallais, as well as banks such as the Old Bank (Hugh Godfray and Sons) and the Joint Stock Bank (Matthews, de Carteret and Co.). The cod merchant Raulin Robin's bankruptcy saw his capital assets valued at £31,233 in 1886 and this included £27,295 capital investment, not an untypical figure for Jersey merchants at the time. [69] His house was valued at the same time at £10,120. [70] These were the wealthiest people in the Island, a distinct group in the rating lists of no more than about 50 in 1820, although by 1890 nearer 300. St Clement illustrates the point. The Seigneur of Samarés had paid five times the amount of the ratepayer next on the list in 1805; by 1890, without diminution of lands on his part, this figure had been reduced to just over double. Significantly, the next largest rate payer in 1890 was the Jersey Eastern Railway Company. [71]

Below this small group of wealthy inhabitants lay a sprawl of farmers, small merchants and those of independent means. The majority of this group were ratepayers and often principaux. Rate lists differentiated between principaux and ordinary ratepayers, but in terms .of assessing wealth among this middle grouping it is as wise to ignore the distinction and concentrate on the figures. An individual's placing on the rate list depended on several variables. The line which divided principaux from ratepayers was arbitrarily drawn and often had as much to do with political persuasion as individual wealth. So in St Martin in 1811, for instance, the rate was set at 12 Quarters and out of a total of 260 ratepayers only 35 were considered principaux, a selected clique which excluded many members of the middle section. [72] St Brelade in 1811, with its wealthy merchant town of St Aubin, had 55 principaux out of 199 ratepayers and shows a similar pattern of exclusion. [73]

Among this middle section of the population, farmers dominated the rural rate lists in a fashion disproportionate to their number. In St John in 1851 farmers constituted 19 per cent to the artisans' 28 per cent of the working population. [74] Yet in the 1858 rate list the farmers outnumbered the artisans twenty to one. [75] The reason for this lay clearly in the likelihood that farmers would own more land and perhaps more extensive buildings, and in the parish's inability to assess the rates in a concise and uniform way. The result was farmer domination of the parish power base.

In terms of wealth, the middle section of the population were likely to own some land or property, but little capital. A detailed analysis of the Vingtaine des Marais in Grouville between 1851 and 1858 shows that among the 156 head of households 46 were artisans, 47 labourers, 22 farmers, three professional and 38 of independent means or retired. None of the labourers owned either their own property or land. Among the artisans, 16 were rated, including three thatchers,five carpenters and two blacksmiths; 16 of the 22 farmers were rated. As an index to wealth the rate list shows the combined rates of the artisans amounted to 304 Quarters, a figure dwarfed by the 1,208 Quarters of the farmers and the 543 Quarters of the three Professionals. Furthermore, only one artisan, a land-owning publican, was rated for personal wealth. [76]

Analysis of those excluded from the rate list and not poor enough to receive parish relief is virtually impossible because in parish terms their existence is not noted except for baptism, marriage and death and road duty. This main body of the population, including small farmers, artisans and labourers accounted for over half of the population active in the local economy, yet were excluded from the case studies of writers and the general literature of the period.

The tendency to assume that rural parishes consisted of farmers and nothing else largely explains the absence of references to this section of the population in local sources. It was an assumption based in turn on the fact that the countryside abounded with small proprietors. Census returns show how even artisans and labourers often combined their occupation with the cultivation of a small plot of land. However, observers tended to overlook the fact that many of the poorer Jerseymen were really labourers with a bit of land rather than small proprietors. This is illustrated by the 1834 Poor Law Report. When asked how many labourers there were in his parish the Rector of St Saviour, the Reverend Edward Durell, answered: "The farms, not only in my parish, but throughout the whole Island, are generally small. They are for the most part farmed by the landowners themselves. There are very few farmers at Rack-Rent.... ...The agriculture of this Island depends comparatively but little on hired labourers, the greatest of farming labour is done by the farmers themselves and their families". [77] He stated that labourers were a small minority, employed only at harvest times and that, even then, women and children were generally excluded from such work. In doing so he overlooked all those labourers who owned a bit of land. To be fair to Durell, he was answering questions which were not tailored to the Jersey rural scene, but the result was, nonetheless, a misleading picture.

Many nineteenth-century visitors perpetuated the view that rural Jersey was a land of small proprietors, with an insignificant labouring class. This derived, in part, from the absence of obvious English-style agricultural labourers' dwellings. Yet the 1851 census, the earliest that enables such detailed analysis, shows that 28 per cent of the country's working population were labourers. [78] The figure is drawn from a detailed count of six country parishes. The returns did not often stipulate the type of labour involved, but where it did the artisanal trades, notably building and quarrying, dominated. So where did these labourers live ?

In many instances, as noted above, it is possible that labourers were also smallholders, a situation facilitated by the mode of purchase practised in the Island. Known as wheat-rentes, the practice allowed the creation of a perpetual mortgage after a payment of one quarter of the purchasing price. According to C.P. Le Cornu, a leading local agriculturist, small proprietors abounded: "In Jersey almost every family residing in the country cultivate some portion of the land adjoining their houses, if but a garden they grow fruit and vegetables for the markets, and if they have 1 to 2 acres of land they keep a cow, two or three pigs, and some poultry, increasing their stock in proportion to the extent of their occupation". [79] Much of the early activities of the Royal Jersey Agricultural and Horticultural Society, founded in 1833, was aimed at promoting habits of cleanliness and hygiene among the labouring class, encouraging each to "employ his leisure hours in cultivating and ornamenting his little Garden". [80]

As for those labourers who neither rented nor owned smallholdings nothing can be said with certainty. Nonetheless, a study of the census material reveals a pattern. Married labourers and their families are almost without exception listed as separate units. Single labourers tended to either live on the job or lodge. In the parish of St John in 1851, 56 separate units had heads of household who were labourers, whilst 40 individual labourers lodged in households other than their own. Neither house names nor exact locations are provided in the census, but it is often the case that a labouring family appear adjacent on the register to a large farmer. [81] In view of what we know of the historical landscape, this suggests that these labouring units were housed in parts of larger properties, and, most likely, one or more members of the labourer's family would have been employed in some capacity by the proprietor.

A look at poverty in Jersey in the early part of the nineteenth century sheds some light on the experiences of the lower classes. Following the cholera outbreak of 1832, the Jersey Medical Officer stated that the causes of the disease were poor drainage, especially in older St Helier, poverty, hunger and drunkenness. "It would," he concluded, "be somewhat difficult to find a place where in proportion to its magnitude, intemperance had more votaries, or where poverty, demoralisation and squalid misery prevailed to a greater degree". [82] He went on to point out that the majority of the people in these areas were English and Irish labourers, who were not eligible for parish relief.

The medical report makes distinctions essential for any understanding of poverty in the Island, that between rural and urban, and between local and non-local. Nowhere in the countryside could poverty be said to have reached the levels of this description of St Helier. Rural poor were looked after by the parish of their birth. For much of the nineteenth century the urban parishes found themselves fighting to be rid of imported pauperism, of the sort described in the *Jersey Times:* "Yesterday again did the steamer Sir Francis Drake, coming from Plymouth for the second time this season, disembark on our quays a new load of some fifteen indigent Irish people, whose whole wardrobe consisted of the few rags in which they were clad". [83]

The response of the parishes to this imported pauperism, itself a result of Jersey's cheap cost of living and the perceived extent of employment in the Island, was to clamp down on eligibility for poor relief. As early as 1821 the Ecclesiastical Assembly of St Saviour, its southern area rapidly urbanising as St Helier's population spilled out, gave permission to the Church officials to refuse the sacrament of baptism to those born elsewhere so as to avoid the claiming of "civil rights which could subsequently become onerous to the parishioners".[84] In the late 1840s the winters were so severe that the parishes, under petition from the artisans and the urban reformer Pierre Le Sueur, were forced to feed the poor, local and foreign alike, with St Saviour alone giving out 5,301 cabots of wheat and 2,130 cabots of potatoes. [85] The rural poor, as the experiences of the German Occupation of 1940-1945 would later show, were in comparison better off, mainly because of the ability to grow their own produce. It was just as well, since the farmer-dominated parishes had a rather intransigent attitude to the sale of their produce locally when they knew the prices which could be obtained in the export markets, even in time of need. This was evident from the response to the artisans' petition in the winter of 1847 when Connétable Pierre Le Sueur asked the States to curtail exports to feed the population, the farmers response being to defeat the vote, albeit narrowly 14 to 13. [86]

Numerically, those receiving poor relief in rural parishes were a very small fraction of parish populations. In St John in 1817, out of a population of near 2,000, 11 families were receiving regular aid of up to 14 livres tournois per month. [87] To place the sum in context, Samuel Coutanche was willing to pay 2,000 livres in 1811 for a pew in the parish church. [88] According to Quayle writing in 1815, a master carpenter could earn 195 livres a month, a thatcher 156 livres and a woman employed in husbandry, with board, 39 livres. [89] Extra help for the poor was available. In 1819 Marie Hoton (sic) of Herupe, St John, received "2 Chemins de Coton, 1 Flanelle, 1 Jupe, 1 Bed Gown et 2 livres de pain par semaine". The children of Philippe Sare (sic) were given complete outfits. [90]

It is interesting to note that, like rural labourers, designated paupers are to be found on the Census as separate units. In St John in 1851, seven individuals were stated to be paupers. Two children and a young man, stated to be insane, lodged, whilst others lived with family.

Esnouf Carteret, on the other hand, a pauper knitter, aged 24, lived with his grandmother, also a pauper, in what was listed as a separate unit, next door to the Foreign and Travellers' Hotel. [91]

Total poor relief was available only in cases of illness for adults or extreme poverty for children. This involved indoor relief at the Town hospital, at the expense of the parish. Time spent in hospital was thought to ensure that the very poor or infirm "..sont bien nourris, bien entrenus, soignés par un medecin habile en cas de maladie, et instruits dans les devoirs de le religion". [92] In 1846, 111 people were in St Helier's hospital, all of them supported by the Island's parishes. [93] Rare cases of relief involved the parish undertaking to finance a parishioner's passage to emigrate to America, Australia or Canada. [94] Many nineteenth-century writers attributed the low number of parishioners receiving poor relief to the workings of pride. William Plees, writing in 1817, claimed pride to be "more generally operative in small than in large communities. In this island, where the link of affinity is so extended, that passion has great influence". [95] Such a view was supported by Philip Aubin, the Connétable of St Helier, in his evidence to the Crown appointed Commission in 1861, when he suggested that many of the rural poor resorted to living in the Town to try and conceal their poverty. [96] Such a predicament was not eased by the process of applying for aid which entailed a submission of name and details before the Parish Assembly. The only exception to this was the appropriately called 'Les Pauvres Honteux', a fund based on private donations. Application for relief from this fund did not entail the submission of details, although the sum received was necessarily less.

Characteristics of the Jersey People

The Jersey people presented a picture reflecting Norman origins and English loyalties. Writing in 1815, William Berry noted "The generality of the natives have much more the appearance of French than English people, whose manners and customs they seem naturally to have imbibed, or instinctively to inherit, from their Norman extraction. Poor and parsimonious in their living and dress, even their domestic utensils and implements of husbandry are all in the French style". [97] This identity was reinforced by the local language, Norman French or Jèrriais, spoken by the majority of the population to the exclusion of all other. Some English was spoken in the Town by 1800, but was confined to the upper classes. Long separation from Normandy had resulted in Jèrriais becoming what some observers felt was a patois, unrecognisable even to a Norman. [98] It was a spoken tongue without any effective written form, a situation only partially remedied by nationalist writers in the nineteenth century. The fortunes of Jèrriais will be viewed as a crucial indicator of the effect of the English immigrant population on the Island.

To what extent then could the country population be considered Norman in their lifestyles? Everyday life in the countryside, at the beginning of the nineteenth century, was in some respects similar to that of a French peasant. H.D. Inglis, unlike other writers of the period, spent some time among the native population and the picture he portrays in 1834, is one of simplicity, industriousness and austerity. Having entered a farmhouse, "if your visit is made about noon, you will find a good fire burning on the hearth, boiling the soup kettle. The fire is composed of vraic (seaweed), and a few fagots; and the soup which boils in the kettle, is called 'soupe à choux' the staple of Jersey country diet. This soup is made by boiling together as much cabbage, lard, and potatoes, as suffices for the family dinner. Sometimes, but rarely, a little meat is added". [99] Among the more wealthy farmers, Inglis added, occasional deviations from the basic soup were to be observed, but milk and meat were rarely consumed, despite being produced by the household; "a Jersey farmer lives upon that part of the produce of his land, which is the least valuable; and carries the rest to market". An unwillingness to part with ready cash, except for the purchase of tea and sugar, resulted in a poor diet, and one that "suffers sadly, in a comparison with the huge pieces of bacon, the new milk cheese, and the pitchers of ale, which disappear before the farm servants of our English counties". [100]

In costume the country folk appeared typically French. To William Plees this reflected an isolation from the Town: "we not infrequently meet the old farmer, with his large cocked hat, and thin 'queue à la française', and among females, the short jacket or bed gown, and coarse red petticoat, still forms a prevalent though declining costume". [101]

The original Norman link which had established so much of the basis for the Jersey social experience was evident in the rural population but six centuries of separation, albeit not absolute, had resulted in some fundamental changes. Most important in this respect was the absence of a vigorous communal life. Individualism was a characteristic of the Jerseyman, based around the sanctity of the household and rooted in a Calvinist discipline. It was an individualism based in the ownership of land and supported by a non-coerced settlement pattern. The very design of the farming unit with its high surrounding walls and thick oak doors was a physical manifestation of what Dalido, a French sociologist, called a self-imposed "imperméabilité". [102] Only when circumstances demanded did households unite and cooperation take place, but it was a cooperation undertaken within very definite guidelines.

The autonomy of the household was periodically waived, when economic need arose. Certain agricultural tasks, ranging from cider making to the cooking of a local delicacy known as 'nier beurre' (black butter), but more usually the great ploughing and threshing, demanded a pooling of resources in the community. 'La Grande Charrue', the great ploughing, was an operation so large that it demanded the help of extra skilled labour and equipment; ten horses and eight men. [103] A distinct pecking order was observed among the participants, with the proprietor leading the small opening plough and the farmer considered most skilled directing the main plough. In return the host provided a large dinner for his friends and the promise that his help would be forthcoming for similar operations on their farms. [104] It was an exercise in communal cooperation. But, whilst it was common practice and mutually beneficial, Philippe Ahier of Seymour Farm, St Martin, was adamant that it was subject to certain limits. He told the French agriculturist, Galichet, in 1912, "On met à profit le voisinage pour s'entr'aider, non-pour se gêner". [105]

Such neighbourly in-trading reflected a willingness to cooperate between households, but little more than that. The point is illustrated by the efforts of Peter Kropotkin, the Russian anarchist and theoretician, to show how an Island of small proprietors lived in some form of communal harmony. All he could point to as evidence of this cooperation were these seasonal and isolated unions of labour. [106] He was writing in the late nineteenth century, a time when paid labour was employed in agriculture throughout the Island and utilised to meet many of these seasonal demands. The increase in agricultural labourers might be thought to have undermined previous communal practices, but it is more likely that such practices were never particularly popular. Accounts earlier in the century bear out the essential proposition; when pointing to the communal effort, there was little else other than La Grande Charrue. [107]

Individualism did not in itself mean a total absence of communal expression, rather that it was limited in extent and, more often than not, found its outlet within family bounds. Social gatherings on a large scale were rare, several annual fairs, militia reviews and horse races, but nothing on the scale of the great fêtes on the Continent. In part this absence of secular expression and the 'imperméabilité' of the household was rooted in the Calvinist experience of the post-Reformation period. Under the strict Protestant regime social life had been rigidly controlled and the result was a population whose characteristic traits were puritanical and parsimonious. [108] Such a mentality goes a long way to explain the success of Methodism after its introduction in the 1780s, because it offered much that was cherished by the local population: discipline, temperance, strict morality and rustic simplicity.

The Calvinist spirit remained strong until at least the end of the eighteenth century. This can be gauged by the fact that the one area concerned with the Church within the Code of Laws published in 1771, dealt with morality and discipline. The *Réglemens pour l'observation du jour dimanche* demanded that Sunday be kept sacrosanct, detailed fines for non-punctuality for Divine Service and for being caught carrying money or burdens, and restricted licensing hours to a bare minimum. [109] It was a direct continuation of post-

Reformation Calvinism. In similar vein was the parish's stated duty, via the office of Surveillant, to present to the Ecclesiastical Court those thought to be guilty of immoral behaviour. In 1788, 37 of the 43 cases presented to the Ecclesiastical Court were concerned with immorality, mainly sex related, and ranged from Nicolas Arthur being actioned for "l'anticipation de la bénédiction de leur marriage", to Elizabeth Le Gresley being censored for "paillardise". [110] In all cases, the judges, the Dean and several of his rectors, were concerned that the guilty should make peace with the Church, often involving the public showing of remorse at Divine service. [111]

The drinking of alcohol was not totally contrary to the Calvinist creed. Some taverns existed in the countryside but, judging by their location, were often aimed at the labouring class rather than the dispersed farmers. In St John there were three taverns listed in the 1851 Census, among a population of 2,005. One tavern was located near the parish church, the other two at Mont Mado, at that time a thriving granite quarry. The pattern was similar in St Ouen, where four taverns served a population of 2,464. [112] At home, the native farmer might well indulge in home-made cider. Inglis noted cider as the drink of "all rank". [113] For those of a more religious persuasion, the faith and alcohol were ill-suited. Methodism placed a strong emphasis on temperance and self-discipline and, judging by the popularity of that denomination in the countryside, there were many who agreed. Indeed, one of the strongest criticisms to be levied against migrant French labourers, in the later half of the nineteenth century, was their excessive drinking habits. [114] More generally, however, it is unlikely that Jerseymen, who were so parsimonious in every other sphere, including food, were likely to spend much money on alcohol.

Calvinist discipline had a restrictive effect on other forms of enjoyment too. Music appears to have played but a small part in native life. In church, hymns were sung accompanied by various instruments but outside there is no evidence to suggest a music culture. [115] Inglis claimed "The natives do not encourage music", and by this he meant even in the Town. [116] Those folk songs available today appear to be the contrived response of Jersey patriots to cultural challenge in the later nineteenth century. Dancing was likewise anathema to country folk, as the *Quarterly Journal*, half-mockingly, noted in 1842. Whilst dancing was universal in England on occasions such as Christmas it was, said the *Journal*, absent in Jersey; "They say it is inconsistent with the solemn origin of Christmas". [117]

Alongside the more established religions, existed the occult. Witch burnings had occurred in Jersey in the sixteenth century. By the nineteenth century, there is little reference to the occult in any source. However, involvement in the occult appears to have been fairly common, ranging from a mere belief in the spirit world to actual participation in rites and spell-casting. The Reverend Skinner, in Jersey in 1827, noted the general fear of the unknown. He asked a local peasant woman if she could tell him anything about the Armorial representation, near St Martin's Church: "Oui", she replied "il ne vaut rien, il ne faut pas parler de cela parceque c'est quelque chose de mauvais, debous gens ne veulent pas le donner attention". [118] It has been suggested, that the belief in fairies and other supernatural creatures was closely linked to a general apprehension over the Island's many prehistoric burial sites. It is not unusual to find the link between fairies and dolmens reflected in road names, such as Rue à la Dame, in St Saviour, and Le Lavoir des Dames, in St John. The serious nature of these beliefs is not to be doubted. As recently as 1912, a Société Jersiaise archaeological dig at Les Monts Grantez, St Ouen, was temporarily suspended by the actions of an old man, fearful that the excavations would disturb the fairies. [119]

It is difficult to ascertain the extent to which Jersey country folk dabbled in the occult. Today's rural community, not unlike country populations elsewhere, retains a popular belief in the ability of certain of its members to heal. These so-called 'charmers' have long been associated in the Island with the curing of warts. J.H. L'Amy's collection of folklore in the 1920s makes reference to several known charmers. [120] More specifically, the Reverend Thomas Le Neveu, Rector of St Martin, cited cases from the 1840s of countryfolk receiving attention for a range of ailments from individuals believed to possess the power to heal. [121] Black magic was also practised. Le Neveu recounted cases of people he had known who believed a run of bad luck or a misfortune derived from the curse of a malevolent neighbour.[122]

Leisure and communal activities were not determined by religious strictures and individualism alone. The Jersey country population worked a long and arduous day. "The English labourer", remarked Inglis, "is early in the fields, but then he goes to bed betimes. The Jersey farmer, is yet earlier in the fields; but he is also up late. In most of the Jersey country houses, lights are seen in the window at eleven; and in many, even towards midnight". [123] Long hours cut down leisure time. Important Island societies were, not surprisingly, based in the Town of St Helier, but to travel there from the other side of the Island could take some time. The creation of parish-based agricultural societies with open membership, from at least 1848, was as much a reflection on the inconvenient location of the Royal Jersey Agricultural and Horticultural Society as it was of the dislike of the pretensions of certain of its members.[124]

For the majority of country males, spare time was taken up by, if not created for, militia service, church, and, for a lesser number, honorary service for the parish. Of the three, militia service affected the greater number, it being compulsory for all local males aged between 17 and 65. During the course of the nineteenth century, militia service became increasingly unpopular, as the memories of the Napoleonic Wars faded and the raison d'être of a voluntary defence force became progressively undermined. Sunday morning drill was the most unpopular of all activities and Regiment Colonels found themselves continually in the Royal Court presenting defaulters for punishment. [125] Onerous drill duties were exacerbated by friction between the ranks and irritation at how certain individuals managed to be exempted from the Militia altogether.[126] In 1820 over a quarter of the male population served in the Militia. By 1860 the figure had declined to less than one eighth, 97 per cent of which was made up of farmers and artisans.[127]

Nonetheless, the Jersey population found time for some activities other than work. Folk culture generally, as elsewhere, combined religious and pagan with the rhythm of the seasons. In many instances, this meant that practical tasks could acquire a celebratory character. Thus, at Easter, the necessity of collecting the highly prized vraic from the shoreline, for use both as fuel and fertiliser, was turned into a festive occasion, by combining it with the collection of limpets, a prized edible shellfish, allowing families something of a celebratory feast.[128] In similar fashion, La Grande Charrue and the making of black butter were occasions to feast with your friends. The 'veilles', virtually a universal institution in France, had their local origin in the knitting industry. 'Veilles' were essentially winter evenings spent among friends around the fireside, although Inglis reported in the 1830s that the practice had much declined.[129] 'Veilles' also appear to have provided a chance for courtship among young folk, albeit under the watchful eye of their parents.[130]

Celebrations at Christmas and Easter were family centred. "Christmas time is indeed, a week of feasting and merrymaking", wrote Inglis. "On these occasions, there is a family gathering, twenty or thirty perhaps, being assembled, including all who are related to the heads of a family, as far as cousinship. On these occasions the 'soupe à choux' is discarded; fresh pork is substituted for its pickled relative: roast beef, such as would not disgrace the table of an English squire, takes its place. Eating and drinking, although the staple amusement, is not the only one. Cards and dominoes are introduced....while the Christmas song, the laugh, and the jest, go round".[131] Easter was celebrated in similar style, and the feast included local specialities like 'fiottes' and 'mèrvelles'.[132]

Certain celebrations, namely those which involved pranks or tomfoolery, were the prerogative of the young. The 'Dimanche des Brandons', celebrated on the first Sunday in Lent, involving youngsters of both sexes singing and dancing around a bonfire.[133] The eve of St John's Day in June was usually celebrated by the 'Faire Braire les Poets'. The ceremony was observed by John Stead in 1809, and consisted of the assembling of a makeshift brass band from kitchen utensils and the making of as much noise as possible; a "singularly discordant ceremony" was how Plees described it.[134] Both these festivals, and others, had Norman parallels.[135]

With the Breton, and even more so the Norman, the Jersey peasantry shared a past and a present. Even so, in 1815, there was an obvious distinction between the mass of the population and the upper sections who, shared past or not, were determined that their future lay with a different camp. William Berry observed that "with those in the higher circles of life, who are now receiving English educations, and have constant intercourse with Britain," the French influence "is evidently wearing off by degrees". [136]

This apparent difference in attitude among the native population towards their shared origins was further complicated by the growth of the Town and the development of a distinct urban culture. In the Town, the distinction between native and non-native was to become less clear as the nineteenth century progressed. Language, dress, and lifestyle identified the individual's affiliation. This was most evident in dress, the Town costume by the 1830s being "nearly that which is common in English towns". [137] Plees even noted a distinction in the customs practised by Town inhabitants, claiming St Helier festivities, such as Milk-a-Punch Day and the Easter Monday celebrations at Mont Orgueil castle, resembled those of the English working classes. [138] Ansted and Latham, writing in 1862, claimed that St Helier resembled in many respects a typical English Cathedral Town, with the fashion conscious society people doing the rounds of theatre and soirées around the piano. [139]

The lifestyles of the mass of the rural population and the upper sections were clearly different. This had much to do with wealth. Few members of the rural middle classes could afford to lead a life equalling that of the Jersey gentry. In agricultural terms alone, few could afford to pay for purchasing visits to England in search of new machinery, as did the Seigneur of Trinity in 1820. [140] Similarly, few families could afford to make Militia officers out of more than one member of their household, because the cost precluded their fulfilling the social obligations of such a post. Colonel John Le Couteur, himself a high ranking Militia Colonel, admitted that such an action would bring ruin upon a family of limited fortune. [141] The lifestyle demanded of high social positions was expensive, as the numerous banquets, society subscriptions, charitable donations and fashion demands showed.

But there was more to the distinction between the mass of the native population and the upper middle classes than simply wealth. The Jersey upper middle class desired an English lifestyle, saw the possibilities of such in the Town and did their utmost to achieve it. It is not proposed to go into too much detail on this theme here, because it will be treated in the main body of the book. Suffice it to say at this point, that St Helier appeared to offer what the anglophiles of Jersey society required. The Town housed the Queen's Assembly Rooms, one of the major venues for society functions, particularly the grand costume balls which took place once a week during the winter, with the names of those who attended being listed in the local press. [142] As we have noted, all the Island's major organisations and societies were likewise based in St Helier. Geographically, it was an obvious location, but there was more to it than that. The majority of the English society people who came to live in the Island were based in St Helier, and these were the people that a great number of the local elite and the aspiring bourgeoisie wished to emulate.

Institutions

In the previous section, we have observed the Jersey rural population as a people not keen on communal expression. We have seen that a folk culture existed, but that it was constricted by a Calvinist discipline, and by the demands of work and family. The various pressures upon this traditional lifestyle, particularly for an upper middle-class desirous of something different, have also been presented.

One crucial aspect of the Jersey rural community's existence must now be mentioned; that is, the institutional outlet it allowed itself for communal expression. The most tangible unit of everyday existence, apart from the individual household, was the parish, in both its ecclesiastical and civil mould. It is here that we must look for the most precise definition of the rural community. [143]

In the life of the whole rural population the Church played a fundamental rôle. Sunday Services provided the only regular point of contact for parishioners. Within the walls of the church was reflected a veritable image of the hierarchical divisions among parish society. The proximity of the pew to the Rector and the communion table designated the rank, status, and, more relevant, the wealth of its incumbent. In the parish of St Ouen, the three major seigneurs of the parish shared the prime position. In St Peter in 1872, C.P. Le Cornu bemoaned the fact that he had to pay £85 for the La Hague pew in an auction, believing the price to have been pushed up from its true value of £35. [144] Even in 1818, the cheaper pews in St John were fetching as much as £18. [145] In St Saviour, private pews were rented out to the detriment of public seating, there being no apparent provision for the poor. [146]

As the head of the only regular meeting place for the parish population, the Rector found himself in a unique position. His Church was equipped for the parish, for its well defined congregation who all required what only the parson could provide: spiritual and social respectability. If this was not monopoly enough, the church's rôle as a meeting point also gave it control of court and parish announcements, of legal transactions in the 'ouie de paroisse', of the storage of Militia equipment, and of the holding of elections in the porch after Sunday Service.

Clearly, for parishioners, all roads led to the Church. This notion was encapsulated in the saying, "Ch'est-la le chemin d'l'église, ch'est par la qu'les enterrements vont, vous errai l'soin d'prendre par la d'auve le mien". [147] However, the rapid and widespread popularity of Nonconformist creeds, notably Methodism after its introduction in 1783, must shed doubt on the Established Church's ability to perform the tasks demanded of it; this is dealt with at a later stage in the book. In this society of individualism and 'imperméabilite', bound together by a staunch Calvinism and later, for some, a staunch Methodism, there is a curious dearth of evidence relating to details of popular religious practice. Baptism, marriage and burial were no doubt important times for rural families, but the Calvinist conventions imbibed since the post-Reformation Presbyterianism suggest that these occasions were solemn events, with a minimum of ostentation. What can be suggested, however, is that implicit in the make-up of the rural population was a requirement, seemingly at odds with its socio/psychological characteristics, for some manifestation of a collective identity. This was desired as a form of expression, as a reinforcement of communal traditions and values, and, increasingly in the nineteenth century, as a defence of the rural way of life. The parish provided this framework: all communal activities utilised it as such a unit.

Prior to Methodism, religious and secular were co-terminous both physically and mentally. After the 1780s there was an increasing separation of the two. In the religious sphere, this separation was reflected in a divide between Established Church and Nonconformism; in the secular sphere, by an increased differentiation between the body civil and the body ecclesiastic. The shared collective for all remained the parish, redefined, yet essentially the same basic unit which for centuries had provided a framework for Island life.

In an Island as small as Jersey it was possible for the States legislature to be localised enough for the mass of the population to be familiar with its proceedings. In each parish, at least a triumvirate of politicians, the Connétable, the Rector and a Jurat, would be personally known to the people. It is likely that this familiarity would be extended to nearby parishes, through either friends or family attachments. It was a familiarity which no doubt provided a reassurance as to the preservation of one's way of life. The urbanisation of St Helier and of parts of its adjoining parishes and the perception by the rural folk of a body of people with different interests, values, and even language, created two worlds in the Island. These worlds were transcendable on some levels, but distinct nonetheless. It was in this situation that the parish came to the fore, as both a preserver and a buffer against incursion.

The interest in parish politics reflected the importance placed on parish representation in the legislature. The Connétable was the elected delegate, regularly instructed by the Assembly on how to vote on each issue. In 1785 the Parish Assembly of St Clement, prompted by a suggestion in the States regarding an Island tax, deliberated upon the rôle of their leader. The question arose as to whether the Connétable "doit consulter ses Paroissens, ou s'il a le droit, de lui même, de donner son opinion sur le sujet, dans les Etats sans consulter ses dit Paroissens, et qu'il auroit été trouvé alors que apoint auroit été de grand consequence au public, il étoit nécessaire de la remettre à une assemblée des Principaux, officiers et Chefs de Famille".[148] It was agreed that in all matters, with the exceptionof defence, which might demand emergency decisions, the Connétable's stance must be decided by the majority opinion of the Assembly.[149] In all the parishes, acts of the Assembly generally conclude with "Le Connétable été charge de voter dans les Etats...".[150]

The rôle of the Connétable and his officers reflected this strong interest in the affairs of the community. Their rôle was the administration and policing of the parish in paternalist fashion; keeping parish matters within parish hands. Recourse to the instruments of justice outside the parish, that is the Royal Court, was made only when totally necessary. That a defendant's first call to justice was the 'enditement' or jury made up of his own Connétable and twelve of the parish's sworn officers was an extension of this idea, one which lasted until 1863.[151] John Le Couteur, although untypical of the country Connétables, nonetheless settled matters in the traditional manner as Connétable of St Brelade. The argument between Mrs. Gruchy and her two neighbours, whose sheep had allegedly eaten and trodden on her corn, was settled by Le Couteur suggesting they each pay 20 sols for every offending sheep.[152] The incident was not recorded in any official parish book and was judged upon on the spot by the parish arbitrator.

Even for those ineligible to vote in elections, parish politics remained a focus of much attention. For much of the 80 years between 1769 and 1850, the Island found itself divided into hostile political camps. The Rose or Laurel parties, as they had become by the nineteenth century, fiercely opposed every possible parish election. Yet their competition, like the earlier Charlot and Magot struggle of the 1770s, was less about ideas than about personalities. More often than not, opponents in politics were not concerned with policy, but with establishing or retaining parish oligarchies. We shall go into this sphere in some detail in the third section, but here it should be noted how the parish represented the main battle arena for local politics, and how it managed to involve large numbers in every parish.

One must be careful not to present too idyllic a picture of the parish as a natural unit, self-sufficient in justice and administration. The attacks on the many deficiencies and injustices of parish organisation brought by the Crown Commissions of 1848 and 1861, the urban based reformists, and parishioners themselves, will serve to balance the picture. The purpose here is to show how, at its best, the parish provided a useful component in a tight-knit society, a collective framework for a body of individualists. The great strength of the rural bloc rested with its representation in the States. Even after the introduction of elected Deputies in 1854, a deliberate attempt to distinguish between parish and legislature, it tended to be those who had made their way up through the municipal ranks who were elected.[153] The legal relationship between the States and the parishes remained ill-defined. Attempts to amend this state of affairs could be successfully thwarted. At the end of the nineteenth century, the parish had quite successfully warded off all attempts to redefine its rôle, and, with the exception of minor incursions, remained strong enough to ward off all major attempts at centralisation.

A community identity centred on the parish was reinforced by an identity shared at different levels, which could transcend the bounds of party politics and parish loyalty. At a cultural level, a Jersey identity derived from the local tongue, Jèrriais. Unintelligible to outsiders, it was a medium which linked local people to one another and would, during the course of the nineteenth century, be raised as a rallying point in defence of a cultural onslaught by the English language. On a broader plane, there was evidence of a Jersey ethnic or national identity, an identity not necessarily in conflict with loyalty to the English Crown, but an assertion of attachment to local institutions and a degree of self-independence. At a time when other levels of identity had been undermined, this national identity bound Jerseymen together, including even those of the Town. These feelings of allegiance were to trouble urban-based local reformers who found themselves torn between the need to reform and allegiance to their Island.

The parish will be recognised throughout this work as a major index to change in the nineteenth century. In an Island characterised by an absence of communal expression, the parish, as the only institutional representative of a collective identity, reflected the attitudes and responses of the rural population to change and possible threats to the traditional way of life. As a unit of administration, it had a degree of power, manifested most directly through its political representative, over both its own affairs and those of the Island as a whole. During the course of the nineteenth century the rural parishes showed this power collectively in the States against all attempts at major reform.

The parish in its ecclesiastical mould had, for several centuries, proved a community of the faithful. However, the advent of Nonconformism, particularly Methodism in the 1780s, and a growth in secular power, undermined the former comprehensive hold of the Established Church over parish affairs. The collective unit redefined itself increasingly around the contours of the parish civil, and its very strength relied on the fact that the majority of its population continued to live, work and worship within its boundaries. To reach any understanding of the rural community in nineteenth century Jersey it is necessary to view it through the medium of the parish.

Section Two

Change and Challenge

Introduction

For an Island which for centuries had remained relatively isolated and free from major outside influence, the nineteenth century brought many changes and challenges. The advent of the steamship on Channel Island routes after 1824 and the introduction of the Electric Telegraph to Jersey in 1870, in both a real and symbolic sense, represented the forces thrust upon Jersey from the outside. These forces overcame the physical barrier of the sea, so long the defence of the Channel Islands against new peoples and new ideas. In the course of half a century, a once unknown Crown outpost was to be turned into a location familiar to a large body of immigrants, travel writers, economic theorists, tourists and parliamentarians alike.

This section is an attempt to examine the various forces of change and challenge unleashed upon Jersey society in the nineteenth century and to gauge how that society fared. It will be particularly concerned with the response of the traditional country landed interest or, as it is called in this work, the rural community. The importance of this approach is more fully appreciated when we consider that the forces of change, with one major exception - that of Nonconformism - were based in the urban area, the main location of immigrants and a successful economy.

The Napoleonic Wars were in many ways the great unleasher of change in the Island of Jersey. They brought many people to the Island and encouraged an already active capitalist economy to expand and diversify. In the wake of the Wars, the two essential ingredients which laid the foundations for a changing Jersey society were people, in the form of a large body of immigrants, and money, fuelled by a new body of entrepreneurs and workers, ready to build on the experiences of the local merchant and commercial sectors.

Jersey's population increased from a wartime total of 22,000 in 1806 to a nineteenth-century peak 57,000 in 1851. The vast bulk of its immigrant population came from England and its colonies. These immigrants were attracted to the Island by its climate, its cheapness of living, its economic potential and its political affiliations with Britain. Their presence both fuelled and helped foster the relaunch of the Jersey economy in the post-war period. This economy included a significant cod trade and overseas carrying trade, and a shipbuilding industry. The large body of non-natives in the Island provided a force of change by their very presence. As they were English speakers in a land of French speakers and its localised equivalent, Jèrriais, a basic divide was immediately obvious. English was equipped with a body of speakers convinced of its superiority and an academic and grammatical base.

Furthermore, it was supported by the social desires of a section of the local middle class. Jèrriais, by contrast, was a patois with no practised written form. What ensued was a battle of languages, unresolved in the nineteenth century, but by its close turning very much in favour of English. A major tenet of Jersey's identity was thus challenged in an almost unconscious and effortless manner.

Real challenge, however, came with far more conscious effort and was not solely external in origin. Economic growth and the opportunities of the Victorian world produced a native commercial bourgeoisie, whose wealth and desire for political power unleashed a further barrage on Jersey's traditions and historical development. Coupled with the demands of the English middle class, the urban based Jersey bourgeoisie set about an intended course of restructuring and realigning its society to a basis more reflective of the demands of nineteenth-century society. It set about challenging the historical power base of the rural community.

The country bloc, too, benefited from the general expansion of trade and commerce. The rural population developed its own highly specialised and remunerative agricultural industry, one which in the event would outlive the commercial and financial empires of the great local cod houses. In power terms, the country dominance of the local legislature enabled the rural community to regulate Jersey society according to its own social and economic needs. This rural oligarchy became increasingly intolerable to the urban based capitalists.

Yet simultaneous to a challenge to its political base, the rural community faced a seemingly even more direct threat to its traditional structures, in the shape of Nonconformism. The arrival and rapid popularity of dissenting religion, particularly Methodism, threatened to undermine that most cherished of all institutions, the parish, whose existence had for so long been bound up with the Established Church. What made the threat so potent was that it came not from outside, but from within, the result of a conscious effort by members of the rural community to choose a new religion.

The challenge to Jersey society in the nineteenth century was then both external and internal, and composed of threats to the social, economic, religious and cultural spheres. This work, however, is not charting the course of a triumphant challenge to Jersey, because these challenges were not, on the whole, successful. The threats, which at times appeared most potent, were mildened by several factors. Economically, English capital got no where near securing a measure of control over the Jersey economy until at least the 1880s. Any political challenge from locally-based English reformers was weakened by this fact. Native urban reformers found themselves torn between the desire for political power and loyalty to an Island, whose independence and privileges vis-à-vis the English mainland were a main foundation to local commercial wealth. The nonconformist challenge was assimilated by the rural community and the parish recast in a secular mould. Only the cultural challenge was to shown any signs of success by the end of the nineteenth century. We will now turn to examining these forces of challenge in detail.

Chapter 3

The Economic Development of Nineteenth-century Jersey

The nineteenth century was, in many respects, a period of economic success for Jersey. Certainly, it was a success loudly acclaimed by all who visited the Island. In agriculture the potential of the small proprietor, noted by theorists ranging from De Lavergne to Kropotkin, was borne out in triumphs in potato cultivation and livestock rearing, all for a specialised export market and all highly remunerative. [1] Externally, the Newfoundland codfisheries and the world carrying trade, supported by an expanding shipbuilding industry in the Island, made Jersey the fourteenth largest fleet in Britain.

It was no wonder that the author of the article in the *Quarterly Journal* in 1843 was puzzled: "Now, if a political economist was to lay down this doctrine, the population of a country, though far exceeding the number which its soil and fisheries, and manufactures are capable of maintaining, may increase rapidly, export largely, and possess every reasonable comfort, without any direct extraneous support, he would be considered crazy, or ignorant of the first principles of the science which he professes, and yet he would be fully borne out in his assertions by the actual circumstances of Jersey". [2]

The author had not, as he feared, got his economics wrong. He had simply failed to take into account the fact that the Jersey economy had an extra dimension which enabled the local population to overcome the intrinsic hindrances of a small island to sustained economic growth. That dimension was brought about by a number of factors. Firstly, Jersey's geographical location provided the Island with several advantages. Its mild climate was ideal for agriculture. Furthermore, the combination of proximity to France with a close political relationship with England cast the Island as as entrepôt, involved in both legitimate trade and smuggling between its larger neighbours. Secondly, Jersey's historical rôle as a strategic outpost for England resulted in political and economic favours. Most important amongst these in economic terms was the Island's right of free trade with England and its colonies. Together these factors provided the Jersey population with a strong base for economic expansion.

The period from the end of the Napoleonic Wars in 1815 to the financial crash of 1886 witnessed Jersey's most concentrated exploitation of its economic advantages. Trade and commerce were nothing new to the Jersey population and during the course of the nineteenth century this experience was put to good use. The potential for economic development was enhanced by large-scale immigration to the Island which provided a sizeable labour force, a new body of entrepreneurs and a significant local consumer market.

Greater advantage, too, was now to be taken of the Island's trading privileges. Jersey's past mercantile successes had relied on British protection and Parliament's acceptance that the Channel Islands were a part of Britain, and thus entitled to share in its areas of exploitation.[3] The nineteenth century mercantile economy was equally reliant on these privileges. In agriculture too, the fine line between prosperity and mediocre development rested on more than just a favourable climate and industriousness; success was dependent on the ability to export produce to a large market tariff free.

The basis of Jersey's economic success was, however, more precarious than theorists and writers such as De Lavergne and Kropotkin tended to suggest. Trading on the periphery of the great powers and relying on the ability to exploit the Island's political position to achieve economic advantage was an uncertain foundation for an economy. With all factors utilised to the utmost advantage, Jersey traded high among the powers, but in the final reckoning was only a small Island and could have no influence over major policies. Jersey agriculturists, for example, found themselves threatened with the withdrawal of privileges throughout the century, ranging from the Corn Laws to the cattle plague exclusion in the 1860s, but by successful lobbying they managed to avoid the worst. Shipbuilding and the cod fisheries were not so fortunate and in the late 1870s went into rapid decline, the cumulative effect of factors which they often could not control. Agriculture proved more durable than the mercantile and commercial sectors, mainly because it was vested in something not quite so variable as the dictates of the overseas trade, the land. Its progress through the century was apparently one of strength to strength, but the potato blight of 1845, bad harvests in the 1880s and the fluctuations of livestock export revealed shaky foundations, designed for quick profit rather than long term sustenance.

Furthermore, despite the Island's earlier experiences of economic development, the combined forces of English immigrants, a growing entrepreneurial class and an expanding economy represented a degree and range of capitalism and commercialisation unknown to Jersey society and, more pertinently, suggested the potential to overwhelm it. These forces provided the foundations for the challenge to the rural community. Caught in the throes of economic change and expansion itself, the rural bloc found both its political hegemony and its traditional way of life under threat. This challenge was rooted in the frustration of financially powerful merchant and commercial sectors at their inability to find access to power in the Island. This chapter is an attempt to explain how the economic basis for a challenge was created and how it was matched by a rural community which showed itself able to change economically and ensure its interests and power base in the States remained secure.

The Post-Napoleonic Period

The economic challenge to the rural community was not seen immediately. It would take several years after 1815 before the local merchant sector had re-established itself on its pre-war footing, let alone developed and expanded. It would take the English immigrant population even longer before its numerical force was matched by any equivalent economic power.

It was noted in the introductory section how the near-siege conditions of the Napoleonic Wars did not result in a revolutionary departure for the Jersey economy from pre-war trends. Rather, a slight realignment occurred, with a local market augmented by garrison troops and by French exiles ensuring that capitalist profits were maintained. The wartime siege had resulted in prosperity for some, particularly agriculturists, who had exploited high market prices. Nonetheless, some degree of depression was felt in the immediate aftermath of the Wars. The few newspapers of the period point to the effects of deflation as the large garrison, naval squadron and many of the refugees left the Island. Market prices dropped and farmers were not keen to sell locally; it appears that there was some time lapse between the declaration of peace and the return of the French traders with their marketable produce. In November, 1816, an editorial in the *Chronique* demanded that the export of potatoes be restricted to that surplus to local requirements. The paper also noted that grain was in short supply. [4] Claims for action to redress this situation ceased only after the Lieutenant-Governor's assurance that 82,000 cabots of corn would be retained for domestic consumption. [5]

Farmers, too, were concerned. In a speech to the States in 1819, unsuccessfully urging a ban on the importation of French cider to protect local producers, the Reverend Ricard, Rector of St Ouen, portrayed the countryside as in a state of depression. He claimed farmers were unable to find outlets for exports and were facing low prices and a much diminished market in the Island. [6] In what was to become a lasting struggle between town and country, the Connétable of St Helier retorted that the situation was far worse in the Town, with mass unemployment and low wages. Those fortunate enough to be in work were receiving no more than 40 sols a day. Cider, the main drink of the Island, was costing 40 sols a pot. [7]

The urban unemployment felt after 1815 was directly related to the withdrawal of the large wartime population. The merchant sector, experiencing difficulties in trying to re-establish itself, could offer few jobs. The Newfoundland cod-trade had been severely curtailed, despite diversification, with its markets, supply lines and even its centre of production overseas disturbed and now based in the Gaspé Peninsula. [8] Time was required to reorganise and adjust to new circumstances. The situation was exacerbated by the determined efforts of the British Government once and for all to put an end to smuggling in the Islands, a determination which was interrupting the daily flow of trade, although it appears to have affected Guernsey more than Jersey. [9]

By 1820, however, and increasingly throughout the decade, the post-war depression was halted and a basis was created for the expansion and development of the economy on an unprecedented scale. The reversal of depression was heralded and, in the long-term, sustained, by the massive increase in the Island's population. This was primarily the result of a large number of English immigrants choosing to settle in the Island. By 1821 the population had risen from the 1806 wartime figure of 22,855 to 28,600, by 1831 the population numbered 36,582, a growth of over 20 per cent in a decade. It was an increase which, claimed the visiting Mudie, was "almost unprecedented except in single manufacturing towns under very extraordinary circumstances". [10] By 1851 rapid augmentation had continued with the population rising to 57,155. [11]

Precisely who Jersey's early immigrants were is unclear. This is mainly because the earlier censuses give no details as to origins. Mudie estimated in 1839 that at least 3,000 of the immigrants, excluding trades people, were what he called "resident English", that is "those who reside in a place without tie or employment". Three-quarters of this group, he claimed, were half-pay officers and their families. [12] If we look at the Census for 1851, the first source able to give the degree of information required, we see that English immigrants in St Helier, their main location, were dominated by artisans (24 per cent) and labourers (21 per cent). Those of independent means, which by 1851 included few half-pay officers, made up 8 per cent of the group, whilst individuals who classed themselves as professional or managerial accounted for 5 per cent. The remaining 42 per cent were family dependants. [13]

There was much to separate these groups of English people in Jersey. Inglis, writing in 1834, divided the urban population of St Helier into "business and idleness", the English 'residents' (using a definition similar to Mudie's) forming the main part of the latter. [14] He was not far wrong. The most basic divide between English immigrants was based on their reasons for coming to the Island, something which was determined by wealth. For the middle class, Jersey offered a warm climate, proximity to home and, what Inglis, with some exaggeration, called a "great cheapness of living". Jersey was free of any form of taxation and imported goods were free of excise. Thus consumables such as tea could be obtained at half their price in England. Wines and spirits too were available at reduced prices. [15] The author of *Queen of the Isles* claimed, perhaps somewhat optimistically, that those with incomes of between £50 to £100 per annum could expect to be able to save at least 30 per cent by living in the Island. [16]

Such prospects for saving by the English middle class no doubt paled against the realities of life for labourers and small artisans. Whilst aided by the cheapness of imported goods and alcohol, they faced low wages and high rents on property. Jamieson has shown how maritime workers received wages consistently lower than their counterparts on the English mainland. [17] Low wages did not help pay property rents which Inglis estimated to be 25 per cent higher than their English equivalent. [18] It is clear that artisans and labourers came to the Island primarily to find employment.

The experiences of English artisans and labourers are most relevant because they appear to have been the mainstay of the immigrant contribution to the Jersey economy. This is difficult to substantiate for the whole economy, but information is available from both the maritime trades and the agricultural industry. Among the leaders of Jersey industry, it is clear that there was but a small English presence. All the major cod companies, the power-houses of the Island economy, were controlled by Jersey families, and remained that way until their decline in the 1880s. [19] A similar picture emerges from a look at local finance houses. Out of 45 houses listed as 'Banquiers de la Ville' in 1815, only four appear to have an English connection. [20] Of the ten leading shipbuilders in the 1830s, only two were English, these being the yards of Frederick Clarke and Edward Allen. [21] The picture is similar with regard to local ship owners. [22]

To find the English presence in the Jersey economy at this period we must look to the shipyards and to the warehouses of St Helier, St Aubin and Gorey. Here English immigrants plied their trades as ships carpenters, shipwrights, sailmakers and blacksmiths. [23] In 1835, when data are first available, only six per cent of Jersey vessels were manned solely by English crews, but those that were mainly oyster cutters based at Gorey in St Martin. [24] The oyster industry, relatively unskilled and labour intensive, reflects the main thrust of the English presence in the Jersey economy at this time. Gorey was transformed into a village of English labourers and artisans. In a matter of two decades after 1815 the oyster industry there underwent rapid growth and by 1822 was employing 300 vessels, 1,500 British seamen and 1,000 shore staff. [25] Maritime skills were at a premium and by 1832 the village population was significant enough to merit its own Anglican Church (Gouray Church). In the countryside, by contrast, English immigrants were conspicuous by their absence. In 1851 the northern parish of St John counted only 50 English residents out of a total population of 2,005. The more isolated parish of St Ouen had only 30 English residents in a population of 2,464. These figures contrast with St Helier's English population which made up 25 per cent of its total 29,741, and perhaps even more so with the 24 per cent of the only partially urbanised St Saviour. [26]

The English immigrant contribution to the early post-war development of the Jersey economy was thus as a cheap labour force to the urban based industries. Jersey merchants, drawing on this rapidly expanding labour force, were able to recover from wartime and post-war setbacks by making the period 1830 to 1860 the most successful in the Island's trading history. Fish provided Jersey with an entry into the world of trade and exchange. Its export from the Gaspé to the Americas (notably Honduras, Brazil and the West Indies) and Europe (mainly France, Spain, Portugal and Italy) resulted in a return of consumables, raw materials and manufactures, ranging from coffee and sugar to iron and timber. [27] It was the basis of what Ommer has called the Jersey Merchant Triangle. [28]

The Growth of Commerce and Maritime Power

In 1837 an article in the short-lived *Guernsey and Jersey Magazine* claimed that "By far the most important and beneficial branch of the commerce of Jersey are the fisheries on the coasts of British North America. That branch is not only valuable from the direct industry which it promotes, the capital which it employs, and the number of persons who are engaged at the fishery, but it is the root of other indirect industry, and the means of supporting many families. Without her codfishery, the commerce of Jersey would dwindle away". [29] The claim that the codfishery and its related industries provided the basis for Jersey's commercial success in the nineteenth century was well-founded. It is a claim reiterated by Ommer in her study of the merchant triangle, in terms of both infrastructure and capital. It was a claim that the majority of nineteenth-century agriculturists refused to acknowledge.

The cod trade was by far the most important component in the economic structure of nineteenth-century Jersey. In the 1830s it was estimated that the value of the trade to the Island totalled £100,000 per annum, a figure agriculture would not match for another half century. [30] In scale and complexity it remained unequalled, its fleet larger and heavier than any other sea-borne trade and its capital significant enough to diversify into the world-wide carrying trade and into financial and commercial enterprise in the Island. [31]

Unusually for such enterprises with a global network of trade links, claims Ommer, the cod trade made much use of its domestic base. Every sphere of the trade - strategy, marketing, production, support, maintenance and labour - was controlled from the Island. Even where business required operations to be conducted abroad, the large local firms ensured that they were supervised by family members or by individuals incorporated into the trading infrastructure by marriage alliances. [32] In the 1840s, the Robins and the Janvrins, the leading exponents of these closely controlled networks, had such links with London, Liverpool, Halifax and Naples, as well as with each other. [33] An overall business supervision of the trade was provided by the Jersey Chamber of Commerce, established in 1767 by Jersey merchants as a commercial and political watchdog, and as a lobby for their interests. [34]

From the solid foundation of the cod trade the Island developed into a major base for re-export. Shipping brought in raw materials which were assembled and occasionally manufactured in the Island, then sent on to the fisheries. Salt excepted, all other commodities - including flour barrels, cod tubs, biscuits and some clothing - received some degree of processing. [35]

The commodities dealt with by Jersey merchants were carried world-wide by local vessels. By 1846, 372 ships of 33,000 tons were registered in Jersey; 100 of these, ten-tonners based at the fisheries and employing 2,000 seamen. By 1860, 60,000 tons of shipping were registered in Jersey. [36] If we take Jersey non-coastal shipping arriving at the port of London in the year 1840, as an example of the Island's overseas trade, we find that 41 ships had arrived from all parts of the world: from Iberia (five), the Mediterranean (10), North-West Europe (four), North America (two), the Caribbean (three), Honduras (four), South America (nine), the Cape of Good Hope (one), West Africa (two), and India (one). [37]

Shipbuilding developed from within the same local structure through capital investment provided by the great codfishing houses. Between 1815 and 1879, 881 wooden sailing ships (101,638 tons) were built in Jersey yards, the peak year of 1864 accounting for 5.9 per cent of the total tonnage of such vessels built in the United Kingdom. [38]

Indeed, the shipbuilding industry provides a fine example of how the Jersey entrepreneurial class exploited the advantages bestowed upon it by Jersey's peculiar position vis-à-vis Britain. The continuation of Parliament's wartime duties on imported foreign timber and the Channel Islands' exemption from such legislation meant that the raw materials required for shipbuilding were available at a price lower than on the British mainland. The carrying trade's provision of economical transport and cheap labour, already a linchpin in Jersey's cod trade, made for an exploitable advantage. [39] The industry required little capital to sustain it, since a negligible amount of equipment was required for construction, and a trade infrastructure of associated industries in the form of sailmakers, ropemakers and blacksmiths was already present in the ports of St Helier and St Aubin. [40]

Merchant wealth was likewise turned into commercial and financial capital. As early as 1816 the merchant house of P. and F. Janvrin began selling off its assets in the cod trade and became 'Banquiers de la Ville'. By the 1870s Hugh Godfray and Son had developed into the Old Bank, Nicolle, de Ste Croix, Bertram and Company into the Mercantile Union Bank, and Matthews and de Carteret into the Jersey Joint Stock Bank [41] In the commercial sphere the Island's large department stores of Le Gallais and de Gruchy's had a similar beginning. [42]

The carrying trade, shipbuilding industry, service industries, and financial and commercial ventures were in both origin and development a product of the merchant system. The utility of such a linkage system was explained by the President of the Jersey Chamber of Commerce in 1841: "There are employed... as seamen, fishermen and landsmen about 4,000 persons. There are in this Island many families engaged in the making of worsted hose and mitts, wearing apparel, boots and shoes for the use of the fisheries. The trade gives employment to about 8,000 tons of shipping exclusive of those vessels which carry fish to the Brazilian and other markets from this Island". Furthermore, the importance of the merchant system was such that "that trade destroyed, that source of industry dried up, the commerce of this Island would receive a death wound, and many a parent who now, by the industry which this trade supplies, maintains his family in decent pride and honest independence, would probably be obliged to seek relief from the parish, which is a degradation and a stain which a Jerseyman can never forget or overcome". [43]

The success and wealth of the cod trade, expanded and perpetuated by the carrying trade and shipbuilding, as well as by agriculture, although in a slightly different way, combined to make Jersey a generally prosperous society. And it was a prosperity remarked upon by all who visited the Island, from William Plees in 1817 to H.D. Inglis in 1834, to D. Ansted in 1862.[44] It was reflected in the rapid growth of the Town of St Helier which was able to maintain a population of nearly 30,000 in 1851 and the ability of the Island to continue to attract large numbers of immigrants.

The Growth of Agriculture

The circumstances of Jersey agriculture differed fundamentally from those of the externally based economy. Its main resource, the land, was limited and shared between a large number of cultivators. As a result, it sustained high production costs. By merchant standards, agriculture worked within a framework which was restricting and potentially self-defeating, as success resulted in increased population and increased demand on finite resources. However, agriculture was based on the land and the Jersey political structure was dominated by the landed interest. By the 1880s these two considerations enabled local agriculture to avoid the damaging external change that so affected the codfisheries, the world-wide carrying trade and the locally based shipbuilding industry.

Jersey's agricultural success was a subject which interested writers and theorists throughout the nineteenth century. One of the earliest of these writers was Thomas Quayle, who visited the Island in 1813 under a commission from the Board of Agriculture to examine the state of the agriculture practised there. His conclusion was highly favourable: "The directions of the Board to enumerate these [obstacles to improvement], will happily produce a barren chapter. The islands enjoy a beneficent government; protecting them with arms, from the ravage, and the insult of the surrounding foe; fostering their industry; securing to them its fruits according to their own laws; readily acceding to any improvements....extracting from them no revenue; doing nothing positively tending to their oppression". [45] It was an interesting view to take, in that the success of Jersey agriculture was not ascribed in the first instance to the circumstances of the industry itself but to the existence of a benign and watchful State. Others too, were less concerned with the farming and growing, satisfied that the air of prosperity was secured and perpetuated by a moral and political well-being. Dubost, who visited the Island in the 1870s, claimed the Island's degree of political independence and the lack of taxes ensured the success of local agriculture.[46] Peter Kropotkin, writing in 1890, was certain that all was well as long as the Island was free from the evils of Roman law and landlordism.[47]

These statements contain a key insight into the success of agriculture in nineteenth-century Jersey. It was not a matter of fundamental change in agricultural practice. Whilst cider was gradually ousted by the potato as the main cash crop, the average Jersey farm retained its traditional balance between arable and pastoral. Establishments like Bashford's Vinery and Langelliers Nurseries in St Saviour, greenhouse complexes concentrating on a variety of hothouse crops, were a rarity in the century.[48] The cash nexus, long accepted by the rural community, did not lead to a totally capitalist orientated economy. Farming units remained small. At the back of the mind of this conservative body of country people remained the basic peasant need to produce at least some of their own consumables. The capitalist part of their agriculture rarely reached the pinnacles of high farming, aspired to by progressive agriculturists on the English mainland. Whilst Jersey farmers achieved intensive cultivation, high production and high return, their methods showed few signs of the application of scientific advances and were marred by high costs.[49] Without the peculiarities of Jersey's economic and political position, its independence vis-à-vis the English Crown and Parliament, the ability to export tariff free to the United Kingdom, and the willingness whenever any of these rights were threatened to lay claim to them as the price of centuries of loyalty, the success in this industry so marvelled at by visitors to the Island would probably have never been achieved. Throughout the nineteenth century, writers such as Quayle, Dubost and Kropotkin stressed an institutional framework rather than farming as such, as the basis of Jersey agricultural success.

Details of Jersey farming in the nineteenth century are provided by several sources and enable a comprehensive analysis. In his prize-winning essay for the *Journal of the Royal Agricultural Society of England* in 1859, C.P. Le Cornu gave a breakdown of what he called a typical Jersey farm.[50] In area the farm would be near 20 acres (45 vergées), comprising six or eight fields, perhaps with a couple of orchards, averaging between two and three acres in size. In terms of crops and livestock the breakdown would be:

Hay & Pasture	10 acres	Horses	2
Turnips.	2 ..	Cows	6
Mangolds	1 ..	Heifers	6
Parsnips	1 ..	Pigs	8
Carrots	3/4 ..		
Potatoes	2 ..		
Wheat	3 1/4 ..		

In terms of management Le Cornu estimated that four people would be required all-year round and these people generally consisted of family, especially if they were tenant farmers.

Girardin and Morière's excursion to the Island on behalf of the Société Centrale D'Agriculture du Département de la Seine-Inférieure in 1857 provided breakdowns of five farms ranging from Mrs. Le Gallais's 90 acres at Le Moie (sic), St Brelade (used here, to contrast with Le Cornu's example), to Thomas Baudains' rented 20 acres (at £130 per annum) at St Saviour. [51]

Mrs. Le Gallais

Pasture	35.5 acres	Milkers	18
Potatoes	13 ..	Heifers	22
Parsnips/Carrots	13 ..	Calves	25
Turnips	13 ..	Bulls	5
Corn	14 ..	Horses	8
		Pigs	12

Among the samples, in keeping with Le Cornu's basic divide, the mixed farm is the standard unit. An average of the farms in Girardin's study shows a similar pattern:

Crops	per cent	Livestock	per cent
Pasture	46%	Milkers	27.5 %
Potatoes	14%	Heifers	25.7%
Roots	21%	Calves	15%
Corn	19%	Bulls	3%
		Horses	9%
		Pigs	19.8%

In this breakdown pasture clearly dominates the farm set-up. This is not surprising; pasture provided food for the livestock, 167 head on four farms, and played an important part in the rotation system. Quayle did not provide a detailed breakdown of a farm in 1815, but he did note that the rotation followed was one of grain interspersed with roots or pasture: the Norfolk rotation system. [52] The Trinity Manor Farm Diary for 1820/21 shows a similar rotation being followed, as well as revealing the fact that potatoes were as yet relatively unimportant. [53] In the 1857 breakdown, cereal is still an important part of the farming pattern. The small rôle attributed to potatoes probably reflects the effects of the blight of 1845. Le Cornu, writing in 1870, claimed that fear of a further spread of the disease resulted in a drastic decline in potato cultivation which lasted for ten years. [54] Jersey's inclusion in the British Government's agricultural statistics after 1877 enables a comparison to be made between Le Cornu and Girardin's studies and official figures for the late nineteenth century. The returns for 1900 provide a detailed breakdown by parish for both livestock and crops. [55]

Crops	per cent	Livestock	per cent
Pasture	62%	Cattle	59.3%
Potatoes	27%	Horses	11.3%
Roots	1.6%	Sheep	1.2%
Corn	5.9%	Pigs	28.2%
Orchards	3.5%		

The pattern of Jersey agriculture that emerges from the 1900 figures is one of specialisation in two areas, livestock rearing and potato cultivation. This was achieved to the detriment of cereals and root crops, and, to a lesser extent, cider cultivation which was in decline since the beginning of the nineteenth century. The statistics suggest that it was not until after the 1850s that such a pattern took shape, a period which coincides with a shift in potato cultivation away from main crop export towards the production of 'earlies'. This was even more the case after 1880, as the export figures in Fig. 4 show, when the highly specialised early potato, the Jersey Royal, came into production.

The decline of Jersey cider production is a subject which receives scant attention from nineteenth century writers. It will be observed that Le Cornu's breakdown of a typical Jersey farm in 1859 did not include orchards (see *ante*). This is peculiar given the fact that cider export figures, as Figure 4 illustrates, show some strength until at least 1860. Le Cornu's essay, intended as a broad survey of agriculture in the Channel Islands, similarly disregards the cider industry. The extent of his coverage is to note that most farms possessed both an orchard and a cider press. [56] When Bear visited the Island in the 1880s he observed the decline of cider cultivation, but gave no reasons: "The apple orchards have been greatly neglected of late, and are fast disappearing". [57] Only Girardin and Morière, both Normans with an expertise in cider, ascribed any cause to the local decline. They suggested that the increased popularity of beer in England, a result of free trade laws which allowed entry to foreign corn, meant cider was no longer a fashionable beverage. Local consumption had followed English trends, leaving only rural folk to drink cider. [58] It is a plausible theory, but, nonetheless, the fact remains that the once major Jersey cider industry declined with but little comment from Islanders or visitors.

	Potatoes (Tons)	Cattle	Wheat (Qrs)	Cider (Gallons)
1800	-	(1803)406	-	(1803) 222,500
1810	1,400	988	-	-
1820	-	-	-	-
1830	8,679	1,353	(1832) 3,160	191,377
1840	17,670	1,744	7,138	208,531
1850	5,622	1,402	1,561	97,874
1860	2,677	1,138	*	100,049
1870	11,527	1,896	*	4,632
1880	33,043	1,920	*	•
1890	54,109	1,712	*	•
1900				

* *No figures available after 1854 suggesting an end to major corn exports.*

• *No figures available after 1874 suggesting an end to major cider exports. Before 1830 a gap means no data available.*

FIGURE 4: *Major Agricultural Exports in Nineteenth-century Jersey. Source: Export figures 1800-1810 from T. Quayle, op. cit., Apendix p. 323; 1830-1890 from the Almanack du Chronique.*

By the late 1850s, then, it is clear from export statistics and farm surveys that a more streamlined mixed farming became apparent in Jersey agriculture. Early potatoes and cattle rearing worked well together and the importation of guano after 1848 enabled a less rigid rotation, since fertility could be restored in a much shorter period. Pasture was also a good restorer and livestock provided useful manure fertiliser.

Streamlined production for the English market meant that few Jersey farmers were willing to cultivate for local consumption. The production of local consumables now rested with the household garden ,and, by the 1880s, a growing number of outdoor market gardeners, particularly around St Helier. The glasshouse industry which was rapidly developing in nearby Guernsey at this time made but a small appearance in Jersey. [59] This was in part because of Jersey's southerly aspect (unlike that of Guernsey, which slopes northwards) which ensured that sunlight sufficient for the cultivation of early crops could be obtained without recourse to glasshouses. What deterred many from market garden cultivation, at least until the 1880s when some fruit, vegetables and flowers began to be exported, was that local prices paled against the potentially high returns available from export. Le Cornu expressed little surprise at the decline of production for domestic consumption. He observed that a population of near 60,000 in 1859 meant that "it cannot be supposed that the island can produce sufficient for its consumption. France supplies it with oxen, calves, pigs, sheep and poultry, as well as eggs and frequently flour, wheat, barley, oats; but when the French ports are closed against the exportation of grain, flour comes from America, oats and barley from the Baltic. Jersey is chiefly supplied with cattle and grain by the foreigner: it is not to the injury of the Jersey producer, and much to the advantage of the consumer, for both are imported at a lower rate than that at which they could be produced, and the Jersey farmer is left to employ his time and capital in a way more profitable to himself and the island at large". [60]

A view of a selection of imported consummables for the nineteenth century (see Figure 5) reflects the extent to which Jersey's rapidly expanding population relied on outside producers for its food supply. [61] The import figures should be treated with care because they may include cargoes, such as grain or manufactures, brought in by the carrying trade for re-export. Nonetheless, the imports reflect the needs of both a rapidly increasing population and an agricultural industry concentrating increasingly on cultivation for export, particularly on the potato. The number of bullocks imported is a reflection of the Jersey cow's rôle as a dairy producer, rather than as a beef animal. It is interesting to note that potatoes were not imported until after the blight outbreak in 1845. Even when potato cultivation returned, it was concentrated on early potatoes and this necessitated the continued importation of maincrop potatoes to last the winter. Grain also received a great boost in importation, coinciding with the general decline in local production which has been identified. We shall now deal with the two main strands of the agricultural economy in the nineteenth century in some detail.

Livestock Breeding: the Jersey

The Jersey cow was the pride and joy of the nineteenth century Jersey farmer. Acknowledged world-wide for its deer-like beauty, the Jersey was also a productive dairy animal. Export of the animal had taken place in the mid-eighteenth century, but the name of the breed was not well established abroad until the mid-nineteenth century, when increased demand for the

Jersey made livestock breeding a lucrative and steady industry for local agriculturists.

	Grain (Qurts)	Potatoes (Tons)	Bullocks	Sheep	Pigs	Poultry	Butter (Cwt)
1830	33,461*	2,390	4,470	335	16,450	-	-
1840	-	-	3,319	11,957	3,558	36,957	-
1850	18,268	1,528	4,333	14,575	5,812	42,507	3,686
1860	22,450	1,473	4,224	14,713	4,383	62,416	73,858
1870	56,375	2,308	4,682	14,137	2,623	79,577	4,287
1880	114,234	65,784	3,938	8,884	1,355	47,665	3,122
1890	-	-	-	-	-	-	-
1900	-	-	-	-	-	-	-

* *1837 figure. It should be pointed out that it is not known whether the figures were solely for home consumption, as some may have been re-exported.*

• *From this date on• a substantial amount of flour was also imported into Jersey.*

There are no statistics available before 1830. A gap means there is no data available.

FIGURE 5: *Major Consumable Imports in Nineteenth Century Jersey. Source: Almanack du Chronique*

Such was the importance of the early cattle trade to the Island, that the States took steps to protect it in 1786. By an Acte des États of that year, the importation of foreign cattle into Jersey was prohibited. Contravention would result in a penalty of 200 Livres, forfeiture of boat and tackle, and further fines for all the sailors on board. [62] Furthermore, the legislation was renewed on a regular basis. [63] The preamble to the first Acte in 1787 had pointed out how "The scandalous importation of cows etc. from France having become most alarming for the Island, in that it threatens to bring ruin to the commerce between England and Jersey". [64] In 1791, reflecting this concern, the Connétable of St Martin presented a case against a French national, Nicolas Boutar, who was charged with bringing foreign cows into the Island via Rozel Bay. Despite two cows being found on local farms, one in the stable of Jeanne Collas, the other at Philippe Aubin's, the defendant was discharged. [65] By 1827 the States had resorted to paying informers for information relative to the fraudulent importation of French cattle and were successful in the prosecution of one Pierre Le Ruez. [66]

The concern to maintain the isolation of local cattle from those of nearby France was both economic and political. Local cattle were valuable exports. Jerseys had been exported to the English mainland since at least 1751, when a combined shipment of around 250 Channel Island cattle had been transported, and no doubt provided a useful source of income to farmers. [67] The importation of French cattle into England via Jersey was a smuggling ruse, an attempt to plug into the same market. After a short stay in the Island, French cattle were exported to England, thus exploiting Jersey's right to export freely to English markets. In 1853 the *Jersey Times* explained that the risk taken by Breton smugglers as well worth it since their cattle could normally fetch only £3 to £4 in French markets, but by shipping them via Jersey they could realise prices of £12 to £20 in England.[68] Economically, such a strategy was clearly detrimental to local farming interests, but the States were actually more concerned with the fact that this practice was an abuse of a precious trading privilege; free trading rights could not be jeopardised.

The protectionist legislation of the 1780s is now popularly viewed as an attempt to ensure the development of the Jersey as a pure breed, but this does not appear to have been the case. As the agriculturist John Thornton pointed out in 1881, "These Acts did not prohibit the importation of English cattle; both Shorthorns and Ayreshires were introduced"[69] Likewise, a correspondent to the *British Press and Jersey Times* in 1879, who claimed to be an experienced English agriculturist, was convinced that animals had been brought in from Guernsey.[70] The breeding potential of isolating a promising breed was only ever secondary to the more general fear of losing economic privileges.

The cattle exported as early as 1751 were a response to the demand for extra livestock in English agriculture, rather than to a demand for a quality breed.[71] One of the earliest works on cattle, Bradley's 1729 *Gentleman and Farmer's Guide*, had made no mention of the Channel Islands.[72] By 1786, Culley's *Observations on Livestock* mentioned a breed by the name of Alderneys, a term which for some fifty years was to represent all Channel Island cattle, but stressed its lack of significance as a commercial breed.[73] In fact early successes for the Jersey breed in the English market in the late eighteenth and early nineteenth centuries were as so-called 'lawn-cows', animals purchased to prettify the parklands of the gentry and provide them with rich creamy milk.[74] Jersey breeders were to have to wait another half century before the Jersey cow became established as an animal of note.

According to Quayle in 1815 the Jersey agriculturist had in his grasp a useful marketable commodity second in local estimation only to vraic, the seaweed used for fertiliser. This amounted to quite a rating, given the value placed on the right to collect vraic (see the Introductory section). Quayle observed that the Jersey cow "seems to be a constant object of his thoughts and attention....that attention she certainly deserves, but she absorbs it too exclusively: his horse he treats unkindly; his sheep, most barbarously; but on the idolised cow, his affections are riveted as firmly as those of an eastern Bramin on the same animal".[75] Yet, doted on or not, the breed was neglected and its potential unrealised. Quayle pointed out how "no individual has attempted, by the selection of cattle, and breeding ,from them to attain any particular object".[76]

It is difficult to ascertain how influential Quayle's substantial volume was in both swaying local opinion and in influencing the future development of the breed. He was optimistic about the potential of the Jersey, but concerned about the limitations local circumstances might place upon its improvement. [77] Mr. Bertram, of Grouville, told Quayle that the money received on a cow in its lifetime was around £30, and the expense of keeping it, allowing for two vergées of land for each cow, £18. Prices such as £15 for a two year old heifer and up to £25 for a four year old cow in the local market alone made sales worthwhile. [78] The market forces could, said Quayle, prove a beneficial influence, "but hitherto no persevering systematical experimenter has attempted, by a careful selection of individuals, and attention to their crosses, to improve this breed....From the narrow limits of each dairy farm, and small quantity of pasture in the occupation of any one person, it is not likely that such an attempt will be speedily made". [79]

Quayle sounded rather like a disciple of Arthur Young in his belief that the small and independent farming units of Jersey would act as an obstacle to the progress of the breed, and in many respects he was vindicated. Progress for the Jersey breed came through an organisation which attempted to transcend the influence of inward looking units and push forward the ideals of high farming. The Royal Jersey Agricultural and Horticultural Society was founded in 1833 with the specific intention of creating "a spirit of industry and emulation" among local farmers. [80] The Society was established on the initiative of several of Jersey's leading gentleman farmers, notably Colonel John Le Couteur, General Helier Touzel and the Bailiff, Thomas Le Breton. [81] Its exact beginnings are unclear, but it had a precursor in the shape of a society established in 1790, still in existence by the time Quayle visited the Island, "but certainly not with many external signs of animation; rather it is to be feared in that state which has been characterised as "un sommeil éternel". [82] The Royal Jersey Agricultural and Horticultural Society proved more enduring. Within a couple of decades, the Society's scientific experiments, its education programme and official recognition of its efforts from English agriculturists had helped raise local cattle breeding from a random trade to a specialised export industry.

How much the Royal Jersey Agricultural and Horticultural Society's ideas on improved methods and practices were disseminated to the main body of the farming community is not easy to gauge. In England at this time, agricultural societies were proving both popular and advantageous to the agricultural industry, improving livestock breeding and advancing the use of machinery. Nevertheless, these societies were, for the main part, preaching to the converted and they often ignored the smaller farmer, something which worked against the spread of agricultural advances. [83] The Royal Jersey Agricultural and Horticultural Society was not without problems as regards its relationship with smaller farmers, as we shall see later in this chapter, but its general influence was aided by several factors. The smallness of the Island facilitated an easy dissemination of ideas. Word of mouth and the realisation that there was money to be made from pure bred livestock would have spread new ideas. This local network was strengthened by the Island's newspapers which regularly carried adverts for agronomic literature, articles on farming and reports on the activities of the Society. [84] Ultimately, however, the influence of the Royal Jersey Agricultural and Horticultural Society on local cattle breeding may be judged by the improvement made evident in the breed.

The first attempt by the Royal Jersey Agricultural and Horticultural Society to assess the standard of local cattle was a show held in April, 1833, where 49 animals were shown by a handful of farmers. The judges' impressions underlined the defects in the breed and the need for improvement. [85] The response of the Society was the establishment of a strict model by which cows and bulls could be judged. In 1834, a 28 point model (30 in the case of bulls), based on what was considered to be the perfect Jersey in terms of beauty, was introduced.[86] The basic premise of the scale of points was that beauty and finesse of form resulted in a highly marketable cow that was both pleasing to the eye and economically productive: a basic symmetry, particularly of the udder, would utilise the Jersey's natural ability to produce rich and creamy milk.

By 1842 the Royal Jersey Agricultural and Horticultural Society could report on what it called seven years of "Society-coaxed cattle breeding". The Annual Report for that year claimed that the efforts of the Society had "almost caused the ancient characteristic defect of drooping hind quarters of the Jersey cattle to disappear, besides several minor defects and it only remains to give squareness to the hind quarters and roundness to the barrel to render it a most beautiful animal". [87] John Le Couteur, himself a prime mover in the scale of points, reported in an 1844 article for the *Journal of the Royal Agricultural Society of England* that the old Jersey cow of 1800 to 1830 with its hollow back, crooked hind legs and cat ham, scoring at most only 18 points "could still be seen in some pasture", but that a new cow now dominated with "the head of a fawn, a soft eye, her elegant crumpled horn, small ears, yellow thin, a clean neck and throat, fine bones, a fine tail: above all, a well formed capacious udder, with large swelling milk veins". [88]

In 1856 the highest export figure for Island cattle in the nineteenth century was reached when 2,153 animals were exported from Jersey. [89] The animal had finally found a niche in the market-place. Although unable to move away from its image as the rather delicate lawn-cow, in fact trading on this, the Jersey was beginning to be accepted as a productive asset, both in England and the United States. Writing to the *Jersey Times* in 1848, an American agricultural researcher claimed that "The improvement which has taken place in this breed in the Island of Jersey,..., is most remarkable, and in their improved condition for certain purposes, especially for the luxury of cream and butter, it would, I think, be impossible to find a more valuable breed". [90]

The breed was particularly popular in the United States. The *Louisville Farmer's Home Journal* reported in 1878: "A few years ago the Jersey cow was brought prominently before the public as the butter cow par excellence. The crudeness of her form then stood antagonistic to the accepted curve of beauty, the type of fashion being moulded on the Shorthorn idea of beauty. This little cow therefore had not only to prove her real usefulness in the butter dairy, but she had to do it in the face of fashionable prejudice. In the face of this difficulty, still the little cow moved upward in the esteem of the public, selling at prices never extravagantly high, but still ranging only next to the fabulous Shorthorns....The strongest point, however, in favour of this cow is that, while the prices paid for her many years ago.... were more or less speculative, she has found her way into almost every considerable dairy herd in the country". [91] In the monthly bulletin of the American Jersey Cattle Club, which had been established in 1869, it was suggested that "the marked coincidence between the increasing requirements for improved butter making, together with the advancing commercial importance of dairy interests, and the rate at which the Jerseys are coming to the foremost position at agricultural exhibitions, should be accepted by Jersey breeders as a suggestive indication". [92] The Jersey cattle trade developed into that of pedigree export. This was particularly the case after 1866, when the Royal Jersey Agricultural and Horticultural Society established a Herd Book to ascertain pedigree and progeny. [93] Borrowing from the trends developing in England regarding pure bred livestock, exports would now include animals scoring high not only on the scale of points, but also high in pedigree terms, so that buyers could choose to purchase into particular blood strains. [94]

The middle men of this successful trade ranged from local and English dealers to individual farmers who visited Jersey to purchase for their own herd. John Le Bas claimed to be the largest single cattle exporter between 1830 and 1866, and in the latter year alone shipped out 830 animals for English dealers. [95] P. H. Fowler and A. Arnold, both English dealers, were responsible for the major share of exports to the United States. [96] Others, like Mr. Motley of Boston, simply came over to the Island and bought their own cattle, Le Couteur recording that this particular gentleman had bought £500 worth of Jersey stock in a year. [97]

By 1870 the cattle export market had stabilised at an annual figure of just under 2,000 head. In many respects the market was a diminishing one, because as herds became established elsewhere, the need for Jersey born animals declined. This was countered by finding new markets, but it is clear that demand from the large markets of England and the United States had peaked. Direct purchase from Jersey became increasingly limited to buyers who required a particularly pure blood strain or who bought for reasons of snobbishness.

By the1880s some commentators suggested another reason for a planing-off of exports, namely that Jersey breeders had become slaves to the perceived market demand for beauty over production. Local papers carried letters from non-local agriculturists complaining about this tendency. A reprinted article from the New York journal *The Cultivator* made the point: "I have contended for many years that Jersey breeders were making a mistake in breeding for the lawn demand, rather than the churn. The former was the representative of bigger prices than the latter, as fancy is very oft to rule higher than utility. Fashion guides the former and merit the latter. For ten years at least fashion and fancy had the lead, and these ten years have been detrimental to Jersey cattle, if not almost ruinous in many herds". [98] J. Burns Murdoch was of a similar opinion and in a discussion with a local farmer at St Aubin, they were agreed "that the Jersey farmers are breeding too much in, and too much sacrificing size and bone to artificial points of excellence and beauty, which they judge as evidence of purity of breed. I was the more convinced of the truth of this, after witnessing the show of bulls....The animals exhibited were really very pretty, their beauty,however, was more that of the deer than of the bull," while they were "generally led home by women, more like pet sheep than anything". [99] The combined effect of herds becoming established elsewhere and the local preoccupation with breeding for beauty was a levelling off of prices. Le Cornu had reported prices of between £12 to £14 for two year old heifers in 1859. [100] Bear suggested a farmer in the late 1880s would be fortunate to get £15 for an animal of similar age. [101]

Nonetheless, whilst markets were falling off slightly the exports remained fairly buoyant. This was acknowledged at a Royal Jersey Agricultural and Horticultural Society meeting in 1887 and it was suggested that new markets be sought; the chairman pointed out that exports had already reached England, France, Belgium, Canada and the U.S.A.. [102] The first available census of stock is one in 1866 in which the cattle population was numbered at 12,037 head.[103] By 1900 the number had increased by a small amount to 12,272. [104] This means that for this period at least, annual cattle exports amounted to nearly a sixth of the bovine population. This suggests that livestock export provided a steady and remunerative return for farmers. The supply was far more reliable than crops which might fail at harvest, or, in the case of the early potato, mature behind schedule. The demand for this specialist product remained remarkably constant, no doubt strengthened by the scale of points and pedigree herd book.

Subsidiary products from the Jersey cow included milk, butter and, to a lesser extent, meat. Butter was consistently exported from at least 1830 when statistics are available, but by the mid-1870s fell off rather sharply. Rider-Haggard, carrying out agricultural and social research in the Island in 1901, was informed by the Secretary of the Royal Jersey Agricultural and Horticultural Society that the reason for this decline was the preoccupation with the potato. [105] As to milk, little information has been uncovered on this subject. There is uno evidence to suggest the existence of a major dairy in the Island, farmers no doubt making their own provisions for selling privately. With regard to meat, the Jersey breed is not a beef animal and in the nineteenth century was not treated as such. It is unlikely that animals, other than the old and infirm, were slaughtered for this purpose, mainly because of their value on the hoof. Pork, as may be seen from Escard's case studies, was the most popular meat in the local diet, mainly because of its preservative potential and the easy incorporation of pigs into the farming economy. [106]

Livestock export provided a steady source of income for agriculturists in nineteenth-century Jersey. Cattle rearing and breeding worked well alongside the other main component of agriculture in the period, potato cultivation. In the popular mind, at least, the Jersey retained a special place in both the Jerseyman's heart and the local economy. For C.P. Le Cornu, reflecting the traditional favouritism that Quayle had noted in 1815, cattle constituted "the mainstay of agriculture; it is that upon which the farmer chiefly depends for money to pay his rents". [107]

The Potato

The potato was a very different kind of exportable commodity from the Jersey cow, yet the two complemented each other. The potential of the farming unit which combined livestock with arable was exploited from at least the late eighteenth century, but after about 1870 production became streamlined and concentrated on potatoes as the main arable component. Potatoes, particularly 'earlies', could bring high returns, but their realisation depended ultimately on the weather. A late potato harvest, even if delayed only by a matter of weeks, could ruin a whole year's profits. The steadier and regular livestock export provided an essential safety net.

As a cash crop the potato had caught on early in Jersey, produced for export only two decades after its introduction. Quayle noted how this had been achieved despite early prejudice and a preference for the parsnip. But his report in 1815, which shows both main crop and 'early' potatoes being produced, states that the crop was not of a high quality. [108] The prime concern of the cultivator at this time was for a heavy return in weight from the land: 18 tons an acre was not uncommon, and the result was a bulk crop of indiscriminate variety. [109] The only distinction between main crop and 'early' was the time of cultivation and no particular consumer market was targeted. The *Customs Bills of Entry,* available after 1829, confirm that potatoes reached London between September and April. As Figure 6 shows, the bulk of the export was main crop, meaning that the main harvest was in the late autumn of every year. [110]

Year	Month	Tonnage
1829	September	34
	October	207
	November	693
	December	154
1830	January	-
	February	207
	March	100
	April-August	-

FIGURE 6: *Potato Exports from Jersey to London in 1829/1830*

Potato cultivation in the early nineteenth century was rather haphazard. In 1838 the Royal Jersey Agricultural and Horticultural Society reported that "The Committee has seen occasion to regret that the potatoes from this Island did not reach the finest prices in the London market, owing perhaps to the circumstances of various varieties of white potatoes being in cultivation, and the shipment being made in an unequal state of ripeness, the quality could not be so good, nor their properties for boiling so excellent, as if of one good stock".[111] The Society's response to the problem was to introduce to the Island what it believed to be the two finest potato varieties on the London Market, the York Red and the York Kidney, for production trials. Samples of the two varieties were to be cultivated by several members of the Society. If the trials proved successful, the intention was to keep the varieties pure, "so that Potato Merchants may be enabled to name the variety they offer to the London dealers..".[112] The result of the trials is not known and any success is likely to have been dampened by the outbreak of blight in 1845. Nonetheless, the profitability of the later market in 'earlies' was in no small part due to the calibre of the varieties grown. If nothing else, this early exercise in tailoring a product to the market set a useful precedent.

Between 1810 and 1845 potato exports increased steadily, multiplying twelve-fold.[113] This was achieved at the expense of other root crops since cider production, and to a lesser extent grain production, continued to be strong. A manuscript for St Martin in 1848 shows that cider orchards still accounted for 22 per cent of the agricultural land in use in that parish. Cider cultivation was overshadowed by pasture (50 per cent), but well ahead of the 14 per cent cereals and the post-blight potatoes, which accounted for only seven per cent.[114] Parsnips are likely to have been the crop hit hardest by the popularity of potato cultivation. Quayle, as we have observed, noted that the potato had been seen as a crop to rival the parsnip in the late eighteenth century.[115] The link between the two crops could be observed during the blight, when farmers turned to parsnip growing as an alternative to the potato.[116]

Early successes in potato cultivation were abruptly halted by the blight of 1845, an outbreak that was to have a dramatic influence on the crop in both the short and long term. It hit the Island a year after it affected the British crop, first detected in the month of June "when a few cold nights checked the flow of sap and paralysed the plant" and the disease immediately set in with awful rapidity; and so virulent was it that when the time arrived for clearing the ground, in some places every tuber had rotted away, and in others one half of the crop was injured.[117] By January 1846 it was estimated that one third of the crop had been lost, with the resulting scarcity pushing local prices to three times higher than previous years, at 15 pence per cabot.[118] In export terms the disease resulted in a drop from 18,560 tons in 1843/44 (1844/45 not available) to 3,822 tons in 1845/46.[119] The decennial average of exports for the period 1845/46 to 1856 was 4,900 tons compared with 13,500 tons for the preceding ten years.[120] The disease prevailed until at least 1849 when a further major outbreak hit the Island, but then declined in malignancy.[121]

Despite the high prices available due to scarcity the markets remained dull. There was a general feeling among Jersey farmers that a return to potato cultivation would bring unsatisfactory results and that since no effective remedy for the disease had been discovered it might remain in the soil. Farmers turned again to parsnip growing and stock fattening.[122] The result was a further decline, with the decennial export average for 1856 to 1866 set lower than that immediately following the blight, at 4,200 tons.[123]

Blight or not, the Royal Jersey Agricultural and Horticultural Society remained convinced of the financial returns that might be realised from a high quality potato industry. The 1858 Annual Report reviewed the progress of agriculture since the Society's formation, and praised the improvements in livestock rearing and general cultivation. The potato industry was singled out for particular criticism. Exports had dwindled to negligible quantities and the preceding quarter of a century showed farmers unable to perceive the demands of the market. It was recommended that attention be paid to the early market.[124]

The Annual Report of 1859 announced the beginnings of the early potato trade. The first basket of early Jersey potatoes (cultivator unknown) reached its destination, Covent Garden, on April 18th. By early May the Island was producing such a quantity of the crop that "the Steam Packets which perform the General Service on the South-Western Station were found inadequate to transport the goods. In consequence, the Company was obliged to have an extra vessel on the line for upwards of two months. This is besides what was shipped by the Weymouth and Channel Island Company".[125] The trade upon which so much of Jersey agriculture's fortune in the later nineteenth century was to depend had arrived.

The optimism of the Royal Jersey Agricultural and Horticultural Society was a little premature. The potato exports of 1859 were in fact less than those of 1858, 2,211 tons compared with 3,093 tons. [126] The late season of 1860, which did not commence until the end of May, resulted in the Society finally concluding that the potato trade rested on a most precarious footing. [127] In export terms, the potato trade did not fully recover from the reactions to blight until 1868 when 10,184 tons left the Island, a figure which by 1878 had become 27,626 tons. [128] The main focus was by this time the early market. C.P. Le Cornu provided a breakdown of the marketing of the 1868 potato season. It shows that packages of produce (size unknown) left by steam for Southampton, Weymouth and Littlehampton, whilst loose cargoes headed for Plymouth, Cardiff, Liverpool and Barbados (80 tons to the last-named) by sail. The first package left on the 19th March, followed by another on the 24th and four more on the 26th. By the 21st April the season had opened, with 43 packages shipped on the one day. A net return of £55,573 was realised, £44,131 via the steam packets. Including that left for seed and consumption, a gross return of 17s 6d was obtained per vergée of potatoes grown in the Island. [129]

In 1878 production for the early market became even more specialised with the introduction into the Island of the International Kidney Potato. The variety was so successful as a tasty and attractive product that it became the mainstay of the potato industry, under the name of the Royal Jersey Fluke. [130] Between 1881 and 1890, potato exports averaged 49,480 tons per annum; between 1891 and 1900, they averaged 59,914 tons, with a peak total of 66,840 tons in 1891. [131]

Visitors to Jersey in the early months of the year in the 1880s and 1890s could thus observe the whole spectacle of the potato harvest at its most developed. En route to Jersey in 1883, J. Stuart Blackie described a brief stop at one of the harbours in Guernsey: "The whole traffic of a country here passes bodily before [the observer] in the space of an hour; and what struck me most, when brooding over this process from the quarter deck, at Guernsey, was the interminable number of empty casks or barrels that came swinging up from the hold, relay after relay, floundering about in the air....these casks had come from Covent Garden, where they have been disembowelled of their wealth of early potatoes to fit out London dinners, and were come to their native soil to be replenished with fresh stores....These floundering empty casks were the overture, as it were, to the great potato opera, which I saw afterwards played at Jersey....a sight that....stamped the word 'potato' distinctly on the brain of the spectator as the badge of Jersey productiveness and the pledge of Jersey prosperity". [132]

It was to be the trade in 'earlies', particularly after 1880, that brought capital returns to a height which matched the earlier successes of the cod trade, although, naturally, profits were divided between a far great number of producers than the small group of merchant houses. The French agriculturist Dubost could, with some justification, claim in 1879 that "You cannot go 100 yards into the interior without being compelled to admit that you are among past masters at farming". [133]

The Jersey potato industry was not, however, quite as perfect as some commentators may have suggested. There was an essential difference between the ability to cultivate in abundance and the ability to do so economically. There was also the problem of overproduction, one which led to fears of a move towards a damaging monoculture and by the late 1880s had brought a steep decline in market prices. These points will be examined in a later chapter. The point to be stressed here is the successful development of Jersey agriculture into a major industry in the nineteenth century, with a significant market for its goods and a potential for high returns for its endeavours.

Dubost's 'past masters' were a body of over two thousand individuals involved in Jersey agriculture. [134] To the historian, the majority of nineteenth century agriculturists remain anonymous. The few farmers that come to light in any detail do so only because they were singled out for interview or analysis by visiting theorists and writers, and will be examined at a later stage in this book. The purpose of this particular section has been to look more at economics than people, a balance which will be restored. Having looked at the advances of agriculture in some depth, we will now place these within the broader economic structure of the Island and assess the implications of economic change for Jersey society.

The Structure of the Jersey Economy

As already observed in this chapter, the nineteenth-century Jersey economy was based on Jersey's political position vis-à-vis the English Crown and the economic privileges that resulted from it. The Jersey merchant sector pioneered the exploitation of this relationship, and in many ways established its parameters. Agriculture necessarily shared the advantages derived from Jersey's political status, but it did so within the framework created by the merchants. Historically, the landed interest held all political power. For most of the nineteenth century, Jersey merchants held the Island's capital wealth. Not surprisingly, the two blocs stood antagonistic to one another.

Alongside these two blocs stood the immigrant English population. These immigrants came to Jersey for a variety of reasons, but ultimately were united in their desire to take advantage of a booming economy. Control of the Island economy was, however, firmly in the hands of native businessmen and it was to take some time before any significant English influence in this sphere could be obtained. For much of the nineteenth century the chief English rôle in the economy, as we have seen, was to provide artisans and labourers to the

Jersey merchants. The presence, however, of this large body of English residents was to prove of fundamental importance to the conflict between the rural and urban blocs.

The fact that the economic successes of the rural community were won within and relied upon a trading structure that had been developed by the merchant sector caused certain problems. For obvious reasons, this was a dependence that few agriculturists would have cared to admit. Jersey society had developed as a society dominated on all levels by the landed interest. The States retained this dominance throughout the century. To acknowledge the rôle of the merchant sector in the economy and, by extension, in society at large, would have legitimised the demand from this sector for a share in the power structure. The rural community in nineteenth century Jersey was not prepared to make such a concession.

Local merchants provided a broad range of services to the rural community in the nineteenth century. In the merchant function they provided some transport to agriculture and to some extent played the middle-man rôle of purchaser too, notably in their demand for agricultural produce at the fisheries; in the commercial function they brought to the Island a broad range of consumer and industrial goods, much of which, particularly agricultural machinery, was to the advantage of the rural sector; in the financial sphere they provided access to capital and investment facilities, though to what extent this was taken up by agriculturists, it is difficult to quantify.

The Jersey agricultural industry made some use of local merchant transport facilities. It is likely that the first exports of potatoes from the Island went to the Gaspé codfisheries in Canada. Locally grown potatoes were certainly carried by local ships as part of their necessary stores, this being another aspect of the industry's use of its home base.[135] Jersey's carrying trade, on the other hand, was generally more concerned with freight carrying overseas. Local vessels did, nonetheless, carry a share, but not the bulk, of the Island's agricultural produce to its English markets. In 1840 Jersey ships took 44 shipments out of a total of 215 from the Channel Islands (Guernsey took 31) to the port of London. Liverpool (16 shipments), Bristol (17 shipments) and Hull (4 shipments) also had regular visits from Jersey vessels carrying local produce.[136]

If the use of transport facilities to carry produce to the English markets was never a major factor in agriculture's rise, the rural use of merchant lobbying power certainly was. The shared past of Crown-bestowed privileges in trade brought agriculturist and merchant together, and when the rights of free trade came under fire it was not unnatural that lobbying forces would unite. Behind the creation of the merchants' lobbying organisation, the Chamber of Commerce, in 1767 was a belief that the States constitution at the time neither could nor would pursue and protect the Jersey merchant interests to the extent the local merchant body required. [137] By the time agriculturists realised the potential of lobbying power, namely after 1815, they found in the Chamber a skilled and experienced lobbying body.

The Chamber of Commerce's stated purpose was "the well-being of trade, and to support and keep the merchants upon a respectable footing". [138] To this end, a London firm was employed to represent its interests at 'Court', arguing its case and watching for the possibility of restrictive Parliamentary legislation. [139] The Chamber of Commerce was a tight-knit economic organisation, ruthless in its pursuit of profit, as shown by its ability to suppress an attempted ship carpenters' strike in 1786. [140] In the 1780s its membership consisted of the dozen leading merchant families and, to all intents and purposes, it remained this way well into the nineteenth century. [141]

The agricultural equivalent to the Chamber of Commerce was, as we have already seen, the Royal Jersey Agricultural and Horticultural Society, established in 1833. The Society differed from the Chamber in certain important respects. It was not an out-and-out lobbying body, its self-appointed rôle being that of educator and advancer of scientific agriculture and high farming. [142] Furthermore, despite purporting to represent Jersey agriculture as a whole, the Society was essentially a gentleman's organisation. The Society's rules made a clear-cut distinction between members and subscribers. In 1833 members paid membership fees of £1 or more, considerably more than the 10 shillings paid by subscribers, and a difference which entitled them alone to sit on the Board of Management, to vote in Society meetings, to stand for Society office and to compete for certain extra prizes at cattle shows. [143]

The Royal Jersey Agricultural and Horticultural Society chose to speak for the farming community, but from the outset the relationship between the Society's gentleman farmers and the main body of local agriculturists was an uneasy one. After an initial enthusiasm - in 1834 the Society could claim a membership total of 230 - membership fell, as agriculturists showed their disappointment at its gentlemanly pretensions by establishing independent home-spun societies at the parish level throughout the Island in the 1840s and by ending the States grant to the Society in 1842. [144] The Chamber of Commerce, by contrast, was never intended other than as a tight-knit body, representing an entire interest group, and therein lay its lobbying power.

It was not unnatural then that in times when economic privileges came under threat, the experienced Chamber of Commerce came to the fore. Thus, when in May 1819 British Customs sent investigators to discover whether the quantity of cider exported by Jersey could possibly be that produced in the Island alone, that is they suspected it was being supplemented with French produce, the Chamber of Commerce closed ranks with local agriculturists and the officials returned satisfied as to the production capabilities of local agriculture. [145] Again, complaints in 1820 by West Country farmers of a similar nature regarding corn, which finally resulted in Parliament's appointment of a select committee to investigate the matter in 1835, saw the Chamber of Commerce petitioning and lobbying in London alongside the States of Jersey and Guernsey. The joint action resulted in the successful exclusion of the Channel Islands from the restrictions of the Corn Laws. [146]

Making use of the expertise of the Chamber of Commerce made sense, but it was not necessarily a reflection on the inadequacy of the Royal Jersey Agricultural and Horticultural Society. In times of crisis the Society showed itself to be a tireless agitator. This was most evident in the mid-1860s when the British Government placed a ban on the importation of all cattle in a effort to curtail the effect of the rinderpest epidemic in Europe. The Chamber of Commerce was at this time (see the following subsection) unable to expend much effort in the cause of Jersey's rights to free trade but in 1866 the Society, in conjunction with the States of Jersey and Guernsey, managed to secure the exclusion of the Islands from the ban.[147] The concession was such that local breeders were able to benefit from the decline in livestock in England by providing cattle to replace those lost. [148] When forced to, the Royal Jersey Agricultural and Horticultural Society was capable of fighting for the Island's rights.

Any action which might have served to restrict the trading privileges of the Island was a curtailment of merchant activity, and in all such cases the lobbying of the Chamber of Commerce was clearly motivated by self-interest. This was never denied, but what understandably irritated the merchant and commercial sectors was the way in which members of the agricultural industry could calmly expect the Chamber of Commerce to exert all its energies in the pursuit of economic freedom for the Island and subsequently fail to acknowledge the contribution. But the matter went further than ingratitude. The landed interest in the States willingly fought alongside the merchant sector to keep English markets open and trade barriers down, but it equally willingly used its power in the States, as in 1819 and 1835, to impose local tariffs on goods imported into the Island, which, it claimed, were undercutting local producers. [149]

Such selfish behaviour was both damaging and galling to Jersey merchants. It showed an agricultural sector willing to utilise any economic advantage offered it by the merchant sector, but unwilling either to recognise the contribution or reciprocate. The results of this political and economic ambivalence form a major theme in this work. Herein lay the basis for the two main groupings in nineteenth century Jersey: the rural bloc, with its power historically in the land and agriculture, reflected by a strong political base in the States; and the urban bloc, composed of the merchant and commercial classes, its power based on its wealth, but with no real reflection in the political arena. To this latter grouping was added an equally disenfranchised body of English immigrants, who whilst not matching local economic power, derived their voice from their shared experiences as a body of smaller capitalists and consumers. It was a divide originating in the great upheaval Jersey experienced in the economic sphere, which threw up a new body of urban-based middle-class capitalists to challenge centuries of domination by the landed interest.

The Decline of the Merchant Economy

The Jersey merchant economy, far more than its agricultural counterpart with its solid foundation in the land, was excessively reliant on its ability to exploit and manipulate Jersey's trading privileges to their utmost. The vulnerability of trade carried on the periphery of great nations was fully appreciated by those involved: indeed, the establishment of the Chamber of Commerce was a response to such an imbalance. However, by the mid-nineteenth century economic forces and rapid change heralded the decline of the cod-trade and its associated industries. Internal financial collapse in the 1870s and 1880s, a result of local ineptitude, left these sectors equally powerless and marked their departure from local and world trade.

In 1860 the Chamber of Commerce failed to obtain exemption for the Channel Islands from the *Customs Amendment Act,* which laid charges upon goods exported from foreign parts or colonies into Britain, and vice versa.[150] The failure brought closer to home a changing state of affairs which had been eroding the Island's merchant economy from the 1850s. A previous leniency exercised by Parliament in interpreting and applying legislation where it affected the Channel Islands was now apparently absent. Worse was to come. The Anglo-French Treaty of 1860, which effectively brought to a close centuries of animosity between those two states, showed similar disregard for the Island's need for economic favouritism.[151] More significantly, it represented a serious wound to the Island's leverage over England. Much of the constitutional ambivalence so readily manipulated by Jersey capitalists had rested on the Island's position as an outpost in hostile territory, a state of affairs relevant up to the 1850s when defensive harbours were built in Jersey and Alderney to repulse a feared French attack.[152] By the 1860s the Channel was no longer a hostile territory. Circumstances had so changed that the interests of a small Island of little tangible value could now easily be overlooked.

The events of 1860 reflected a changing global state of affairs that was generally detrimental to Island commerce. Technological change, Britain's concern to maximise its own trading profits, the rise of the United States as a great power and the Anglo-French Treaty stripped the Island of its merchant pretensions and demanded a diversification beyond its capabilities. The merchant triangle was subjected to a many fronted attack: in the marketing sphere, by a move away from protectionist policies heralded by the repeal of sugar duties in 1852; in the production sphere, by the 1854 Reciprocity Treaty between Canada and the

United States, which allowed the latter access to the fisheries; and in the home sphere, by the challenge to sail dominance in the carrying trade from steam ships. [153] The heavy capital outlay required to shift the shipbuilding industry into producing iron vessels was beyond the means of the Jersey merchants, and would have been so even at the height of their success. Shipbuilding, too, went into rapid decline. [154]

Undermined by changes over which it could have little control, the merchant sector was further and more directly hit by local financial collapse. In February 1873, the Mercantile Union Bank, one of the larger Island banks, closed with liabilities ten times larger than its assets, including £55,000 worth of notes in circulation. [155] It was joined four months later by the Joint Stock Bank, the bank of the Methodists. [156] In both cases, dishonesty and a lack of legal supervision had enabled over-expenditure, particularly on the Island's harbour development. The use of extensive loan facilities offered by the banks and an inability to repay, immediately resulted in the cod business of De Quetteville of Labrador following the finance houses into liquidation. [157] Worse was to come when, in the beginning of 1886, the Jersey Banking Company, known locally as the 'States' Bank', closed its doors and suspended all payments. Jersey merchants had borrowed heavily in a time of depression from an unlimited credit bank. Unprotected by limited liability legislation, local merchant houses were left in severe financial difficulties. The two greatest Gaspé cod firms, C.R. Robin and Le Boutillier, as well as some smaller firms, found their financial base destroyed, and collapsed. [158] The integrated network of linkages in the cod trade, by which the leading merchant families were inter-connected, brought down the majority of those involved in the industry, including the families of Duheaume, de Gruchy, Gosset, Payn, Clement, Nicolle, Le Brocq and de Ste Croix. [159]

The devastation of the merchant sector and all those involved in its operations was clear from the reaction of the local press. "Le mot CATASTROPHE n'est certes pas exagéré," exclaimed the *Nouvelle Chronique*, "et n'est peut-être en réalité que trop faible pour faire comprendre la secousse fatale au commerce de notre ile, fatale à l'industrie en général, fatale de nombreuses familles qui croyaient leur pain assuré par un emploi régulier. La suspension de paiement de la 'Jersey Banking Company', bien que ce soit un désastre colossal n'est peut-être encore que secondaire de l'éntendue de ses effets déplorables à la fermeture du plus grand, du plus important, du plus ancien des établissements de Jersey. Depuis plus d'un siècle la maison de M.M. Robin et Compagnie avait marché de progrès en progèrs, et si la providence les avait favorisés pendant de longues années d'une grande prospérité, des centaines de capitaines de navires, des milliers de marins et de pêcheurs, des nombreux commis, enfin une belle partie de trois générations de Jersiais a dû rendre témoignage....de la soigneuse excellence de l'administration de cette grande maison du commerce". [160]

The Chamber of Commerce, whose minute book recorded the decline of the cod industry, lamented the inability to expand. It recognised the inherent weakness of a small island; "apart from our shipping interest and our fisheries we are an agricultural and domestic economy". In what was perhaps the most poignant reflection of the collapse of the merchant sector, it was decided instead to turn the attention and expertise of the Chamber to the advancement of the agricultural industry. [161] A year later this was extended to embrace the developing tourist industry. [162]

By contrast, the agricultural industry remained relatively immune from the financial crises of 1873 and 1886, and the general collapse of the cod trade and some of its associated concerns. The only reference made to the bank failure of 1873 by the Royal Jersey Agricultural and Horticultural Society was the criticism of a local merchant exporter of agricultural produce who had ceased trading with liabilities of £14,000. [163] By 1886 the agricultural sector was facing what local observers perceived as a mini-crisis, with falling prices in both livestock and potato exports. The Jersey Banking Company had offered high interest rates and the Jersey Herd Book, a trading unit of the Royal Jersey Agricultural and Horticultural Society, had invested £2,641. Following the 1886 crash, only a quarter of the original sum was recovered. [164] This appears to have been the largest loss experienced by the agricultural industry. Bear stated that the result of the crash for farmers was only "a diminution of great prosperity". [165]

This apparent immunity of the agricultural industry is not surprising. Agriculture was based on small, economically autonomous producers who were not reliant on large sums of capital. The bank crashes may have hit individual savings, but there is no information to this effect. Even if some agriculturists had fortunes comparable to the merchant sector, and it is doubtful that many of them had, given the general nature of the rural economy they would have invested profits in property or land, probably via secure wheat rentes (local mortgages). Furthermore, agriculture's business associations with Jersey based merchant firms had been in some degree of decline since the 1850s. It was in the nature of 'early' potato export that speed of delivery to the consumer was essential. From the outset in 1858, shipment of the crop was by steam packet to Southampton and Weymouth, a service in regular operation as a mail and passenger carrier since 1824. On arrival in England, potatoes were transported to the vast metropolises of London and Birmingham. By the time of peak potato production the advantage of the steamship was augmented by the use of rail for the overland stage. [166] The coming of steam, then, further undermined the local carrying trade, although, as we have observed, English ships dominated from the very outset the transport of Jersey agricultural produce from earlier in the century.

The 'early' potato likewise contributed to the first appearance of major English merchant interest in the Island in the nineteenth century. The specialist nature of the crop, its perishability and short marketing period demanded coordinated handling and this was mainly provided by non-locals. Of the five major merchants advertising in May 1880, for example, only one, Thomas Sauvage, who was acting for G. Bell at Covent Garden, bore a local name. The likes of J.A. Stirling and Company, B. Kedgley and Son, Kneeling and Hunt, and John Figgess, all London based, reflect the English dominance in this sphere of operations. [167]

Whilst considerable criticism in the press was levelled at the English merchant presence, claiming that it was detrimental to local interests, demands for some form of cooperative marketing organisation, though leading to a meeting of the Royal Jersey Agricultural and Horticultural Society and the Chamber of Commerce to this end in 1879, appear to have come to nothing. [168] Here was an example of the Jersey individualism, discussed in the First Section, undermining cooperation.

In a wider sense the arrival of English merchants and purchasing agents heralded the introduction of larger English concerns. This was most apparent in the financial sphere, with the takeover of the small local banks by the likes of the London and Midland Bank in 1897 and the London, County and Westminster Bank in 1918. [169] Such moves were in the nature of filling the vacuum left by the demise of the great cod houses, so long the giants in the Jersey economy, but were also built upon half a century of hard work and experience by English immigrants.

From at least the 1850s, there were signs of an emerging English capitalist presence further up the local economic ladder. Although the rôle of English immigrant in the Jersey economy was still predominantly in the artisanal and labouring spheres, local trade directories reveal a slight shift in this pattern by the mid-century. In 1849, for example, four of the eight banks listed in the *British Press Almanack* were drawing capital from English banks on the mainland. Out of 30 locally based insurance firms, 10 were English. [170] Such a presence provided an introduction to the Island for larger English capital concerns after the 1880s.

Nonetheless, the crashes of the 1870s and 1880s left agriculture very much at the economic helm. Jersey's rural economy rested on more solid foundations than did its external trade. Its concentration on high priced cash crops, utilising its natural advantages, kept competition with English and European growers within manageable bounds. Similarly, the fact that Jersey's agricultural exports amounted to but a small share of the English market - a mere drop in the ocean, as the Royal Jersey Agricultural and Horticultural Society continually maintained - meant English agriculturists were not concerned enough to challenge the Island's right to free trade with the mainland.[171] Bear was keen to stress in 1888 that English growers continued to regard Jersey growers as "foreign competitors", but if they did, they tended not to show it.[172] The export of potatoes and cattle, and increasingly in the last decade of the nineteenth century, market garden crops, tended not to upset the sensibilities of English growers in the way that corn and, to a lesser extent, cider had done earlier in the century.

That agriculture successfully outlived its merchant rivals was a reflection of the two sectors' different structures and differing susceptibility to external changes, rather than of a greater expertise in business management. The merchant empire, if it can be called that, lived on the periphery of other economies and ultimately fell victim to its precarious position. It was ironic that the *Customs Consolidation Act* of 1876 simultaneously confirmed Jersey's internal rights to continue as before in its trading with Britain and ended the right of its merchants to trade duty free between the colonies and the mainland: the Act levied a charge on all goods exported to or imported from Britain, excepting the direct produce of the Channel Islands.[173]

During the course of the nineteenth century, the Jersey economy expanded on an unprecedented scale. In human terms alone, the rapid population growth experienced both as cause and result of economic transformation reflects the scale of that change and the potential threat it brought to traditional Jersey society. Jersey, for the first time in its history, now had a significant urban population, many of whom were non-local in origin. This urban community had its experiences, attitudes and wealth rooted in things other than the land, so long the basis for the Jersey social, political and economic structure. It is not surprising that the differences between the urban and rural blocs resulted in friction.

The threat to nineteenth-century Jersey society, derived from economic expansion, was mildened by factors present in that expansion. The native population of Jersey retained control of the commercial sector up to at least the 1880s, when the financial crashes and fall of the great cod houses allowed the emergence of a English commercial presence. Up to that date the English presence remained predominantly in the artisanal and labouring spheres. The English contribution to political challenge would come from the relatively small independent business community, a challenge that was necessarily weakened by its small size and lack of economic clout. This left the onus for political challenge on the native commercial sector, a challenge which, as we shall see, was itself undermined by several factors. As for the rural community, its historical political power was now matched by a vibrant agricultural economy which by 1880 had shown itself to be more stable than the urban economy. This combination of political and economic power was to place the nineteenth century rural community in a strong position.

In this chapter we have attempted to present the economic basis to the various challenges thrust upon Jersey society in the nineteenth century. A major part of this book will examine what occurred as a result of this economic growth and expansion.

Chapter 4

Religion and the Church

It is reflective of the variety of forces unleashed upon Jersey society in the nineteenth century that those which affected the Church, primarily Nonconformism and the increasing secularisation of the parish, had very little directly to do with the development of the economy outlined in the previous chapter. Nonetheless, operating in tandem, both Nonconformism and economic transformation were potentially disruptive to society and successful in creating a basis for change. The major distinction between the two was that Nonconformism, although originating from outside the Island, remained essentially an internal affair, threatening only a readjustment of the inner workings of Jersey without ever challenging the whole.

From at least the thirteenth century, when documented evidence is available, to the late eighteenth century the Established Church in Jersey was in an enviable position. It was equipped for all aspects of parish life, social, political and religious. A staunch Calvinism, introduced at the Reformation, meant a close supervision of the everyday life of the congregation. Ecclesiastical authority was coupled with a monopoly control over many of the civil functions of the parish, a combination which effectively left the rector, except perhaps in a strong seigniorial area such as St Ouen, as potentially a more powerful figure than any of his parishioners.

From the 1770s this position of near dominance was challenged and subsequently eroded both by the introduction and spread of Methodism and the increasing autonomy of the body civil in the parish. Although not the first Nonconformist denomination to enter the Island - there had been a Quaker presence since at least 1740 - Methodism succeeded in providing an alternative to the Established Church and proved to be the catalyst to the widespread introduction and acceptance of various Nonconformist bodies, including Presbyterians, Independents, Baptists and Roman Catholics. [1] In turn, the spread of Nonconformism undermined, too, the secular rôle of the Established Church, it being no longer possible for the Church to claim to represent the whole parish. Along with such factors as the growth in population and the resulting need for a more complex parish infrastructure, Nonconformism thus contributed to the ascendancy of the body civil in the parish during the course of the nineteenth century.

This chapter will examine the Nonconformist challenge to the Established Church in nineteenth century Jersey. It will show a Church at the end of the eighteenth century which was powerful at all levels of society, but undermined by the hide-bound nature of its ecclesiastic establishment and morally weakened by its political excesses in the secular sphere. Methodism is presented as a response by a section of Jersey society to these excesses. Its arrival in Jersey in 1784 and its rapid success, particularly in the countryside, established the basis for a challenge to the Established Church's previous monopoly.

We observed in the introductory section the powerful position of the Established Church in Jersey. This power was apparent until well into the nineteenth century. Nonconformism and an increasing secularisation of parish functions undermined this position. If we are to understand these two processes, it is necessary to examine the Established Church in some detail, paying attention to the constitution of the clergy, attitudes to the Church and the public image of that Church.

The Clergy

As a body the nineteenth-century Established Church clergymen formed a fairly uniform group, although shared social backgrounds did not prevent independence and individuality, often tantamount to parochialism. The difference between the small size of the living available in the Island and the opulence, by Jersey standards at least, of clergy households suggests that the majority of clergymen came from the ranks of the upper middle-class. Family wealth was required to maintain the sort of clergy households disclosed by the census of 1851. Most of the twelve rectors had at least two domestics, the Reverend Charles Marett, Rector of St Clement (1842-1876) , had six, including a cook, a dairymaid and a chambermaid.[2]

The middle-class nature of the local clergy is further reflected in their family connections. An analysis of the sixty Jersey rectors between 1770 and 1900 reveals that at least half of them were connected to leading members of the upper middle-class, either by birth or marriage. Thus the Reverend Charles Le Touzel, Rector of St Martin (1799-1818), was the son of Jean Le Touzel, a Major in the Militia, and Elizabeth du Parcq, sister of the Reverend Jean du Parcq, Rector of St Ouen. The Reverend Edouard Falle, Rector of St Martin (1829-1881), married the daughter of the Reverend George Balleine, a former Rector of St Martin, and fathered a future dean of Jersey. The Reverend Charles Marett, Rector of St Saviour (1876-1895), was the son of a Colonel in the Militia and the nephew of Rear Admiral Charles Bertram.[3]

As a clue to personal wealth it is worthwhile noting that it was not uncommon for clergymen to contribute substantially towards various causes within their own church. In 1865 the Reverend Balleine donated a significant sum to the new pews being installed in his church at St Mary, whilst the Reverend Ahier in 1842 made by far the largest contribution in his parish of £62 towards the cost of an organ for his church at Trinity.[4]

Nonetheless, it would have been possible for individuals from poorer backgrounds to have become clergymen, since the requisite degree could be obtained with the aid of various local scholarships to Oxford and Cambridge. Thus, the Reverend Philippe Filleul, the son of a St Clement's farmer, reached Pembroke College, Oxford, with the help of the Don Baudains in 1813. [5] In a more general sense, though, the poor parson of the English mould is not quite appropriate to Jersey, finding parallel perhaps only in curates to parish rectors and, later in the nineteenth century, vicars of newly created ecclesiastical districts, such as St Matthew's in St Lawrence (1842) and St Mark's in St Helier (1844).

The ecclesiastical living available to the twelve rectors was modest. This was a result of early feudal appropriation, and was small enough, claimed Inglis in 1834, to make them "a working clergy". [6] The incumbent of each parish church received small tithes from the land, known as 'novales' or 'deserts', and various fees, such as those for the burial service. Only 10 per cent of the great tithes on the good corn land was received by the rectors, since these had fallen initially to lay hands, then to various abbeys on the Continent and finally, after the Reformation, to the Crown. [7] In 1853 the death of the Governor of Jersey, Lord Beresford, and the Crown's decision to discontinue the office resulted in the rectors sharing his portion of the great tithes, to the estimated total value of £300. [8] The other main contributor to the living was the Island's glebe land which totalled 167 vergées, of which individual parish shares ranged from 4 to 26 vergées. [9]

Further information on clergy finances is contained in a group of letters directed at a Reverend Clement in England in 1830. The anonymous author saw little reason for poverty among local rectors, since agricultural productivity ensured bountiful tithes. The production of local apples and potatoes was so considerable, he claimed, "as to afford them a decent maintenance without pressing on some of the poorest of their parishioners....It is said that the income of none of them is much less than £200 a year: of course it varies with the size and productiveness of the parish....[but thanks to] the comparative cheapness of things here to what they are in England, it may go a considerable deal further, thus placing them all in a state of respectability and ease". [10] H.D. Inglis offered a slightly smaller figure, suggesting that the small tithes alone fetched no more than £120. [11]

Whatever the state of their finances, the livings of local clergymen were enhanced by accommodation provided by the parish. This perk, suggested the eighteenth century clergyman Philippe Falle, was "but one particular wherein they are little eased". [12] It was surely more than that. Most rectories were of a size consistent with that of a small gentleman's residence. The potential new rectory at St Ouen's in 1763 was described in detail to the Parish Assembly as comprising a large main house, "offices, le Jardin de devant la Maison, le Jardin planté à Pommiers, la pépinière, la pièce de terre au sud dudt. Jardin, le petit Becquet de terre...., du pressoir". [13] Along with these often large rectories came the assurance that repair would be undertaken by the parish. This was guaranteed by the Trésor, a parish fund for the upkeep of the church. [14] Nonetheless, whilst repairs were the responsibility of the parish, the rector was required to keep the place visually appealing. This the Reverend George Balleine, installed in the new rectory at St Ouen in 1816, discovered when he was served with an Ordre de Justice for neglect of the property, particularly the garden and specifically the trees which he was summoned to replace or restore. [15]

Moderately well-off or not, some rectors attempted to boost their finances by a variety of means. It is quite likely that several rectories were run as farms; the Reverend Marett's staff at St Clement included two farm labourers, described as his servants. [16] Similarly, the rectories at St Brelade and St John show signs of having been farms at one time, and St Ouen's Rectory was a farm in use in 1838, as was St Saviour's earlier in the century. [17] The Reverend Poingdestre found it necessary to combine his rôle as vicar of St Matthew's Church, in St Lawrence, with the position of Regent of the school of St Anastase, in St Peter, though, due to the dire circumstances of the latter institution, he complained that he was continually out of pocket. [18]

Perhaps the best indication of the state of finances for the majority of the Established clergy is revealed in their concern over the future of feudal dues. The main part of their income was feudal, and the suggestion in 1833 of a possible Parliamentary move to commute tithes and the extension of this to the Island, resulted in a petition en masse to the King from the Island's clergy. Whilst they agreed in principle with a commutation, they could not, they claimed, do so in practice because of the poverty of their benefices. [19] The award to the rectors of the former Governor's portion of the great tithes in 1853 made them all the more intransigent on the subject. [20]

The requirement in the Ecclesiastical Canons that the Jersey clergy be local men in practice meant that a rector's experience was, with the exception of training, generally limited to the Island. [21] Of the sixty parish rectors who served in Jersey between 1770 and 1900 it appears that only three had served in a similar capacity elsewhere, namely England. One of those, François Jeune, stayed in Jersey for six years only (parish of St Saviour 1838-1844) and returned to England, where he became Bishop of Peterborough. Three rectors of the sixty, the Reverend Boudier at St Ouen (1785-1794), the Reverend Dupré at St John (1809-1818) and Dean Corbet Hue (1823-1837) were absentee. Only ten of the number appear to have been vicars prior to receiving their own parish, all locally. [22]

Once appointed to a parish, a Jersey rector was likely to stay there for some considerable length of time. Out of sixty rectors in the period 1770-1900, thirty-five served in one parish only, twenty-one in two parishes, three men served in three parishes, one served in four. The average term of office in a parish in the same period lasted twenty-three years. Whilst it is likely that a rank order of rectorships existed, the only real clue as to what parishes the Church considered more important than others comes from the appointment of deans. With the exception of one appointment at St Martin (François Le Couteur 1789-1808), Jersey deans served in either the parish of St Saviour or St Helier, the latter because of its position as effective capital of the Island and the former possibly because of its earlier importance as a centre of the Jersey Church in the twelfth century. [23] It is likely that smaller parishes, particularly St Mary and St Clement, carried less prestige.

The analysis of incumbents gives little clue to a hierarchy. An average stay of a rector in St Mary of twenty-four years, for instance, compares quite favourably with the figure of eighteen years in St Helier and twenty years in St Saviour. For no obvious reason, rectors at St John stayed for the shortest time, eleven years on average, whilst the parish of Trinity was served by only three clergymen in the whole period, giving an average of forty-five years per rector.

Information regarding the personalities and behaviour of the clergy is scant. That which exists, of necessity, reflects on the activities of the more outspoken individuals among the local clergy, usually in the political arena. More often than not, attention is drawn to particular rectors because of lengthy disputes with members of their parish. The majority of clergymen in the late eighteenth and nineteenth centuries remain somewhat anonymous, which may indicate good parish relations or their lack of interest in politics. Occasional testimonies favourable to the parish rector exist, such as that of St Ouen's Ecclesiastical Assembly in 1859, and that of St Peter in 1813, which stressed how "by a strict attention to his various duties and the precepts inculcated from his pulpit he [the Reverend Francois Ricard] has contributed largely to the peace and good understanding which this parish has for a long time enjoyed".[24] But they are not abundant.

Attitudes to the Church and Clergy

That the Connétable of St Peter might recognise the contribution of the Rector to the tranquillity of parish life and that St Peter was generally considered a parish where politics divided people less than elsewhere, was no coincidence.[25] Clearly, the attitudes and political stance of a parish rector influenced the way he was viewed and treated by his parishioners. The experience of the Reverend Edouard Le Vavasseur dit Durell is a case in point. Appointed Rector of St Saviour in 1819, Durell was a Rose Party man in a parish dominated by Laurel supporters. Undeterred by the situation, he led an active political life, becoming editor of the Rose Party paper *The Gazette* in 1823. His political stance, however, made him many enemies in the parish and resulted in his ultimate downfall in 1841, when he was suspended from duty by the Ecclesiastical Court. This followed a long legal battle concerning an accusation made by several of his parishioners, never proved one way or the other, alleging homosexual activities. [26] Regardless of the case against him, Durell's past intransigence and strong political views lost him much potential support. His insistence on turning his appearance before the Ecclesiastical Court into a courtroom drama did not endear him to his peers, who were likewise unimpressed by the attempts of his advocate (Pierre Le Sueur) to outwit them. [27]

It must be noted that the incidence of clerical politics coincides with periods of particular political ferment. Thus, Durell was active during the stormiest phase of the Laurel and Rose conflict in the early nineteenth century. Likewise, the Reverend Thomas Sivret joined some of his fellow rectors in the Magots, the democrats, against the Charlots in the equally politically virulent period of the 1780s, an allegiance which prompted the leading Charlot and Lieutenant-Bailiff, W.C. Lemprière, to complain to the Privy Council. "The clergy", he lamented, "are the great patriots of the day, who conscientiously sacrifice every consideration to what they call Liberty, that is the pleasure of throwing everything into confusion by their ill-fated interference in Politicks. Your Lordship will no doubt admire their zeal when you know that on Sunday they marched in a public Market Place with blue cockades in a disgraceful and undignified manner, huzzaing for Liberty like Bacchanalians, and wearing the badge even in the Pulpit, no doubt with a view of inspiring their auditors with Christian meekness and moderation". [28] Lemprière was not alone in his dislike of Church involvement in politics. To be fair to the clergy, they sat in the States and in times of political crisis or injustice it was not unnatural that they should wish to take part. The pulpit provided an ideal platform to express political opinion, as the Reverend Jean Lemprière showed the congregation of St Helier in 1789 with his Magot rhetoric. [29]

Individuals like Durell took their political involvement too far, but even a moderate involvement in politics could be seen to conflict with the rector's position as spiritual leader and moral guide. It is likely that many felt like Inglis, who regretted the clergy's legislative rôle because it "affects the usefulness of the clergy, which necessarily depends greatly, upon their moral influence over their respective flocks": where a great diversity of opinion existed the clergy were of necessity "brought into ill odour with a part of their parishioners". [30]

If politically active clergymen reflected poorly on the Church's position in the community, then no doubt clerical in-fighting did even more harm to its public image. Such outbursts varied in scale and occurred only occasionally. Two examples will illustrate. In 1794 the Reverend Bertram of St Brelade actioned the Reverend Ricard of St John for the unsanctioned burial of several soldiers in the cemetery at St Brelade. In his capacity as Chaplain to the 67th. Regiment Ricard had buried soldiers elsewhere in parish cemeteries, particularly St Ouen and Grouville, with similar disregard, and Bertram's complaint was followed by remonstrances from the Rectors of St Ouen and Grouville. The complaints were two-fold, firstly that Ricard had violated the others' parish jurisdiction and, secondly, caused them the loss of the necessary fees. The case was settled amicably, but was a stern warning as to the inviolability of the ecclesiastical parish. [31]

The case against the Reverend Ricard involved little more than a territorial clash between ministers, settled by recourse to the Ecclesiastical Assembly. Damage to the Church's public image could be minimised in this way. The Dupré case went a step further. Appointed Dean in 1802, the Reverend Edouard Dupré was a staunch Laurel supporter in the increasingly Rose orientated parish of St Helier. His first ten years as Dean were marred by many clashes with parishioners. [32] By 1812, the situation had reached such proportions that a group of the congregation petitioned the Privy Council for permission to build an alternative venue to practice their faith. In 1813 the Council agreed to the request, adding that the founders had the right to appoint their own minister. [33] St Paul's Church was opened on 14th December 1817 by the Rector of St Ouen, the Reverend François Ricard, an act that so angered the Dean that he forbade all clergy entry to the building and the church was closed. [34] The response of the founders was to find a French minister of the French Église Réformée, who was willing to take Anglican Orders, but his attempts to preach in St Paul's were greeted with excommunication by the Dean. The case then went to the Royal Court, who backed the parishioners and negated the right of the Dean, who presided over the Ecclesiastical Court, to interfere. An appeal by the Church authorities to the Privy Council in 1819 resulted in a reversal and an upholding of the Ecclesiastical Court's right to administer its own justice. [35] Meantime, the Church had suffered seven years of bad publicity.

Cases such as this, and the already mentioned Durell case (1836-41), were damaging to the Church, even if in all three cases its right to put its own house in order was vindicated. In similar fashion, the activities and intransigence of the Reverend Abraham Le Sueur in the parish of Grouville in the latter half of the nineteenth century, particularly over the parochial school, and his choice to fight his battles through the columns of local newspapers, meant unnecessary and undesirable publicity. [36] Nonconformist congregations, by contrast, did not wash their dirty laundry in public.

The Durell and Dupré cases took matters to the extreme, but they were representative of the high incidence of conflict between rectors and their parishioners. These struggles were political, social and "religious. A Jersey rector could expect his behaviour during Sunday service to be scrutinised as closely as his actions outside the parish church, and disagreements in either sphere could provide the basis for a long feud.

Pew ownership reflected this blurring of distinction between religious and secular. The ability to own a pew within a church gave its owner a vested interest in that building and anything that might occur to undermine or devalue that investment would not be tolerated. This meant in effect that a rector, already circumscribed in his movements by the Ecclesiastical Assembly, had to tread warily within his own church. In 1833 the Rector of St Ouen, the Reverend Philippe Payn, found himself served with an Ordre de Justice at the instigation of one of his parishioners. Jean Arthur claimed that as the owner of two pews "situés dans la partie méridionale de l'Eglise de St Ouen" and, by all accounts, "tres-advantageusement placés rélativement à la situation et la position de la chaire et du pupitre du Ministre", he was most dismayed to see that the said pulpit and desk had been moved. The movement of furniture had been undertaken to better serve the interests of the congregation as a whole. Arthur's point was that his pew had been greatly reduced in value; he did not stipulate whether the loss was religious or financial. Condemned to pay £100 compensation to Arthur for the decrease in the value of his property or to return the moved furniture to its former location, the Ecclesiastical Assembly voted for the latter. [37]

The behaviour of the parish rector was under constant scrutiny and any deviation from that expected of him was reported to the competent authority. In most cases, attacks on an individual rector represented a disgruntled sectional interest, in the same way as parish elections were often challenged by the defeated. The Reverend Amice Bisson of St Lawrence found himself on two such charges before the Ecclesiastical Court in 1782 and 1802, when the Surveillants of the parish claimed he was guilty of a variety of offences, mainly drink related, which included negligence and political bias at election time; on both occasions he escaped on a technicality. [38] One incident was enough to spark a lengthy struggle, such as that between the Reverend William Duheaume and a section of his parishioners in Trinity, whereby a disputed electionof church officers resulted in his being described as "tant en Assemblée de paroisse que dans le public....un scandale à l'Eglise". [39]

In the parish of St Ouen secular-religious conflict was particularly acute through three successive rectorates between 1789 and 1820. Parishioners charged all three incumbents with failing to act in the manner required of them by the parish. In the first case, which involved the Reverend Jean Boudier, there was some substance to the parish case. Appointed in 1785, Boudier had appeared in the parish only twice (August 1786 and September 1787) prior to charges being brought before the Ecclesiastical Court in 1789. [40] Whilst the Ecclesiastical Canons specifically forbade pluralities, a minority of rectors had taken this to mean no more than one living in Jersey. [41] In true rural parish fashion, the major complaint regarding Boudier's absence was that it deprived the parish of a political representative in the States, as well as leaving the presbytery in a state that disgraced the parish; there was no mention of a spiritual loss. [42] The parish followed the matter through in the Ecclesiastical Court and Boudier was finally relieved of his position, a judgement based on the 24th Canon which empowered the dean to sequestrate the living of a rector in certain circumstances. [43]

Subsequent rectors of the parish encountered an intransigent congregation. The Reverend George du Heaume faced civil interference to a degree which forced him to take parish officers, including the Connétable, to both the Ecclesiastical and Royal Courts. [44] In the parish only three years, the Reverend George Balleine was there long enough to be accused by the Surveillants of malpractice, namely deserting the church and congregation immediately prior to Divine Service, an accusation of which he was found innocent. [45] His replacement, the Reverend Francois Ricard, finding himself in court at least three times, faced similar charges of malpractice, but, as a former Connétable of St Ouen himself (1785-1790) prior to taking Holy Orders, he replied in kind and accused leading municipal officers, including the Seigneur of St Ouen, Charles Le Maistre, of insulting and irreligious behaviour. [46] To illustrate the triviality of some of these charges, one dispute centred on whether or not the Church door should have been closed during a storm, and whose right it was to perform such a task. [47] The four ministers had lasted a total of 38 years, in an Island where as we have noted, between 1770 and 1900, the average rector stayed 23 years in a parish. [48]

The parish of St Ouen between 1785 and 1823 is a good example of how a combination of antagonistic forces and a powerful body civil could make life difficult for the clergyman, if he did not toe the line. For a Parish Assembly unhappy with its present incumbent, whether because of personality clash or the refusal of the rector to subject himself to its way of thinking, the only option was to find points of conflict. Generally speaking, however, the result was a policy both ineffective and trivial, and one which contrasted with the ability to take relatively speedy and effective action against an undesirable Connétable at triennial elections. This is illustrated by the 34 years of the Reverend Abraham Le Sueur in the parish of Grouville and the 51 years of the Reverend William Duheaume in the parish of Trinity, incumbencies which were sullied by ineffectual charges of misconduct and counter charges of unwarranted interference. [49] Even when an effective way was found to be rid of an unpopular rector, as in the case of the Reverend Durell, accused of sodomy, the resulting case was dragged out for five years; even then his loss of position was related more to his stupidity in reaction to the charges than to their actual content. [50] Likewise, the Durell case showed how the suspension of a rector from office caused no end of problems: parish affairs were disrupted, since church officers could not be elected without his presiding over the Ecclesiastical Assembly, and Sunday services were temporarily suspended when Durell refused to hand over the keys to the church. [51]

Parish records, then, contain more examples of clergymen at odds with their congregations than of exemplary pastors beloved of their flocks. Indeed, the Established Church offered little evidence of spirituality in the conventional sense. If the parish church could be said in any sense to represent the self-image of the community in the late eighteenth and early nineteenth century it was of a local, stable world, where social hierarchy was reflected in the arrangement of the pews: multiple ownership in the case of the wealthy, basic seating (at the expense of the Trésor) at the back for the less well-off. [52] If an inability to purchase a pew was not enough of a social indicator, it might be reinforced by exclusion from a parish election at the church door after Divine Service, as Philippe Ami discovered in the parish of St Brelade in 1826, when he faced a rigorous interrogation by Jurat Benest on the grounds of his "being a poor man". [53]

The external image of the church was no more imposing than its inner spiritual life. As we shall see in discussing Church attempts at regeneration from the mid-nineteenth century, church buildings were generally in a bad state of disrepair. In one of the letters written to the Reverend Clement in 1828, the parish churches of Jersey were described "as remarkable for nothing, but the sad state in which they are suffered to remain. They are all of them stone structures, with a stone spire, or square tower: the interior is of low, heavy Norman or Gothic architecture, and consists of narrow aisles, and a vestibule. The walls are of stone, white washed; and the pews are of dirty deal, unpainted; stained with the splashes of the last white-washing, overwrought with spiders' webs, and the flooring of many of them literally worn out and broken up, disclosing the bare earth, as if the footsteps had trodden it unrepaired. The whole appearance of the greater part of them is so chill and humid as to fill one with apprehension of catarrhs, and rheums, and agues". [54] A resident of twenty years claimed in 1841 that whilst "in general, their situation is highly attractive.... scarcely will the interior of any of the churches repay a visit to them". [55]

Furthermore, added the writer to the Reverend Clement, "Not one of them has an organ except the town church. I cannot tell if this is a remnant of a Presbyterianism, which was once established here, or proceeds from the parsimony of the people. It must be the latter, as the ritual is now the same. In some of them the singers are assisted by a flute or a clarionet, but as the performers are not paid for their services, these aids are somewhat wanting. When this is the case, and the congregation not very numerous, the psalmody is so dissonant, that the imagination is carried back to the coventides of the puritans". [56]

This then was the Established Church of late eighteenth and early nineteenth-century Jersey. It was a Church of great influence in Jersey society, both on an Island level, through its representation in the States and the Ecclesiastical Court, and on a parish level, through its control of spiritual and secular life. With the church in its various capacities as a spiritual house, meeting place, and storeroom, and the cemetery, with that continuity of the living and the dead among those whose families had for generations lived in the same parish, the rector found himself literally at the centre of the community.

Yet, for all its influence the Church's image was tarnished in several important respects. The general picture that emerges is one of an hide-bound establishment lacking in vitality and freshness, of a Church whose spiritual rôle was discredited by the political excesses of its clergy and of an institution which reflected the hierarchical divisions of society often to the prejudice of the less-privileged.

Ultimately, however, the Established Church presented a powerful opponent to any individual or institution that chose to fight. An editorial in the English press in 1873 suggested that the power of the Church in Jersey was such that the only realistic option available to parishioners who found themselves at odds with it was recourse to religious dissent. [57]. It is a remark which has equal poignancy if applied to the 1770s, because it was in that decade that a section of the rural community chose the path of Nonconformism. Therewith began the transformation of the parish into an essentially civil unit, a development which by the end of the nineteenth century had significantly reduced the Established Church's secular rôle to a bare minimum. This growth of municipal power will be examined in a later chapter.

The move to Nonconformism, the people it involved and why they chose to move away from the Established Church will now be examined. It is a process that took place against the backdrop of the Established Church as presented. Nonconformism, particularly Methodism, will be analysed from the perspective of its challenge to the traditional rôle of the Established Church in the Jersey parish.

The Arrival of Methodism

Methodism came to Jersey via Newfoundland in 1774, when two Jersey traders, Pierre Le Sueur and Jean Tentin, returned to the Island newly converted to the new creed. The urban spread of the faith was facilitated by the arrival of English garrisons in 1779 and 1783, both of which contained some Methodists. With the second garrison came a bilingual preacher, Robert Brackenbury, reflecting the linguistic problems English troops faced in trying to follow their new religion and the division that would ultimately result in a decision to divide Methodist Jersey into circuits, sometime before 1810, one English and one French. The joining of Jean de Quetteville, a Jerseyman, with Brackenbury, created the team that was largely responsible for the spread of Methodism in the Island. [58]

In the Town, Methodism caught on among what Guiton called "de simple artisans". [59] Worship was based around small group meetings in private houses. So it remained until the near-ruined, but privately owned, Chapelle des Pas, on the outskirts of the urban area, was made available. From 1790 until 1813, when a chapel was built in Don Street, a private town residence provided the base for meetings, the medieval chapel proving inadequate. [60]

In the countryside conversion followed a similar pattern to the Town. A handful of lay-preachers, particularly Jean de Quetteville, toured the countryside, preaching to assembled groups. The preachers relied on the rural network of kinship and friendship, as well as the organisation of women like Jeanne Perrot, a Huguenot refugee from 1740, and Mme Montbrun. [61] Early successes in country parishes relied on this personal contact. Thus, the converts in the parish of St Mary, who were numerous enough for Wesley to come and preach to them during his brief visit in 1787, were the result of a contact between the Town and a Mme Le Couteur, in whose house the meetings were held. By 1802, the numbers were such that the meetings were moved to the north of the parish, at the house of a Mme. Lemprière. In 1809 there were two alternative meeting places in the parish, by 1815 a chapel had been established. [62]

Between 1784 and 1808 Methodism spread to the eleven country parishes. Progress was delayed only by early opposition in the parishes of St Peter, St Clement and Grouville in the 1790s and the decision to retreat rather than force the issue. [63] In all parishes the same pattern was followed: small groups in private houses. For the lay-preacher the pace was fast, with de Quetteville in 1783 spending his Sundays preaching in St Ouen, St Mary and St John. [64] By 1787 the Wesleyan Conference recorded 200 members in Jersey; by 1791 this had risen to 316. [65]

The population at large appears initially to have adopted a tolerant attitude to Nonconformism. This tolerance extended to all Protestant denominations present in the Island: Methodists, Baptists, Calvinists and Bible Christians. There were cases of persecution. Adam Clarke, a visiting English preacher, found himself a victim of mob violence in St Aubin in 1783, but this appears to have been the result of drunken privateers and ignorance, as opposed to real opposition. [66] In the countryside, Jean de Quetteville encountered isolated areas of opposition: "Aux landes de St Ouen, je fus jeté par terre avec violence, et empêché d'aller dans la maison ou j'allais pour prêcher. À St Jean je fus menacé furieusement par un des principaux de la paroisse, tandis que le maitre de la maison était prêt à prendre son sabre pour me défendre". [67] The decision to avoid potentially hostile areas, such as St Peter and St Clement, no doubt minimalised the possibility of clashes. For country folk who had made a conscious choice to become dissenters, opposition was often a case of enduring gibes like "À tout pécheur miséricorde, À tout Méthodiste-la corde". [68]

Opposition tended to be on an individual basis. Jean e Quetteville's parents disapproved of his religious activities and as a result refused to lend him a horse to travel to his preaching places. [69] In similar vein was the experience of Charles Blampied, a stone-cutter from Trinity, whose conversion to Methodism was a result of his first marriage, but after imprisonment for his faith, his father-in-law by second marriage gave him a stern warning as to the limits of tolerance of a respectable woman; gaol went beyond those limits. [70]

The real challenge to Methodism and Nonconformism generally came not from the population at grass root level, but from the State in its civil capacity, and for reasons which were not directly to do with religion. Charles Blampied's imprisonment in 1794 for refusing to attend Sunday Militia drill, on grounds of conscience, marked the limit of official tolerance.[71] The Court decision was a little out of step with normal practice, since defaulters were generally fined. Within the course of a year Blampied was gaoled three times, 24 days in total, for successive defaults: he refused to pay any fines on the grounds that he was committing no wrong. [72] Following his third imprisonment in June 1796, a petition, signed by 29 leading members of the Nonconformist body, was presented to the States demanding tolerance. [73] Within just over a decade, local Methodism was presenting a united front in the Island.

Six days later, the Royal Court responded to the petition by gaoling an 18 year old Methodist defaulter from St Ouen. [74] Unperturbed, local Methodists continued to default. [75] By 1798 the States decided that it was time to make a stand against such insubordination. In an Acte des États it stressed the gravity of the refusal to perform Militia drills and ruled that defaulters were to be banished from the Island until they showed themselves willing to conform to military requirements; individuals would be given eight days grace to reconsider.[76]

The response of the States and the Royal Court to Nonconformism was based on the perceived threat to their authority, rather than on religious premise. No doubt the fact that Jersey was at war with the French and military efficiency a priority lessened official tolerance, particularly since Methodists questioned only the day chosen for drill, not their duty to serve in the Militia. Nonetheless, the penalty was a severe one. By contrast, the civil authorities in Guernsey showed how such antagonism could be avoided, when the Governor created a separate company of Methodists for Alderney, known as the 'Army of Gideon'. [77]

The Jersey response to what was perceived as the Methodist threat to civil order is explained partially by the Lieutenant-Governor's belief that it came from outside the Island. "Why do they come amongst us ?", wrote General Gordon in 1798, ironically perhaps, since many of the Methodists from England were a part of his garrison. [78] It has been suggested that the attempted suppression of the Methodist challenge to Militia rules, an attack in no real degree extended to their right to religious dissent, was a fear carried from the French Revolution and the revolt of the lower orders. [79] Such a theory is reinforced by the fact that the Militia were, following an acte of the States in 1795, given responsibility to suppress civil disorder. The acte had been a response to certain notices discovered in St Helier calling the people " à la révolte, au sang, et au carnage". [80]

The Methodists responded to the threat of banishment with an appeal by the Jersey body of members to the Privy Council. The local nature of the appeal undermined somewhat the Lieutenant-Governor's theory regarding Nonconformists as outsiders. The Privy Council replied with an overruling of the States' decision, which enabled militiamen to drill on days other than Sundays on grounds of conscience. [81] Within nine years of the judgement the Methodist precedent was followed by Philip Arthur, an Anglican, who claimed the right to avail himself of the 1798 ruling. His claim was refused by the Royal Court, but succeeded on appeal when the Privy Council clarified its ruling to include all militiamen. [82] Never keen to be outdone, the Royal Court refused to extend the 1810 ruling to officers and stripped Captain Charles Bertram of his commission in the East Regiment when he refused to perform Sunday drill. [83]

Methodism in the Militia during a crisis situation had been heavily opposed by the States and the Royal Court, mainly because of its potential threat to internal discipline and civil order. It was also viewed, to a certain extent, as a threat visited upon the Island from the outside: the authorities would respond in a similar way to the attempts of English immigrants to force reform in Jersey institutions in the mid-nineteenth century. However, opposition to a civil threat did not of necessity mean opposition to Methodism as a religion. This can be gauged in two respects: firstly by the attitude of some leading members of Jersey society to Methodism, and secondly by the contrasting attitude of the authorities to Catholicism, present in the Island amongst Royalist refugees from the French Revolution.

When the States met in 1798 to discuss banishing Militia defaulters, at least two members opposed this attack on Methodism. The most significant opposition came from the Reverend Edouard Dupré, Rector of St Helier and Dean from 1802 to 1823. Dupré took a sympathetic attitude towards Methodism, even inviting Coke, a close aide to Wesley, to preach in the Town Church during his visit to Jersey in December 1785. [84] Why he should have been sympathetic to the Methodist religion, it is difficult to say. Unlike the similarly sympathetic Reverend François Jeune, Dean from 1838 to 1844, there is no obvious family connection with Nonconformism. More likely, is that from a purely theological point of view Duprè had few points of conflict with the Wesleyans, the group that was to remain dominant in Jersey Methodism. Among the New Dissent (as opposed to the more radical Old Dissent of groups such as the Quakers) Wesleyans were the closest to the Church of England in theology, the major difference being the stress they placed on preaching. [85] The non-radical dissent of the Wesleyans made it easier for the Established Church to accept their presence in the Island.

As regards the exiled French priests the Dean represented the official line, toleration of them as refugees but containment of them as Roman Catholics. The refusal of many French Catholic priests to take the oath of allegiance to the Civil Constitution of Clergy of 1791 resulted in 2,200 of them, including three bishops, being exiled in Jersey; the number was reduced to 1,800 after 1795. [86] The Royal Court stipulated that the conditions of exile were that the Catholic faith be practised privately, with no attempt to proselytise the native population. [87] The order was abused, ironically, by a Jerseyman, Matthieu de Gruchy, who had converted to Catholicism and been ordained as a priest in France. Several rural families in St Martin complained about de Gruchy's activities and the authorities responded by arresting the Bishop of Tréguier in 1795. The situation was calmed by the expulsion of de Gruchy. [88] As regards Methodism, there was never any comparable move to oppose religious practice or attempts to convert.

As one further example of a leading member of Jersey society sympathetic to the dilemma Methodists faced as regards Militia drill, we must note the actions of Jurat Nicholas Messervy. In the States debate of 1798 Messervy showed himself opposed to the whole idea of banishing local people. [89] As a Colonel in the East Militia Regiment he took this a stage further and attempted to help Pierre Le Sueur Jnr, son of the Methodist preacher, who had been actioned by the St Helier Regiment for three drill defaults. Messervy's compromise was to allow Le Sueur to drill on a day other than Sunday for the East Regiment. The Royal Court overruled this, stating that it contravened the regulation governing place of domicile. [90] Nonetheless, Messervy's example showed that people in positions of power were willing to come forward and respect the views of local Methodists.

As a body, the clergy did not react uniformly to Methodism. Only the Rector of St Mary, the Reverend Francois Valpy, showed any obvious sign of opposition, when he interrupted a meeting in his parish and engaged the preacher in a theological dispute. [91] It is possible that the early opposition in the parishes of St Peter, St Clement and Grouville, was the result of clerical influence. Throughout the nineteenth century hostility or opposition to Methodism from the clergy came only from individual rectors. The Ecclesiastical Court never attempted to censure any individual over his or her desire to choose their religion. As the Reverend Durell noted in his notes to the 1837 edition of Falle's *History of Jersey*, "It cannot be expected that with an increased population, and in the present state of society, a perfect conformity should have continued. Dissenters are now numerous... The 22nd Canon against Nonconformists", giving the Church power of censure and discipline, "remains unrepealed, but it has virtually ceased to exist". [92]

The Organisation of Nonconformism

Notwithstanding the problems regarding Sunday Militia drill, Methodism and the other Nonconformist denominations continued to gain in popularity. In the Town there were some initial problems over a place to worship. These derived from the refusal of the States to pass a building contract "au nom de la société', which in effect meant that any place of worship would have to be owned by an individual and subject to the various claims of inheritance and bankruptcy. [93] This was no doubt intransigence on the part of the States, although it reflected in part genuine difficulties arising from Jersey's distinctive property laws. A chapel was finally opened in Don Street in 1813. [94]

In the countryside a Wesleyan chapel had already been opened in December 1809 in the parish of St Ouen. This was followed by Six Rues Chapel in St Lawrence in 1811. [95] By 1819 six parishes had their own Methodist chapels; by 1838, with the building of a chapel at La Rocque, all twelve parishes had their own places of worship. By 1887 there were at least 36 dissenting places of worship in the Island, 23 of them Methodist, 17 of those outside St Helier.[96]

The way in which the small groups of people worshipping together became a large number of chapels scattered throughout the Island tells us much about the organisational skills and community spirit engendered by Methodism, even after only a relatively short presence in the Island. Examples in two country parishes will illustrate. Dissent was introduced to the parish of St Mary in 1784. By 1815, the newly-converted had built a small chapel (150 seats), the plot of land being provided by a principal of the parish, Jean Binet. By 1828, the demand was such that a new chapel, Bethlehem (300 seats), was built, the congregation raising the necessary £100. [97] Methodism in the parish of Trinity showed a similar rate of growth. An initial donation of land resulted in the building of Ebenezer Chapel (120 seats) in 1809. By 1826 this had been replaced by a larger building (400 seats), with one member contributing two-thirds of the building costs. [98]

In the Congregational Church, known locally as L'Eglise Indépendante, the pattern of growth parallelled that of the Methodists, although on a much smaller scale. The only Free Church place of worship in the countryside was at Sion, St John, established in 1809, following a gift of land from one Jean Le Sueur, a principal of the parish. The church itself cost £250 and consisted of granite walls, a thatched roof and earthen floor. Membership totalled 62 members. [99]

The only primary sources relating to a Methodist chapel to be found for this early period are the records of Sion Chapel, situated on the St John/Trinity boundary, from 1826 onward. Our information is further, but not as fully, supported by a pamphlet on La Rocque Methodist

Chapel, written in 1932 by one of the chapel's elders. The work is useful because it is based on the chapel account books (now missing) and on the memories of its members. [100] The study states that no minutes of the trustees could be located for the nineteenth century. This absence of primary source material is matched by all the Island's chapels. [101]

Methodism had come to the Sion area around 1800. This appears to be a late arrival since the area was located amidst other cell groups, and by 1820 three prayer groups were flourishing in the Vingtaines of Hérupe (St. John), Mont à l'Abbé (St. Helier) and Augrès (Trinity). The obvious place to build a chapel was at a point central to the three areas, but this was deferred for some time because the Independent Chapel mentioned above occupied a nearby site (built circa 1809), and it was not wished to upset the Calvinists. The chapel was finally built in 1826. [102]

To avoid the problems of inheritance and other property laws Sion chapel, like other Methodist chapels, resorted to legal devices. The chapel was built and supervised by a trust, which meant its ownership was taken out of individual hands and placed in the control of a body of trustees. These trustees were elected elders, who became the official and legal representatives of the building and its funds. The eleven Sion trustees were all male, lived in either St John or Trinity, and owned property or land. Eight of them were farmers and one a full-time, locally-born, preacher. [103] Money had been borrowed to pay for the chapel from a fund referred to as La Banque des Chapelles, a central Methodist fund, probably the precursor to the Joint Stock Bank, known locally as the Methodist Bank, which went en désastre in 1874. [104]

La Rocque, the other locality on which fuller records exist, had to wait until 1838 for its Methodist chapel, but Methodism had been present in the area since 1808. The experience of Nonconformists in this area was closely tied up with that of the English population in the village of Gorey. This population was made up of people employed in the oyster trade. Nonconformism in Gorey received a rowdy reception. Services had to be suspended between 1817 and 1822, and were only resumed under the protection of Connétable Charles Bertram. It may be that, as in the town of St Aubin, sailors were a little less inclined to be tolerant towards dissenters; certainly, their behaviour stands in marked contrast to the reaction from country folk. By 1832 the situation had calmed and Salem Chapel was built in the village. [105]

The residents of La Rocque, however, felt that their number warranted a chapel of their own. In 1837, 17 members pledged £74 towards the construction of a place of worship. In the event the building cost £300, half that sum being provided by locals, the other half by a bank loan. By 1865 the chapel was free from debt. The eight trustees were farmers to a man. [106]

One very striking aspect of the day-to-day organisation of Sion Methodist Chapel is its similarity to both the Ecclesiastical Assembly of a parish and the running of an Anglican church. The Assemblée des Séquestres de la Chapelle met several times a year, depending on requirements, and was presided over by an elder or, more generally, by the Prédicateur Ambulant; in 1835 this was Jean Du Putron. [107] Meetings were held in the chapel and their domain included all matters concerned with the building and its congregation.

The internal running of the chapel emphasised the communal aspect. Money collected at Communion went to a fund known as 'les pauvres', which was dispersed among deserving members of the chapel and the poor of the neighbourhood. The treasurer of this fund in 1844 was a woman, Madame Le Quesne, which would have been unthinkable in the parish hierarchy, but among the Methodists reflected the important rôle women played, and had played from the start in organising meetings. [108] To a certain degree their participation was limited to activities traditionally expected of women, as, for example, when they were asked to organise the major fund-raising bazaar in 1876. Similarly, at La Rocque, half the teachers at the Sunday school established there in 1840 were women. Nonetheless, some like Madame Le Quesne, albeit in the minority, achieved the position of elder. [109] There is no evidence that a woman was ever a lay preacher in the nineteenth century. [110]

Members of a chapel were individuals who, the trustees considered, had shown their commitment to the Nonconformist creed by regular attendance, devotion and, no doubt, contribution. When, in 1876, the old chapel at Sion was felt to be too small, the Séquestres were charged "de visiter les membres et les amis de la congrégation" for their opinion on a new chapel. [111] The resulting fund-raising, including the bazaar, made £333, a sum which was temporarily invested in the Channel Island Bank and the Hampshire Bank. [112]

Again, looking at the organisation of the Independent Church at Sion, within sight of the Methodist place of worship, we find a parallel organisation of trustees running the church, electing pastors, assessing the suitability of members and auditing the accounts. [113] Managing an organisation distinct from the Established Church, which in the parish utilised municipal manpower and funds, clearly required heavy lay involvement.

Who then were these Nonconformists? Inglis, writing in 1834, stated that Methodists, Independents and Baptists were present in Jersey in large number, "especially of the lower classes, and of the country people". [114] The Methodist Jersey-French circuit baptismal records for 1831 to 1852 show that 50 per cent of the children received into the Church had fathers who were artisans, 23 per cent labourers and 17 per cent farmers. Out of 562 baptisms 55 children had fathers who listed themselves as professional, many of them schoolteachers. [115] Methodists represented a fair cross-section of the population, excluding the upper sections of the social scale. In the parish of St John, for instance, the 1851 Census material shows

shows artisans as 28 per cent of the working population, in Methodist baptisms as 26.5 per cent; labourers by the Census as 24 per cent, by baptisms 38 per cent; and farmers, by Census 19 per cent, by baptisms 32 per cent . Out of the 68 families in St John with children baptised as Methodists between 1831 and 1852 only two, listed as professional, were outside these three categories. [116]

The baptismal figures also reveal that Methodism varied from parish to parish in terms of popularity. Between 1831 and 1852 65 families in the parish of Trinity had children baptised in the Methodist faith, whilst St Peter had 53. St Saviour, on the other hand, had only 14 families, St Lawrence had 16, and St Mary 17. Such figures permit a very approximate view of the strength of dissent in individual parishes. Bearing in mind that the figures include only Methodist and Independent families of child rearing age, we see that in St John there were at least 68 Nonconformist families out of a total of 413 families (1851 figure). In St Ouen there were at least 24 Nonconformist families out of a total of 436 families.

Certain difficulties are involved in assessing numbers as a guide to the influence of Methodism in the community. In Methodist chapels and other Nonconformist places of worship, including St John's Independent Church, there was a definite distinction between fully-fledged members, that is those considered worthy of the title by the elders and formally admitted as such, and attenders, sometimes known as 'listeners' or 'amis' of the church. [117] Only members were included in official totals. On the other hand, considering the process of choice involved, it would be legitimate to take as Methodists those who regularly attended Methodists chapels. It is a great disappointment to the historian that Jersey, whilst subjected to the decennial censuses carried out in England and Wales, was not included in the 1851 Census of Religious Worship. Some idea of how strong attendance was in the Established Church would have been useful in this context.

Lelièvre gives official Methodist membership totals, as recorded in the *Magasin Methodiste*, in his work in 1885. These figures state that the number of fully-fledged Methodists in Jersey society was never higher than 2,435 in the peak year of 1870, that is 4.3 per cent of the total population. The French circuit, predominantly in the countryside, dominated the English circuit on average by four to one. If we match the official figure with the existence of listeners and the known proportion of Methodist families in individual parishes, which vary from 5-15 per cent, then an estimate of Methodists as constituting 10 per cent. of the rural population seems plausible. [118] However, the size of Methodist chapels in the Island and widespread rebuilding to match popular demand suggest this to be a conservative estimate. Every country parish had a Methodist chapel by 1838, and every one of those chapels was either extended, rebuilt or joined by another in the same parish by 1881. Methodism was offering more seats in an increasing number of chapels to a country population which, as we shall see in a later chapter, was remarkably stable in size throughout the nineteenth century. The seating capacity of Bethlehem Chapel in St Mary was 400 in 1826 in a parish population of 977 (1831 figure). Ebenezer Chapel in Trinity, offered 400 places to a population of 2,098 (1831 figure). In 1911 the Wesleyan Chapel Committee for the Jersey/French circuit recorded that it offered 7,128 seats to the public in 19 chapels, and 5,533 of these were for renting. [119] These figures suggest that whilst 10 per cent as an estimate of the numerical strength of Methodism has some sound basis, it is but a conservative one. It must also be borne in mind that these figures do not include any other Nonconformist faith.

The Reasons for Nonconformism in Jersey

Why then did at least 10 per cent of the rural population, a significant interest group in itself, feel it necessary to leave the Established Church, a move which weakened, indeed in certain respects severed, their traditional links with both its secular and religious manifestations, and turn to another denomination? This question is best answered by setting what we know of Methodism in the Island against the backdrop of conditions in the Established Church in the period it came under challenge.

The main sources on Methodism in nineteenth century Jersey, Lelièvre and Guiton, are vague as to what caused people to move away from the Established Church. Both are at pains to point out that the eighteenth century was a period of religious mediocrity, but fail to substantiate the claim, preferring instead general statements like "le triomphe de l'anglicanisme fut aussi celui de l'indifférence et du formalisme". [120] Nonetheless, if we combine what we have already mentioned regarding the condition of the Established Church and its clergy at the end of the eighteenth century with similar studies in England and Wales, we may have a clearer picture.

The exodus from the Established faith in Jersey was the result of a dissatisfaction with the Church, as regards both its public image and its dealings with members of its flock. We have noted the high political profile of certain clergymen, the poor condition of parish churches and the faithful reflection of society's hierarchical divisions within the church, much to the detriment of the poor. These factors were common to the origins of Nonconformism in England. Obviously, we must distinguish between the Jersey brand of Methodism and some of the fiercer struggles experienced in England, particularly in cities like Manchester and Liverpool. Nonetheless, there is a similarity in that many historians have suggested that Methodism was not a truly revolutionary religious challenge, that is, it was never as far away from the Established Church as contemporary polemics and tracts might suggest. [121] In Jersey we have a similar situation. The condition of the Established Church clearly upset the sensibilities of a section of Jersey society. These people chose to reconstruct a faith more akin to their spiritual and social desires; an all-embracing religion that they believed was once present in the Jersey of 'temps passé'.

One point that should be made is that Methodism in Jersey was successful because it was allowed to be. As J. Obelkevich shows in his study of South Lindsey in the nineteenth century, the success of Nonconformism depended very much on how strictly controlled a parish was, by either parson or squire, or both. In closed parishes, where such power was strong, it was difficult for people to move away from the Church of England; in open parishes it was easier to do so. [122] In nineteenth-century Jersey, although by no means comparable in geographical extent or dispersed settlement to South Lindsey, the parishes appear to fall into the category of 'open'.

Methodism could grow strong, it seemed, where the Established Church was weak. [123] There is no evidence in any parish to suggest that any rector showed any overwhelming inclination to oppose the spread of Nonconformism in any major way. Local seigneurs, as we noted in the introductory section, did not possess the requisite power to interfere in their tenants' religious preferences, even if they were so disposed. Both the Church on an Island level and the States had such a power of censorship. As we have seen, however, the States showed themselves concerned with Nonconformists only when they seemed to threaten their own authority. The Ecclesiastical Court possessed the power and the prerogative, both through Canon 22 and the Code of 1771, to censure and punish those going against the rules or wishes of the Church; it showed no desire to do so.

But clearly, whilst a helpful environment aided the growth of Nonconformism, it does not explain it. [124] To a certain extent, a Church dominated, as Jersey Methodism was, by artisans, labourers and farmers was a Church of the dispossessed, or at least the disadvantaged. The essential difference between the communal identification offered by the parish church and the Methodist chapel was that in the latter spiritual commitment entitled one to become an active member of that community, regardless of status.

However, the argument that Nonconformism represented a Church of the dispossessed goes only so far. Becoming a Methodist was not a total rejection of social hierarchy; after all, chapels had their own power structures and not everyone could become an elder. In Sion and La Rocque the trustees were farmers or property owners to a man; there is no mention of artisans or labourers. [125] Similarly, as we have seen, the internal church hierarchy reflected in pew ownership in the Established Church was paralleled in Methodist chapels, albeit not to the same extreme. [126]

Spiritually too, as we have noted, the move to Methodism from Anglicanism was not a radical departure. The emphasis on preaching, and, more importantly, lay preaching, meant that country congregations received their dose of spiritual refreshment from their own peers and domesticity was emphasised from the very outset. An 1858 list of preachers for the Jersey/French circuit shows that 21 chapels had 30 Jerseymen at their disposal, individuals who moved on a regular weekly basis from chapel to chapel. [127] In the parish of St John for 1851, Peter Lesbirel, a 58 year-old proprietor (of 2 acres) living near Sion, stated his occupation as lay preacher. A few hundred yards away at the Calvinist Independent chapel lived Clement de Faye, minister, with his wife. Three miles to the north-west lived the parish rector, Samuel Wright M.A., Jersey-born of English parents, with his coachman, house servant and 2 acres of glebe land. The difference was finite, but it did exist. [128]

In attempting to understand the appeal of Methodism in Jersey, we must pay heed to the fact that it was never far away from the Established Church, either spiritually or socially. Methodism was not so much a rejection of the religious community as defined within the Established Church, as a reaffirmation of an essence that it was believed to have lost.

The recreation of some form of alternative religious community was facilitated by the unique identity of the Jersey Methodist movement. This identity derived from the relative isolation of the Channel Islands and the French language. The need or desire to create a rural Church is reflected in the early decision to keep the Jersey-French circuit and the English circuit more or less distinct. De Quetteville appreciated this and as early as 1795 replaced the only existing Nonconformist hymns, those of the Huguenots, with a collection of 467 hymns, either translated or written by the author. [129] By 1818 he had published an extended version, as well as starting the *Magasin Methodiste*, an evangelical monthly, which contained biographies of local ministers and members, bible interpretations and news from home and abroad. [130]

Lay-preachers from the country, chapels built by united effort and a collection of hymns and periodicals unique to the congregation created an alternative framework for a community. In the popular mentality of the rural folk, the Methodists became recognised as an entity in themselves, in no way apart from the parish community, but to some degree distinct. As Galichet suggested in 1912, much of this derived from an obvious morality. [131] This was expressed in staunch temperance, strict observance of the Sabbath and conservative dress. Galichet's case study of P.J. Brée of La Sente, Grouville, showed a typical Jersey Methodist, but also a typical member of the rural bourgeoisie. His house was a major point of pride and included a library, with maps and ancient charts on the wall. He was wealthy and staunchly independent, heavily involved in church and local politics. Yet his staunch Methodism could distinguish him from his peers as an anecdote suggested: following success at an agricultural show several fellow farmers had suggested that the only way for him to regain his hat, taken in jest, was to join them in a celebratory drink; the hat was never retrieved. [132]

Caesariensis, writing anonymously in 1917 of his experiences in the Church in Jersey in the latter half of the nineteenth century, was to suggest that "religious differences, in and out the pulpit, between Anglican and Nonconformist were limited to religious matters", and did not interfere with personal friendships. [133] Generally speaking, this appears to have been the case, and could apply equally well to the first half of the nineteenth century. It was a situation of general understanding that becomes all the more obvious when contrasted with attitudes towards Catholicism. Not only was Catholicism alien as a religion to Jersey, but it arrived with Irish and French immigrants and stayed with them. Unions of protestants such as the Jersey Protestant Alliance, united against Popish Nonconformists. [134] Methodism was neither particularly alien nor was it restricted to non-locals. The appeal of Methodism to everyday rural folk and its success in all corners of the Island made it difficult to single out and attack.

Whoever Caesariensis was, he gave more of a clue to the understanding of Methodism, and the sort of challenge it presented to the Established Church, than he may have realised. The non-contentiousness of rural Nonconformism in nineteenth century Jersey must be stressed. The challenge it presented to the Established Church was not an active or conscious one. Methodists did not spend time writing anti-Anglican polemics in the *Magasin Methodiste*, let alone in the local press, or actively lobbying in the States and parishes for the reform of Church and society. The Methodists' statement was made with their feet.

Nonetheless, the fact that at least 10 per cent of the rural population chose to reject the existing religious community was significant enough to constitute a challenge to the Established Church and society as a whole. It could not be otherwise. Dissenters were making a conscious move away from the traditional communal unit. The parish in its every facet was closely bound up with the Established Church. Nonconformism was in effect challenging the very basis of the rural community.

Chapter 5

Language and Anglicisation

The most obvious vestige of Jersey's Norman past to the visitor or immigrant in early nineteenth-century Jersey was its language, Norman French or as it was known locally Jèrriais or Jersey French. In structure and particularly vocabulary Jèrriais was significantly different from French, the official language of the law. Within the Island itself Jèrriais varied considerably, six distinct areas being recognised. [1] Despite six centuries of effective rule under the English Crown, geographical isolation from the English mainland and regular contact with France meant that the English language remained a rarely used medium until the beginning of the French Wars.

Jersey's linguistic isolation was ended by the Napoleonic Wars. The introduction of a large garrison force and a significant English-speaking wartime population between 1793 and 1815, followed by the arrival of a large body of British immigrants into the Island, particularly in the period up to 1860, introduced the English language to Jersey society en masse. The language was not wholly foreign to the population. Past centuries had seen local contact with a range of English speakers - garrison troops, merchants, religious officials and Crown representatives - while certain members of the gentry had received their education in England, notably clergymen and military officers. Such contact, however, in no way prepared Islanders for the arrival of a substantial body of English speakers. The majority of the Jersey population remained unfamiliar with the English language.

Jèrriais, essentially a spoken tongue in the local context and without any firm dictionary basis, found itself challenged by a standardised language with a large body of speakers. English immigrants to the Island were convinced of the superiority of their language and showed no inclination to learn the local vernacular. This linguistic self-righteousness was shared by a section of the Jersey middle class, notably those educated or trained in England. English was identified as the language of commercial success and moral and intellectual advancement. [2] These tendencies were enhanced by the attitude of the British authorities who began to see the advantages of an anglicised Jersey.

The fortunes of Jèrriais and French in the nineteenth century provide both an index and a mirror to the challenge faced by the Jersey identity from what we might call the anglicisation process. As we shall see, it was a challenge which showed Jersey society at its most vulnerable, that is where institutional defences - in this case the educational structure - were weak and Islanders were forced to resort to a cultural defence.

Jèrriais: the State of the Local Language

Jersey-Norman French reflected the long past Norman link. It was an association severed incompletely in 1204 and regularly renewed by an interchange of trade and, up to 1620, by religious organisation. Nonetheless, Jersey was to all intents and purposes an enemy of France for much of the six centuries after its separation from Normandy and the once shared language was disjoined from its roots. The linguistic result, as the Guernsey resident William Berry noted in 1815, was a Norman-French "corrupted rather than improved". [3] The Reverend Edouard Durell, a local rector, agreed: "The language is bad provincial French, with some local peculiarities, and a few English words. It does not seem to have been altered for some centuries, and indeed it is more likely to become extinct than be improved". [4] With no effective academic or literary basis Jèrriais had developed into "a heterogeneous compound of antiquated French, intermixed with modern expressions and gallicised English words, so that it might be termed a kind of 'lingua franca'; and it is pronounced, especially in the country districts, with a most abominable 'patois'. The different parishes even vary in these respects, so that there are more dialects in the language of Jersey than in the ancient Greek". [5]

Apart from the statements of a few observers like Berry and Durell, there is little known about Jèrriais before the nineteenth century. There appears to have been no lexicographical work undertaken before this period and modern dictionaries have shed no light on the early structural condition of the language nor on its grammatical differences from French. [6] Nineteenth-century visitors stand alone as the providers of detailed analyses of Jèrriais.

To these outsiders, indeed, to some local commentators too, Jèrriais appeared ill-organised and corrupted. The Reverend Skinner noted the local tongue in his diary in 1827: "among the peasants it is become so much a dialect,..., that the French themselves cannot hold conversation with a native". [7] Quayle detailed the basic differences between Jèrriais and French pronunciation, most evident in "the 'ch', which is often sounded 'k', as in 'kemise' and 'cat', for 'chemise' and 'chat': in the 'ç', which is sounded 'sh': as in 'plache' and 'faction', for 'place' and 'façon'. The 'oi', already noticed, pronounced as 'ai'; and in a singular corruption of 'r', between two vowels, which becomes a sound, in some degree, resembling that of the English 'th', in thus; as in 'pethe', 'methe', for 'père' and 'mère'; but partaking also of the sound of 'z'. Inter parish dialect differs in the sound of vowels and in the use of a few words". [8]

It was Thomas Quayle alone, however, who made a different, indeed a potentially positive point about Jèrriais. "In many instances," he claimed, "it is evident, that the words in use in these islands are less dissimilar from the parent Latin, and from the least corrupted of the jargons derived from it, the Italian, than is the modern French. 'Vaque, querbon, quemin, pêsson, bêre', for instance, bear a stronger resemblance to the same terms in Latin and in Italian, than the French 'vache, charbon, chemin, poisson, boire". [9] It would not be until the later nineteenth century, when Jèrriais came to be regarded as an important aspect of the Island's identity, that such positive thoughts as regards the local tongue would emanate from Jersey sources.

Alongside the predominant "barbarous dialect of French", as Inglis called Jèrriais, which was spoken by all, was a familiarity with English among the gentry and sections of the commercial classes which well preceded the French Wars. [10] The three major sources on local enclosure, Poingdestre, Dumaresq and Falle, all published their late seventeenth century volumes on Jersey in the English language. [11] Indeed, Philippe Falle noted a local familiarity with English: "Albeit French be our ordinary language, there are few gentlemen, merchants or considerable inhabitants, but speak English tolerably. The better to attain it, they are sent young to England. And among the inferior sort who have not the like means of going abroad, many make a shift to get a good smattering of it in the Island itself. More especially in the town of St Helier, what with this, what with the confluence of the officers and soldiers of the garrison, one hears well-nigh as much English spoken as French". [12]

That English was not a language foreign to Jersey ears is further evidenced by the comments of authors visiting the Island during and immediately after the French Wars. "The English idiom", remarked Quayle, "appears frequently in their own dialect". [13] William Plees pointed out that English was "becoming daily more and more prevalent; the necessity of comprehending the soldiery has made it understood, even by the market women". [14]

Most familiar with the English language was the native gentry. Quayle spoke highly of their pronunciation and fluency, despite some "Gallicisms". [15] Berry, however, suggested that only a select few had attained a thorough mastery. [16] By 1834 H.D. Inglis, who had spent several years in Jersey, maintained that "Although the English language be sufficiently comprehended for the purpose of intercourse, it is certainly not understood by many in its purity". [17] All were agreed, however, that the majority of the rural community remained essentially ignorant of English. One writer went further and said that those countrymen who spoke it were considered to exhibit an "affected superiority". [18] Thus, for the majority of natives in the early nineteenth century, Jèrriais remained the dominant language.

The Challenge to the Local Language

In linguistic terms a large number of English speakers was bound to present a challenge to the local language. In the Jersey context the immigrant challenge to the language was accentuated by several factors. Perhaps most important among these was that Jersey constituted a lone preserve of Norman French within a kingdom where English held sway. Before the nineteenth century the use of French in many contexts - unlike the use of Celtic languages - had gone virtually unquestioned, as an aspect of Jersey's quasi-independence. It reflected both Jersey's insular location and the feeling of the Crown that this was the most likely way to retain the loyalty of these important outposts.

After 1815, however, the sheer expense of the Napoleonic Wars and a gradual but sure shift in maritime strategy during the course of the nineteenth century changed the way many of those in positions of power viewed the Island. J.R. MacCulloch's review of the British empire in 1837 included a stinging attack on the Channel Islands. His complaints centred on the heavy cost of defending the area. This view was representative of the more widely held belief, and one that gained ground during the course of the century, that the Channel Islands gained much more than did England out of their rather peculiar relationship. [19] Whilst Wellington's *Memorandum* (see above, Chapter 1) had re-emphasised the strategic significance of the Islands, the application of steam to warfare suggested that the natural defences of winds, rocks and tides were no longer reliable. [20] This point was stressed by the Lieutenant-Governor of Guernsey to Sir George Grey at the Home Office in 1843 when he pointed out that such defences would "disappear as obstacles before steam". An alternative approach was required and he was not the first to suggest that "Every measure therefore, which, without shocking the prejudices of the population at large, tends to render the Islands thoroughly English, should be adopted, the encouragement of the use of English is obviously one of them". [21]

These views had found an earlier expression. In 1817 the visiting writer William Plees had argued along very similar lines, stressing the centripetal forces of national uniformity as "the natural strength of every country", rooted in "that intellectual band by which the inhabitants are united in sentiment; and in cordial and personal loyalty; the results of animated affection. Loyal indeed, and in eminent degree, the islanders have always been: but from their former comparatively trifling intercourse with Great Britain, and from the dissimilitude of language, their attachment to the mother country, and to the sovereign, seems in those days to have sprung chiefly from hereditary impression; scarcely from any genuine sympathy of heart towards the English themselves, in preference to the natives of other countries, or from congeniality, or approximation of character". [22] Inglis, writing in 1834, took the argument a step further, and linked future economic prosperity and the continuance of "general happiness" to the need for a thorough anglicisation of the Island.[23]

The extent to which these ideas, which gave defence and security requirements as necessitating anglicisation, permeated the corridors of power in England is difficult to assess. At the very least, much of the relationship between the Island and the Privy Council might be viewed in the context of the desirability of anglicisation from the latter's standpoint. The dispatch of the investigative Commissions of 1847 and 1861 are, as we shall see in the following chapter, examples of an attempt to reform what was alien to the British system.[24] It ran counter to the habit of leniency which had marked the relationship between the Crown, anxious to retain the loyalty of a useful outpost, and the Channel Islands since 1204. This suggests that there was more to the new attitude than merely the advent of steam and its application to war. That officials like the Lieutenant-Governor of Guernsey could claim in 1846 that "it cannot be wise that the young advocats should go to French law colleges for their education, making there French friendships, adopting French principles, and bringing back French views of policy and government to British Islands within two hours steaming of France", when this was a centuries old practice, reflected a concern not so much for military objectives, but that these British Islands had developed along different lines from the Mother Country.[25] It is apparent that English was now being seen as an increasingly essential part of loyalty to the English Crown. This reflected the growing nationalism of the nineteenth century: the year of the quote (1846) saw the setting up of a Commission to enquire into the knowledge of English among Welsh school-children.

The renewed interest in the development and present state of affairs in Jersey derived from the fact that the Island was by the 1830s home to a significant English population. As we have observed in Chapter 3, the reasons for the immigration of such a broad-based group were social and economic, but aided by a feeling common to newcomers and natives that the Island was an extension of Britain. Quayle, writing of Jerseymen, stressed this idea of the extension: "England, and everything English, is dear to them: thence are derived their habits of life; thither the majority of their youth resort for education, and for preferment: our books are their study: our notions they have thoroughly imbibed; and English hearts beat in their bosoms".[26]

Yet, such a picture was misleading. There were surface similarities between England and Jersey, but the basic structures of government, law and municipal organisation were different. And, perhaps more importantly, the language of the Island was different.

Military arguments and the presence of a large body of English immigrants in the Island were supported in the anglicisation process by a section of the Jersey gentry and middle-class. The support of these local anglophiles was instrumental in ensuring the success of the English language. It was against these people that the Jersey press levelled charges of pretension and materialism, accusing them of undermining linguistic identity.[27] The prime movers were generally men who had received an education in England and often followed a successful military career, represented in official life by those such as Colonel Sir John Le Couteur, Viscount and Aide-de-Camp to the Queen, and Lieutenant-General Touzel, the Crown Receiver. Ecclesiastically, it was represented by anglophiles such as the Reverend Thomas Le Neveu of the predominantly rural St Martin, whose parish magazine established in 1890 was printed in English, and the Reverend Abraham Le Sueur, of Grouville, a leading advocate of the English language and the first to suggest its use in the legislature in the 1880s.[28]

The motives behind certain members of the gentry's desire to anglicise were both social and economic. Instilled with the political and social ideals of a country which was seen as very much in the ascendancy, individuals like John Le Couteur strove to introduce England to Jersey. This was not surprising, Le Couteur had made his life, wealth and success in an English mould. A Captain in the British Army he returned to Jersey in 1816 where he was appointed Aide-de-Camp to Sir Colin Halkett (1821), and then to King William IV, a close friend from his schooldays, and Queen Victoria. As a leading agriculturist, his main work *On the Varieties, Properties and Classification of Wheat* (London 1836) resulted in his election as a Fellow of the Royal Society in 1845. He was also a leading politician, serving as a Connétable and a Jurat, and receiving a knighthood for lifelong services to Crown and country in 1872.[29]

The English language was an introduction to this world of commercial success and moral advancement. It was with some pride that Le Couteur noted in 1847 that the ability of many of the children of "St. Aubin [in St Brelade] to speak English was the responsibility of his family, who had established a Sunday School there in 1814, and of the local gentry, who had promoted the study by offering prizes as inducements.[30] Similarly, when Queen Victoria, during her visit to the Island in 1846, noted her approval of the local language, which she felt sounded like Welsh, Le Couteur was quick to point out that whilst the language of conversation in the country was the vernacular, there were English schools in every parish.[31] Even earlier than this, in the 1830s, H.D. Inglis had noted that it was already difficult to separate the local and English upper-classes, be it by dress, manner or appearance. The local lower order, by contrast, were distinguished by their pronounced "French air".[32]

Anglophile pretensions could be observed even in some local institutions. Nowhere was this more so than in the Royal Jersey Agricultural and Horticultural Society. Established in 1833, the Society reflected the Jersey gentry's striving to emulate a gentlemanly association of the English Victorian mould. The founding members were Jerseymen of long established families, yet keen to follow the path to English gentleman status. The proceedings of the Society, in stark contrast to every other rural institution, were in English and at the first showing of livestock in 1834 those wishing to exhibit animals were required to forward a letter of entry in English.[33] It was as if with so many rôle models around in the form of resident English gentry, it was necessary to make every effort at emulation. By 1856 the *Jersey Times*, an English language paper, reported with some glee that all the important associations and societies of the Island had English names and used that language in which to converse.[34]

The Carus Wilson Case: the mid-Century State of the Language.

The first significant clash between the English and Jersey communities was not long in coming. In 1844 the Carus Wilson case openly revealed a situation that had been building up since the early 1830s. Wilson, a pamphleteer and political activist, was charged with and subsequently found guilty by the Royal Court of having written a libellous letter in the *Jersey Gazette.* [35] The incident in itself was minor, but it sparked off a major debate on the English presence in the Island. Wilson, like his associate A.J. Le Cras, was a political agitator, belonging to a body of immigrants derided by the *Chronique* as unrepresentative of Englishmen in the Island. [36] In Court, Wilson showed himself scornful of the Jersey legal system, which he considered antiquated, and the refusal to allow the court hearing to be conducted in English resulted in a further outburst directed at the simplistic and uncultured nature of the local language.

The case provided ideal ammunition for all sections of the press. English newspapers, established as early as 1822 with the *British Press,* took up the defence of Wilson on the grounds that his treatment at the hands of the prison authorities was representative of the way the political system worked against English residents. [37] The Jersey papers too saw it as an opportune time to assess the influence of the immigrant population.

The parish of St Helier, whose urban nature made it in many ways representative of both camps, found itself in the rôle of conciliator. In a parish meeting of "constituans et de résidans anglais" it resolved to try to restore the peace. The Assembly concluded in English: "this meeting highly appreciates the social and general advantages accruing from the residence of large numbers of our British fellow subjects in this Island....and feels most anxious that the greatest cordiality and good feeling should continually exist between the Residents and the Native Inhabitants". [38]

The *Chronique* was less concerned with conciliation and directed an attack on the attempts by the immigrant population to anglicise Jersey institutions and traditions. [39] The Jersey language was, claimed the paper, the bastion of its nationality. It was appreciated that "le contact journalier des habitans avec les Anglais et les Français, et plus encore depuis la navigation à la vapeur, a un peu modifié l'habitude de cette langue: mais dans le fond le jersiais est toujours la langue dans laquelle l'on aime à s'exprimer". [40]

In the columns of the newspapers the state of the French language, both the official French and Jersiais, now became the touchstone of the Island's identity. In 1856, following a Privy Council demand that proposed legislation, which was sent for official ratification, be forwarded in English, the *Jersey Times* reflected on the laments of the Jersey French language press: "In all the higher class and in very many of the middle-class native families of the Island, what is the language of society and the hearth? Really, if as our contemporary [*Le*

Chronique] would seem to assert, Jersey 'nationality' depends on the maintenance of French as the language of the country, that nationality is already half relegated to the 'olden time'".[41] By 1868 the now amalgamated *British Press and Jersey Times,* the major English readers' newspaper in the Island, could gloat: "Judged by encroachments on its language, Jersey is in a bad way....French holds its ground in the States, in the law courts, in the parochial assemblies, and generally in the country parts. But the capital is the seat of the national life, the organ of the national thought, and the indicator of the national career. Where shall we look for the French language there?".[42]

Newspapers aside, the language of the Town area, mainly St Helier, but including a part of St Saviour, St Clement and St Lawrence, was predominantly English by 1868, if not by 1856. As Likeman has shown from her study of school log books the language of instruction was determined by the language of the neighbourhood and in St Helier this was predominantly English.[43] St Mark's school, in the north of St Helier, was opened in 1846, but French was not introduced there until States legislation made it financially difficult not to do so in 1867; even then, the Headmaster thought it necessary to obtain parental permission first.[44]

The advance of English was observed by the Royal Commission of 1861. Of the 70 or more witnesses examined by the Commission, only four (including one Jurat) demanded that they be allowed to give evidence in French. The witnesses were primarily middle-class, although many, including the Connétables, were from the country. The Commissioners observed that it was "admitted on all levels that of late the English language has been gaining ground on French; so much so, that in St Helier, particularly among the rising generation, it predominates".[45]

It is likely that, in some spheres at least, English was becoming the language of commerce. In a town with a large immigrant population it was necessary for rural visitors to be at least familiar with English usage. English potato merchants advertised in English.[46] The Commissioners of 1861 noted that "in St Helier, merchant books are kept and banking business transacted in English".[47]

Yet interchange between town and country was essentially a one-sided affair and predominantly for commercial reasons only. Few country folk went to Town for social reasons. Local farmers showed their displeasure at the English pretensions of the Royal Jersey Agricultural and Horticultural Society in the 1840s with the creation of competing parish societies.[48] The *Chronique* gave its impression of country feeling in 1857, stating "les habitants de nos campagnes ne peuvent voir avec plaisir cet esprit d'envahissement qui se manifeste de toutes parts et qui ne tend riens moins qu' à nous ravir notre ancienne langue pour y substituer la langue anglaise".[49]

In the countryside Jèrriais dominated everyday communication and French proper remained the medium for Church services and Parish Assembly minutes. In the latter, at least, the written word was often an odd mixture of patois with occasional English words. Quayle noted anglo-gallicisms like "éducation compulsoire", used in the place of "instruction obligatoire". [50] The Report of the Commissioners in 1861 made the distinction between town and country, and suggested that "with the exception of the old inhabitants of remoter parishes, it is probably true that most Jersey born persons are competent enough in English to converse in it. Many speak both English and French indifferently, and often local dialect besides". [51] Among the poorer country folk, it was suggested, English never formed the language of conversation. [52]

The Rôle of Education

Among those aware of the challenge to Jersey's linguistic identity, the area recognised as being of key importance was education. The education of Jersey children would determine the future of Jèrriais. Yet those who wished to create some form of educational insurance for the future faced several major, and, as it turned out, insurmountable problems. The most fundamental of these was the broad chasm between the Jèrriais of the countryside and the French of the Courts. Jèrriais was a patois, not a language, and, without an academic grammatical base, a medium with so much internal variation could not immediately be taught. French proper could be taught, but the experiences of country schools show that it could prove almost as foreign as English to patois speaking children.

In the country schools both English and French proved a problem for students brought up speaking only patois. At Trinity Parish School the Inspector's Report for 1897 noted how the children could speak neither English nor French. [53] The suggestion by the 1886 Inspector that the purchase of English Bibles and Prayer Books would help the school in its endeavour to teach the English language went to the heart of the problem. At school, children faced an emphasis on the learning of the English language, at Church they were awarded French Bibles as Sunday School prizes, and at home they conversed with their family in patois. [54]

Urban children apparently faced less of a linguistic dilemma. An unofficial document, considered competent by the Commissioners of 1861, showed that in eleven voluntarily supported schools in St Helier the average daily attendance was 1,282, out of which only 175 pupils spoke French alone. [55]

The basic problem of focus faced by country schoolchildren encapsulated the Island's linguistic situation. Each of the three languages existed because it had a specific and clearly delineated reason for doing so. Of the three, Jèrriais was structurally the weakest because it did not have a readily accessible written form, although scholars would later give it one.[56] French proper had a clear institutional rôle to play in the judicial and legislative system and for that very reason was easier to retain as a part of the general institutional rebuttal of any attempts to anglicise.

A major obstacle in the way of local attempts to obtain a uniformity of language teaching was posed by the Island's education structure. It was a structure divided between numerous institutions whose strong independence thwarted all attempts at centralisation. Up to 1882 education was provided by numerous independent schools of a religious, charitable, private or parochial nature. The 1819 Select Committee Report on the Education of the Poor reported the availability of educational facilities in every parish, ranging from St Martin's Parish School, which made provision for the poor, to a Sunday School alone in St John and a "great number of schools" in St Ouen.[57] The wide diversity was a result of the challenge to the Church's monopoly over education in the late eighteenth century.

By the Ecclesiastical Canons the Church was given sole control over education. Each parish was to have one schoolmaster only, chosen by the Ecclesiastical Assembly.[58] The schoolmaster's duty was to "instruire les enfans à lire, escrire, prier Dieu, respondre au Catéchisme: les duiront aux bonnes Moeurs, les conduiront au Presche, et Priers Publiques, les y faisant comporter comme il appartient".[59] By the mid-eighteenth century this monopoly was under fire from individuals and parish rectors wishing to teach. In 1787 the Trinity schoolmaster, Charles Dorey, actioned George Ahier in the Ecclesiastical Court for opening a private school in his parish. In his judgement, the Dean ruled that Ahier was in breach of ecclesiastical law, but three of the rectors sitting as assessors protested, particularly the Rector of St John (the Reverend Thomas Sivret), on the grounds that the existing law was detrimental to the people.[60] This resulted in the breaking of the Church's monopoly.

However, freedom from Church control resulted in a proliferation of independent institutions. By 1820 the Select Committee Report counted 62 of these schools.[61] This was something which worked against a uniform education policy and proved detrimental to the French language.

The changing fortunes of the Church in education are made evident by the experiences of the two medieval religious sponsored schools, St Anastase in St Peter and St Mannelier in St Saviour. Originally funded by English benefactors in the fifteenth century to provide a free education for the less well-off, the two schools were, by the nineteenth century, ill-funded and in poor condition.[62] In an attempt to place the colleges on an "efficient and respectable footing" both had taken on fee paying scholars, an action which brought the school regents and the Church much criticism.[63] It was clear that both schools required extra financing, something the Church appeared unable to provide and something the States were reluctant to do because it was an ecclesiastical sphere of influence. The Reverend Robert Mallet, Regent of St Mannelier in 1859, claimed the problem derived from the clergy guarding their authority too jealously. [64] The Reverend George Poingdestre, Regent of St Anastase, was as bitter as Mallet, but went a step further and refused local clergy the authority to visit and examine the school. [65] In Guernsey a similar situation existed regarding Elizabeth College, but was resolved when "the old patent was given a new rôle" and the college was turned into a States public school. [66] In Jersey the Island's educational flagship became Victoria College, built in 1852 very much along the lines of an English public school and, relevantly, overlooking St Helier. For a school intake which was to be dominated, as we shall see, by the children of English immigrants, two small colleges located out in the depths of the countryside and built initially for poor students would clearly not have suited requirements.

The experiences of St Mannelier and St Anastase reflected how internal disputes between the clergy and the reluctance of the States to tread on ecclesiastical toes could result in a stalemate. It also gave one further insight, provided by the Reverend Poingdestre, as to how country folk viewed education. Country parents wished for a basic education and nothing more. Any pretensions either school may have had for public school-like standards were undermined by parental refusal to pay for grammar books and their distaste for the teaching of classics. Furthermore, the demands of the family always took priority over those of school, and in harvest time this meant an empty classroom. [67]

Some form of centralised education structure was essential if language was to be taught in a uniform way, but the closest Jersey came to this was via Privy Council financing. The Privy Council provided a limited amount of finance for primary education, particularly after 1839 through its newly established Committee of Education. [68] The States' rôle was nearly non-existent. An Education Committee had been established in 1794, but appears never to have functioned. [69] After 1836, some States money was allocated towards this sphere and limited contributions were made. [70]

Both the strong parish system and country attitudes to education worked against any form of centralised control. The Reverend Philippe Filleul, of St Helier, pointed out to the 1861 Commission that "the education of the people in the country in former times and at the present time, has been carried on chiefly by private individuals establishing schools. The children generally of the country people are sent to those private schools. Our people are a very thrifty and economical people; they value education up to a certain point; so far as they are aware of its importance, they are anxious to obtain it for their children; they have generally paid for them, and that constitutes a great difficulty in the way of establishing public schools". [71] The Reverend Poingdestre, Regent of St Anastase School at St Peter, likewise pointed out that country folk preferred to pay for their children's education. [72]

The parish in its civil capacity bore no legal responsibility to provide schools for the children of parishioners. Nonetheless, many parishes chose to do so. By 1861 only four parishes did not have central parish schools, that is, schools supported by parental payment and intermittent donations from the States or the Administrator of Impôts (an independent fund derived from excise on wines and spirits). [73] These schools were, in the words of the Commissioners, "of modern establishment". In the parish of St Mary, one of the four without such a school, there were four private schools, all operating independently. [74]

From the point of view of an overall educational strategy, parish schools proved something of a problem. In certain respects the link between parish and education worked well in the country, parishes utilising the relationship to provide for pauper children, as in St John and St Martin. [75] More often than not, however, education policy fell foul of petty parochial squabbles. This occurred at its worst in Grouville, where the Reverend Abraham Le Sueur's conflict with parents and the civil officers of the parish over who should control the parish school resulted in its closing down in 1863. [76] It is also clear that parishes disliked the centralised interference implicit in blanket legislation. The parish of St John illustrated a common parish concern when in 1893 it complained about the States' decision to make primary education compulsory. The Parish Assembly felt that such a policy could only be detrimental to parish independence and the "contrôle naturel des parents". [77]

A further decentralisation and independence in education was fostered by Nonconformist schools. As early as 1818 the Methodists, no doubt following the lead of the Established Church in this sphere, had set up a Sunday School in St Brelade and were teaching eighteen pupils.[78] In the country, schools were associated with the chapels and like the École des Bethlehem (1902), established alongside the chapel of the same name (1829). What Methodism was doing in the country, Catholicism was striving to do in the Town, albeit alongside Anglican and National Society institutions. Competition was a natural outcome, best reflected in the struggle in 1861 for a grant from the Assembly of Governor, Bailiff and Jurats between St Ouen's Wesleyan School, judging by inspection reports one of the Island's leading schools, and St Ouen's central school, a grant they both received. [79]

The dice were clearly loaded against an overall education strategy. The issue was settled by the financial problems of the States, culminating in the bank crashes of 1873 and 1886. The Island was forced to rely on outside financial aid. The problem with such a reliance was that it did not come without conditions. In 1872 the Privy Council withdrew its educational funding in an attempt to coerce the States into following Parliament's 1870 *Elementary Education Act* (the States had little option but to comply) meant regular visits from Her Majesty's Inspectors, whose purpose was to assess the schools and their pupils, in English.[80]

It was to be, however, the desires of the anglophile gentry and upper middle class which created the greatest obstacle to a comprehensive educational response to the language question. The establishment of Victoria College in 1852 as the pride of the education system and an attempt to emulate the public schools of the English mainland, represented the apex of the desire to anglicise. Its existence as the foremost college in the Island ensured that the English language remained as the principal medium of education.

The three prime movers behind the college project, which was conceived as a plan to commemorate Victoria's visit in 1846, were the Lieutenant-Governor, General James Reynett, Colonel John Le Couteur and General Helier Touzel, the Crown Receiver. Reynett was convinced that such a college would strengthen "the attachment of the inhabitants to the British connection and authority". [81] The intention was made clear in a letter from Dean Jeune, Master of Pembroke College, Oxford, approached for his opinion on the matter: "The youths of the upper and middle classes are, generally speaking, sent to French Colleges, or to English schools. Of the former....what all among ourselves admit, that they do not afford the moral or religious or intellectual training which English parents (and English in heart are the inhabitants of Jersey) deem suitable for their children". Furthermore, he added that whilst a low standard of educational facilities was suffered by all, it affected far more "those which, for the sake of all, ought to be pre-eminent in knowledge and virtue". [82]

Victoria College became a focus for the struggle between those determined to anglicise and those opposed to it, the outcome of which reflected the power and influence of the former. Prominent critics of anglicisation, like Francois Godfray and the Bailiff, John de Veulle, fought fiercely to have French taught on an equal basis with English and for the States to have an equal say in the running of the College with the Assembly of Governor, Jurats and Bailiff. They failed. Victoria College opened in 1852 as the institution envisaged by those desiring a public school of the English mould. [83] In 1860 the *Chronique* reported that the gentry had their way, only 60 of the 200 students being Jersey boys. [84]

Appraisal of the Challenge

The English language came to nineteenth-century Jersey in force. It was backed by a substantial body of immigrant speakers. As the experiences of Wales and Ireland showed, it was in the nature of English settlement to assume the primacy of its own tongue. [85] There is little evidence to suggest that English residents in Jersey attempted to learn French, let alone Jèrriais. For example, Englishmen never wrote letters in the French language press. Yet to be fair, it was not difficult to live in the Island speaking only English and this situation was further facilitated by a willingness on the part of the local population to converse in that tongue.

The rôle of the local gentry and middle class in undermining Jèrriais was crucial. Whilst, to an extent, the effectiveness of this challenge to Jèrriais was the result of certain weaknesses inherent in the language, particularly its lack of a written form, and certain institutional difficulties, such as British Government pressure, much of it must be attributed to the pretensions of local anglophiles. The establishment of Victoria College in 1852 fully reflected these desires. François-Victor Hugo, an astute observer of Jersey society, realised that much of the desire to relegate the language was based on shame: "Brave Normans of the Channel Islands, who blush to speak as your forefathers did and who teach your children English, who replace old French road names by English ones, who zealously turn the thatched house of your ancestors into a Saxon cottage, know that your patois is venerable and sacred". [86]

It was an embarrassment based on the rustic associations of Jèrriais, the language of the soil, insufficient in vocabulary for higher conversation. This was most evident in Guernsey in the late 1840s, when prominent ex-military members of society found themselves and the local language incompatible they claimed that their degree of expression was hindered by the limitation of the language and resorted to the language of their education and career. [87] English came to Jersey as a godsend to the middle-class. It arrived as both the language of the immigrant and the language of Victorian England and the British empire. For these sections of Jersey society, particularly those educated in England, the English language held fortunes told and untold, and their vision of it as the language of the educated and the wealthy was ably supported by those English residents of independent means and gentlemanly values.

English, then, was regarded as the language of progress on every level. The *Chronique* went further than this, suggesting local anglophiles believed that success and anglicisation were one and the same. [88] Material and spiritual gain lay with the ability of Islanders to master the English language. It was a connection implicit in Le Couteur's conversation with the Queen: that the patois was the language of the bucolic, but that help was on the way. [89]

The future determinant of the destiny of Jèrriais, despite its continued existence in the countryside, was education. That had been decided by both conscious effort, the rôle of the Privy Council and the desires of the anglophiles, and local factors, namely the non-academic basis of the local tongue and the facility with which elements of the English education system could be grafted onto a local infrastructure.

Nonetheless, a change of language would come only by popular acceptance. Jèrriais survived as long as it served a communicative need for the rural community. This much was noted by the *Chronique* in 1855: the challenge was there and it was the responsibility of the local intelligentsia to defend the Jersey tongue, particularly via education. [90] In the third section we will examine in more detail the implications of the success of the English language in the Island and the efforts made by sections of Jersey society to preserve their linguistic identity.

Chapter 6

The Political Challenge

Jersey's political and legal structure had developed to meet the needs of the Island's landed interest. It was a structure which originated in the Island's position as a half-way house between Normandy and England, a position reflected in Jersey's mix of dependency and self-government. By the beginning of the nineteenth century, despite some late eighteenth century altercations which had resulted in the Code of 1771 (see the Introductory Section), the States and the Royal Court still resembled institutions of delegated feudal power. These institutions had experienced little of the reforming momentum experienced elsewhere in Europe and on all levels remained dominated by judicial and legislative overlap. Jersey's political structure had developed in a state of isolation and as a result was archaic and inward looking.

Economic transformation and the immigrant influx of the nineteenth century brought a variety of forces to bear upon Jersey's political structure. The growth of local merchant wealth and of a significant commercial class shifted the balance of economic power away from the country to the Town. Alongside the native urban classes was a large English immigrant population whose language, cultural presence and, to a lesser extent, economic influence was most evident by the mid-nineteenth century. These new elements in Jersey society were important both numerically and in terms of wealth but politically they were restricted by an infrastructure ill-suited to their requirements. A fast growing and dynamic commercial population found its progress barred by the powerful traditional landed interest. Some form of conflict between the old and new in Jersey society was inevitable. This conflict found its loudest expression in the reform movement of the nineteenth century.

This chapter will examine the pressures for reform which developed in Jersey in this period, and the groups behind these moves. It will look at the intervention of the British Parliament and seek to explain why this intervention had far less impact than some reformers had hoped and many Islanders had feared.

In the nineteenth century Jersey came of age politically. Its political evolution was a transition from the mere "body of petitioners" of 1771, noted by Le Herissier, to a quasi-independent state.[1] It was a process which involved a shift in power from the English Crown to the Jersey States, leaving the Crown's rôle closer to that of constitutional monarch than feudal lord. Yet autonomy was not complete. Ultimate authority over Jersey moved from the Crown to Parliament. This was not an obvious shift, however, in view of Parliament's reluctance to interfere directly in the Island's affairs.

It has been suggested that one reason for the transference of power from the Crown to the States, apart from the more general decline in power of the monarchy vis-à-vis the popularly elected legislature in England, was that the Crown was impressed by Jersey's ability to govern itself. [2] Nonetheless, whilst such developments were taking place in the nineteenth century, the Crown via the Privy Council still maintained its rôle as ratifier of local legislation and watchdog of internal developments. It was in this capacity that the Privy Council, responding to perceived popular dissatisfaction in Jersey and Parliamentary demands, put considerable pressure on the Island to reform and clarify its judicial and legislative institutions. Implicit in this pressure was a belief that reform should be along the lines of the English model. Nineteenth century Jersey thus won greater control over its own affairs despite more overt interventions from the English mainland than ever before.

From a local point of view, development towards near self-rule was less apparent than the growing interference in the Island's internal affairs. The areas affected were the judiciary, particularly the rôle of the Jurats, and many aspects of municipal government, including policing and political representation. These spheres of local power were precisely those which the rural community identified as the bastions of its independence. Attempted interference was viewed as a major and direct challenge, more obvious and discernible than that posed, as we have seen, by an expanding economy and population and a changing language base.

The threat of reform derived from both locals and English immigrants. Many Jerseymen preferred to view the threat as one derived from immigrants alone. Unaccustomed to the local political and legal framework and, in fairness, often victim to its arbitrary applications and abuses, these English residents appeared to some natives to exercise undue influence on the local commercial sector, which in turn agitated for reform. This reforming group was in fact dominated by locals, mainly the urban based middle-class, a factor which made it less inclined towards agitation of an anti-Jersey kind. In direct contrast to this mainstream reforming body, a group of hard-core English reformists, led by Abraham Le Cras, of Jersey parentage, but brought up in England, believed that the strength of the rural bloc in the States and the unwillingness of local reformers to go beyond the bounds of loyalty, left only one course open: direct petitioning of both the Crown in Council and the British Parliament.

As a result of pressure from both interest groups, more significantly and persistently from Le Cras's agitators, the Jersey community found itself subjected to two Royal Commissions in 1847 and 1861. And it experienced a near constitutional crisis in 1852, when the Privy Council forwarded reforming legislation to the Island, legislation which had neither been initiated in the Island nor drawn up in consultation with its government. [3] Such moves were felt to represent a strong threat to Jersey's independence precisely because they were aimed at its major institutional structures and derived from a source which might, in the final event, force the reform. By the 1860s the combination of internal agitation and external pressure raised the threat of just such an intervention when it appeared that the British Parliament itself was considering direct pressure to impose change on the Island.

The English in Jersey

In 1883 the visiting John Stuart Blackie recounted an Englishman's comments on Jersey: "Only one thing this green little gem of the sea requires to make it perfect, a full participation in the benefits of English law". To this the Governor was said to have replied, "The absence of English law, specially of the English land laws, is the very thing to which the men of Jersey with good reason attribute their notable prosperity". [4] The anecdote reveals much of the reason for conflict between the local Jersey population and the immigrant English population.

The Island that English immigrants chose to live in, often to retire to, during the course of the nineteenth century, was one of beauty, mild climate and prosperity. It was also an Island which had remained thoroughly feudalised, ruled by an ill-defined Norman legal structure, and inhabited by people well versed in defending themselves and their institutions. In many respects it was an alien environment. English residents could find themselves subjected to a host of laws, regulations and procedures which they had never heard of, could not understand because they were in a foreign language and could do little to remedy because they had no access to the local power structure. Such a state of affairs came as something of a shock to many who had chosen the Island thinking it merely an extension of the English mainland.

By 1851 these English immigrants numbered almost 12,000, in an Island of 57,000 people. The English presence was concentrated in the parish of St Helier where they constituted over 7,000 of the urban population of 30,000. Excluding family dependents in St Helier, some 3,000 in total, 41 per cent of the English residents were by occupation artisans, 38 per cent labourers, 7 per cent professional or small businessmen and 14 per cent were people of independent means. [5] It was a population significant enough to maintain two major thrice-weekly English newspapers, the *Jersey Times* and the *British Press*. As we have seen in the chapter on language, the English residents' influence could be gauged by the amount of English heard in the Town area. The wealthier members of the English community could be observed in a Georgian and Regency setting around the areas of St Mark's and St James'.

Whilst the local French newspapers were inclined to lump all the English residents together as one body, there is little to suggest that any great degree of unity or affinity existed between them. Three broad categories can be made out: the upper middle-class of independent means; the commercial middle class; and the English labourers and artisans.

At the top of this social ladder were those of independent means, many of whom chose Jersey as a place of retirement. [6] These people did not play an active part in anything local other than the social life of the upper middle-class, much of which they created themselves, along the lines of Victorian England. Balls at the Queen's Assembly Rooms, Music Halls and social calls to fellow gentry reflected a life, claimed Inglis, marked by idleness and a need "to get quit of time". [7] These people remained generally aloof and uninterested in the political sphere, content occasionally to lend a signature to a petition, but not actively involved in the demand for reform.

Of the English working class and artisans resident in the Island we know little, except that they were forced to work for a living in a variety of essentially urban-based jobs. They were without a voice in the community and, in many ways, without rights in the parish, as those seeking poor welfare discovered to their cost. [8] The English middle-class championed its own interests in protests and demands for reform, mostly to do with property and access to power, not those of its working class compatriots.

It is to the independent business section of the English middle-class that we must look to find the origins of discontent with the Island's political and legal system. By 1850, as we have seen in Chapter Three, there was a growing middle section of professionals and small businessmen in St Helier who were English. That this body formed a significant interest group can be gauged by the eagerness of the local urban bloc to placate them in times of confrontation. In the wake of the Carus Wilson case of 1844 (see the previous chapter) the Civil Assembly of St Helier showed itself keen to make peace, stressing the social and economic advantages derived from the English immigrant population. [9]

Even within this group, however, a distinction can be made between a small body around Le Cras and the larger corpus of English resident reformers. Of the latter, its presence and its pressure for change were often evident and noted, but it generally contented itself with an anonymous rôle behind the main body of native reformers. What we do know about this body derives from several celebrated legal cases, evidence to the Commissions in 1847 and 1861 and the parish records of St Helier. The Le Cras group, by contrast, remained distinct and non-local, both in membership and methods and was never representative of a significant section of the English residents.

English reformers, be they from the larger, anonymous body or Le Cras' group, became disgruntled with the Jersey system of laws and traditions, a system they came increasingly to believe was designed to work against outsiders. They were not alone in this feeling, but were distinct from local reformers in the belief that the English system of business, government and justice was superior to all other. Such an attitude was observed by Charles

Le Quesne prior to the visit of the Royal Commission in 1846, when he noted "the system pursued in the Channel Islands is very different from that practised in England, and English lawyers being naturally accustomed to view their own as approaching perfection, there would not only be a natural bias..., but also a kind of prejudice against a system which although old, was of a different character". [10] This immigrant belief in the superiority of all things English separated English reformers from the native reformist bloc and ultimately served to undermine their effectiveness.

The Objects of Complaint: States, Jurats and the Parish Police

The English middle class came to Jersey primarily to make money. In a booming economy this was quite possible and, as any glance at the advertisements of a mid-nineteenth-century newspaper will show, English capitalists carved themselves a reasonably sized niche. However, the balance of political power did not fairly reflect economic power, and English businessmen, like their Jersey counterparts, found themselves faced with an infrastructure unsuited to the demands of a modern commercial economy, and controlled by rural interests powerful enough to ward off attempts to change it. Such a situation was exacerbated for Englishmen by their belief that the Jersey system not only ignored economic realities, but actually worked against economic expansion and the accumulation of wealth. The major grievances were the composition of the States, the legal structure, the administration of justice and the arbitrary power of the parish authorities.

Historically, the States of Jersey had developed as a legislature which gave equal representation to each of the twelve parishes. Thus, the rector, Connétable and Jurat from every parish sat in the States. However, a power structure based on the equality of all parishes conceded little to the changes of the nineteenth century, and the Town's disproportionate share of the Island's population and wealth was not reflected in its representation in the States.

The composition of the States meant that a like-minded rural community could effectively outvote the Town by eleven to one. In real terms this was lessened because some parishes, notably St Brelade, which shared a merchant and urban population with St Helier, occasionally voted with the Town. Furthermore, the clergy were very much a law unto themselves and it is difficult to discern a particular line of voting amongst them. Connétables and Jurats, however, were men selected from parish cliques and could be relied upon to form a rural caucus.

The country majority in the States was remarked upon at an annual dinner of the Royal Jersey Agricultural and Horticultural Society in 1858. The Bailiff was quoted as having claimed that as nearly all the members of the legislature were landowners, and a large proportion cultivated their own land, it was unlikely that Jersey agriculture would ever suffer. "Assuredly", commented the *British Press and Jersey Times*, with some irony, "our agriculture need have no fear on that score; not until a St Ouen's farmer grows cabbages or potatoes in the Royal Square will the States, constituted on the present footing, neglect country interests". [11]

The States was a target for criticism on two counts. Firstly, its composition made any reform which was not of obvious benefit to the countryside unlikely. Anything which involved a financial contribution from the States or the parishes, or was designed to be of direct benefit to the Town, had small chance of success. Secondly, States legislation tended to reflect country concerns, often to the detriment of the commercial population. This was particularly so over economic policy and will be examined in this chapter from the point of view of tariffs.

As regards justice and the law, the grounds for complaint were an antiquated legal system and the perpetuation of judicial and legislative overlap, most evident in the office of Jurat. The basis of the law was the Coûtume de Normandie, essentially concerned with land, and some principles of Roman Law, where the Coûtume was inadequate. The situation was further complicated by the fact that the law had no formal basis other than sparse records of Court decisions, civil since 1524 and criminal from only 1797. [12] By the nineteenth century the Jersey judicial system combined Coûtume and English law according to no set pattern.

The problem with an ad hoc common law was that it resulted in inconsistency. This was further compounded by the absence of any guiding legislation. As a general reflection on the state of the legal system, Le Herissier uses the example of the development of the law on murder to illustrate how Jersey law often blurred the distinction between English and Norman law according to no set pattern. In the thirteenth century Norman customary law, on a basis of reciprocity, demanded the loss of life or limb as the only punishment for homicide. The use of local judicial discretion in the sixteenth century meant that by the seventeenth century the Court distinguished between types of homicide, only murder now carrying the death penalty. Strictly speaking, this was an unjustified deviation from the Coûtume. By the eighteenth century, Jersey had moved even closer to the English system in practice. [13]

The weakness of the States as a subordinate legislature, the confusion between judiciary and legislature up to at least 1771 and inaction on the part of the Privy Council thus resulted in a political and legal system that was outmoded and contradictory. [14]

The twelve Jurats operated within this system. They were popularly elected judges who also sat in the States, and proved the major targets for criticism in the nineteenth century. The Jurats reflected Jersey's close combination of judicial and legislative functions. The Code of

1771 had made some attempt at a separation of powers and as a result the Royal Court had lost its right to legislate. [15] But the overlap had been but partially remedied and the Jurats remained with a foot in both camps. Judicial integrity was thus undermined from the outset. It was further debased by several other factors. Firstly, a knowledge of the law was not a requirement of the office. Secondly, most Jurats were high profile politicians. Members of the office had always been enmeshed in local politics and many of them were former Connétables.

Partisanship amongst the Jurats was commonplace and a natural result of the constitution of the office. Discussing a forthcoming parish meeting in St Lawrence in 1819 to nominate candidates for Jurat, the *Chronique* stipulated that it was vital "qu'on devaity choisir une personne de la campagne". [16] Two years prior to this a parish election for Centenier had been annulled because of Jurat Philippe Marett's interference. [17] Political bias was then extended to the Royal Court where it was widely claimed that a Laurel Jurat would never convict a fellow Laurel, nor a Rose party man his own fellows. [18]

The calibre of Jurats and their adequacy for the post was not of major concern for the electorate, but nonetheless it perturbed some observers. In 1870 a correspondent to the English press told of his confusion over the election of Jurat Picot whom he had thought to be the son of a former Jurat, "a learned man", only to find it was John Picot Esq. of St John, which dismayed him. "Well surely the magistracy of the Island must be going a begging to look for a judge in a cider store...He may be a good man, but how about the law? Where has he learnt to be a B.A. or an M.A. Nowhere, except in his Uncle Tessier's cider store". [19]

It is not to be doubted that Jurats were popular among the local population. Indeed, the populist nature of the office could prove a source of concern for the established political hierarchy. The election of Thomas Anley in 1807 by the largest majority ever known resulted in the Royal Court attempting to refuse his admission to the bench, on the grounds that his past "conduct had been violent and tumultuous", and his loyalty "suspect by speeches culpable". Anley was of humble origin and earned his living as a butcher's book-keeper, suggesting an element of social snobbery in the Court decision, but it was his populist stance as the representative of the parish of St Helier and his defiance of what he saw as the oligarchic power of the Court that most troubled them. It was a popularity that gained him the support of 1,942 electors in a petition against the Court's refusal. [20]

The result of the Anley election was the appointment of the Royal Commission of 1811, called for by the Royal Court to inquire into the method of appointing Jurats. The Commission. in practice a small deputation from the Privy Council, declined the Court's request to make Jurat election the responsibility of an electoral college. It stressed instead the populist nature of the office and the common desire that it should remain so. [21]

Jurats popularly elected, politically involved and often without a legal background, found themselves deliberating on the law in the Royal Court and creating it in the States. Their potential inadequacy and partisanship made judicial decisions an automatic target for criticism and challenge. From a purely legal point of view, the 1847 Commission pointed out that in the absence of legal training Jurats used "individual notions of justice". [22] The result was, in their cited example, a murder conviction in which two of the Jurats were so against capital punishment that they proposed transportation, even though no punishment other than death or loss of limb was recognised for such a crime. [23] Whilst seemingly humane, such judgements were problematic because they were based on no fixed principles of law. It would be no exaggeration to claim that the vast majority of petitions to the Privy Council or members of Parliament demanding political change in nineteenth-century Jersey pointed to the Jurats as the major cause of dissatisfaction and the overwhelming obstacle to reform. Litigants and defendants alike could rely on no uniform and consistent justice, and honourable as Jurats may have been, their partisan election, absence of legal experience and political rôle in the States, left them open to criticism and attack from those unsuccessful in the court. Targeted as a main subject for reform, Jurats then found themselves defending their office in the legislature. As Sergeant Piggott, M.P. for Reading, claimed in 1861, "From the very nature of the case the reform could not be expected to proceed from the States, because the Jurats took the most active and influential part in the proceedings of the States". [24]

If a legally-based justice was problematic in the Court, it was potentially even more so when dispensed by the parish authorities. English residents came to an Island essentially controlled by the parishes. Through the rating system and policing function it was possible for a small clique to retain and exercise all power in the parish. Assessing the rate determined the constitution of the assembly and rating was the responsibility of the ruling assembly. Injustice in the parish affected all the inhabitants and this was reflected in complaints to the Commissions of 1847 and 1861. What most affected English residents, as with regard to the judiciary, was the arbitrary exercise of power and their inability to find access to it.

A small and powerful body of individuals could obtain control of a parish assembly. Parish police officers were in an ideal position to form such a clique. In the parish of St Helier in 1846, for example, there were 382 members of the parish assembly. Of this number 31 were police and ex-police voting ex-officio who would have been unable to vote by virtue of rate paid. Only 11 police officers could have voted by the rating system. This meant in effect that 12 per cent of the assembly were parish officers and this not counting ex-police who voted by virtue of rate. [25] As a share of the assembly's voting power 12 per cent is seemingly insignificant, but what concerned people was the potential in such a group for a hard-core oligarchy. This becomes apparent if we look at St Ouen, albeit a place where few

English residents lived, but a parish where 26 out of a Parish Assembly of 48 were police. [26]

The 1847 Commission concluded that such a coherent body in the assembly could become the nucleus of a police party, and like the Jurats, police were enmeshed in party politics. [27] This in turn led to abuses in setting the rate, enabling a ruling clique to perpetuate its control. Philip Godfray's evidence to the Commission explained the process of fixing the rate, and how manipulation of the lower ratepayers was the key to success. By altering the minimum rate required to obtain voting eligibility a ruling clique could gain supporters and exclude opponents. In Rose dominated St Helier, he claimed, the Laurel party had defeated its rivals in an election for Jurat by 97 to 85. However, it was a close thing. An analysis of those rated at the minimum requirement showed how Rose supporters had been packed in for extra support, numbering 60 to the Laurel's seven. Slightly below the rating figure set for that particular year, claimed Godfray, was a large body of Laurelites, all deliberately excluded.[28]

As to the functions of the honorary police, they must have seemed similar to English police magistrates, possessing powers of discretion which the Commissioners of 1847 suggested would in England be considered incompatible with the duties of a police officer.[29] Several witnesses, including the police officers themselves, revealed how Centeniers, the grass root enforcers, assumed quasi-magisterial powers without even a basic legal background. Centenier Duparcq of St Saviour gave evidence of how he dealt with a case of a forged bank-note, when he made the offender pay the holder and then burnt the note. The Connétable was not informed and as far as Duparcq was concerned his immediate punishment of the offender ended the matter. [30] Centenier Abraham Aubin, also from St Saviour, had searched the house of a woman and then gaoled her on no other pretext than a complaint of 'immorality' from the son of her lover, whom she intended to marry. [31]

The specific complaints to the Commissions of 1847 and 1861 appeared trivial, minor incidents of police officers overstepping the mark. But behind them lay a concern for the fact that honorary police appeared to have unlimited powers of discretion and that whilst the human touch was a heart-warming reflection of communal self-regulation, it also allowed injustice and, at worst, abuse.

The concerns outlined in this subsection were reflected in several major incidents, events which, as we shall see, strengthened the hand of those opposed on principle to the Island's institutions.

The Grounds for Complaint: Case Studies

Clearly there were grounds for complaint against all of the basic institutions of the Island. The power structure was dominated by the rural community. In the States country politicians simply reinforced the power of the judiciary and the parish, and as an obvious result failed to reform. Abuse of power, whether intentional or produced by archaic structures, affected the whole population, local and immigrant alike. We will now look at some specific incidents which illustrate the basis for the demand for Jersey reform, beginning with the power of the rural bloc, as expressed in its economic policy.

The growing differences in outlook, priorities and perceptions between the rural and urban community were most evident in the economic sphere, where conflicting attitudes to the workings of market forces were as much about power as economics. On the one side lay the traditionalist agricultural interest, on the other the urban middle class, made up of the merchant/commercial sector and the English immigrant population. As the Queen's Receiver, General Helier Touzel, explained to the 1848 Commission, the division between town and country could be observed in the prevalent opinion that "whatever sum of money is applied to the improvement of the town is so much withdrawn from the country; forgetting that every improvement to the town improves themselves. There is a degree of jealousy unaccountable between the country parishes and the town. It is very difficult to persuade the country parishes that it is to their advantage to improve the town". [32] The problem for the urban community was that the rural community dominated the organs of power.

As an illustration of Touzel's comment we might look to the parish of St Ouen and its attitude to the proposed harbour developments in St Helier in 1840. The Parish Assembly instructed the Chef de Police, acting as Connétable because of a disputed election, to vote in favour of the extensions but to oppose all moves for a general levy to pay for it. It was pointed out, by the Parish Assembly, that the parish had voted for similar modernisation in 1838 and that these extensions had resulted in substantial benefits for the commercial classes (of which the members of the Parish Assembly did not consider themselves a part), who in turn should pay for the latest improvements. [33] Five months later,when the States was searching for ways to finance the scheme, the Parish Assembly thwarted all suggestions other than an increase in the împot on imported alcohol. This particular change was beneficial to the country bloc in that it raised prices for outside competitors in the local market and left the rural population, who drank their own cider, unaffected. [34] In May 1843, the same ambivalent attitude was evident when the parish calmly demanded money from the States to finance the construction of the new Chasse du Manoir, a lengthy road which was to link up the extremes of St Ouen. [35]

In this conflict of outlook and attitudes the countryside was by far the more intransigent. It was determined to maintain high returns on agricultural produce even at the expense of the urban population and unwilling to view the opinions and reform attempts of the urban based merchant classes as anything other than a challenge to the traditional Jersey way of life. On the ending of the French Wars in 1814, for example, the country parishes demanded that the local market be protected from cheap French goods. This was greeted with dismay by the *principaux* of St Helier. They feared the impact on local consumers, "considérant que l'intérêt des cultivateurs et celui des commerçans et des habitans des Villes doivent être les mêmes, et qu'ils doivent se réunir pour le bien commun". [36] This argument totally failed to persuade the rural bloc, despite the suggestion by the Connétable of St Helier that tariff barriers might affect the carrying trade and thus have repercussions for agriculture. [37]

In 1835 the rural bloc was again calling for a tariff barrier covering agricultural produce. This time the demand formed the basis of a petition signed by 1,625 "country folk", presented to the States by François Godfray, the former Connétable of St Helier. The concern was that French goods, namely pigs, bacon, poultry, fruit and vegetables, were underpricing local produce in the market-place. [38] It was somewhat disingenuous for an industry which concentrated on the export market in England to identify competition in the local market-place as the cause of difficulties. In the parish assemblies .the reasons for the current state of affairs were stated as local high production costs, especially high labour charges, and falling potato prices on the mainland due to competition; a tariff was required to enable producers to salvage some profits in the local market. [39] The reaction of the urban population was one of incredulity at both the reasons given and the absence of gratitude for the efforts of both the parish of St Helier and the Chamber of Commerce in keeping English markets open and tariff-free to local producers, only to find their own markets facing closure to competition. [40] It was claimed in the *Jersey Times* that the English residents, who constituted two-fifths of the population (an exaggeration), were providing 300,000 livres per annum to the Island economy and deserved better treatment. [41]

For most of the time the economic policies required by the Town, that is the merchant and commercial interests, were the same as those required by the country. The ability to export to English markets free of restraint was the mainstay of the carrying trade, as it was of Jersey agriculture. To this end the Chamber of Commerce exerted its energies and considerable talents on behalf of country and town alike. The shared needs of local exporters were reflected in the joint efforts of the Chamber of Commerce, the Royal Jersey Agricultural and Horticultural Society and the States of Jersey to persuade a Parliamentary Select Committee, inquiring into the local corn trade in 1835, that the Island should be excluded from the corn laws, and that its trading privileges vis-à-vis the United Kingdom should be confirmed. [42]

Yet there was more to the merchant economy than export alone and therein lay the potential for conflict with country interests. The carrying trade depended on a constant flow of imports, most of which were brought to the Island by local ships, and, after some degree of processing, re-exported world-wide. Similarly, as Jersey agriculture became more specialised and less corn was grown, the carrying trade was required to bring in the necessary grain along with the other consumables and consumer goods. Import tariffs increased freight charges, which then increased consumer prices and, in a knock-on effect, the merchant and commercial sectors faced demands for higher wages. [43]

The problems caused by the selfishness and intransigence of the agricultural sector were evident as early as 1816. The post French Wars' depression resulted in a local food shortage but farmers were eager to export. The situation required the intervention of the Lieutenant-Governor, under his emergency powers, to ensure a sufficient quantity of potatoes and grain was retained for local consumption. [44] More serious was the grain riot of 1847, when labourers and artisans from the Town, numbering several hundred, marched to the Town Mill at Les Grands Vaux and broke open several grain wagons, necessitating garrison troops to restore order. The long term explanation for this outburst was the 1840s depression of trade but the immediate cause was the refusal of the rural-dominated States to stop grain being exported in a time of crisis. [45]

Import levies, therefore, amounted to anti-consumer activity and St Helier, which housed the greater part of the population and the main organs of government, commerce and trade, suffered on a scale which the country never experienced. Matters periodically came to a head, as in 1836. Propositions to halt the importation of foreign cider, considered detrimental to local sales, and the levying of an all-Island rate as a means of periodic funding, in which St Helier would contribute one-fifth of the total, genuinely angered the inhabitants of the Town: "il semble que les Etats du pays ont eu en contemplation de faire cesser la bonne intelligence qui existait entre la ville et la campagne". [46]

Urban victories over rural protectionist policies, such as those of 1816 and 1828, when the Connétable of St Helier managed to persuade the States to suspend corn exports temporarily lest the poor would suffer, were rare. [47] Furthermore, for each victory there was a price to pay. For example, the States' agreement to finance the new harbour developments of 1839 and 1847 was not so surprising as it first appeared. The commercial benefits of an extended and modernised harbour were appreciated in the country, as we have seen in St Ouen, but, as François Godfray in his rôle as rural spokesman pointed out to the States, parishes were not willing to to pay for it: funds would have to come from import duties and harbour duties. [48] The feeling of powerlessness, on the part of St Helier's Parish Assembly, was such that it attempted the novel argument of pointing out "que le corps législatif de cette Île a perdu de vue que la paroisse de St Helier ne se borne pas à la Ville seulement; qu'elle possède une campagne fort étendue faisant partie de ladite paroisse," (the Vingtaines of Mont à l'Abbé, Mont Cochon and parts of Mont au Prêtre and the Canton du Rouge Bouillon) "et qui méritait, aussi bien que les autres campagnes de l'île, la bien veillance des Etats". The result of the proposed legislation would be "une partie considerable de ladite paroisse, se trouveraient victimes d'une loi qui a été formée exclusivement pour servir les intérêts de la campagne au detriment de la Ville". [49] It was an argument which had little effect.

The issue of tariffs and the States' economic policy provide a specific illustration of a general situation in which the interests of the urban population always came second to the demands of the rural community. It was a situation which affected the social and economic welfare of local town dweller and immigrant alike. More crucially, the power of the landed interest in the States left the urban community powerless to do anything about it.

The intransigence of the States on economic policy was a direct assault on commercial interests and urban life but many problems simply derived from a legal and political system that was archaic. In what became known as the Dodd and Merrifield case the principles involved and the long term repercussions illustrated very clearly how the legal system could catch the unwary English businessmen.

In 1854 Grantham Dodd, an English solicitor practising in Jersey, found himself imprisoned at the suit of one of his clients in England, the Atwood family, on a charge of maladministration of trust funds. Dodd had been appointed trustee of a settlement left to the family, under the terms of which the wife was entitled to the annual profits of a certain property. The family's demand for the whole sum of the settlement, Dodd's refusal to pay it, and the Royal Court's inability to compel him to do so, resulted in the family having Dodd imprisoned as a debtor under Jersey law. [50]

Grantham Dodd spent three years in gaol, the result of incessant delays in court hearings and a family appeal against a ruling in his favour. He was finally released in January 1857, after a personal petition to the House of Commons and the cessation of the payment of gaoler's fees by the Attwood family - it being a condition of incarceration for debt that the debtor be maintained by the creditor. On appeal, the Royal Court ruled that Dodd should never have been arrested in the first instance and, secondly, that the court had no jurisdiction over what was primarily an English suit. [51]

The case had been further complicated by the attempts of Dodd, in need of money and awaiting the results of the appeal of his creditors, to serve a creditor's writ of his own. This writ was served out of the Court of Common Pleas in England, against one Walter Baltas, also resident in Jersey. The latter's response was to obtain a Royal Court decision as to the illegality of such a writ in the Island and Dodd was joined in gaol by his clerk, John Merrifield. [52]

Paradoxically, considering its subsidiary nature to the first offence, Baltas' suit enabled Dodd, by use of *Habeas Corpus*, to obtain a hearing before the Lord Chancellor in Chancery. Here it was shown that writs issued out of the Court of Common Pleas were legally enforceable in Jersey and that Dodd and Merrifield (particularly Merrifield, whose only rôle was to carry out his employer's instructions) were wrongly imprisoned. In the Baltas' case, Dodd was totally exonerated by English law. In the Atwood case, however, Dodd was not so fortunate. By English law, under which the trust was drawn up, he had committed no crime but he had been imprisoned by Jersey law and there he would have to stay until the Royal Court ruled otherwise. [53]

The details of the case are important for several reasons. In the first instance, Dodd found himself victim of both the absence of law, in the case of the original English trust, and the ridiculous nature of creditors' rights in the Island. [54] Secondly, the fact that the case was able to go before the Lord Chancellor, as opposed to the normal course of appeal to the Privy Council which would have probably resulted in less interest, brought to the attention of many the antiquated and discriminatory nature of some of the laws in Jersey. In this respect, the earlier Carus Wilson case had already resulted in public concern being expressed in England as to the state of the laws and their administration in the Island. [55] Finally, and more specifically, one of Dodd and Merrifield's advocates, Serjeant Pigott, was the man who as an M.P. would in 1861 and 1862 press Parliament so adamantly to force the reform of the Island's judiciary.

Dodd had been incarcerated by the arbitrary judgement of the Jurats. This was not the only case of this kind. Captain Rigby Collins found himself likewise gaoled by his creditors for debts incurred in England. He was interned for over two years without charges being brought and his attempted defence was hamstrung by the Royal Court's inability to call witnesses from outside the Island. [56] Captain Peter Brouard, a merchant, found his ship, worth £2,000, confiscated and sold at the suit of a creditor in 1834. Eight years on, the Privy Council reversed the original Royal Court judgement but Brouard was unable to retrieve any funds because the necessary witnesses were outside the Island and the Royal Court was powerless to force their return. [57]

The Widow Bond Case was of a different nature, but equally a check on individual freedom and the pursuit of commerce. In 1850 the Seigneur of Collette des Augrès, François Godfray, claimed one year's rental of a livery stable in 'année de succession', a feudal privilege relating to the death of a tenant without lineal heirs, from the widow of its former operator, an English small businessman.

The stable had been let at £30 per annum and after a deduction for wheat rentes owed (i.e. the mortgage), the sum remaining was £14. Godfray claimed the larger sum and disclaimed any liability to discharge the rentes. [58]

Godfray's claim was in effect a double one, the enjoyment of the land discharged of all rentes and the enjoyment of those same rentes. The Commission of 1861 suggested that such a double claim was unfounded, the seigneur being in no case "entitled to more than the entire profits of the tenement holden to him".[59] It was further argued that whilst such a claim may have been that which was originally intended by feudal law, with the lord coming in by 'title paramount', it should have been modified by force of circumstance and the changing position of the landholder vis-à-vis the seigneur.[60]

The operation of the feudal system in St Helier reflected an anachronism in terms of the changing social and economic environment. On certain fiefs, notably the Fief de la Fosse, the absence of rural land left the seigneur exacting dues from an urban population, most of whom were not local and were unfamiliar with the situation.[61] The near farcical nature of such a state of affairs was noted by Friedrich Engels during one of his visits: "There is a lot of amusement to be got out of this posthumous feudal set-up by the way, and the whole mess is endlessly ridiculous. A modern advocate as 'Seigneur' and the shopkeepers of St Helier as 'vassals' - the masquerade is quite a joke. The fellows are now holding feudal courts: the 'prévôt du seigneur' is a 'carver' and 'gilder' who can't speak a word of French and, although he is in second command, doesn't understand a thing that is going on. The 'Seigneur' threatens his disobedient vassals, who are 60-70 per cent of the whole number, with confiscation of their houses. And the vassals - 'drapers' and 'tallow-chandlers' - threaten to counteract force with force. Voila the present state of affairs".[62]

The situation was not quite so humourous for those like the Widow Bond. A press campaign and subscription fund financed an unsuccessful challenge in the Court; the judgement came ten years after the first claim.[63] The feudal law to which the Bond family had fallen victim was but one of a body of local land laws, the workings of which urban-based capitalists saw as restrictive and discriminatory. And, indeed, a consistent claim from reformists was that these property laws should be changed to allow the disposal of real estate, particularly acquired property, by will.[64] This, for instance, would have enabled people to avoid the 'année de succession', a practice which took advantage of those unfortunate enough to die without lineal heirs.

Property was not a good investment. As the preamble to the *Loi (1834) sur le Retrait Foncier* pointed out, it was subject to various claims and laws, feudal or otherwise, and people preferred to buy via rentes.[65] Purchase by wheat rentes was a peculiarly Jersey system which resembled both the English mortgage and share market. Land could pass from vendor to purchaser without cash changing hands. Instead, the purchaser was bound to pay an annual charge upon what amounted to a perpetual mortgage. The system was designed for an economy short of capital. It also gave considerable security to the debtor, because provided he paid the interest due on the rente the creditor could not call it in. However, it was a lengthy process unsuited to capitalist requirements, particularly since, once instigated, it was difficult to get out of the transaction. Until the passing of the *Loi (1880) sur la Propriété*

Foncière the debtor could not pay off the debt . The only way to disencumber property of rentes was by purchasing other rentes from a third party and transferring them ('assignation') to the creditor. [66] It was also complicated, as a view of any list of comparative rent values will show. [67] The major problem, however, was that purchase via rentes left everything the debtor owned liable for 'decret' (bankruptcy) or default and, since extended liability operated, a purchaser could find his property liable for the debts of the previous owner. [68] As Charles Trebeck, an Englishman resident in Jersey for fourteen years, pointed out, building or buying a house in the Island could prove a most hazardous experience. [69]

A demand for a change to the local land laws became a part of the reform programme. A petition in 1846, signed by 1,116 landowners and capitalists, stressed that increased demand on property had seen real estate prices soar and that freedom of commerce demanded the loosening of restrictions. It would, suggested the petitioners, "be useful and politic to profit and experience, and to encourage capitalists to employ their capital in the purchase of freehold estates, 'immeubles', in freeing that kind of property from the impediments which still exist, and which so notoriously restrict commerce". [70]

Within this petition can be seen the conflict of interests between a rural community whose land laws had evolved to ensure that property remained within the family and a predominantly urban capitalist community, who viewed property as another means of investment. The 'retrait lignager', abolished in 1834, is a good example of such a law, enabling as it did the repurchase of a property sold from the family estate for the original purchase price, providing it occurred within a year and a day of the original transaction. [71] But reform was slow since a rural dominated legislature was keen to preserve its land laws. Even the *Loi (1851) sur les Testaments 'D'Immeubles,* which enabled limited entail and liberated property for those in special circumstances, was a small reform in a large body of land law. As the preamble noted, the concern was for proprietors n 'ayant enfans ni autres descendans", not capitalists. [72]

By comparison with the legal system and antiquated commercial practices the parish could seem trivial as a source of injustice. Nonetheless, victims of rating abuse and police injustice could feel equally aggrieved. The experience of Stephen Thomas, an English merchant in St Helier, is a case in point. In the 1850s, desirous of a vote in the Parish Assembly, he applied to be rated. His property qualifications were verified by a principal of the parish, François Bertram. Without apparent reason, Centenier Le Cronier, the Chef de Police, declared "C'est ce bougre la: je propose qu'il ne i soit admis", and his admission was duly refused. [73] His only course of appeal was application to the Royal Court, where he could swear on oath the extent of his property. The disadvantage of such an action was that, due to the prevailing rate law, appellants were taxed to half the amount of their property value, considerably more than other ratepayers. [74]

Similarly, encounters with the parish police from St Helier were highly unpredictable, often reliant on the vagaries of personal prejudice. A reporter from the *Miroir*, for example, told the Commissioners of 1861 how his allegations of an assault against him had been ignored by the honorary police. The apparent cause of the assault was a story that had appeared in the newspaper. The police took the view that the attack had been justified and refused to press charges. Charles Manin, on the other hand, found himself arrested by Centenier Slater for the non-payment of a dog licence. He was placed in gaol for two days at the discretion of the Centenier, prior to a Court appearance which ruled that the arrest was unlawful. [75]

These examples of the grievances of the resident English population, highlighted both in the local press and petitions despatched from the Island to the Privy Council and the House of Commons, range from wrongful incarceration and discriminatory laws, to arbitrary interpretations of the law. They took place within a political system that discriminated against the urban and commercial community. From at least the 1830s, these grievances became the basis for a demand for reform. The feelings such restrictions and injustice engendered in the English resident community were perhaps best expressed in the surprise shown by the London based *Morning Chronicle* following various recommendations in the 1861 Commissioners' Report. "The character of these recommendations is curious in the extreme", the paper commented. "One of them is 'that parties be allowed, by consent, to resort to trial by jury'. The next is that 'the Court have full power to allow in any part of the particular case the use of such language as may seem conducive to justice'. All simply establish rules recognised for centuries everywhere else". [76] It was feelings like these that gave rise to the drive for reform.

The Drive for Reform

The drive for reform presented a number of difficulties for English residents. From early on, their interests and concerns were expressed in their own newspapers, the *British Press* from 1822 and the *Jersey Times* from 1832. But the press constituted an ineffectual lobby, for it lacked any effective access to the organs of political decision making. To a large extent, however, the difficulties of foreigners in a strange land were off-set by the fact that their concerns about injustice and commercial restriction were shared by a substantial body of mainly Town-based Jerseymen. By allowing the ruling oligarchy of St Helier, which after at least 1833 can be said to have been dominated by the urban bloc, to represent their attitudes and their demands for reform, English immigrants gained an effective forum.

After 1833 the urban bloc, as a body sharing common ideas and ambitions, became the representative of commerce, both local and immigrant English. The reformers sought to restructure Jersey society by bringing about increased popular political representation for the Town, a uniform system of justice, land laws which enabled commercial speculation, and a professional police force to safeguard commercial and private property in St Helier. It was a pragmatic programme, concentrating on practical needs rather than the finer points of political philosophy and economic science.

Yet the basis for consensus went only so far. The local element in the urban bloc was ever conscious that whilst a wide reform of the Island's institutions was clearly necessary both for commercial and political reasons, that reform should never undermine the basic tenets of the Jersey constitution. In political terms this precluded seeking external help, other than through the recognised channels of appeal to the Crown in Council. For native reformers Parliamentary intervention was unthinkable. For some English immigrants, this state of affairs and the minor and anonymous rôle to which they were confined, was unsatisfactory. One small group of English reformers led by the agitator A.J. Le Cras therefore chose to agitate outside the Jersey system.

The potential conflict of allegiances among native reformers can be observed in the many petitions presented by the urban bloc. Even when the names of petitioners are missing it is possible to determine the extent to which a 'Jersey' influence shaped the argument. A good example of this is an 1848 petition asking for an increase in the number of States' members, particularly for the parish of St Helier. The argument is framed in a style which demands reform, yet is careful not to over-criticise the existing situation. It stresses the heavy workload of present members of the legislature and notes how, because of great changes since the Napoleonic Wars, "D'autres idées, des principes différents, ont succédé à ceux qui guidaient les hommes d'une autre époque.... Au milieu de ce progrès général, la plupart de nos institutions sont demeurées à-peu-près stationnaires".[77] The petition is not an obvious challenge to authority.

The local fear of an open challenge to the Island's authority and the accepted means of lobbying for reform was something English reformists must have understood. The choice facing them was to accept the traditional path to reform and so gain the support of local reformists, or go against it and face their opposition. The majority chose to go with the parish, but it was a choice which left them without any tangible influence. No English resident appears to have attained political office anywhere in the Island during the nineteenth century. In St Helier the parish police force in 1846 numbered 36, but only two officers were English and they held the relatively minor posts of Officier du Connétable and Vingtenier.[78]

It could be argued that Englishmen had no desire to be parish policemen and preferred to use their influence via the parish assembly. The St Helier rate list for 1858 shows a fairly strong English representation. In the Vingtaine of Canton de Ville (the centre of St Helier) for instance, 318 out of a total number of 1,559 ratepayers were English. [79] Yet, as the parish records show, committees appointed by the principaux, set up for a variety of tasks and the main workhorses of the parish, show no sign of an English presence. The Comité des Constituans appointed to inquire into tax reform in the Town parish in 1838 consisted of 11 members, all Jerseymen; the Comité appointed to inquire into a new cemetery in 1854 had 15 members, all local. [80]

All that remained for English residents seeking reform was a vote in the Parish Assembly. If such a vote could ever be put to good use then arguably it was in the case of Pierre Le Sueur, Connétable of St Helier 1839-1853. Le Sueur was the darling of the English residents. The English press' testimonial to him in 1848 showed how the immigrant population considered him a reformer in the English mould, always speaking to his English parishioners in their language. An inscribed plate presented to him by grateful parishioners claimed Le Sueur's successes as "The new Law of Civil Procedure, by which the costs of lawsuits are greatly lessened; the new Criminal Code, now in progress through the States; the legislative blows already aimed, and, we hope, to be eventually successful against the abominable systems of unredeemable mortgages and seigneurial privileges which still oppress and disgrace the country; the New Harbours; the Drainage of the Town, and its many improvements; the Hospital Chapel and Schools....". [81]

Le Sueur's advantage was that he had a foot in both camps. A Jerseyman and leading advocate, he was also a Town dweller from birth and appreciated what the great expansion of commerce and population was doing both to his parish and the Island as a whole. The triumph of his predecessor, the nonconformist Pierre Perrot, over the leading Laurelite, Francois Godfray, in the elections of 1833 marked the beginnings of the local reforming lobby.

In November 1834 a meeting at the Regent Road Theatre in St Helier resulted in the establishment of a Reform Society to work closely alongside the parish of St Helier, in which Le Sueur was to play a major rôle. The demands of the Society were as follows: an end to the judicial and legislative overlap, particularly the rôle of the Jurats in the States; the dismissal of the Crown appointed clergy from the legislature; political representation for St Helier proportional to its share of the population and reflecting its commercial importance; clarification of the parish rating system; and the creation of smaller courts to deal with minor offences and the recovery of debts. [82]

The Reform Society was not an organised institution as such, rather a loose representation of the Parish Assembly of St Helier and any members of country parishes who wished to join. Thus, those present at a meeting at the British Hotel in 1839 were described as "St. Helier electors and country principals". [83] Its main work was discussing, canvassing and petitioning. On occasion a significant number of like-minded voters could be assembled. In 1839, 3,500 signatures were obtained for a petition to the Governor and States which demanded an increase in the number of elected members of the legislature. Three principaux from each parish had been requested to ascertain the views and gain the support of their Assemblies; only the parishes of St John, Trinity and Grouville refused to become involved.[84]

In this way English reformers were able to join a larger body of reformers with at least some political clout. The demand for a full-time police force gives an interesting insight into the workings of the relationship. It was felt by many, claimed several witnesses to the 1847 Commission, that a town of 28,000 people, as a place of much commerce, required an official all-day watch and protection force.[85] The suggestion had been mooted in the St Helier Parish Assembly as early as 1839.[86] A petition, dated around 1850, set out the case for such a force. It was signed by 507 "Natives and British Inhabitants", 286 of the latter, including 47 retired high ranking army and naval officers.[87] Yet, alongside arguments stressing the need for such a force were others expressing the concern of native Islanders that any such force should not be allowed to infringe the power of that most cherished of institutions, the parish, and that the burden of supporting such an organisation should be the responsibility of those who required it.

The movement for reform thus reflected a careful balancing of conflicting interests and allegiances. This requirement may well explain, in many respects, Le Sueur's lack of major success, despite what many believed to be his influence over a majority of rural Connétables.[88] He presented proposals for major reforms five times between 1841 and 1850, reflecting the early demands of the Reform Society in 1834. They included the demand for a paid police force for the Town, a court of petty debts and a police magistrate; all were quashed by the rural majority in the States.[89] It is unfortunate that we have few details on the actual debates in the States - Jersey has never had any Hansard-type recorder - but if they reflected the arguments of the rural and urban blocs outside, expressed in newspapers, parish assemblies and in evidence to the Commissioners of 1847 and 1861, we can assume that a rural bloc was attempting to balance reformist demands against their potentially unwelcome repercussions for the balance of power in the Island.

Already by 1830, however, one important group of English reformists, more sceptical about the possibilities of reform from within, adopted a different strategy, that of direct engagement of the English authorities. It was to prove a move of fundamental importance to the cause of Jersey reform. From at least 1830, therefore, pressure for reform derived from two very different groups: that of the internal reformers, led by Pierre Le Sueur, dedicated to changing Jersey's archaic structures, but not at the price of external interference; and that of A.J. Le Cras, obsessed with the evils of the Jersey system and willing to invoke even the help of Parliament in his quest for change.

The group led and dominated by A.J. Le Cras originated in the local reformist paper, the *English and Foreign News.* The paper was joined by a further Le Cras newspaper, the *Patriot,* in 1831. In style the papers, like the *Jersey Independent* (1855) run by the Chartist George Julian Harney, were radical and anti-Jersey, and were in stark contrast to the more popular and staid *Jersey Times* and *British Press* (amalgamated 1870), both of whose reforming spirit was checked by a concern to maintain gentlemanly standards.

Le Cras represented the type of agitator despised by local reformers. Pierre Le Sueur's biographer, himself an ardent Rose supporter, made the point, contrasting him with "des réformateurs modérés qui désiraient sincèrement améliorer les institutions de leur pays. Mais il en était d'autres qu'on peut appeler les 'anti-Jersiais', qui, eux, voulaient non réformer, mais bouleverser; qui ne respectaient ni nos lois, ni notre langue, ni nos moeurs; qui, par caprice ou par intérêt, voulaient nous assujettir aux lois anglaises, et saper par sa base notre constitution; qui pétitionnaient non pour réformes, mais pour l'anéantissement de notre nationalité....Son plus chaud partisan était M. Abraham Jones Le Cras." [90]

The attitude of English residents to Le Cras is not so obvious. The more serious upmarket English press (records available after 1848) paid little heed to him either way. This is perhaps not surprising, since whilst his intentions may have been admired, his methods would have been deplored. Le Cras remained very much a legend in his own newspapers. It is difficult to be exact about numbers as regards his followers or fellow reformers since his was a very personal campaign. Even after the formation of the Jersey Reform Committee in 1859 he remained the front man for the organisation. He certainly associated himself with the causes of Carus Wilson, and other such newsworthy individuals as Grantham Dodd and Peter Collins, but this was perhaps a ploy to advance his arguments. [91]

Why Le Cras was so committed to changing Jersey society, though perhaps undermining is a more appropriate word is unclear. He told the 1861 Commission, in a five day long examination, that he was born of a Jersey family in Salisbury and moved to the Island sometime in his late teens, where his skill with a pen led him into journalism. [92] He never made it clear whether he considered himself an Englishman or a Jerseyman, although neither side in Jersey claimed him as their own. "For forty years," he added, "I have made the laws of the island my study. I have made a compilation of about 3,000 Orders in Council and from 5-6,000 Acts of the Court. Those are the means by which I have acquired my information".[93] His vast accumulation of material was presented in several major works, beginning in 1839 with *The Laws, Customs and Privileges in the Island of Jersey,* and followed by *Manorial Rights in Jersey* (1856) and *The Constitution of Jersey* (1857). This was supported by a stream of pamphlets and letters to the British Government and Privy Council. [94]

Le Cras' basic premise was that the Island's independence, as reflected in its legislature and judiciary, was "founded on fraud and usurpation", and rested on the ability of the Island to cajole privileges and rights out of London by exploiting its isolated position and English ignorance of the realities of the local situation. [95] In the preface to his first work in 1839, he claimed its aim was "purely for the purpose of exhibiting to the world the scandalous nature of the laws....and the wretched manner in which they are administered; in the fervent hope, that it will provoke enquiry, and be the means of causing such abuses as shall be proved to exist, to be forthwith reformed". [96]

Le Cras' campaign was legalistic and personal. His programme of reform had no economic dimension. His failure to integrate his programme with the needs and demands of the commercial classes, although there is no evidence to suggest that this had ever been his intention, lessened his chances of real long-term success. His determination to invoke external help undermined his chances of working with the urban bloc. Locally, as Pierre Le Sueur's biographer suggested, he was seen as a cranky, but dangerous, antiquarian. The only other major interest in his life, which may give some clue to his reforming zeal, was religion. He was a devout Swedenborgian and a writer of religious tracts. [97] There is no doubt, however, that he was unchallenged as Jersey's most effective political agitator.

In 1840 Le Cras, supported by a minority of the 15,000 English inhabitants in Jersey, successfully challenged the States over their right to naturalise aliens, forcing the Island to petition the Crown to ratify all former acts of naturalisation. [98] It was a technicality he had discovered via his researches and his success spurred him to wider, although as it turned out generally less successful, attempts at reform. In 1844, with the desire for a paid police force in mind, he formed the British Protection Society which published a list of tradesmen involved in the honorary police force and organised a boycott of them. [99]

In 1846 Le Cras struck lucky when a letter to the M.P. for Bath, a former Jersey resident, brought the issue of Jersey reform before Parliament. A Parliamentary question on Le Cras's behalf resulted in a demand in the House for an inquiry to be set up into the criminal law of the Islands. The British Government's response was to recommend to the Crown that a Royal Commission be appointed. [100] The stage appeared to be set at last for fundamental reforms.

The Royal Commissions of 1847 and 1861

The *Royal Commission Appointed to Inquire into the Criminal Law of Jersey* arrived in the Island in August 1846. Its brief was to ascertain the basis of criminal law in the Island, and in this capacity they examined the judiciary at parish and Island level, and the honorary system. Both institutions came in for heavy criticism.

Distaste for this unwelcome incursion of a group of English barristers, commissioned to inquire and probe, was evident at all levels of Jersey society, and will be examined in the context of local responses, in the next chapter. For present purposes, it is worth noting how the *Chronique* reflected local feelings. In an editorial in 1846 the paper proclaimed that it had never before seen such a "motley crew of restless agitators" appearing before the Commission deliberately to criticise and undermine local institutions.[101] In the event, Jersey witnesses outnumbered resident English agitators by over two to one.[102]

The idea of a Commission was not particularly new. There were many precedents, the most recent the already mentioned Commission of 1811. A Commission was a nineteenth-century version of the medieval Crown's justices, precursors to the office of Bailiff, who would visit the Island on similar missions.[103] There was a feeling, however, that this one represented something more, arising out of two decades of unprecedented pressure to reform, pressure which was not solely local.

It would be too much to suggest that Le Cras and his small band of agitators were solely responsible for the arrival of the Commission. The investigation was a response to obvious discontent, rooted in the urban bloc and reflected in its attempts to force reform through the States. There had been a long stream of petitions, both personal appeals like that of Rigby Collins (see p. 149) in 1842 and more general appeals like that of the Jersey Reform Society in 1839, requesting an extension of popular representation in the States. Such petitions involved, as a matter of course, the Governor, the Crown representative in the Island, and the Privy Council. Some petitioners, like Le Cras with his stream of correspondence in the 1830s and 1840s, went direct to the Home Office or to M.P.s known to them.[104]

However, in the context of the Commissions of 1847 and 1861, Le Cras' rôle was central. As a political agitator he knew no rival in the Island; even George Julian Harney, for all his Chartist experience, remained very much on the periphery of the demand for reform.[105] Le Cras was astute enough to realise that not all parliamentary members were ardent admirers of the loyal outposts just off the French coast. Such members were likewise aware, from newspapers and legal periodicals, of the experiences of English residents like Grantham Dodd and Carus Wilson, who had gone to live in Jersey and fallen foul of the Island's authorities.

The Commissioners appreciated that many of the witnesses called before them had an axe to grind. In their report they noted that "So strong are the feelings of the extreme reforming party, that it was urged upon us to recommend measures which would stop little short of an absolute adoption of the English Law and an annexation of the Island to an English circuit....On the other hand, there is a very numerous party, to whom the mere fact of a change conveys a suspicion of an intention to subvert the constitution of the Island, or at least, to favour one party at the expense of another". [106]

The Report of the Commissioners, who were acutely aware that they viewed Jersey institutions through the eyes of English barristers, gave a wide-ranging and thorough assessment of the criminal law, both in theory and in practice. [107] Throughout, the populist nature of local institutions and offices, and the pronounced overlap between judicial and legislative, were criticised as producing inefficiency, poor administration and, most importantly, injustice. The Jurat system was targeted for special concern, and it was recommended that it be replaced by Crown-appointed professional magistrates. [108] The honorary police, it was suggested, should be replaced by a paid police force, "independent of the Parochial Assemblies". [109] The two reforms would be strengthened by the drawing up of a code of judicial and penal procedure. [110]

"The inhabitants of the Island," concluded the Commissioners, "have a right to ask that this state of things should not remain. And it appears to us that it may be remedied with little difficulty, and inconvenience, or shock to any feeling or even prejudice". [111] They felt this to be an important point to make and, in support of this, quoted the observation of Robert Pipon Marett (later Bailiff 1880-1884) that previous reform endeavour had failed at the outset through neglecting to "s'accommode[r] au génie du peuple pour lequel elle est faite". [112]

The conclusions of the Commission broadly embraced the local reformist demands of the 1830s and 1840s. If a common strain ran through the recommendations it was that the Jersey institutions in question should be generally rearranged, to a greater or lesser degree, along the lines of the English legal system. Yet the immediate local response was a petition in counterweight to the Report. This petition, despatched in 1848, signed by numerous Islanders and pleading for non-interference in local affairs, reflected the fear of outside pressure predicted by the Commissioners. It was claimed that the response to their recommendations was "The greatest alarm....throughout the Island; public meetings were held in every Parish, and a petition, to the Queen's Most Excellent Majesty in Council, against the proposed change was soon covered with 6,000 signatures". [113] The conflict of allegiances between the desire for reform and the wish to prevent any external interference was most evident in the Parish Assembly of St Helier, where the "agitation de la population du pays" was greeted with dismay by reformers. [114]

However, the recommendations of the Commission were just that, recommendations only, and this was appreciated, albeit with some trepidation, by the Jersey authorities. In the case of the local reformist body, demands for action were increased, not appeased. In 1849 a numerous body of merchants and tradesmen of St Helier petitioned the Lieutenant-Governor, complaining about "the deafness of the States to the trading sector's desires", namely the need for a full-time police force and a court of petty debts. [115] In November 1850 a large meeting at the Temperance Hall in St Helier reiterated the reformist demands for a court for petty debts and a paid police force; a petition was forwarded to Sir George Grey, Secretary of State at the Home Office, and Her Majesty in Council. [116] Le Cras was likewise actively petitioning the English authorities for the implementation of the recommended reforms. [117]

On the 11th February, 1852, the Privy Council responded to the recommendations of the Commission and the clamours for implementation with three Orders in Council proposing the establishment of a police court for minor offences, a petty debts court and a town police force. [118] This was communicated direct to the Royal Court, although it contained no order for registration, which was the usual Privy Council response to locally-initiated legislation. It appeared that the States as a quasi-independent legislature had been effectively bypassed. The reaction of the States and the Island as a whole was outrage at such direct interference.[119]

The States of Jersey suspended the orders. It pointed out that as recently as 1835 the House of Commons' *Report on the Channel Islands and the Corn Laws*, appointed to investigate West Country complaints regarding the smuggling of French grain via the Islands, had shown that the Islands had never abused their rights and that these should, therefore, not be infringed. The Parliamentary Committee had concluded "that it would not be expedient to abrogate or infringe the islands' rights, and which were conferred upon them in consideration of the signal service which, at various periods of history, they have rendered to the crown and people of this country". [120] The States similarly emphasised the democratic rights of the Jersey population and the need for the assent of their representatives to laws and taxes that affected the Island. [121]

The Three Orders in Council were, however, interpreted as a heavy nudge, if not a threat, and the States simultaneously initiated six acts of its own to incorporate the demanded reforms. The six acts established a paid police force, allowed for more Centeniers in St Helier and St Martin (the latter because it had to police Gorey village and the St Catherine's defence works), established a petty debts court and a police court for minor offences, as well as introducing certain clarifications of the legal process. [122] After a constitutional wrangle the States had acceded to the reforms forced upon it, although it gave them the appearance of an Island initiative. In return, the Privy Council upheld the right of the States to be the "exclusive legislative authority, competent to fix or change the municipal law of the Island". The Crown in Council retained its prerogative control. [123]

In the wake of Privy Council pressure the States thus did make some reforming gestures. And in 1856 political representation was extended with the introduction of 14 Deputies, four of them for St Helier, a minimal recognition of its large share of the population. [124] But these were reforms forced upon the States. There was no attempt to introduce several of the major reforms recommended by the 1847 Commission, particularly the divorce of political from judicial authority and the abolition of the Jurats. The reforms of 1853 and 1856 were a minimalist response to placate the Privy Council.

The clamour for reform evident in the 1840s was not as obvious in the 1850s. This was in part because of the six acts of 1853 which had met some of the reformists' demands, notably the establishment of a court of petty debts and a professional police force for the Town. It was also a defensive reaction against the threat to Island independence implied by the Privy Council action. This had long been appreciated by Pierre Le Sueur who, whilst an ardent reformer in the 1840s, realised the difficulty of combining reforming zeal with defence of local institutions. An inability to pursue reform through the States left appeal to the Privy Council as the only alternative but this was simultaneously an open invitation to interfere in local affairs. Le Sueur's early death in 1853 at the age of 41 removed a great mediator between the local and English populations, as well as a mover of reforms. [125]

Le Cras, keen to involve outside authority in local affairs, remained dissatisfied; for him anglicisation seemed the only acceptable course, and in 1850 he left the Island for his native England. He claimed he was forced to do so because his house in Les Vaux was being "assessed through party spirit at exorbitant rate" and his security threatened, "through the corruption and irresponsibility of the police". [126] But by 1853 he had returned to the Island and was agitating again, publishing several major works and sending yet another stream of correspondence to the Home Office and selected Members of Parliament. [127]

Convinced that Parliament had the right to legislate for Jersey, Le Cras in 1859 enlisted the support of George Hadfield, M.P. for Sheffield, urging a new inquiry into the "civil, municipal and ecclesiastical laws of the island". [128] Le Cras believed further pressure might be forthcoming, provided it could be shown that the abuses remained and that the Island was unable or unwilling to reform. In February 1859 Hadfield's questions in the Commons resulted, with apparent ease, in the appointment of a Royal Commission to inquire into the matters raised by Le Cras, the civil, municipal and ecclesiastical laws of Jersey. [129] Hadfield claimed to be representing a large body of Islanders, although the two petitions which had a direct influence were signed by relatively small numbers, 329 and 410. [130]

The new inquiry, which visited the Island in June 1859 and March 1861 followed the pattern of its 1847 predecessor, relying primarily on oral examination. Over 100 residents were interviewed, including 25 non-locals, whose prime reason for attending was to highlight specific and usually personal complaints. These included some of the cases already mentioned, such as those of Grantham Dodd and Peter Brouard. Local witnesses were called primarily to provide expert evidence. [131]

Written depositions were also accepted, including one from the newly formed Jersey Reform Committee. Created at a meeting of reformers in St Helier in July 1859, the Committee was directed by Le Cras. [132] In true Le Cras style, two one hundred page memorials were directed to the Commissioners, asking for the abolition of the Royal Court and the assimilation of English law in the Island.

The conclusions and 88 recommendations of the 1861 Commission reflected its wide brief. For instance, the recent moves of the States towards allowing commutation of seigniorial rights were applauded. [133] In the sphere of the parish it was suggested that the establishment of independent assessors and auditors would avoid potential abuse in rating and accounting. [134] Yet, as with the 1847 Commission, deep concern was expressed over the constitution of the Royal Court and a remedy suggested in the appointment of paid judges to replace the Jurats. It was also recommended that trial be by jury and that use of the English language should be allowed in Court. [135]

The theme common to both Commissions was criticism of the continued overlap of judicial and legislative rôles at Island and parish level alike. In no way was the 1861 Commission a challenge to the Privy Council assurance of 1853 regarding the right of the Jersey population to initiate its own legislation. Its purpose was to examine the system of local government and law, in theory and practice, and to bring to the attention of the local authorities its weaknesses and abuses.

The 1847 and 1861 Commissions, but especially the latter with its wider brief, both provide detailed information on the inner workings of many spheres of Jersey society. They are perhaps most significant for the light their criticisms throw on specific local institutions and for the response such criticism evoked. But their after effects were very different. The direct result of the 1847 Commission, as we have seen, was Privy Council pressure in 1852 for certain reforms. The Commission of 1861 had no such obvious repercussions.

Following the 1861 Commission it appeared that Jersey institutions had survived the demand for reform. Two major inquiries had come and gone and the only obvious repercussions were the minor reforms of 1853. Jersey had successfully defended its constitutional integrity. But Le Cras was too dedicated to the cause of root and branch reform to be satiated by such a minimalist response. Once again his petitioning of Parliament was to pay off. This time, however, no inquiry was appointed. It appeared that Parliamentary patience with the Island had finally run out; unprecedented Parliamentary intervention loomed large on the Jersey horizon.

The Rôle of Parliament

Both the Commissions of 1847 and 1861 were initiated in directives of the British Government, acting in response to the questions of Members of Parliament. This was peculiar, since Parliament had previously shown little interest in the internal affairs of Jersey, other than those which concerned defence and trade. It was a centuries old practice that the Crown should look after what were, after all, its dependencies.

The Channel Islands were, nonetheless, very much in the Parliamentary eye during the 1840s and 1850s. The construction of the so-called 'harbours of refuge' in Jersey and Alderney proved a source of much conflict, with many M.P.s' viewing the project as costly and unnecessarily antagonistic to the French. [136] Similarly, the Dodd and Merrifield case, which came up before the Lord Chancellor, and the Carus Wilson case, which interested legal circles because of its relevance to *Habeas Corpus*, brought more attention to the Island. For a selected group of M.Ps. and Government representatives, petitioning and correspondence increased this awareness.

The fact that a large body of English immigrants now resided in Jersey no doubt intensified interest and justified concern in the Island's internal affairs. We observed in the chapter on Language how certain Crown representatives had stressed the utility of an increased conformity with the United Kingdom. This was most evident in 1872 when the Privy Council withdrew its educational funding to force the Island to adopt Parliament's 1870 Elementary Education Act. [137]Parliamentarians were clearly not strangers to the Island of Jersey.

The Jersey Reform Committee, keen to exploit such an interest, chose to ignore the possibility of a positive reaction from the local authorities to the 1861 Commissioners' Report and attempted to persuade Parliament to intervene directly in Jersey affairs. [138] In so doing it stole the Report's thunder, although no doubt the action was precipitated by a belief that the 1861 Commission would be as relatively ineffectual as that of 1847. It is equally possible that Le Cras believed that the threat of direct Parliamentary intervention, coupled with the Report, would bring about a reform of the judiciary by the States. [139]

The diligence and industriousness of the Le Cras reformist group paid off again in May 1861. Within weeks of the publication of the latest Commission Report, Sergeant Piggott, M.P. for Reading, sought leave from the House of Commons, "to bring in a Bill to amend the constitution, practice and procedure of the Court of the Island of Jersey". It was a move prompted, he claimed, by there being "no probability of Crown initiated reform" and "not the least likelihood" of its coming from Jersey. [140] On behalf of the Government, Sir George Lewis agreed with Pigott's assertions as to the urgency for reform in the Island, claiming that "if ten Commissions, composed of competent men, were appointed....they would all be obliged to arrive at similar conclusions". However, he added, in a statement which represented the official line towards the Island, that it was not customary for Parliament to legislate directly for the Island, pressures were mounting in Jersey itself, and it was only a matter of time before reforms were introduced. [141]

The Government line prevailed at the second reading of Pigott's bill, which was suspended for a period to allow internal reform. [142] Several M.P.'s remained unconvinced by arguments that Parliament had no right of intervention and that the Jersey authorities could be relied upon to reform themselves and, in April, 1864, the Jersey Court Bill was reintroduced for a second reading by the M.P. for Southwark, John Locke. Jersey, it was claimed, had had more than enough time. [143]

The reintroduction of Pigott's bill was only one of several threats that hung over the Jersey authorities in 1864, testimony to the efforts of the reformists. In January 1864, following the resignation of two Jurats through ill-health, the States had sought the customary ratification from the Privy Council and permission to call an election. But simultaneously, a petition was forwarded by 279 leading "Landed Proprietors and Merchants", asking for ratification to be withheld, to force a reform of the judiciary. It was followed by a similar petition from Le Cras' Reform Committee. [144] Ratification was refused. It was admitted in the Privy Council response that the final petition had been the catalyst for action; although signed by a relatively small number it was no doubt the final straw. A communication from Sir George Grey, at the Home Office, delivered a blatant threat to the Jersey authorities: if no moves towards a reform of the judiciary were mooted, the Government would find it difficult to oppose Locke's second reading. [145] Within this threat lay the most blatant challenge to Jersey's independence. Conformity with the wishes of Parliament had become the price of retention of privileges. Not surprisingly, because it had little real choice, the States' reassurance was forthcoming and Locke was apparently persuaded to postpone any further action. [146]

Yet, once again, the Island showed itself to be in control of the situation. Centuries of exploiting the Island's strategic position and of extracting liberties from the Crown had left a heritage of experience in diplomacy and manipulation. By what amounted to a master-stroke, the States was able simultaneously to honour its agreement to Parliament and continue to block external pressure.

What lay behind Parliamentary pressure, the Privy Council's refusal to ratify the resignations and Grey's threats was the belief that popular desire for reform in the Island was widespread. In fact this was not so. The States exploited this belief to its advantage. In January 1865 an Island-wide plebiscite of ratepayers was held on the abolition of the office of Jurat and its replacement by a paid judiciary. The result was overwhelmingly in favour of the Jurats, 2,298 voting against a new judiciary and only 180 for it. The parish of St Helier provided 62 per cent of the 180 votes, and even then brought a vote of 81 per cent for retention. In the parishes of St Mary, St Ouen and St Peter no votes at all were recorded against the present system. [147]

The plebiscite of 1865 was the major turning point in the nineteenth-century struggle for reform. It marked the end of external pressure on Jersey for reform. It likewise marked the end of Le Cras' political agitation. Locally a reformist lobby continued to thrive but no longer provided a challenge on the scale experienced in the previous forty years. The rural community had successfully thwarted all attempts to undermine its power and the traditional institutions from whence this power derived. The nineteenth-century reform movement was to all intents and purposes laid to rest.

The question remains as to how the Island managed to avoid direct intervention to force major reform. The 1865 plebiscite, whilst conducted fairly, was in many ways a sham, asking the principaux of the Island's parishes whether or not they wished to see their own power and traditions undermined. Le Cras' Reform Committee attempted to have the plebiscite quashed on the grounds that illicit pressures had been brought to bear on the voters; the ballot paper was so worded that it suggested the proposed reform would result in taxation. [148] But he was missing the point. There was no need to cajole the ruling bloc into voting against external meddling in local affairs.

Perhaps the most puzzling aspect of the affair was Parliament's willingness to accept the referendum as an answer to its threats of intervention. The Jersey authorities were allowed to escape very easily and lightly and this must have been expected by the British Government. Apparently convinced of the popular base to the office of Jurat, Parliament suddenly ceased to be interested in the internal affairs of Jersey.

Throughout the three sessions of the Jersey Court Bill Parliament's right to intervene was much disputed. This was a question which troubled successive governments between at least 1846 and 1864. As Sir George Lewis put it in 1861, "If Jersey were an integral part of the United Kingdom....he should not hesitate to lay on the table a Bill dealing with the question [of reform]. But the difficulty lay in the fact that Jersey was only a dependency of the Crown. It was a separate appendage from the United Kingdom, and it had not been the custom of Parliament habitually to legislate with regard to that island. He could not suppose that any inhabitant was so little master of his sense or understanding as to deny the power of Parliament to legislate with regard to it; but what was disputed was the power of the Crown by Orders in Council to make constitutional changes in the laws of the island". [149]

The Privy Council, too, was restricted. The three Ordres du Conseil of 1852, however, remain a puzzle, and were certainly an attempt directly to influence reform in the Island. What is more difficult to explain is the manner in which the States gave way to this pressure, whereas the attempt in 1864 to withhold ratification of the two Jurats' resignations was met by a constitutional appeal to the Lord Chancellor. [150] It is possible that the more superficial reforms of 1852, which added minor institutions and did not affect the overall power structure, were viewed with less suspicion than the threatened constitutional changes to the judiciary. Their implementation also resulted in the Privy Council's reaffirmation of the Island's rights of independence and internal regulation. Over the events of the 1860s the Law Lords, like the British Government, ruled that permission for the Jurats to resign should not be withheld, nor used as a constitutional lever, even though they were "strongly of the opinion that a complete change in the constitution of the Royal Court is absolutely necessary for the welfare of the Island". [151]

In the absence of clear constitutional rights recourse was made by both Parliament and the Privy Council to the argument of popular demand. Sir George Lewis suggested that "there was a limit to the forbearance of Parliament; and, owing to the increased number of English residents in the Channel Islands, consequent on the increased facilities of communication, the attachment to old customs no longer prevailed there to the same extent. He, therefore, regarded the question mainly as a question of time". [152] In the course of the second reading, he acknowledged that in the absence of recognisable local dissatisfaction on a large scale, Parliament could do little. [153] The Commissions of 1847 and 1861 were a response to perceived popular discontent, as was the withholding of assent to the resignations in 1864. But, ultimately, such a premise enabled a rural bloc whose power base was popular to defend its most cherished institutions.

The British Government paid no more than lip service to the reform of Jersey institutions. It seems that the post-reform Parliament of 1832, so keen to investigate and reform the skeletons in their own cupboard, were not interested in interfering in Jersey's affairs. This would explain how in all three cases the impetus for some form of Parliamentary action came from private members. It also reflected Parliament's respect for the constitutional relationship between the Island and the Crown, something with which it showed no intention of interfering.

Just how popular the demand for reform was locally is difficult to assess, mainly because local reformers took care not to overstep the bounds of allegiance to Jersey institutions. Recourse to the Privy Council was an acceptable means of seeking redress. The general feeling appears to have been that induced external interference might go a great deal further than locals intended. In this respect, recourse to Parliament went beyond the acceptable bounds, because it would be recognising a jurisdiction which might well challenge the Island's claim to semi-independence.

It is an interesting reflection on the local reformists, particularly the upper-middle class, that it was John Le Couteur who presented the 1864 petition for reform of the judiciary. A scholar of reform, rather than an active agitator, his independent opinions and willingness not to see a threat to independence around every corner, were thought highly enough of for the English solicitor Edward Flower to dedicate his work on *Habeas Corpus* to him. [154] Yet even Le Couteur, a former Connétable and Jurat himself, and a man with much influence, realised that a reform of the magnitude required could only be achieved from the outside.

As to the small group of non-local reformers who chose not to join the urban bloc's attempts at internal lobbying, their continued petitioning of Parliament reflected a willingness and, no doubt, a need to seek redress outside the normal boundaries. Extreme cases of misfortune, abuse and prejudice, like those of Grantham Dodd and Peter Brouard, proved the catalyst for external interference. In this respect A.J. Le Cras must stand alone as the most industrious and effective agitator, but his influence was probably little greater in real terms than that of English residents who chose the more locally-acceptable path to reform and remained largely hidden behind the leading lights of parish politics, such as Pierre Le Sueur. Le Cras' influence was limited to mobilising Parliament. The groundswell of popular support he used to justify external interference was never as strong as he claimed. Few resident English turned up to complain to the Commissions of 1847 and 1861.

Parliament had made it clear that it would intervene in Jersey affairs only on the presumption of united urban dissatisfaction. Le Cras was beaten because this did not exist. He remained isolated from the body of native reformers whose reforming zeal was undermined by feelings of loyalty and allegiance to the Island and its traditional structures. Pierre Le Sueur and the reformers he led refused to abandon the parish-based political culture within which they worked. This meant, in effect, that Jersey reformers chose to fight the rural bloc on its own territory with the result that they found the landed interest unyielding in the demand for reform. In the next section we will examine what lay behind this local allegiance to the parish system and how it circumscribed the native demand for reform.

Section 3

Defence and Continuity

Introduction

In this previous section we have examined the various forces of change and challenge unleashed upon Jersey society in the nineteenth century, an economic and demographic expansion after 1815. In the last chapter we showed how in its most specific form - Le Cras' campaign to change the Jersey constitution - this challenge foundered on the English reformers' alienation of all sections of the native population, including potential allies in the commercial sector. This section is intended to balance the emphasis on essentially English pressures hitherto with a detailed look at the local population. The positive defences and the more inert influences of continuity within Jersey society - which formed the Island's reaction to the challenges - is also discussed. In this way the development of the rural and urban blocs, as separate and identifiable entities, and their seemingly ambivalent relationship will be set in its fully rounded context.

The Jersey parish was a crucial indicator of local attitudes and reactions to change. As a major organ of local government and community in the island, it was rightly perceived by reformers as the bastion of rural power. It became the focus of the rural/urban conflict, a dispute centred on power and economics, but confused by competing loyalties. All challenges to the parish and attempts to curtail its power were stoutly and successfully repulsed. Reforming townsmen found themselves hamstrung by the fact that their desire for change was undermined by an unwillingness to show themselves disloyal to local institutions and independence. This dilemma was most apparent in Pierre Le Sueur's politics and ultimately served to undermine the cause of reform. By the end of the century, the parish as an institution had not only been successfully defended, but significantly augmented in power.

Parish power reflected but one aspect of a rural community which by self-discipline and strict traditional practices was able to regulate the countryside. Demographic stability provided an important means of continuity for the rural community. Despite a rapid population growth rate in the Island as a whole, particularly between 1821 and 1851 when the population doubled, the countryside retained a relatively stable population. With a high internal growth rate, this rural stability was ensured by emigration and by internal migration to the Town. Enforced seigneurialism and local inheritance practices, that stressed the importance of retaining an undivided family patrimony, meant the countryside showed itself inhospitable to English immigrants and few settled there. Nineteenth-century rural Jersey accommodated but few of the island's increasing number of inhabitants.

Yet demographic stability belied certain changes in the countryside, namely the arrival of French immigrants and an increase in the number of tenant farmers. Breton labourers were brought over to Jersey to meet the demands of the booming agricultural industry, but many decided to stay and farm their own units. These Bretons contributed to a growing trend towards tenant farming in the late nineteenth century. By the 1880s these Bretons and tenant farmers loomed large enough to concern the guardians of Jersey agriculture and the landed tradition. This concern as based on the belief that tenant farmers wee upsetting the delicately balanced rural economy, be it by the demand for land , that forced up rents, or by single-minded profit orientation. However, it was underpinned by racial prejudice and fears as to the ability of the larger landowners to control this increasingly independent class of small farmers. This conclusion is supported by the finding that agriculture, in fact, remained the basic unit of capitalism. Despite fears of monoculture, the traditional balance of livestock and crop cultivation were retained.

An inhospitable environment to English immigrants, a powerful communal framework and a disciplined family structure, most evident in the practice of inheritance, provided powerful barriers to external influence. However, certain forces proved more than a match for such barriers, and enjoined compromise, if not long-term defeat. In this section the challenges of Nonconformism and the English Language and culture are brought together in comparison to show how two very different elements forced a compromise in a society. Elsewhere such a compromise showed itself , both structurally and institutionally, well able to defend itself. Nonconformism is analysed particularly from the way its non-contentiousness and the toleration this engendered resulted in the reconstruction of the parish onto a more civil footing, which whilst effectively assimilating the challenge within traditional bounds had certain implications for the rôle of the parish in the community.

The challenge of the English language and culture, on the other hand, revealed the inadequacy of the rural bloc in dealing with a force which did not operate within the framework of understanding an control. Local society was linguistically and culturally weak, a situation which left the Island easy prey to a powerful and well-defined English language and culture. Pressure from the United Kingdom, particularly as regards education funding and the anglophile desires of a section of the local middle class, confounded any concerted institutional defence. Jerseymen struggled to find more intangible barriers and this section will examine their attempts to harness Jerriais and construct a national or ethnic identity as a means of cultural defence. The long-term effects of these challenges in the nineteenth century, strongly contrasted with institutional challenges, were to leave this formally isolated and unique Island culturally and linguistically weakened.

We will now turn to examining these forces of defence and continuity in detail.

Chapter 7

The Parish: Politics and the Question of Reform

It is not surprising that the major target for institutional reform in the nineteenth century was the parish, in its various aspects. Both the 1847 and 1861 Commissions pointed to a municipal organisation much in need of reform, particularly in its policing and rating functions. Local and English resident reformists alike identified the parish as the bastion of native rural power and defender of many of the abuses and restraints that they despised. Parishioners too, fought and litigated over elections, perceived corruption and malpractice. All recognised the parish as the major institutional component in Jersey society, which in its positive aspect provided access to power and justice for its parishioners, yet, on its darker side, excluded many from their democratic rights and blocked all attempts to adjust the Island infrastructure to meet the demands of modernisation.

The urban community required the structures of Jersey society to be realigned onto a footing more suited to its economic and political requirements. However, the cause of local reform was hamstrung from the outset by two important considerations. Firstly, as we observed in the previous chapter, it was realised from an early stage that effective restructuring would have required outside pressure from the Privy Council, if not Parliament. This was a price local reformers were unwilling to pay, because to have invoked external interference would have undermined the Island's independence, upon which so much of the Island's commercial success was built. Secondly, and more crucially, local urban reformers were in many respects as attached to Jersey's institutions and its populist political culture as members of the rural community.

Pierre Le Sueur's rôle in the reform movement of the nineteenth century can be understood only in the context of local parish politics. In this chapter we will examine what this parish-based political culture meant to the local population and why urban reformers like Le Sueur chose to fight within its framework, rather than seek external help to force reform upon the States. Through the experiences of Le Sueur it will be shown that, far from being at opposite ends of the political spectrum, the rural and local urban communities still found more to unite than divide them. In the face of attacks upon traditional structures, particularly by A.J. Le Cras and by Parliament, rural and local urban interests became reconciled. A shared past with their countrymen and a belief in the ability of the Island to sort out its own problems ultimately undermined the ability of the urban reformers to achieve major change. The Jersey parish remained as the major institutional structure of Jersey society.

The Power of the Parish

Even a community which puts a premium on individualism needs some form of corporate power to represent its interests and regulate its affairs. For centuries, as observed in the Introductory Section, Jersey society had cast the parish in this rôle. By the nineteenth century the parish was a most powerful institution, representing its members on all levels and paramount as the most succinct definition of the community.

What then lay behind the popular belief in the parish? In his nineteenth-century work on the constitutional history of Jersey, Charles Le Quesne attempted to answer the question in terms of the honorary system. He suggested that the motive behind the desire of parishioners to take up honorary service for their parish was its "incentive to manliness and virtue. If young men exhibit qualities which procure for them the esteem and approbation of their neighbours, these have means of testifying their regard and confidence by electing them to some of the parochial offices; and if, in some of the inferior offices, they acquit themselves of their duties with fidelity, a reward awaits them in higher office". [1]

It would be cynical not to accept Le Quesne's explanation. Yet, the rewards of honorary office necessarily involved power and the rôle of the parish in Jersey society was such that it could amount to the power of mini-government, with the same mixture of judicial and legislative authority evident at Island level. It was what the Commissioners of 1847 called a "mixtion de pouvoirs", the undefined powers which, on a humorous level, allowed Thomas Le Cornu, Connètable of St Ouen, to include gin as a legitimate parish expenditure, but on a more serious level, allowed Centenier Thomas Slater, of St Helier, to arrest and imprison (two days solitary) Charles Manin for being drunk and disorderly, without any recourse to the judiciary. [2]

In the context of the party politics which prevailed throughout the majority of the Island's parishes for at east the first half of the nineteenth century, such ill-defined and unrestricted power was appealing and worth fighting for. After all, as J. Carré concluded, The Constable is always a party man, be he Rose or be he Laurel, it is not therefore too much to suppose, for whoever has studied human nature will readily conceive the possibility, that the Constable will be disposed to be lenient with those he knows to be his friends, and to be cold, [dedaigneux], if not absolutely provokingly harsh towards his political opponents". [3]

Once in power a faction could utilise its multiple powers to ensure its stay was long and fruitful. Rate lists were manipulated to determine the electorate, whilst the policing function was used as an effective threat against political opposition. Not surprisingly, most criticism of parish malpractice and bias was directed against rates assessment and policing. A.J. Le Cras's short departure from Jersey in 1850 was, he claimed, a result of the St Helier parish authorities doing their utmost to make his life difficult, be it by over-rating his house at Les Vaux or failing to respond to any calls he might make requesting police help. [4]

The virulence of parish politics, particularly in the earlier decades of the nineteenth century, reflected this power. In the Larbalestier/Le Maistre election for Connétable in Trinity in 1818, 252 votes were cast out of a possible 325. Yet, over 3,000 people were stated to be present at the polls.[5] Parishioners or otherwise, over 2,500 people were concerned enough over the outcome of the election to participate, even though they could not vote. This mass involvement and the competitive spirit it engendered prompted the Reverend Durell, in his preface to the 1837 edition of Falle's *Account of the Island of Jersey*, to lament, "Unhappily if we were to present a separate History of that period, it would contain little more than an account of the virulence of parties, the oppression of the subject by the perversion of justice, and the political rancour and personal hatred, which have carried their dissensions into the bosom of private families".[6] Durell's view was coloured by his own professional demise, the result of his mixing religion with politics (see Chapter 4), but there was an element of truth in what he said. John Le Couteur, resigning from office as Connétable of St Brelade in 1832, also noted the volatile political situation: "I have given up my post of Constable in good time to escape from a stormy sea of politics which now disgraces us".[7]

The situation referred to by both Durell and Le Couteur was the division of the Island into two hostile political camps. H.D. Inglis, writing in 1834, described this division as being one of "two factions, calling themselves Laurel and Rose; which in their mutual animosity and extreme blindness resemble the Guelfs and Ghibellines of the Middle Ages. ...It is utterly impossible for anyone unacquainted with Jersey to form any idea of the length to which each party spirit is carried there. It not only taints the fountains of public justice, but enters into the most private relations of life".[8] The two factions originated in the struggle between the judiciary and legislature in the late eighteenth century, in part remedied by a separation of the two functions in the Code of 1771. The factions were two groups whose identity rested on allegiance to the major players, Charles Lemprière, Lieutenant-Bailiff, and Jean Dumaresq, Connétable of St Peter.[9] By the early nineteenth century, after a party political lull during the Napoleonic Wars, Lemprière's Charlots or Conservatives had become the Laurel party, and Dumaresq's Magots or Progressives the Rose party.

By the 1830s, Rose and Laurel party politics had reached most of the Island's parishes, and individual parishes could be identified by the allegiance of their ruling oligarchy. As in the Charlot and the Magot days, leadership was again vested in the major players in the political arena: François Godfray for the Laurels; Pierre Le Sueur for the Roses.

Godfray and Le Sueur were the leading politicians of their day, as well as the Island's leading barristers. Within one year of practising at the bar, Godfray's gift for fiery rhetoric resulted in his nomination by the Laurel party as a candidate for Connétable of St Helier, where, at the age of twenty-three, he defeated the Rose candidate, Pierre Perrot.[10] For the next thirty-three years Godfray sat in the States: as Connétable of St Helier 1830-1833, as Connétable of St Martin 1834-1841, and as Connétable and Deputy for St Saviour 1842-1868.

Le Sueur, like Godfray, received his legal education in Paris, and his political rise was rapid. He was elected Connétable of St Helier in 1839 and remained in office until his early death in 1853. His style was less fiery than Godfray's, and he made his name defending in major court cases, including that of fellow Rose-supporter the Reverend Edouard Durell, Rector of St Saviour, who was accused of sodomy in the 1830s. He was elected Connétable at the age of twenty-nine and took the mantle of leader of the Rose party from the Nonconformist Connétable of St Helier, Pierre Perrot. [11].

Godfray and Le Sueur epitomised their respective parties. Both men took a major part in their party newspapers: the *Constitutionel* with its laurel symbol, from 1820, and the *Chronique* with its rose as a headpiece, from 1825. [12] Pierre Le Sueur was clearly the more popular of the two men, his liberal reformism embracing local commercial interests and a major section of the English residents and his personality and openness to reason gaining him support in the country. François Godfray, by contrast, had a less broad appeal. Labelled the 'Baron of Bagatelle - a name referring to the fact that he owned seventeen fiefs in his lifetime, and enforced his feudal rights with the full power of the law - by the English Press, he was by all accounts an unreasonable man; indeed, he was accused in 1832 of challenging the Bailiff to a duel following an altercation in the States. [13] Nonetheless, his willingness to represent rural interests, however unpopular they might be in the Town, brought him much rural support. [14]

Yet to read the *Chronique* or the *Constitutionnel*, or to study the political careers of Le Sueur and Godfray, is not to observe two very different political persuasions or concepts of how society should be organised. Both men shared a fundamental belief in the Island's basic institutions and its right to clean out its own house. They disagreed on the popular operation of those institutions and the speed of necessary reform. It was a difference reflected in their origins: Godfray coming from a privileged middle-class background, Le Sueur the son of a town blacksmith. In practice, this meant that the men sat opposite each other over most local issues. [15] However, in the context of popular party politics, the dominance of personality as a shaper of attitudes and policy meant in effect that there was often little to distinguish Rose from Laurel.

As a look at Figure 7, a map of nineteenth-century party dominance, reveals, party politics did not divide the Island into simple rural and urban blocs. On the contrary, much of rural Jersey was dominated by the Rose party. The Laurel party even managed to control St Helier between 1827 and 1834. In a parish arena where politics were personalised, party labels were interchangeable. Likewise, they were not wholly binding. When St Helier electors met country parish representatives in 1839 and decided to petition for more popular representation in the States, allegiance to the Rose Party did not stop the parishes of Trinity and St John from abstaining along with Laurelite Grouville. [16] Similarly, it was possible for some parishes, like St Peter in the first sixteen years of the nineteenth century, to remain immune and independent from party divisions altogether. [17]

The Rose and Laurel parties were not parties in the sense of political organisations with an official structure and a coherent body of ideas. Rather they represented groups of people who identified with each other on a personal level, these allegiances often the result of family affiliations. The personalities of the leading politicians were more important than ideas. One might support François Godfray because he delivered a speech full of invective at the local parish hall; one might support Pierre Le Sueur because he defended a parishioner in the Royal Court. It is no coincidence in such personality-dominant politics, that the only two Jerseymen considered worthy of biographies by their contemporaries in the nineteenth century were Le Sueur and Godfray. [18]

The personal nature of political allegiance was noted in 1846 by the Lieutenant-Governor, Sir Edward Gibbs. He claimed that Pierre Le Sueur, "as Advocate of the Royal Court and from being Constable of St Helier's parish, possesses a controlling influence over about three-fourths of the other constables, who with one exception are plain uneducated farmers". [19] The exception he referred to was François Godfray, at that time Connétable of St Saviour. The description of the other Connétables was supported by John Le Couteur: "The Constables as a class of men are perfectly respectable as to character, but frequently not possessing weight or education enough to prevent their being led. The leading gentry of the island will not act as Constables, unfortunately, considering the situation beneath them". [20]

It may have been the worldly experiences of Gibbs and Le Couteur that led them to regard Connétables as country bumpkins, educated locally as opposed to abroad, concerned only with petty parochial matters and never quite *au fait* with the broader concepts of social and economic policy, but there must have been some truth in it too. Le Sueur and Godfray, by contrast, were learned, educated and wealthy. They knew how to communicate with the Jersey people, both on a personal level and through their partisan papers. They commanded respect, which in the political sphere became loyalty.

Families in their extended form tended to share the same affiliations. As in the Namierite view of politics in eighteenth-century England, political affiliations were not shaped so much by issues of principle as by family connection. W.L. de Gruchy, writing of his experiences in the later nineteenth century, pointed out how prospective political candidates needed only a list of family names to determine whom it was worthwhile to canvass, those of the opposite political persuasion were not worth the effort. [21] For the young Henry Coutanche, marrying into the staunch Rose family of the Hammonds of La Chasse, St Lawrence, meant becoming one, even if his previous inclination had been towards the Laurel camp. In 1872 he was elected Deputy for St Lawrence on a Rose ticket. [22] Pierre Le Sueur told the Commissioners in 1847 that his voting against Charles Sullivan for director of the Hospital resulted in a formerly staunch Rose family becoming Laurel, a shift which enabled revenge by the promotion of attacks against him. [23]

Family affiliation and personality-dominant politics notwithstanding, a comparison of the records of Jersey's rural parish assemblies in the nineteenth century reveals successive oligarchies whose policies and general attitudes are remarkably similar. Without the newspapers it would be impossible to distinguish Rose dominated parishes from Laurel ones. The most pronounced distinction between parish assemblies in the period is that between St Helier and the country parishes, between urban and rural. In this distinction social and economic policies come to the fore and the allegiances to the camps of Pierre Le Sueur and Francois Godfray become more strictly defined and restricted to Town and country respectively. Serious politics in nineteenth-century Jersey, that is, when economic interests or spheres of power came under threat, had very little to do with the Rose and Laurel parties.

Nonetheless, the importance of the Rose and Laurel parties lay in their ability to politicise the parishioners of even the most distant rural parishes. The result was fiercely contested elections and parishes divided to the extent of each party having a separate tavern, as in St Martin with *The Rose* and *The Crown* one either side of the parish church. [24]

There is no doubt that parish politics were fierce, even allowing for the hyperbole and exaggeration of the partisan press. Conflicting accounts in the local press make it difficult to separate truth from political exaggeration. This is illustrated by the description of the Gibaut/Nicolle election in St John in 1825, which varied from the *Chronique's* report of the agitation of a vast band of hoodlums to the *Constitutional's* claim that everything passed "fort tranquillement". [25] Nonetheless, John Le Couteur's experience of election was a major factor in his decision not to stand for a second term as Connétable of St Brelade. He noted in his diary: "As I find John Pipon is doing everything he can against me, and I am told it is by threats and promises, I commence from today making and securing my own votes....Colonel Pipon came up to me and said he heard that I was 'making use' of his name. I told him in this manner, that if he made votes against me by threats and promises I would report it to the General in order that it might be brought before the Court. We had high words, but I ended by repeating the same thing from the Market Place to the Hospital". [26] On the day of the election, after Sunday service, "I motioned and requested R.C. Remon [the opposing candidate] to come and stand by me. That would have been too friendly by half, so he declined. Colonel John

Pipon stood at the foot of the stairs, trying to hold up a threatening look to the voters who should dare to vote for me....Some looked their Colonel eye to eye....others more nervous passed." [27]

Colonel Pipon's intentions were obvious and his ability to intimidate voters in a parish where he was both a major fief holder - his family held the Fief of Noirmont - and a high ranking Militia officer cannot be doubted, particularly in an open ballot. François Godfray himself was not above pressurising voters who were his tenants, as his attempts, albeit unsuccessful, on the Fief of Chesnel in St John in 1841 showed. [28]

Contested results were commonplace and accusations of vote fixing, threatening behaviour and ungentlemanly practice resulted in numerous court cases. Between 1800 and 1850 the result of one out of every six elections was challenged in the Royal Court. [29] In the parishes of St Ouen (1819-1836) and St Martin (1844-1862) the electorates were without an elected Connétable for over 17 years, because of disputed results; the Chef de Police was obliged to serve in a dual capacity as active policeman and head of the parish. In 1840 the States attempted to settle the problem of parishes being left unrepresented during the course of long court cases, by allowing officers elected by the majority to be sworn in immediately and fulfil their obligations, until it was ruled otherwise. Ironically, the legislation was temporarily halted by the appeal of an unsuccessful candidate in an election for Connétable. Ratification of the Act was withheld by the Privy Council on the grounds that the law would prejudice Philip Duheaume's case pending over an election at St Ouen, where he had lost by three votes. [30]

Once in office a Connétable and his supporters worked hard to ensure their stay was a long one. A minor adjustment to the rating level, which determined the size of the electorate, could make a vital contribution to the election result. Indeed, the preamble to a weak legislative attempt in 1835 to preclude such manipulation noted "que souvent ceux qui formaient la majorité dans les Assemblées de Paroisse, abusant du pouvoir que la loi leur a confié, ont, à la veille d'une élection, dans la vue de favoriser leur candidat, obtenu une rectification du Rât Paroissial". [31] The potential result of such an action was that a ruling clique became an oligarchy, or, as the 1847 Commission put it, the nucleus of a police party, opposition to which of necessity became an anti-police party. [32]

As Figure 7 shows, a ruling oligarchy could maintain control of a parish for a long period, although party dominance most likely belies internal divisions and changes over a number of years in the constitution of the dominant elite. Nineteenth-century Connétables served, on average, terms of six years, that is two electoral terms (an interesting comparison with parish rectors who served, on average, 23 years in a parish: see Chapter 4). Party dominance was clearly carried through from Connétable to Connétable. However, one difficulty in

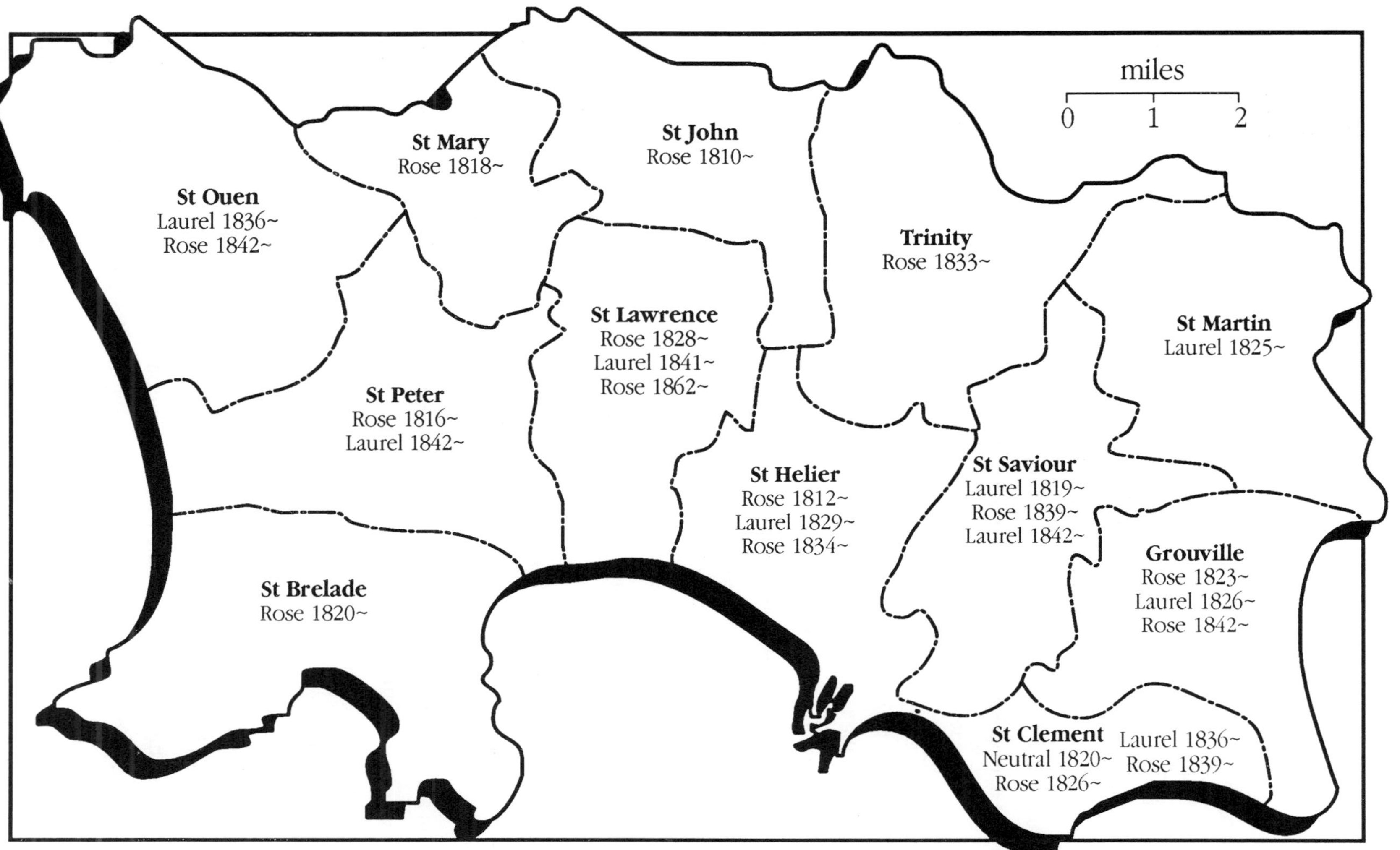

Party dominance by Parish 1810 ~ 1862. ***FIGURE 7.*** *A Map of Parish Politics in Nineteenth-century Jersey* **SOURCE:** *Chronique de Jersey le Constitutionnel.*

ascertaining the extent of party dominance in any one parish is the way in which the interest in the Laurel and Rose factions ebbed and flowed. While St Martin continued to be a Laurel dominated political hotbed for much of the nineteenth century, and St Helier, perhaps not surprisingly, remained Rose dominated, in the other parishes of the Island it is less easy to discern a pattern, other than a general dying down of party politics after about 1850.

The potential for a self-supporting oligarchy to entrench itself was made all the more likely by a clause in the *Loi (1804) sur les Assemblées Paroissiales*, which gave all serving honorary police officers the right to vote in Parish Assemblies, to be extended in the case of Connétables and Centeniers to former officers. [33] The result was, if we take 1847 as an example, that policemen who by rate would have been ineligible to vote outnumbered those who would have been eligible by five to one. In ten parishes, excluding St Helier and St Martin, this police vote accounted for at least one quarter of the Parish Assembly's voting power; in three parishes, St Ouen, St Mary and St Lawrence, its voting power was extended to one half of the total. [34] These figures substantiate the St Ouen's Connétable Thomas Le Cornu's description of the state of his parish and its record of rate assessment in 1861: "It shows that the parish assembly do what they please, upon any point, and that the greatest absurdity might be proposed there and carried by the majority". [35] Earlier in the century, the Reverend Edouard Dupré, Dean of Jersey, had complained to the Commission of 1811 about this very problem, claiming it resulted in men of property (by which one assumes he meant the local gentry) being effectively outvoted by members of the police. [36]

The Reverend Dupré's comment sheds an interesting light on the parish oligarchy. Connétables, and even less so their inferior officers, did not in hierarchical terms represent the leading members of rural society. That is, the parish oligarchy was not controlled by or made up of the wealthiest or most educated of the parish. This much is stated by John Le Couteur and Lieutenant-Governor Gibbs. If we examine the Connétables in the nineteenth century we discover that they were, for the main part, landed proprietors, but accepting that the seigneurs were among the largest landowners in the Island, the absence of lords of the manor is marked. Between 1750 and 1900, something like 27 seigneurs held the post of Connétable out of total of 270 in that office. Twelve of these seigneurs served before 1800. Similarly, only fifteen lawyers and seven Militia Colonels (the most senior local rank) served as Connétables between 1750 and 1900.

There is little detailed information forthcoming on the backgrounds of socially less distinguished Connétables. However, it is apparent that the Connétables constituted a middle-class clique, limited to certain families in each parish. St Mary provides the most extreme example of such clan dominance. The Arthur family, large landowners based at La Falaise, La Pompe and Le Rondin, accounted for 62 years of St Mary's Connetablés in the nineteenth century. Indeed, in 1842 the Arthur family provided the parish's Connétable and two Centeniers. If many gentlemen did not wish to take up the office then perhaps it was, as Le Couteur suggested, that they considered "the situation beneath them". [37] Prior to his election, Le Couteur's friend Thomas Le Breton, Bailiff of Jersey, had suggested "that it would not be quite dignified in a Colonel being a Constable". [38]

The result of such a situation was then, as the Reverend Dupré and Thomas Le Cornu suggested, a parish assembly able to manipulate all parishioners, even the wealthiest members. Thus Philippe Duheaume, a farmer at St Ouen and one of the largest ratepayers, claimed he was ill-treated within his parish because of his unpopularity among the ruling clique. His wealth made it difficult for the parish oligarchy to exclude him from the rate list and thereby from the political arena, so instead, claimed Duheaume, he was subjected to police harassment. [39] Similarly, the Seigneur of St Ouen found his feudal privilege of granting tavern licences in the parish, for which he received a fee, under fire from the Parish Assembly in the late eighteenth century and only with great difficulty obtained a compromise solution.[40]

The parish could be a most powerful instrument in the hands of an unscrupulous oligarchy. For those victim to such an abuse of power there was little chance of respite, at least not until their party came to power. Virulent parish politics were a reflection of this power, as were the desires of the various local factions to obtain control of their Parish Assembly. Yet, as potentially powerful as the parish may have been, it is equally clear that oligarchy rule did not result in massive corruption and the perversion of justice. When talking about abuse in the parish system in nineteenth century Jersey we are really talking about favouritism rather than oppression.

Attitudes to the Parish and the Drive for Reform

This verdict seems to be confirmed by popular attitudes. It is apparent that despite continual disputes about rate assessment and election results, which few parishes escaped, there was no general dissatisfaction with the parish. Complaints in the newspapers amounted to no more than gripes and groans of a partisan and relatively minor nature. The parish was seen as representing and defending the interests of the parishioners. It was an institution well worth preserving.

The great forums for complaints about the parish were the Commissions of 1847 and 1861. It was to the Commissioners that English residents, local townsmen and Parliament looked to highlight the defective nature of Jersey's municipal structure. Yet, seen as a whole, the evidence given to the Commissioners was a vindication of the belief Jerseymen placed in the parish system. Criticism of the policing function was limited and generally absent from the country parishes. Complaints about rate assessment, on the other hand, were more numerous. Some witnesses went to great lengths to prove that rating abuse existed, even providing complex calculations. [41] John Mallet tabulated that the total rateable value of real property in St Ouen was 16,000 quarters, whereas the rate assessment was for only 1,600 quarters; an appreciable gap by any standard. [42] François Bertram, a St Helier merchant, criticised the biased nature of the very system, claiming it was often the wealthy who suffered at the hands of an arbitrary Parish Assembly. [43]

Occasionally, effective action was taken against rate manipulation. Thus the Royal Court ruled against the parish of Trinity in 1835, stating that providing the property owned was sufficient for rating purposes there could be no grounds for excluding individuals from the rate list. [44] In St Ouen, too, Philippe Duheaume was successful in having a rate assessment meeting ruled invalid in 1831 because it took place prior to the passing of the annual accounts. Rates were supposed to be based on the needs of parish finances for the forthcoming year; the setting of rates before the accounts had been ratified was clearly an attempt to manipulate the electorate. Yet it took Duheaume twelve years to obtain a judgement. [45] More generally, however, the only options open to these victims of rating abuse prior to 1879 were silence or, as Stephen Thomas of St Helier told the Commissioners of 1847, a costly appeal to the Royal Court for a rectification. Furthermore, on appeal the only means of redress open to the Royal Court was an order that the appellant be assessed at half the rateable value of his property, considerably more than he would have been otherwise charged. [46].

Rate abuse was clearly a source of much complaint. Yet even the Commissioners of 1861, whilst pointing out the potential for such abuse in the parish system, which often stemmed from personal animosities and self- interest, conceded that this was "the necessary price to be paid for a system of self-government and local independence and self-reliance". [47]

That Jerseymen were generally satisfied with this system, despite certain abuses in its everyday operation, can be shown in several other ways too. For instance, actual prosecutions for abuse of parish authority were few. A.J. Le Cras was convinced that this situation represented the Island looking after its own. "Notwithstanding the numerous complaints which are brought against them ("our political police") to the Crown Officers", he claimed, "only one member of the force, Mr. Ching (St. Helier), has been brought before the Court for the last fourteen years! The motive alleged is that punishment would never follow". [48] The conviction of Centenier Thomas Slater of St Martin for wrongful arrest in 1871 was seen in similar vein by the English press, which claimed it as a moral victory against the indiscriminate powers of parish police. [49] On the other hand, it is possible that the actual number of complaints was small. Those who brought their grievances to the Commission of 1861 were generally bringing complaints about neglect by the police, rather than accusations of discrimination or abuse. In the political climate that prevailed, convictions on such evidence would have been difficult to secure. [50]

Contested elections likewise rarely journeyed right the way through the legal process, one or other of the parties generally conceding. Occasionally, litigants were persistent, as in St Lawrence in 1801 when Jean Poingdestre actioned Philippe Marett, who had beaten him in the election for Connétable by three votes. A Court decision came four years later, against Poingdestre, but in the meantime the parish had gone those four years without a Connétable. [51]

The evidence given to the Commissioners of 1847 and 1861 thus showed a rural community attached to its institutions and a political culture rooted in the legally unrestrained power of the parish. Here was the parish as described by Philippe Falle in the early eighteenth century, a communal organisation thriving on the belief parishioners placed in it. [52]

More significantly, however, as we saw in Chapter 6, the evidence given to the Commissioners showed that, despite widespread discontent with the workings of local institutions, including the parish, native reformists did not require a complete restructuring. Many Town-based reformists were in fact as attached to local institutions as their counterparts in the rural community. None more so than Pierre Le Sueur.

When Pierre Le Sueur, the Connétable of St Helier, whose popularity encompassed English and local reformer alike, was asked by the Commission of 1847 whether he thought that the parish system, the combination of political and peace keeping functions, and the honorary police generally, were beneficial to state and society, his answer rested on two premises. In the first instance, he pointed to the pecuniary question, namely the way in which an honorary service provided a range of services that the state might otherwise find it difficult to afford. Secondly, and he seemed to have some difficulty explaining this, he emphasised the significance of the system as a moral rather than a coercive force in society. The public image and efficiency of the honory police was diminished he felt, by the attacks of the media and the resulting popular feeling. Such opposition originated in political and personal spite, often as a result of an honorary servant carrying out his duty. [53]

Here then was the leader of the local reform movement expressing praise for the value of what was essentially a rural unit in the context of the Town. The broad local attachment to the Island's institutions, represented by Le Sueur's words, had overwhelming repercussions for the cause of reform in the Island. From the outset local reformers were to be hamstrung in the pursuit of their cause by an unwillingness to activate any substantial external interference in local affairs. Thus in a situation of often intense urban dissatisfaction with the operation of local institutions to the detriment of the Town, local reformers were forced to find the main part of the solution from within the Island.

In Pierre Le Sueur was the one hope of a degree of conciliation and accommodation between the Town and the rural bloc on the question of reform. Le Sueur combined a commitment to the cause of reform with a belief in the viability of local institutions. More importantly, his position as leader of the Rose party gave him widespread popular support. His quandary was how to obtain the required reform, for which the support of at least a section of the rural community was required, without alienating his Rose supporters in the country, the effect of which could only be to strengthen a rural/urban divide.

A political clash in 1839 between Pierre Le Sueur and the country States members, led by François Godfray, shows how very difficult Le Sueur's task was. Between 1832 and 1839 the problems aged and often ill Jurats faced in attending meetings of the States and the resulting difficulties the States encountered in obtaining the requisite quorum, meant that the legislature was meeting, on average, no more than five times a year. At a time when States business was growing to meet the demands of a large population and a booming economy, this state of affairs began to prove intolerable. In 1836 François Godfray moved that the quorum should be lowered from the full complement of the house to a sitting of 24 out of the 36 members. [54] Pierre Le Sueur opposed the proposition, albeit unsuccessfully. He appreciated the need for the States to meet on a more regular basis but felt a lower quorum would only serve to further undermine the urban vote. On its present footing, Le Sueur believed his powers of influence and persuasion gave him at least a chance of success in a full legislature. [55]

Le Sueur's belief in his ability to influence the Rose Party Connétables and Jurats was not misplaced, as we have seen, but there was clearly a cut-off point, where such allegiance was superseded by a loyalty to country interests. This cut-off point arose whenever the political or economic priorities of urban and rural blocs were at odds, such as the disputes over the question of tariffs in the first half of the nineteenth century (see Chapter 6). Le Sueur's pursuit of local reform placed an increasing strain on his Rose support in the country.

Le Sueur's hope to reform by a moderate programme, as outlined in Chapter 6, was vain. The whole ethos of Jersey political culture was populistic and therefore suspicious of his rational, moderate policy with its consequently elitist, anglophile overtones. Rose and Laurel voters were not interested in rational arguments. Their politics went little beyond mass participation in party issues. The niceties of liberal argument in the States held little sway over country Connétables of relatively humble status and intellect. At the most basic level, the rural community was motivated by the need to retain country power and profits. This was something François Godfray, as a man himself motivated more by raw politics than debate, understood and it was behind him that the rural bloc closed ranks.

The intransigence of the rural bloc when faced with rational arguments and moderate policies can be observed in its complex dealings with the Royal Jersey Agricultural and Horticultural Society. This institution claimed to represent the agricultural interest, and its efforts to improve the industry scientifically were considerable (see Chapter 3). It was also a tireless pressure group, as seen for example, in its response to Parliament's proposed corn bill in 1835, which threatened to end the Channel Islands' free trade agreement with the United Kingdom. The Society forwarded a petition stressing the Island's charters and privileges, and pointed out "that within the last twenty years the commerce of this Island has increased in a degree probably unequalled in any other spot of equal magnitude on the Globe....That it is alone to be attributed to that most sound of all mercantile principles, freedom from restraints which has caused an unlimited foreign commerce and given an extraordinary impulse to the Capital and Industry of this Island". [56]

The petition was not unlike the numerous representations from the Chamber of Commerce aimed at similar concessions and therein lay the potential for conflict. The Royal Jersey Agricultural and Horticultural Society, like the earlier elitist Chamber of Commerce, was essentially a gentleman's society in the English mould and, whilst it was more than willing to fight to retain export privileges, its economics were far more reasonable than those demanded by the more conservative sections of the rural bloc. François Godfray, the great defender of vested rural interests, presented the 1835 petition. Yet, the measure of agreement reached between the rural bloc and the Society on this issue was not to last.

Godfray was not long in falling out with the Society. He and many of his rural supporters were not keen that the States should subsidise the inducements awarded by the Society for agricultural improvement. The prizes were given to those who contributed to the advance of Island agriculture, be it by the example of their husbandry or by turning out the best animal at the Society's annual show. Godfray claimed that the prizes went to those who did not need the money. In a letter to the *Constitutionnel* in 1838 he requested an explanation as to why funds voted from the public treasury were directed towards prizes subsequently won by the Bailiff, John de Veulle, and the Attorney-General, J.W. Dupré. [57] John Le Couteur, in a letter to Jurat Le Quesne in 1837, had claimed that the States' funding, much of which had gone towards prizes for cottagers, was justified: "None but a prejudiced eye can help perceiving that its [the Island's] general husbandry has advanced. The clean and improved state of the land of the more wealthy farmers has opened the eyes of their poorer neighbours....I lament that a gentleman of Mr Godfray's talents, should so little comprehend the nature of agriculture, it can only be attributable to the prejudices of an early French education". [58] Nonetheless, whilst the grant had been awarded on the condition that all Islanders be eligible to enter the competition, the Society noted that its members also provided some funds towards prizes and that with regard to these funds it "would have been unjust to treat non-subscribers on an equal privilege basis". [59] The initial States grant of 100 in 1834 (somewhat smaller than the sum which subscriptions had provided) was eventually withdrawn in 1842.[60] The unity of the rural bloc on a populist issue had thus been established.

The country parishes showed their displeasure at the Society's social pretensions which matched neither their social inclinations nor their purses. By 1843 subscribers to the Royal Jersey Agricultural and Horticultural Society had been reduced to almost half the original figure of 250 in 1833. [61] By 1846 two parishes, St John and St Clement, had set up their own parish based agricultural societies. They were soon followed by all the country parishes. [62] In the local press it was suggested that something must be wrong with the central body if the zeal and independence of the parish bodies was anything to go by. [63] The Society was slow to respond, but it aimed at a reconciliation and by the 1880s this could be said to have been achieved. By 1883 membership had risen to 511. Nonetheless, the formal division between large and small landowners was retained, with only 100 members being qualified to sit on the committee. [64] In its first fifty years the Society had faced more than its fair share of country intransigence.

The effect of Pierre Le Sueur's moderate programme of reform similarly caused rural Jerseymen to close ranks. Threats to the rural bloc showed how country parishes of the Rose persuasion were continually willing to forsake loyalty to Pierre Le Sueur and the Rose party and adopt a stance more akin to Laurelite politics in defence of their interests. In this respect, a Rose party oligarchy in St John was not much different from a Laurel dominated St Clement (1836-1839) or St Ouen (1836-1842). When it came to protectionist economic policies for the local market or defence against incursions of parish power there was little to separate country parishes. Thus to look at the Parish Assembly of St John in December, 1846, (a meeting against ideas mooted in the Town to abolish the honorary system) and those of St Clement in August, 1848, (a meeting to formulate a programme of opposition to the Report of the Commissioners of 1847) and St Ouen in June, 1840, (where parishioners refused to contribute to the Town harbour), is to observe parishes whose party affiliations had been discarded for a far more basic and binding allegiance, that of the rural bloc. [65]

The drive for reform, as we have seen, was generally a failure. Pierre Le Sueur's moderate programme failed to obtain any of the major reforms required by the Town. What then must be the verdict on Le Sueur?

It is clear that Pierre Le Sueur overestimated his own ability to sway public opinion. However, given the circumstances, namely the strength of the rural bloc in the States and the decision of native reformers to work within the system, he had little alternative other than to move for reform with his powers of persuasion and argument. His popular following within local party politics must have given him some hope of obtaining a measure of country support.

Le Sueur's dilemma was that of a conflict of allegiances. He was not alone in this regard. In an island where even Colonel John Le Couteur, a committed anglophile generally at pains to elevate himself above local conflicts, could exhibit a staunch parochialism, the divisions between town and country were obviously complex. In a petition to the Privy Council in 1840, demanding an end to the favouritism shown to St Helier's harbour and recognition of St Brelade's right to an equal share of the impôts, Le Couteur pointed out that "Our case has never been fairly debated in Jersey....when our representative has risen in the States, to express the wishes and claims of his Parishioners, the Gallery have saluted him with hoots and hisses which have wholly disconcerted him, indeed, in this and other popular cases, the States far from being indiscriminately open, are governed by the Gallery....The Townspeople being on the spot, take possession of the seats, and if the country people, when having an opposite interest, wished to get in to answer clamour by clamour, they could not, which is so far fortunate".[66] For Le Sueur the problem was even more poignant. He was the only individual in mid-nineteenth-century Jersey with the potential to bridge the gap between a reformist Town and a conservative countryside.

If there was a miscalculation on Le Sueur's part, it was in his failure to understand that a rational programme of reform ill-suited the ethos of Jersey political culture. That reform which was achieved was forced by pressure from the Privy Council in the 1850s. This pressure was the sort of power politics that the rural community understood and to which it responded. Liberal arguments and moderation held little sway in the countryside. By the end of the nineteenth century, rural control of the States and the overlap of legislative and judicial power, evident all at levels of Jersey, society, remained more or less intact. The politics of the parish prevailed.

Accommodation and Limited Reform

The sudden death of Pierre Le Sueur in 1853 at the age of 41 brought the era of reform, at least in its fullest form, to an untimely end.[67] His departure also brought closer the demise of local party politics; the Rose and Laurel parties had been so tied up with the personalities of the two main protagonists that the loss of Le Sueur undermined much of its raison d'être.

The Laurels remained headed by François Godfray. Le Sueur's death left him as the leading politician, and he used the mantle to introduce some limited reform.[68] That change which was instigated drew much from the tireless efforts of Le Sueur in the 1830s and 1840s. Indeed, his death coincided with, in certain respects perhaps even caused, these moves to a partial reform.

Some reform was, as has been seen in Chapter 6, forced upon the rural bloc by the Privy Council in 1852 and this blatant threat of intervention was taken up as a basis for further minor concessions to the urban community. It was accommodation, but the fact that the reform was rural dispensed and rural controlled meant that in reality it amounted to little. The logical means to redress the unequal share of power between the Town and the rural community was by an increase in popular representation in St Helier's favour. This required a replacement of the existing equality-of-parish pattern with something more representative of St Helier's share of the Island's population and wealth. Electoral reform had been mooted as early as 1784 when 'l'Ami d'une réforme' had suggested a change in the constitution of the assembly, the number of elected representatives from each parish to be based on its value to the Island economy. [69] The issue was brought to the fore of the Jersey reformist agenda in the 1830s and 1840s.

In the reformist demands of this period the argument for an economic basis to popular representation distinguished the commercial element of the urban bloc from the political reformers. The Parish Assembly of St Helier reflected both. The economic argument was not unreasonable. In 1836 the rural bloc chose to assess the Town's contribution to an all-Island rate on the basis that its greater wealth meant it should pay more than other parishes. This resulted in outrage from the Chamber of Commerce and the Parish Assembly. [70] Not surprisingly, there followed a demand from the Town for political representation to be similarly based on parish wealth and contribution to the Island economy. [71]

Pierre Le Sueur's concept of political representation was far more concerned with the number of popularly elected members. In the early years of his political career in the 1830s he lobbied for the introduction of parish Centeniers to the States to undermine the rôle of the non-elected clergy and the Jurats. The idea was turned down by the Parish Assembly of St Helier, but it is interesting to note that Le Sueur's feelings on the subject were similar to those of François Godfray, who actually presented the successful 1854 legislation which created the office of Deputy. [72]

In the event, the *Jersey Times'* lament that the introduction of States Deputies would be achieved only when the Connétables could be persuaded to "quietly allow their franchise to be made at once beautifully less", appeared unnecessary. [73] The *Loi (1854) sur l'augmentation du nombre des membres des Etats* was passed without any real opposition from the country. [74] Its instigation marked a real triumph for the lobbying power of local reformers who had roused the Privy Council into appointing the Commission of 1846, which recommended the reconstitution of the legislature. [75] The threat of Privy Council interference in the wake of the three Orders in Council of 1852, was no doubt a major influence.

Nonetheless, the reform passed through the States because the rural bloc allowed it to do so. Indeed, the country played a major rôle, not only in François Godfray's presentation of the Projet, but in the longer term lobbying, since eight rural parishes had joined with Pierre Le Sueur and the Jersey Reform Society in 1839 to forward a petition signed by 3,500 for an increase in popular representation. [76]

The Deputies were the first members of the legislature whose sole electoral purpose was to serve in the States. Out of fourteen Deputies, St Helier gained three and the other parishes got one each. Article 8 of the Law attempted to make the Deputy distinct from the Parish Assembly and the Connétable; he was to have no parish function as such. [77] Like the other members of the legislature, the Deputies would combine their rôle in the States with another occupation.

If the Town felt it had gained a victory, the celebrations were marred by several considerations. In the first instance, St Helier remained potentially out-voted by the country's barely diminished voting power. Secondly, the apparent readiness of the parish oligarchies to have their voting powers lessened was undermined, as predicted by the English press, by the Island's Parish Assemblies adopting the office of Deputy as one of their own. To observe the roll lists of Deputies after 1854, with the possible exception of St Helier, is to see a veritable reflection of the parish clique.

In 1860 François Godfray was almost the Parish Assembly incarnate and his election as Deputy for St Saviour seemed to prove that the office had been embraced as yet another parish representative. His immediate predecessor, the Wesleyan reformist Elie Neel, had gone even further in the parish direction, suggesting a regular electors' surgery prior to States meetings to discuss voting and lines of argument. The *Jersey Times*, dismayed at the prospect of such "familiar electoral evenings", could only warn, "If he carries out these cosy meetings his general views will have a tendency to be narrowed into local ones and he himself to be reduced to a sort of second Constable". [78]

By 1885 it is clear that the parishioners of St John considered their Deputy as just another representative. The Parish Assembly decided that being insufficiently acquainted with the subject to be discussed in the forthcoming session of the States "elle leur laisse [the Deputy and the Connétable] avec confiance toute liberté d'action". [79] The parish of Trinity, by contrast, was not quite so blatant in its treatment of the Deputy, suggesting it had "a l'unaminité chargé le Connétable de voter, dans les Etats, contre la demande des Petitionnaires" (in this case, a demand for the reform of the Royal Court)" priant le Recteur et le Deputé d'en faire autant". [80] Nonetheless, it was clear in both parishes that the office of Deputy had been embraced within the traditions of the honorary system.

From an urban point of view, one of the most fruitful developments resulting from the introduction of the office of Deputy was the formation of a local Reform League, which put up three candidates in the first St Helier election in 1857 and won two seats. One of those victorious, Clement Hemery, showed the parish link by becoming Connétable of St Helier in 1873. [81] The Reform League, nonetheless, reflected the local consciousness for home-spun reform and naturally became the acceptable face of such reform.

The increase in popular representation had been achieved with rural support and it follows that reforms without such ease of passage through the States found progress difficult. The *Loi (1854) sur l Police Salariée* is a case in point. [82] The demand for a paid police force had run alongside the demand for increased political representation in the 1830s, but it had not gained the support of the country reformers. The rural opposition to such a proposal was understandable since it threatened to undermine a major rôle of the parish, its honorary police force. It was obvious, claimed the Parish Assembly of St Ouen in 1846, that a paid police force "entrainerait des frais considérables, et ne saurait offrir aux personnes des citoyens ni aux propriétés plus de sécurité que n'offre la police telle qu'elle existe aujourd'hui, et dont les fonctions sont gratuites. Qu'en détruisant la police actuelle, ce serait saper par les fondemons toutes les institutions à l'ombre et que l'égide desquelles le pays à atteint le haut degré de prosperité ou nous voyens aujourd'hui". [83]

The considerable growth of the Town had by 1840 resulted in a serious law and order problem. The Commissioners of 1847 were given statistics which showed that between 1835 and 1845, 2,112 offenders appeared before the Royal Court, 1,264 of whom were English, Irish and Scottish, and 178 foreigners. [84] In 1840 the States responded with legislation which increased the number of St Helier Centeniers and increased the powers of the subordinate officers of Vingteniers and Officiers du Connétable. [85] It was a traditional response to a modern problem. But reformers were demanding a round-the-clock protection force, and did not consider the changes adequate. [86]

In the event the *Trois Ordres du Conseil* of 1852 forced the establishment of a salaried police force and the legislation was included in the States compromise of *Six Actes des États*[87] Yet, despite the external pressure of 1852, the new police force was fashioned so as to present no threat to traditional structures. The new force did not have the extensive powers of the honorary police, its officers were the salaried equivalent of Officiers du Connétable. Likewise, there was little freedom from parish control as officers were to be chosen by a States Committee and under the direct control of the Connétable of St Helier.

Reflecting the view, noted in 1848 by General Touzel, the Queen's Receiver, that the country would not pay for anything which had no obvious direct benefit to itself, the cost of the salaried police was to be met jointly by the revenue of the Port (one third) and the ratepayers of St Helier (two thirds). [88] By 1860, however, the distinction between town and country had become even finer when it was decided that the police rate should be raised "sur celles de la Ville de St Hélier en raison du montant du loyer,....et sur celles des Vingtaines Rurales en raison de la moitié du loyer". [89]

The legislation establishing the salaried police force and the elective office of Deputy, and the way these institutions were developed and adapted by both the rural and urban communities tell us much about what divided or united the two blocs and how concessions and limited compromise could minimise the potential for conflict.

The local desire to thwart the kind of external involvement most successfully mobilised by A.J. Le Cras and to introduce limited reforms was sufficient to soften temporarily the rural/ urban divide. [90] This is most evident in the partisan newspapers, whose general silence on local divisions during the visit of the 1847 Commissioners showed a concern for the image the Island might project which transcended the perpetual need to score points in the political sphere. The *Chronique* joyfully proclaimed that "Rosiers et Lauriers, sont également désireux de coopérer à la défense de la cause commune". [91] The Parish of St Helier was as concerned as any of the country parishes about the implications of the Crown appointed Commission of 1847. [92]

By 1852 both party politics and rural/urban confrontation had resumed, although Rose and Laurel affiliation was in diminished form (see Figure 7.). [93] The general truce had been too much for that most political of parishes, St Martin, whose parishioners continued to contest elections with traditional vigour. [94] The Island-wide elections for Deputy in 1857, however, generated little political rancour. [95] This, and the general decline of party politics, were in large part the result of the sudden death of Pierre Le Sueur in 1853. Nonetheless, party politics and traditions of partisan voting could still influence events up to the 1870s and 1880s, as Rose candidates in St Helier discovered to their disadvantage in the more rural parts of the parish, but generally such divisions become less easy to discern. [96]

The demise of party politics had but little effect on the power of the rural bloc in the States and its support in the parishes. When exasperated St Helier ratepayers petitioned the Queen in 1880 for more Deputies for the Town they claimed it was a last ditch attempt, after being thwarted so many times in the States "by a large majority entirely composed of country members". [97]

Law books for the nineteenth century provide further evidence of how the rural community forestalled any movements towards a reform of the parish structure and its everyday running by making minimalist and superficial changes. The recommendations of both the Commission of 1847 and of 1861 that the more abusable workings of the parish, namely rate assessment and parish finances, be effectively reformed were to all intents and purposes evaded. In 1900 it was still technically possible for the rate lists to be manipulated and elections to be influenced.

In 1879 the *Loi sur la Taxation du Rât* established oathed Comités de Taxation in every parish to assess the rateable value of every property in the parish on a regular basis.[98] A show was made of the fact that the Royal Court was regulating proceedings, when at the first oath-taking of members in 1880, the younger of two members from the St Brelade's committee, who were shown to be related by marriage, was forced to stand down because of the potential for abuse.[99] In reality, however, the committees were just a delegation of parish power to its trusted members, paralleled by committee delegation in other parish business, and the potential for abuse remained.

Elections and questions of procedure received much legislative treatment. As early as 1814 an amendment to the *Loi (1804) sur les Assemblées Paroissiales*, which had provided the first statutory definition of the parish, stipulated that prior to all elections a "billet de convocation" had to be produced, recorded and followed to the letter in parish meetings, interrupted only by motions proposed from the floor.[100] Similarly, some form of order was established regarding the manipulation of rates to vary the size of the electorate. By the *Loi (1835) sur le Rât Paroissial et les Élections Publiques* the revision of rate lists immediately prior to elections was prohibited. At the same time, the Royal Court was given official status as the court of electoral appeal and its new powers included the ability to inspect voting lists.[101] In 1859 Centeniers were excluded from voting in elections and parish meetings ex-officio.[102] And in 1897 the election ballot was made secret.[103]

Nonetheless, this body of legislative guidelines and definitions, aimed at the parish, left a communal structure generally free of statutory restriction and reliant on common law and tradition for its everyday running. Only the *Loi (1804) sur les Assemblées Paroissiales* had made any attempt at a definition of the parish and, even this, had only involved its two chief officers, the Rector and the Connétable.[104]

The power of the parish could be observed in the landscape. Throughout the Island magnificent new municipal halls, such as those of St Saviour (1890) and St John (1912), and substantial parish schools, like St Mary's (1901), were established. These buildings shared the pre-eminence of the parish centre with the church, which for so long had stood alone as the focus of the community.[105] This change in the landscape reflected a parish that had grown at the expense of the Church, a Church which found its religious rôle challenged by Nonconformism and its secular rôle increasingly restricted by law.[106] It reflected a rural bloc that had successfully staved off attack on its power base.

The rural community in nineteenth-century Jersey managed to retain both its power and its institutional structures relatively unscathed. This successful defence was most evident in its most important communal unit, the parish, which hung on to, indeed strengthened, its position amidst the Jersey community. It was a position reached with few concessions to the demands for reform. More significantly, it was a state of affairs obtained with the tacit support of the native urban reformists.

Far from the picture of large scale abuse and injustice presented by some observers, the Jersey parish was an institution cherished by the members of its community. Virulent party politics reflected a healthy involvement in a communal outlet for a society whose major characteristic was individualism. Hostility between political camps and inter-parish rivalries ran deep but was based on personal and family allegiances. These affinities could easily be transcended in the defence of the rural bloc.

From the outset native urban reformers found themselves in a difficult quandary. From the 1830s onwards it became apparent that the degree of pressure required to force the desired reforms necessitated external involvement. Heavy lobbying, particularly by the outcast Le Cras movement, and a perceived groundswell of popular discontent activated these external forces, most ominously in the shape of Parliament. The native urban bloc was now faced with more than simple realignment of its traditional structures; those very structures now seemed in danger. Furthermore, the possibility of external interference raised a threat to the Island's hard won independence, viewed by many as the very basis to Jersey's nineteenth-century commercial success.

Pierre Le Sueur attempted to obtain the required reform by moderate means. Generally speaking, this policy was ineffectual and bore minimal fruit and even then only after Le Sueur's death and the intervention of the Privy Council. A moderate and rational reform programme held little sway amongst a rural community whose political ethos was populistic. The rural bloc remained motivated only by the need to retain power and profits.

In the event the urban native reformers were obliged to quell the forces of Parliament and the Privy Council that they themselves had helped to activate. The rural/urban divide which had originated in the rapid changes undergone by Jersey in the earlier part of the century, was transcended by a more basic allegiance to the Island and its traditional institutions. Reconciliation was achieved by this basic accord between the Le Sueur and Godfray camps. In this shared past and affiliation to local independence lay the failure of the nineteenth-century reform movement in Jersey.

Chapter 8

Demographic Patterns: Urban Change and Rural Stability

If one thing maintained continuity within the rural community during the course of the nineteenth century it was demographic stability. In the face of a dramatic increase in the Island's population, the result of large scale English immigration, rural Jersey retained a stable population. This was to have certain implications for the rural community's ability to isolate itself from anglicising influence and retain its identity.

Between 1821 and 1851 the population of Jersey doubled from 28,600 to a peak century figure of 57,155. [1] Rural parishes played but a small part in the increase. The main thrust of demographic change derived from the large number of English immigrants who chose to settle in the Island. By 1851 they numbered almost 12,000, constituting 21 per cent of Jersey's total population.

Yet, despite the small size of the Island, English immigration did not advance beyond the southern hills. St Helier, the main port of entry for immigrants, remained their main location. The spread of urban settlement was along the southern coastline, bringing significant English populations to the southern parts of St Saviour, St Lawrence and St Clement. The majority of rural parishes, however, remained comparatively isolated from these changes. English immigrants simply did not venture into the domain of the rural community in any great number. A landscape of intensive agriculture and widespread individual ownership held little interest or prospect of economic gain for English residents, and it was popularly believed that no Englishman could ever farm in Jersey. [2] In 1851 the relatively accessible parish of St John, for example, numbered only 50 English people in a population of 2,021. St Saviour's English population, by stark contrast, made up a quarter of its residents.

The absence of an English presence in the countryside ensured the maintenance of a relatively undisturbed native culture. Even parishes with English urban settlement in their southern extremes were able, often to a great extent, to discount immigrant influence. The French language, for instance, could remain substantially unaffected, the only contact coming through those who visited the Town. Similarly, Parish Assemblies could make decisions about Jersey's social and economic policy without having to consider English interests.

But rural demographic stability did not mean demographic inactivity. In fact natural increase rates in the countryside were healthy. Population growth was regulated by a combination of migration, the traditions of peasant proprietorship and local land laws. In the face of a limited supply of land and family wealth, rural folk thus ensured the perpetuity of the household by actively discouraging younger children from remaining tied to the family home.

By the 1880s this rural self-regulation was put to the test when French migrant workers decided to settle in the Jersey countryside. If parish populations were to remain steady, the influx of Bretons required a corresponding outflow of natives, the prospect of which bore the hallmarks of a cultural threat. This immigration, as the next chapter will show, was to play a rôle in focusing the attention of the rural community on the nature of its identity.

Population Movements 1800-1881

The three decades after 1821 marked the demographic transformation of Jersey. Large scale immigration took place, mainly English in origin and covering a broad occupational strata. As Figure 8 shows, the result of this influx was the doubling of the Jersey population in thirty years.

1806	1821	1831	1841	1851
22,855	28,600	36,582	47,544	57,155*

**Local census reports occasionally differ in exact totals, although the numbers involved are small.*
FIGURE 8: *The Population of Jersey 1806-1851*

It is interesting to note that the early increase between 1806 and 1821 was not only sustained up to 1851, but actually accelerated, suggesting that the economic potential of a large population drew in more people than ever before. The net immigration figure, obtained by correlating the statistics for natural increase and total population change, shows that the influx of 4,344 between 1821 and 1831 was more than matched by the 7,513 between 1831 and 1841 (See Figure 9.). In the latter period, Jersey was hit quite severely by an attack of cholera in 1832, causing the death of nearly one per cent (348) of the people, mainly in the urban parts of St Helier which sustained 77 per cent of the mortalities. [3]

In the period 1841 to 1851 the rate of population increase diminished slightly, with a smaller net immigration of 5,476. This period marks the beginning of major local emigration to the British colonies, although it is clear that substantial numbers of outsiders were still choosing the Island as a place to live. [4] A causative factor in the slight decrease in net immigration was the economic crisis of the 1840s, a period of commercial slump and low wages which culminated in the ship-carpenters' Town Mills riot in St Helier in 1847. [5] There was also a further cholera outbreak in 1849 which claimed 300 lives. [6]

Year	Natural Increase	Total Change in Population	Net Immigration
1821-31	3,638	7,982	+4,344
1831-41	3,448	10,962	+7,513
1841-51	4,000	9,476	+5,476
1851-61	4,035	-1,407	-5,442
1861-71	3,401	1,014	-2,387
1871-81	1,864	-2,073	-1,237
1891-1901	2,069	-1,9426	-4,011

FIGURE 9. *Net Immigration in Jersey 1821-1901.*

In such a small Island the substantial population increase might be expected to have been spread throughout the territory but, on the contrary, it was absorbed almost solely by St Helier and parts of the surrounding parishes, notably St Saviour (see Figures 10. and 11. for population data for St Helier and the Island's country parishes in the nineteenth century). In 1821 St Helier, already growing as a result of the French Wars, contained 36 per cent of the Island's population. By 1841 this had increased to 50 per cent, reaching an all-time high for the period under review in 1871, ironically at a time of population decline, with 54 per cent. This figure was sustained with only marginal loss until the end of the century.

The parish of St Saviour, whose boundaries include some of the lowland area upon which the Town of St Helier rests, was the only other parish to increase its share in population. Yet, a marginal increase in share, from 5.9 per cent in 1821 to 7.4 per cent in 1881, belied a population that grew from 1,687 to 3,890 in the same period. That the increase was mainly made up of immigrants and migrants can be gauged from the fact that St Saviour's natural increase between these years contributed only 463 people to a growth of 2,203. The parish of St John, in strong contrast, saw its population stagnate: 1,657 in 1821, to 1,699 in 1881. Its share of the total population decreased from 5.8 per cent to 3 per cent. The natural increase in the same period was 1,051, a figure which shows that many St Jeannais left the parish in search of a life elsewhere.

The rapid population increase of 1821-1851, sustained by substantial immigration (see Figure 9), suffered a reverse in the period 1851-1861, when the total Island population dropped by 1,407. A slight stabilisation in the period 1861-1871 was followed by the greatest decennial loss of the century in the period 1871-1881, when the fall was 4,182. A further decrease of 2,073 was experienced between 1881 and 1891, with a small drop of 1,942 in the following decade. The census figures show a net emigration from Jersey of nearly 14,000

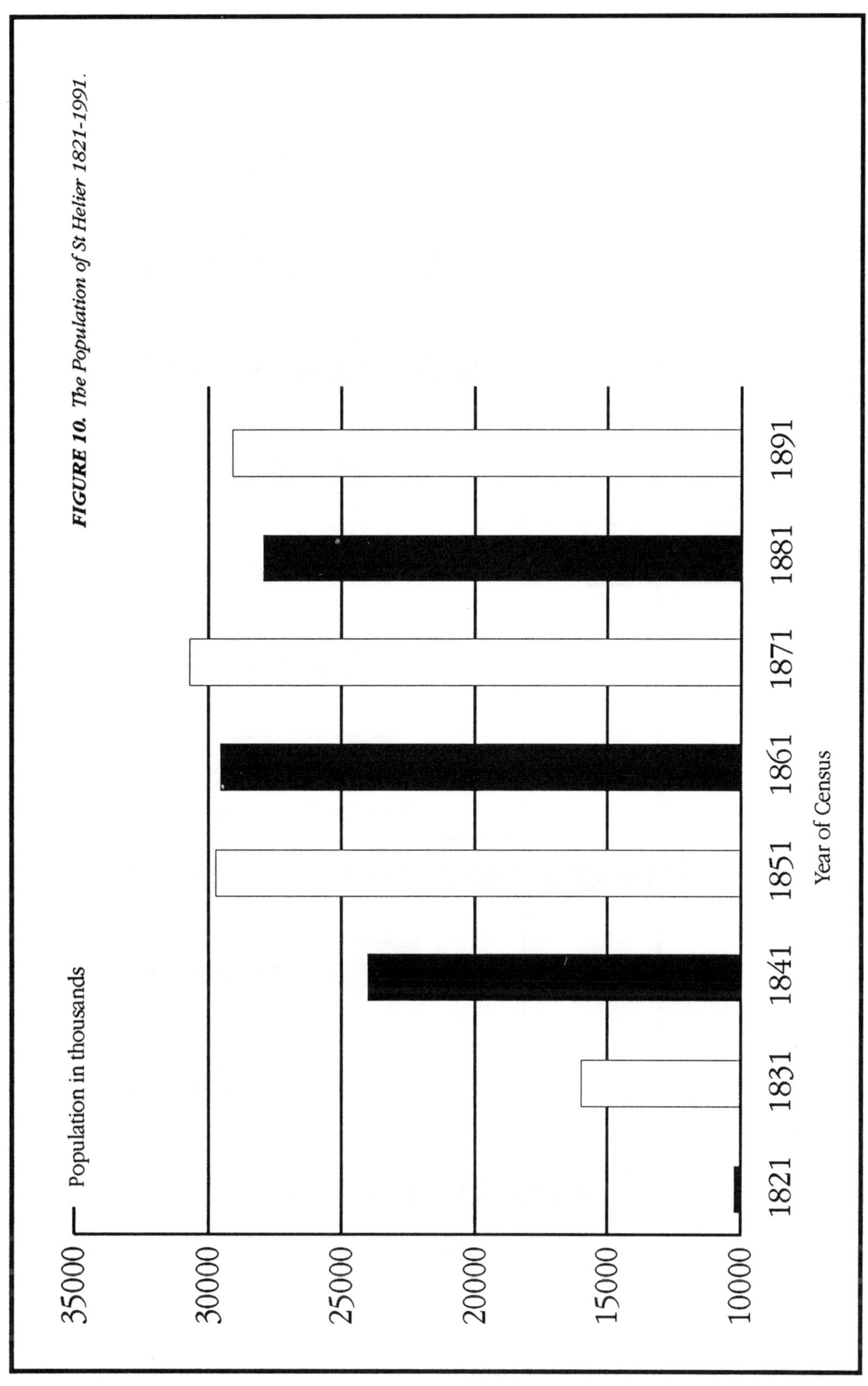

FIGURE 10. *The Population of St Helier 1821-1991.*

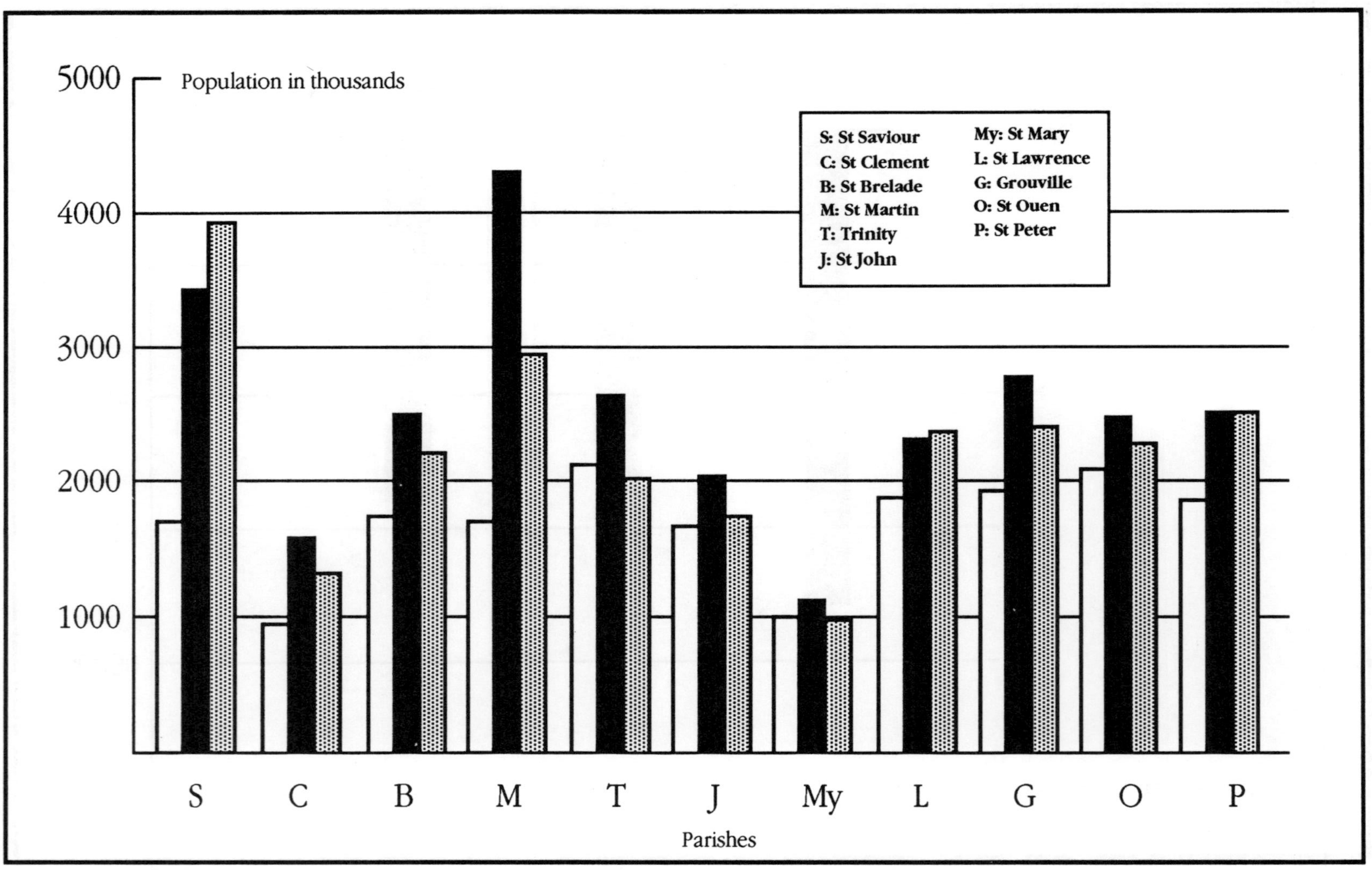

***FIGURE 11.** Parish Populations (excluding St Helier) 1821, 1851 and 1881.*

between 1851 and 1881 . Most of this loss was made up of artisans of non-local origin and their families, forced to leave the Island in search of work elsewhere. Some of this loss, and we cannot be certain as to a figure, included local artisans.

In the period 1851 to 1881, only St Saviour, St Peter and St Lawrence did not experience a decrease in population, their urban zones providing a catchment area for both internal migration away from the country and the movement outwards from St Helier. Of those parishes seeing a decrease the parish of St Martin lost by far the highest number, over 32 per cent of its 1851 population; this is largely explained by the completion of the St Catherine's harbour project and the decline of the Gorey oyster fisheries which resulted in the dispersal of a large labour force numbering, at its peak, over 3,000 people. [7] In every parish which lost population the major loss was experienced among the artisanal group, which more than outweighed gains in the same parishes in the number of labourers.

The decline in population, particularly non-local, in the latter half of the nineteenth century was a direct result of the economic crises and the collapse of the external trading structure in the 1870s and 1880s. The cod trade, carrying trade and shipbuilding industry were the major employers of artisans and labourers in the Island. The scale of these industries for such a small Island reflected their world-wide scope, but this breadth of operation left them subject to influences outside their control. From about 1850 a shift in the maritime policies of the great powers and rapid technological change left the Jersey merchant sector unable to adapt at the pace required.

The collapse of the sugar market in the West Indies and the advent of the iron hulled steamship undermined the carrying trade by cutting freight charges. It also destroyed the successful local shipbuilding industry, which was unable to raise the amount of capital investment required to convert from wooden to iron construction. The many sided attack on the merchant triangle was completed by the local bank crashes of 1873 and 1886 which silenced the large trading concerns, most notably the firm of C.R. Robin. The collapse of the merchant and commercial sector, which in the codfisheries alone had employed 4,000 workers in the 1840s, left a large urban workforce of artisans and labourers unemployed. [8] Whilst the port of St Helier, busy with agricultural export, tourism and consumer imports, required many of the various trades offered by such a work-force, it would have offered work to only a section of them. Some of those left unemployed in St Helier moved on in search of work elsewhere, mainly men and their families who were non-local in origin.

A sample study of the population of St Helier in 1851 and 1881 enables an analysis of this outflow. [9] Overall, St Helier, which in real terms lost only 6 per cent of its population in the period, saw its non-local inhabitants decrease by 7 per cent. With the exception of French and foreign (that is, not English, Irish or Channel Island) immigrants, who increased their share of St Helier's population in the same period from 2.2 per cent to 7 per cent and from 0.8 per cent to 3 per cent respectively, all non-local groups had decreased in number by 1881. The English immigrant share of the Town decreased from 24.5 per cent to 17.6 per cent, Irish residents from 5.4 per cent to 4 per cent, and settlers from the other Channel Islands from 3 per cent to 2.4 per cent. St Helier's population of Jersey rural origins decreased by 2 per cent, although no obvious pattern emerges. Some parishes, like St Lawrence, St Mary and St Brelade, increased their presence in St Helier, while that of others, like St John and St Clement, declined. The main St Lawrence increase was in labourers, the main St Brelade's increase was in artisans and labourers.

The sample study of St Helier shows the non-local artisans (excluding the French, who were poorly represented in this group) to be the occupational group hardest hit by economic recession, declining by 19 per cent. This contrasts with non-local labourers who increased by 9 per cent. Clearly artisans left the Island in significant numbers in this period.

The rural contribution to emigration is difficult to quantify, as is its connection with the economic crises in the post-1850 period. Nonetheless, like the parish of St Helier, each of the eight country parishes that experienced population loss did so in its artisanal workforce, and in a countryside which as yet remained generally isolated from non-local inhabitants this meant a loss of its indigenous inhabitants. St John, for instance, saw its number of artisans almost halved from 260 in 1851 to 164 in 1881. Again, labourers by contrast increased from 208 to 279, farmers, too, experiencing an increase.

In documentation other than census material rural artisans are conspicuous by their absence, something which hinders understanding of their movements. Census material reveals that as a group they were scattered around the countryside. If we look at St John in 1851, a totally rural parish, male artisans numbered 187 and included: 48 carpenters, 31 cobblers, 16 blacksmiths, 13 stone masons, ten shipwrights, two thatchers and one baker. If we add to this the 73 women who listed their occupation as dressmaker, we have a significant skilled labour force in a parish of 2,021 people. By 1881 the 260 strong artisanal force of 1851 had decreased to 164.

Tracing the St John-born population between 1851 and 1881 gives some guide to what may have happened to country artisans. In the five St Helier districts studied St John's born people made up 1.9 per cent of the 1851 population and were composed of 29 per cent labourers, 13 per cent artisans, 10 per cent independent, 6 per cent managerial, 2 per cent farmers and 40 per cent dependents. If these figures can be taken as a fair representation of the St Jeannais presence in the whole of St Helier, then they numbered roughly 565 individuals. By 1881 the St John's presence in these districts had declined to 1.4 per cent of the population, its biggest decrease being in labourers, whose number halved over the period. Numerically the artisan population stayed the same. The total St Jeannais population in the Town had decreased to roughly 392. The nearby partially urbanised parishes of St Saviour and St Clement show an increase in their St John's presence in the same period. St Saviour's population in 1851 included 19 people from St John, three of whom were artisans. By 1881 this figure had increased to 43, with six artisans. In St Clement a population which had actually declined by 15 per cent between 1851 and 1881 saw its St John's-born artisans rise from three to nine. However, the rest of the Island shows a different pattern. St Ouen, a wholly rural parish, increased its share of St John's-born people from 16 to 31, but it was an increase composed of labourers. Both Grouville and St Brelade experienced a decline in their St John's presence.

So where did all the parish-based St John's artisans of 1851 go? This is a difficult question to answer with certainty. Some of these artisans took advantage of the agricultural boom in the 1880s and became farmers. It would appear that agriculture remained fairly immune from the commercial problems of 1873 and 1886. It certainly aroused little concern from the Royal Jersey Agricultural and Horticultural Society. [10] The rural industry had experienced its own problems in the wake of the potato blight of 1848 and, as we observed in Chapter 3, agriculture did not fully recover until the 1880s. But the number of people employed in agriculture, both farmers and labourers, increased between 1851 and 1881. In St John's Vingtaine de Douet in 1881 at least five individuals listed as young artisans in 1851 had become farmers. Others too must have taken this path.

But agriculture does not hold all the answers. Bearing in mind the fact that the country remained comparatively unaffected by the economic difficulties of the 1870s and 1880s, we must seek other reasons for the decline in country artisans. It is possible that some of the services offered by country artisans were being offered increasingly by the Town, necessitating a move to a more urban environment, such as St Saviour or St Clement, or a change of profession.

It is clear, however, that a number of St Jeannais must have left the Island. As a rough guide to this exodus, we can combine natural increase figures with parish population statistics and the estimated effect of natural mortality rates. Between 1851 and 1881 St John had a natural increase of 389 people. If no-one had left the parish, its 1881 population total would have been at least 2,410 instead of 1,699. In other words, there was an outflow of some 711 St Jeannais in the period. The country parishes, as we have seen, account for a certain number of this group, roughly 270, if an average is taken of the parishes analysed. But where did the other 441 go? Some must have gone to St Helier, but its St Jeannais population was in decline, down from 565 in 1851 to 392 in 1881. The latter figure would have included some infill of those St Jeannais who died in the thirty year period, but equally there must have been

St John's born individuals present in both counts. Given the steep decline in the Town's share of St Jeannais, it is a reasonable assumption that it took only a small proportion of the 441. It follows, therefore, that several hundred St Jeannais must have gone abroad in the period. Jerseymen, as will become apparent in the following sub-section, were taking advantage of the opportunities of the New World.

Patterns of Emigration and Immigration

Explicit information about emigration from the Island is derived mainly from the newspapers. The letters from the colonies which newspapers printed, and their general coverage of the potential of Australia, Canada and the United States, reflect public interest in the possibility of leaving Jersey. The correspondence from abroad appealed mainly to two groups, artisans with a skilled trade, and those experienced in agriculture.

Artisans were in demand abroad. One young man, writing in 1889, declared, "Being in the same position as a number of young men in Jersey and seeing no prospect of advancement before me, I have been latterly turning my attention towards other countries with a view to emigration". He contacted an ex-Centenier living in Texas in the United States, who replied "I wish to say that if you know any good carpenters (ship preferred) to do heavy bridge work on the railroads, I could find work for quite a number at 10s and 12s a day, board and lodging costing £4 a month".[11] Joshua Le Sueur, writing from Australia in 1853, stated that carpenters could earn up to 25s a day, watchmakers £2 a day and sailmakers 30s.[12] To artisans like the shipwrights who were earning 3s per day in 1853, such possibilities must have sounded most alluring.[13]

To country folk the colonies offered cheap and unlimited land. From the town of Marion, Iowa, in 1849, a local man detailed the requirements for fitting out a farm and six months provision: "Now here is your farm of 200 vergées, of which 100 vergées is cultivated and fenced, and good stock to begin with, and a house and stables built, for £200. Our passage from Jersey to Liverpool, from Liverpool to New Orleans and from Marion, State of Iowa, for four persons, cost about £50, provisions included, of course with strict economy". The editorial response to this no doubt paralleled what many were thinking, "Now, how many young country men in Jersey may have 18 quarters (wheat rentes) or the value of £300. What a fine chance there would be in such a country as this to become a great farmer and live in the "enjoyment of plenty".[14]

For some, as elsewhere in the British Isles, the impetus to leave was magnified by the possibilities of a quick path to riches in the wake of the Australian Gold Rush in 1851. In February, 1852, the schooner *Adolphus Yates* left Guernsey with a group of six to dig for gold, passage and diggings support being provided free in return for a share of the find.[15] In Jersey

95 people left the Island for Australia on the *Exact*, a special Ecclesiastical Court sitting being necessary to ensure all had the necessary registry documents. [16] In all, it has been estimated that as many as 6,000 people may have left the Channel Islands for Australia between 1852 and 1855. [17]

If the emigrants on the *Exact* (See Figure 12) can be taken as being representative of both emigration in the 1850s and the type of people going to Australia, it is interesting to note that Jersey-born people constituted 71 of the 95 passengers. Nearly half of this group were artisans, mainly carpenters, and only eight of them were taking family along. Perhaps curiously, there were no labourers, although in general terms this may be related to problems encountered in raising the necessary fare. [18] Ironically, since the passenger list of the *Exact* provides a rare source in this field, it appears that the ship arrived in Melbourne with only a few of its passengers still aboard, after an administrative dispute had flared up in Bahia, Brazil en route. [19]

Profession	Jersey	England	France	Other
Professional	2	1	1	-
Merchant	4	3	1	1
Farmer	11	1	-	-
Artisan	32	4	-	-
Labourer	-	-	-	-
Dependent	22	10	2	-

FIGURE 12. *Passengers Emigrating to Australia on the Brig Exact 1852. Source CJ 19/6/1852*

Parish authorities were occasionally asked to lend fare money to prospective emigrants. In St Helier in 1852 19 inmates of the Jersey Hospital, all natives of St Helier aged between 17 and 31, requested the Connétable, Pierre Le Sueur, to finance their emigration (destination unknown) on the grounds of "finding it impossible here in Jersey to provide for our necessities". [20] In the parish of St John in 1832 the Assembly agreed to finance the cost of a move to England for the daughter of Charles Le Gros, a pauper. [21]

Other sources, including, as we have seen, census figures, suggest that artisans generally dominate emigrant figures. An extreme example of this is the emigration of 86 carpenters, serving in the East Regiment of the Royal Jersey Militia, who in 1854 decided to depart en masse for Australia. [22] The only other passenger list discovered in the newspapers bears out this picture. It also shows English residents in Jersey forming only a small proportion of emigrating groups. [23]

Passenger lists, however, relate to only a part of a much wider phenomenon and care must be taken in using them to quantify emigration. They do not take into account indirect emigration, which may have appealed to English or Irish residents in Jersey wishing to bid farewell to family on the mainland before going further afield. Similarly, whilst the example of the *Exact* would lead us to believe that English residents formed only a small part of the exodus, Jamieson finds that in Guernsey the majority of people leaving the Island in the 1850s were non-local artisans hit by harsh economic conditions. [24] One thing is certain, the possibilities of emigration were brought to public attention by a variety of means, be it newspaper correspondence from the colonies, adverts from the Queensland and Canadian Government Offices for assisted passage, or the series of lectures in the Queen's Assembly Rooms, St Helier in 1853. [25]

Disillusionment with Australia in the wake of the Gold Rush meant a return to what was probably the major destination of local emigrants in the nineteenth century, North America. It was a logical destination considering Jersey's strong trading links with Canada and an association which continued to this day, easily observed in the *Revue d'Histoire de la Gaspésie* which carries many articles, mainly genealogical, on local families who settled there. [26]

Channel Islanders loomed significant enough to have a separate column in the Canadian Census of 1851, although Jamieson suggests that this was prompted by their economic significance rather than the size of their population. He likewise suggests that in real terms the Channel Island presence - it is difficult to separate Jersey from Guernsey - was never large, numbering, for instance, only 271 out of 15,500 in Gaspé County in 1871. [27] Nonetheless, a total figure of 900 Channel Islanders in Newfoundland as a whole in 1836 shows that whilst the numbers were small in Canadian terms, they were significant in terms of the Islands' populations. [28]

The detailed attention paid by the press to emigration when there were general economic difficulties was not so marked in the later time of stress in the 1870s and 1880s, when the agrarian economy was healthier. By this time the demographic pattern set by migration flows had become established, characterised by the movement of rural people both to the Town and abroad and by differential immigrationlof English speakers to the southern coastal strip and of French speakers to the interior.

Figure 13, tabulated from the Censuses of 1851 and 1881, shows a sample of parish populations by origins, ranging from the more urbanised parishes of St Saviour and St Clement, compared with the more rural St Ouen, St John and St Brelade. It may be observed that the proportion of indigenous inhabitants in each parish increases the further away the parish is situated from the Town. Thus St Ouen indigenous population accounts for 86 per cent of the people within its boundaries. St John, a little closer to the Town, counts 69 per cent of its population as parish born, St Brelade and Grouville, closer still and partially urbanised along their southern coastline, in the form of the town of St Aubin and Gorey village, just over 50 per cent. St.Saviour has only a 30 per cent indigenous population. The sample study of St Helier reveals an indigenous population figure of 48 per cent.

Parish	French		English		Indigenous	
	1851	1881	1851	1881	1851	1881
St. Saviour	7%	11%	24%	13%	30%	28%
St. Clement	6%	9%	11%	8%	55%	45%
St. Brelade	3%	6%	16%	14%	55%	49%
St. John	3%	10%	3%	2%	69%	60%
Grouville	6%	10%	13%	9%	54%	51%
St. Ouen	1%	6%	1%	1%	86%	77%

FIGURE 13. ***The English, French and Indigenous Presence (by Percentage) in Six Parishes 1851-1881***

Looking at it another way we see that St Ouen's English population in 1851 amounted to 31 people out of a total of 2,217; its total non-local population constituting 8 per cent. St Saviour's English population numbered 478 out of 3,569, its total foreign population reaching 32 per cent.

Few English people, therefore, chose to live in the countryside at this mid-century period. For the English upper middle-class the relative wilds of St Ouen would have had little to offer and for those with money enough to build fine residences the southern slopes of the Island, with easy access to the social life and shopping areas of St Helier, as well as the likelihood of familiarity with the English language, were clearly more attractive. The language factor may also explain the almost complete absence of English agricultural labourers, although the cheap and communal living Breton labourers were probably economically more attractive to farmers, who could with parsimonious ease furnish them with the barest minimum of shelter and supplies.

An analysis of the working English population of St Ouen in 1851 shows that it included 13 labourers (domestic, road and agricultural), two artisans and two of independent means. Nine of these lived in their own households, five of them being married to local girls. A look at married couples in St John, using two sample districts in 1851, reveals that out of 91 married couples in the sample districts, ten had no Jersey connection (seven being French) and only one woman was married to an Englishman. The majority of English residents in this particular instance were living in the only proto-urban area of the north of the parish, around the church.

English residents in the Jersey countryside were most likely to be labourers, without local ties and, if in their own household, living near the parish centre, the closest they might find to a village. Variations in this pattern were limited to parishes with urban areas, such as Grouville with Gorey village or St Martin with its non-local labour force, brought over for the St Catherine's harbour works.

The French population in the Jersey countryside in 1851 was not particularly large and of the six parishes analysed only St John had more French than English residents. The demand for the French as a migratory labour force was to come some time later, particularly in the 1880s. In 1851 the French presence was small. If we look to St Ouen we find its French population of 24 individuals in 1851 composed of 15 male agricultural labourers, five of them married to local girls and one to a French woman. Two farmers, two artisans, a man of independent means and four dependants completed the picture. French people were not concentrated in any particular part of the parish.

In 1851 the country parishes were generally free from foreign presence on any scale. The rural community neither consciously nor unconsciously encouraged non-locals into its territory. It is interesting to note that the only family living in St Ouen to have children who were born in England was the Seigneur of the Fief de St Ouen, John Malet.

To live in St Saviour, by contrast, could mean a fundamentally more cosmopolitan existence. When the number of non-Islanders exceeded those of parish descent, by 32 per cent to 28 per cent, as it did in 1851, the chances of contact, interaction and influence with English immigrants were much higher. Nonetheless, if we take an extreme example of a highly urbanised area such as the Dicq in St Saviour, we see that integration between local and non-locals is not pronounced. Of 185 married couples 67 were local and 87 were non-local. Only 13 locals were married to English born partners. Even when living alongside each other locals and non-locals were generally two distinct groups in 1851.

By 1881 rural isolation from the outside world ended when the countryside came under increasing pressure from an influx of French labourers keen to become tenant farmers. The French presence in the Island of roughly 2,100 in 1851 numbered 4,300 by 1881. In all of the six rural parishes examined in detail the French presence increased noticeably in these 30 years (See Figure 13). In St Ouen the French presence rose from 24 in 1851 to 122 in 1881, and this in a parish where the population had decreased in the same period from 2,464 to 2,217. In the parish of St John the French component of the population increased from 68 to 159, again in a declining total. In the more urban parishes of St Saviour, St Clement and

St Brelade the percentage increase in French residents was significantly smaller than in the rural parishes.

If we examine St Ouen a little more closely we see that the influx of French immigrants was overwhelmingly one of agricultural labourers. In 1881, 75 out of 87 French immigrants working in the parish were farm labourers. The English section of the parish populations, as we have already noted with regard to emigration, declined in all parishes.

At the period of high French immigration, the indigenous section and the overall totals of parish populations were in decline. It was a period of economic expansion for agriculture with an intensification of production and competition for land. French immigrants desired land and, although restricted to leasing because foreigners could not purchase real estate in the Island, their influence on the rural landscape was soon felt. The result, said Bear, was that "rents have been forced up to an extravagant extent by the eager competition of Brittany peasants who have been trained in the art of living on next to nothing,....Under such circumstances, young Jerseymen who inherit land are tempted to let it and to supplement the income which they thus obtain by engaging in commercial or other pursuits. Many of them shrink from the unremitting and arduous labour in which their parents have spent their lives". [30]

The economic outcome of such a situation will be discussed in the next chapter but, for demographic purposes we must note that the influx of French settlers did not destabilise parish populations. Indigenous parish populations decreased almost correspondingly, as if a perceived limit to what was demographically and socially viable was being tacitly observed.

The picture is made clearer by looking at the occupational structure for the same six parishes in Figure 14. In three of the four parishes the number of farmers increased in the period, and so did labourers, as we might expect considering the link between the two occupations. In the two rural areas it is the artisanal groups that have declined, and in all areas there is a substantial decrease in the number of dependants, reflecting a decrease in the rate of natural increase (See Figure 9).

As in the 1840s and 1850s internal migration and emigration were the options chosen by rural artisans. Country parishes remained demographically stable but, in terms of composition and occupational structure their populations looked quite different from those of 1851. Socially and economically the increased French presence was to be perceived by the rural community as a threat to its way of life. It was the first external intrusion upon the Jersey countryside in the nineteenth century.

1. Rural

Occupation	St Ouen		St. John	
	1851	1881	1851	1881
Independent Means	9%	6%	65%	8%
Professional	1%	1 %	25%	2%
Farmer	8%	13%	9%	12%
Artisan	11%	10%	14%	10%
Labourer	13%	17%	15%	19%
Dependants	58%	53%	54%	49%

2. Tending to Urban

Occupation	St. Saviour		St. Clement	
	1851	1881	1851	1881
Independent Means	9%	9%	6%	7%
Professional	3%	3%	1%	2%
Farmer	3%	3%	3%	7%
Artisan	10%	10%	16%	16%
Labourer	21%	23%	19%	23%
Dependants	54%	52%	55%	45%

FIGURE 14. *Simplified Occupational Structure of Four Parishes 1851-81*

Inheritance and the Laws on Property

Whilst the French presence appeared to loom large in the countryside in the 1880s any destabilising consequences were contained by the inability of foreigners to purchase real estate in the Island. Not unusually for a rural society much store was set on land ownership. The system of small *propriëtaires* depended for its survival on its inheritance practices which, in turn, in the nineteenth century, relied on the rural bloc's ability to avoid legislative change to its traditional method of handing down the family patrimony. It was this ability to prevent change in inheritance patterns and the land laws that ensured the demographic and structural stability of rural Jersey in the nineteenth century.

As in other spheres of Jersey life dear to the local population, the laws of inheritance changed little in the course of the century. The change that did occur was a minimal response to the demands for the reform of a system designed primarily for a rural society. The property laws were further safeguarded by a body of seigneurs set on commercial exploitation of their feudal rights, an ability which depended on the maintenance of the *status quo* in this sphere. Whilst seigneurialism was unpopular with the tenantry, legislative attempts at abolition were undermined by a fear that this would have a profound effect on property prices and the land laws.

The Jersey 'partage' was based on Norman customary law and in theory struck a mean between primogeniture and gavelkind. The inheritance laws were first codified in 1771. The 'prérogatives d'ainesse' were paramount and associated with the necessity of forestalling any trends towards excessive fragmentation. In the 'partage des héritages', if there was only one property 'tête de partie' the eldest son inherited the house and the farm buildings, as well as 30 perches for a 'jardin potager'. If the land amounted to no more than 40 vergées in total, the eldest claimed the whole unit. Over and above the rights of the eldest, he also had the choice share (one-tenth) of land above 40 vergées. If necessary, the inheritance was augmented by certain allowances to be claimed from the estate to meet various duties on the property, particularly seigneurial rentes and the 'musquet' allowance, the latter to meet the Militia requirement that every household contain several weapons. Compensation was also available for the eldest should there be any 'rentes foncières' (irredeemable ground rents) charged upon the property inherited. What remained was shared between the younger children, with a bias against females. Each parish had six 'apprécieurs' to oversee the various divisions of inheritance. [31]

Whilst codification was thus already weighted towards avoiding fragmentation, family practice leaned even further in that direction. Younger sons unable to make much use of their minute shares were prepared to come to some form of arrangement with the eldest, allowing the family holding to remain as one unit. The Reverend Edouard Durell explained the practice in 1837: "Where the shares are small the younger children do not think of farming them, but sell them to the elder brother for money or rents, and go into business". [32] Writing half a century later William Bear acknowledged how the practice had continued: "the subdivision of landed property fostered by law, which forbids the willing of land and requires its division among all the children of a deceased owner, has been counteracted by sensible family arrangements". [33] The popular interpretation of the inheritance laws, J. Stuart Blackie suggested in 1883, was "the golden mean between the two extremes of petty parcelling 'morcellement' and monstrous accumulation that have in practice been developed in this domain". [34]

The acceptance of traditional family practice was expected of younger sons. J.J. de Carteret, who was born in 1840 at Vale Farm, St Peter, recollected that as a young man he felt obliged to follow such an arrangement: "The eldest son it will be recollected is born in

England, a sort of fixture, he is born in the 'possessive case', whereas the other sons are as it were born in the 'accusative'. The first is born in the full possession of the lion's share of all the property, the others have much to 'accuse' the law for, and like veritable chickens they instinctively scatter as soon as they can scratch the worm for themselves". At seventeen he left the farm to work in the Town in a merchant's office. Within three years, his migration became an emigration to England and then, in 1869, on to the United States. Perhaps most interesting is his definition of the local form of inheritance as identical with that of England.[35]

The younger members of the family were expected to make way for the eldest. Thus upon the death of Thomas Le Seelleur of Le Villot in St Martin in 1816, three of his daughters ceded their shares in "meubles et héritages" to their elder brother Thomas. A younger brother, George, followed suit, although he did so on condition that Thomas took on the responsibility for all debts and dues upon the property. Fortunately for the younger members of the family in this particular instance, they were otherwise provided for: George inherited a property from another relative and Thomas senior had provided for his daughters with investments in rentes. Both brothers had to pay the dower due to their mother.[36]

Other families were not quite so fortunate. As one local correspondent put it, giving way to the eldest often meant taking up a trade, joining the merchant navy, becoming clerks or labourers in the codfisheries or, ultimately, emigrating to the colonies.[37] If we look to Philippe Ahier's household at Seymour Farm, St Martin, in the early 1900s, we observe that this was the case. Philippe's eldest son was married and farming nearby. It was accepted that on his father's retirement, six years away, he would return to the family patrimony. The second son had departed for Canada at the age of 19, this, the family claimed, being expected of him. The third son remained on the farm, receiving a wage, but it was accepted that he and his three sisters, two of who were trainee seamstresses, would have to leave when the eldest returned. The fourth son was considered the brains of the family and had joined the Merchant Navy as a midshipman (sic). The youngest son, twenty years old, was sickly due to tuberculosis and was not expected to live. In all cases, there was a tacit acceptance of the rôle expected of each individual in the family.[38]

In practice, then, Jersey inheritance did not, as J.J. de Carteret had pointed out, seem that much different from English primogeniture. However, the Jersey legal background with its special complexities, could not be ignored. This was particularly so with the land law's provisions on the transfer of property which applied to urban real estate as much they did country property.

For those unaccustomed to restrictive practices or intent on property speculation the Jersey property laws could prove something of a hindrance. Complicated purchasing practices, a restriction on the ability to entail and the liability of real estate to a host of claims, made property hazardous as a commercial speculation. A prospective purchaser in the Island reflected on the process in 1862: "Inquiring as to purchase money, an intimation which was Greek to me; that I could have the house and its appurtenances for so many quarters....From what I could gather, it seemed to me that if I wanted to buy one villa it was absolutely necessary for me to have a sort of lien or mortgage upon some other property and for my mortgage on that I should exchange with another person his mortgage on the property I wished to purchase, and thus be entitled to the denomination of 'owner' of the property....Why is it necessary for me to resort to the old fashioned system of barter and give my vendor an exchange in kind ?". [39]

As regards entail of real estate, even though the popular interpretation of inheritance was tantamount to this, it was not allowed by law. As A.J. Le Cras pointed out, in one of his many crusading petitions, a businessman could bequeath personal property without restriction but if he owned the smallest of houses the law forced him to leave it to his lineal heirs. [40] Only where a person had neither children nor descendants could he devise by will both his acquired property 'conquêts et acquêts' and any inherited real estate transmitted through an ancestor who now had no descendant living. Le Cras exaggerated the situation as regards personal property, although the law as to personalty was more liberal than that which governed real estate. The right to dispose of personal estate by will was limited to one third part. The remaining two thirds, as a matter of law, descended one third to the widow and one third to the children or descendants. As with real estate, restrictions on the entail of personal wealth were lifted in the absence of children or descendants.

Jersey's property laws were designed to meet the needs of an agricultural community of small land holders and the 'partage' had little to offer urban dwellers. As one Guernseyman pointed out about the similar predicament of his own Island, "If the interests of Agriculture require that sons in general and more particularly the eldest son, should inherit the larger portion of real property situated in rural districts, the same reasons do not exist to extend this principle to all the real property throughout the town parish". His solution to the problem was a simple one. By re-establishing the medieval 'barrières', he argued, so as to define the town of St Peter Port within certain boundaries, with exemption from the inheritance laws practised in the country, the interests of town and country could be reconciled. The idea was not pursued. [41]

There was some pressure for reform of Jersey's land laws, particularly from urban based capitalists but it was undermined by a complex of interests. A profitable seigneurial exploitation relied on the same property laws upon which the rural community appeared to thrive. François Godfray, probably the largest single fief holder in the Island in the period, put the connection to the States, claiming that the abolition of seigneurial rights would undermine the very basis of property in the Island. [42] What he really meant was that these rights were too valuable for the seigneurs to lose. In 1864 the *Chronique* estimated seigneurial rights in St Helier alone to be worth £35,000. [43] In the Projet de Loi of 1886 which intended to abolish all seigneurial rights, the recommended compensation for the whole Island was £43,000. This was rejected by the seigneurs as being far below the real value. [44] Nonetheless, in a legislature dominated by the landed interest the threat that abolition of seigneurial rights might have drastic consequences for the local land laws was bound to have some effect. [45]

The inability or unwillingness to crush seigneurialism at its root was compensated for by some tinkering with the land laws. Nonetheless, the premise underlying these reforms remained the "conservation du bien dans la famille", which in practice meant they resulted in little change. The *Loi (1851) sur les Testament D'Immeubles* allowed limited entail for those without children or descendants. [46] The *Loi (1850) sur les Successions: Droit d'Ainesse* attempted to rectify some of the more blatant inequalities in the partage. The eldest no longer took one tenth of the land, instead taking a share which amounted to one-tenth the value of the remaining property, that is, after his advantages as the 'aine'. The likelihood of variable land values within an estate had caused previous practice to give unfair advantage to the eldest. [47] In 1851 the *Loi sur les Partage des Successions* gave equality of treatment to females in the sharing out after the 'prerogatives d'ainesse'. [48] Finally, and quite relevant to the whole question of potential fragmentation of holdings as property prices soared, the *Loi (1891) sur les Partages d'Héritages* further modified the laws of succession. If the eldest chose a property with five vergées or less attached to it, that is a reduction from the 40 vergées of 1771, the whole was his to keep. [49] The now unpopular musket allowance was abolished. [50]

There was no attempt to introduce a formal right to entail property. With the exception of the limited rights included in the 1851 legislation, the only other change came in 1891 when a man without children or descendants was empowered to leave the usufruct of his property to his widow. [51]

If the laws of property and inheritance changed little during the course of the nineteenth century it was in part because of an absence of any major reforming agitation towards this end. Compared with other concerns, particularly the legislative and judicial overlap that continued to dominate the Jersey administrative structure, the laws of 'partage' attracted relatively little concern. This contrasted strongly with seigneurialism which, as one might expect, had the potential to cause a strong reaction, as the three attempts at abolition of 1848, 1864 and 1886 reflect. [52]

If we take the recommendations of the Commission of 1861 as a reliable touchstone, a major change of the property laws was not seen as a priority. What was required, it was suggested, was a rationalisation of the relevant laws and the eradication of some of the abuses that emanated from them. [53] It was recommended, for instance, to extend the *Loi (1851) sur les Testaments D'Immeubles* to enable those dying without descendants to entail inherited as well as purchased property. [54]

Some of the recommendations bore fruit in what was to be the most extensive piece of property legislation in the nineteenth century. The *Loi (1880) sur la Propriété Foncière* was in main part a result of the efforts of R.P. Marett, Attorney-General and a leading member of the Jersey Reform Party, a group which took over the mantle of reform from Pierre Le Sueur and his followers. The law was intended as a clarification of the laws of real estate and the claims upon it. This included the complicated system of rentes and liability in bankruptcy, the latter now being limited to one property only. [55]

The laws of inheritance remained unchanged. By the 1880s, laws championed as the root of a contented society of small-holders, were being hoisted as the banner of commercial success. J. Stuart Blackie claimed that the inheritance laws were responsible for the "striking contrast between the prosperity of the Channel Islands and the state of Ireland". [56] Foster Zincke echoed the conclusion, referring to agricultural exports as "astonishing amounts which could not have been produced without the division of land which obtains throughout the islands". [57] With a belief in the possibilities of such a link, the rural community, not generally inclined to reform traditional structures and practices, would have proved most intransigent towards any moves for change.

The inheritance laws and the popular interpretation of them helped to regulate the size of parish populations in the country. The absence of any real change to these laws ensured that this demographic stability was continued through the structural changes experienced in the 1880s as an increasing number of French immigrants chose to settle in the Jersey countryside.

Conclusion

The importance of demographic stability to the rural community was that it enabled an extension of continuity with the past. Jersey parishes retained the populations with which they were comfortable. It was the long standing practice of rural households to regulate the handing down of family property in the most economically feasible way; younger siblings expected to move into other occupations or leave the Island for a life elsewhere. The resultant stability and self-discipline provided an unconscious barrier against immigrant incursion. For some parishes, at least up to 1851, this amounted to effective isolation from the outside world. English immigrants simply did not venture into the Jersey countryside. It was a hostile place of foreign language and individualist Jersey residents, which offered little either socially or economically; a far cry from cosmopolitan St Helier.

This immunity from English settlement was no doubt a powerful factor in shaping attitudes and, for most rural parishes, the distinction between town and country could not have been greater. Rural folk found it genuinely difficult to comprehend urban criticism of Jersey society. In an Island where political power was shared equally between the parishes, the rural bloc's domination of the land mass, whatever its share of the population, could easily seem an egalitarian division of power. It certainly provided a good line of defence.

The laws of inheritance were perceived as the root of rural stability and success. Any major change to the basic premise of limited primogeniture was unthinkable. Ironically, the lucrative seigneurialism pursued by commercially minded fief holders utilised those very same laws. This close link ensured the perpetuation of seigneurial exploitation, even though it affected the rural community as much as it did the Town.

By the 1880s, however, capitalist expansion in the countryside brought in a French migrant labour force, the first significant incursion into the rural parishes. With agriculture in the ascendant and the number of those making a living from the land on the increase, many Breton migrants decided to stay and, in so doing, created a class of tenant farmers. Demographically, the parishes remained stable, those choosing a life other than agriculture moving on to St Helier or the colonies.

The French presence, as we shall see in the next chapter, was the first force to concern the rural community from the inside. Previously the various challenges to Jersey society had been kept at a distance. The reaction of the rural community was to undo much of the defensive work provided by demographic stability against anglicisation and modernisation.

Chapter 9

The Maintenance of Small~Scale Agriculture

The maintenance of small-scale agriculture in Jersey throughout the nineteenth century, in a period of economic transformation and success, tells us much about the socio-economic structure of the rural community. The small-holding had been and remained the basic unit of rural capitalism. The pattern of land-use and ownership established by Enclosure sometime in the late sixteenth and early seventeenth centuries, of small fields, high hedges and an intricate network of dissecting lanes, remained effectively the same into the twentieth century (See the Introductory Section). This landscape was not easily changed and the resulting structural stability tempered the challenges effected by economic achievement and the desire for profit.

By the 1880s peasant proprietorship was under threat from an increasing number of tenant farmers, including many Breton immigrants, who were willing to pay the high rents that economic prosperity demanded. The traditional land-owning class saw in the growth of tenantry a cause for alarm. Tenants threatened to replace peasant proprietorship with a class of farmers ignorant of responsibility and agricultural sense and desirous only of hard cash. High rents in turn meant that even the smallest of inheritances could be turned into economic units and leased out. The promise of large profits, warned many observers, turned members of the rural community away from common sense towards reckless greed, manifested in monoculture, high rents and the willingness to replace their own labour with that of a tenant class.

It will be argued that whilst such tendencies were present, particularly after the successes of the 'early potato' in the 1880s, and in some ways challenged the traditional practices of a normally conservative countryside, their overall effect in the nineteenth century was minimal. The rural community regulated itself demographically, as we have seen in Chapter 8, and a dispersed ownership pattern, even if altered by a tendency to tenant farming, meant a dispersed distribution of economic gain. No small group of landowners came to achieve a monopoly of resource or return. To the observer, outwardly at least, the rural landscape was one little changed over the course of the century.

Difficulties of the late Nineteenth-century Economy

The Royal Jersey Agricultural and Horticultural Society's Annual Report in 1858 had warned farmers to "study the wants of local markets". As early as this, in terms of the progress of agriculture in the nineteenth century, a concern was being expressed for the blindness that capitalist agriculturists were wont to experience in pursuit of profit. This blindness, claimed the Report, could be seen in both livestock rearing, in the beautifying of the Jersey cow to the detriment of its milking quality and in crop cultivation where the single-minded mono-cultivation of the potato ignored the need for traditional balanced farming. [1]

By 1886 the warning of 1858 had turned to major criticism. The Society now felt obliged to protest at "the ruthless manner in which what was formerly regarded as the proper equilibrium in well managed farming has been upset." [2] The 1886 Report was stimulated by a local reverse in the English potato markets owing to a glut and the Society resolved to "earnestly ask the farmer if he is acting wisely in trusting almost entirely to such an expensive and precarious crop as the potato". [3] The Report also expressed a concern for the decline in previously increasing cattle exports. Fears for Jersey's economic future were all the more poignant since the Report followed, as we have seen in Chapter 3, the 1886 crash of Jersey's major finance house, a crisis that finally put an end to Jersey's declining merchant economy.

The 1870s and 1880s witnessed Jersey potato cultivation at its most popular. The introduction of a new potato variety, the Royal Jersey Fluke, and the targeting of the 'early' market in England resulted in an 1880 export figure of 33,043 tons of potatoes; 15,000 tons more than the previous highest total of 1840, in the pre-blight period. In 1891 the largest potato lift in the nineteenth century saw a record export of 66,840 tons. [4]

The potentials of potato cultivation were such that between 1851 and 1881 the number of farmers in the Island increased by 35 per cent. These farmers cultivated a crop whose export figures averaged 49,480 tons per annum in the 1880s and 59,941 tons in the 1890s. What attracted these agriculturists was the money to be made. In 1873, with the early market just discovered, a 17,113 ton export had fetched £300,000, that is, £17 per ton. [5]

By the 1880s, however, potato profits were not so high. Using local farmer Joshua Le Gros' calculations for William Bear we can tabulate that 1887 had been an exceptional year for that decade, yet had brought a return of only £437,917 for an export of 50,670 tons, that is £8 a ton, a figure far short of that for 1873. [6] In a bad year, however, such as 1888 which had a combination of a late season and increased competition, the return could be even less, 60,527 tons realising only £4 a ton. Another bad harvest in 1892 showed just how precarious the trade could be. [7]

Reduced profits in the potato industry were matched by a slump in livestock export. In 1881 1,882 Jersey cows had been exported world-wide. By 1885 this figure, in what had been a relatively stable market since about 1830, had decreased to 1,516. In 1886 it dropped to 1,213. Prices followed suit; farmers were lucky, claimed Bear, to get an 1850s figure for 1880s stock. The demand for Island cattle had fallen off "chiefly because Jerseys have been extensively bred for some years in America and elsewhere... the English demand has fallen off for the same reason". [8]

The fear of the Royal Jersey Agricultural and Horticultural Society was that well-balanced high farming, aided by half a century of Society instruction and inducement, had lost out to the desire for quick profit from the potato. The criticism of the short-sightedness of the farming sector was repeated by agricultural observers. J. Burns Murdoch, as early as 1843, had criticised the way cattle breeders were already becoming slaves to a short-term market.[9] By the 1880s, attention had turned to the potato. William Bear claimed, in 1888, that "The future of Jersey growing is now somewhat doubtful, its recent high standard of prosperity having depended to a very great extent upon the remunerativeness of the potato crop". [10] John Coleman warned, "One or two years like the present will have a salutary effect in checking production". [11]

William Bear's researches for an article in the *Quarterly Review* in 1888 made him disclose the fears of what he called Jersey's experienced farmers, who claimed that smaller farmers were engaging in uneconomic practice to the detriment of their own holdings and Jersey agriculture generally. This involved neglecting the previous balance of crop and livestock by devoting a disproportionate share of the land to the potato only. The resulting inability to provide sufficient pasture for livestock and a subsequent decline in vital manure necessitated a heavy expenditure to make good the loss. "Probably," said Bear, "when hay and straw are cheap, and potatoes sell fairly, the profits on the latter crop more than make up for the expenditure on imported fodder; but last year high prices had to be paid for both hay and straw". [12]

Such a false economy was exacerbated by high production costs. Joshua Le Gros provided Bear with a breakdown (See Figure 15) showing the cost of growing a vergée of potatoes in 1888. [13] By Le Gros's estimation £50 an acre was required to make a viable profit; on smaller holdings the figure was even higher. [14] Captain Le Brocq told Rider Haggard that £50 an acre made potato cultivation speculative, and so it appears. [15] The 1887 potato export of 50,670 tons was lifted from 6,488 acres and returned £434,917 or £67 an acre, well above Le Gros requirement, but that was accepted to be an exceptionally good season. [16] A market price of over £8 a ton in 1887 was only £4 a ton in 1888. [17]

The earlier the crop reached the markets the higher the returns were, but much depended on the reliability of Jersey's milder climate to ensure an absence of frost. Neither early harvesting nor high yield guaranteed high prices because so much depended on how the competition had been affected by the weather. In every harvest the difference between high and reasonable profits was determined by the date on which the competitors, namely

Cost	Per Vergée			Per Acre		
	£	**s**	**d**	**£**	**s**	**d**
Rent	4			9		
Seed	4			9		
Scotch Manure	4			9		
Guano/Artificial Manure	4			9		
Planting	1			2	5	
Digging	1	5		2	16	3
Carting	0	12		1	7	
Ploughing, Hoeing, Picking	1	3		2	11	9
Total	**20**			**45**		

FIGURE 15: *The Cost of Growing a Vergée of Potatoes in 1888*

The speculative nature of the crop lay in the need for the harvested potato to reach the English markets before both British and Continental competitors. The actual marketing period was very short, on average little more than two months. Rider Haggard provided a breakdown for the 1900 season. (See Figure 16):[18]

Wks	Date of Shipments	No. of Packages	Tons	Average Weekly Price per Ton		Weekly Totals
				£	**s**	**£**
1	April 30 ~ May 12	7,449	185	31	4	5,772
2	May 14 ~ 19	26,499	885	19	10	17,257
3	May 23 ~ 26	50,899	1,700	16	5	27,625
4	May 28 ~ June 2	98,838	4,942	10	18	54,073
5	June 4 ~ 9	184,077	10,226	8	-	81,978
6	June 11 ~ 16	201,786	11,210	7	3	80,151
7	June 18 ~ 23	194,046	11,414	7	7	84,083
8	June 25 ~ 30	154,845	9,109	7	11	69,076
9	July 2 ~ 7	61,771	3,633	6	3	22,433
10	July 9 ~ 14	11,686	688	4	17	3,359
11	July 16 ~ 21	347	20	3	-	60
Totals		**992,243**	**54,012**			**445,872**

FIGURE 16: *The Marketing Period for Jersey Royal Potatoes 1900*

France, Portugal, Cornwall and the Scilly Isles, reached the market. The difference between profit and loss was dependent on the timing of English maincrop competition. The maincrop potatoes usually arrived on the market in mid to late July, after which the market price dropped below that viable to export from the Island. [19] A successful potato season for Jersey growers was one of mild weather in the Island, poor weather elsewhere and one in which the bulk of the local crop had been exported before the month of July.

There was clearly cause for concern. Rural Jersey in the 1880s was an economic maelstrom of eager capitalists seeking high returns and, in so doing, they forced up land prices and over-produced for a limited market. "High prices", said Coleman, "have greatly stimulated production, until at the present time thee is a danger that the supply will exceed demand, and consequently, prices range so low that the crop will not pay the cost of cultivation, much less leave, as formally, a large balance of profit" [20]. The *British Press and Jersey Times* agreed, stating that the potato traffic had caused large sums of money to be handled; future prospects were being sacrificed to immediate contact with hard cash. [21] The doyens of Jersey agriculture sought to find those responsible.

All the eyes of accusation turned to the smallholder. Experienced farmers claimed in 1886 that "many of the small holders of land devote too much of it to the potato crop, and frequently lose by so doing. For instance, they have to pay considerable amounts for hay and straw imported from France for their cattle. Many of them grow potatoes year after year for several years on the same land, which is only saved from deterioration by a heavy expenditure in manures". [22] To these small farmers, claimed the Royal Jersey Agricultural and Horticultural Society, the principles of high farming, in which a sound balance of enterprise was essential, appeared "erroneous, and in fact have frequently been denounced as such". [23]

Figure 17 is an attempt to determine to what extent smallholders were coming to dominate the Jersey agricultural scene between 1851 and 1914. [24] Quayle's rough estimate of the average farm in 1815 was between 50 and 60 vergées. [25] An average farmer (67 per cent of the total) in 1851 was most likely to work a unit of between 11 and 45 vergées. Around 19 per cent of those claiming to farm did so on units of less than 11 vergées. As C.P. Le Cornu suggested, in 1859, large farms (his figure was 150 vergées or more) were few in number. [26]

It is most interesting to observe that between 1851 and 1881 there is a slight aggrandisement of holding, the number of farm units above 45 vergées growing at the expense of those smaller. This development concurs with a period of strain followed by recovery in the agricultural industry in the wake of the potato blight. However, by 1914, as predicted by those fearful for the future of agriculture, the successes of the potato saw a larger swing back to the smaller holding, with those farming under 11 vergées now constituting 32 per cent of all land-users.

Size of Holding in Vergées

Year	1-11	11-45	45-112	112-
1851	19%	67 %	13%	1%
1881	17%	60%	21%	2%
1914	32%	56%	11%	1%

FIGURE 17. *The Size of Landholdings 1851-1914*

Between 1881 and 1914 there was then a general shift towards smaller land-holdings. What in effect did this mean? It did not mean that units of owned property were necessarily diminishing in size, rather that the units used by individual cultivators were becoming smaller. As evidence to this fact we must point to Figures 18, 19 and 20 which show the percentage of farmers renting land after 1891 and the extent of land this involved.

Year	Owned	Rented	Owned/Rented
1891	35%	50%14%	
1896	29%	52%	18 %
1914	27%	[73 per cent	]*

** A joint figure only is available for 1914.*

FIGURE 18. *Type of Landholding 1891-1914*

Year	Owned	Rented
1891	43%	57%
1896	38%t	62 %
1900	35%	65 %

FIGURE 19. *Distribution of Land Between Owned and Rented 1891-1900*

Size of Unit (Vergées)	Number of Farmers	Owned	Rented
$2\frac{1}{2}$ ~ 10	617	28%	72 %
11 ~ 45	1072	26 %	74%
46 ~ 112	209	30 %	70%
113 ~ 225	6	67 %	33 %

FIGURE 20. *Owners & Tenants by Size of Holding 1914: Source: Abstract of Parish Returns 1891-1914, Public Record Office 14/325.*

The pace or degree of change is difficult to assess since the statistical information available for the nineteenth century concerns only the last decade. No doubt a certain percentage of cottagers and small farmers had rented land in the early parts of the century, but as the Reverend Durell had noted in his reply to the Poor Law Commission, "The farms, not only in my parish, but throughout the whole island, are generally small. They are for the most part farmed by the landowners themselves. There are very few farmers at Rack-rent". [27] The other obstacle to the historian in this respect is the absence of leases which might prove an important source on the early part of the century. Coleman suggested that it had long been the practice of large proprietors to let their land out as several small farms, averaging 30 to 50 vergées, but that unless the lease was for nine years or more, and the usual length he claimed was between four and six, it was not registered. [28] One further piece of evidence which shows that tenant farmers existed in the earlier part of the century is that both Thomas Quayle and William Plees, writing in 1815 and 1817 respectively, gave some detailed analysis of agricultural rents. [29]

Nonetheless, even though the figures available cover only a short period of time, some significant change was taking place. It is clear from Figure 18 that between 1891 and 1914, and probably from earlier than this, tenant farmers were increasing at the expense of owner-occupiers. Those who owned and rented were also increasing, although at a slower pace. The tenants' share of the land, just in the decade between 1891 and 1900, increased by 8 per cent. By 1914 those involved in renting at least some land outnumbered others by more than two to one, except in the very largest farm category.

As regards holding size (see Figure 17), the census statistics available for housebuilding reflect only a minor change. Those parishes with a major increase in their number of dwellings between 1821 and 1881 - St Saviour (up 481), St Martin (up 301), St Brelade (up 151), St Lawrence (up 152), Grouville (up 152) - are, with the possible exception of St Martin (see the chapter on demography), those with urban developments on their southern coastlines. In St John (up 72), Trinity (up 51) and St Ouen (up 25), the numbers are smaller. None of these figures differentiate between farm or private house.

The overall picture derived from these statistics is that by the end of the nineteenth century tenants were at least equal in number to proprietors and that the average size of holding was, as it had probably been throughout the century, less than 45 vergées, although with an increasing tendency to be less than 11 vergées.

The smallholder was, as many feared, on the increase, although he was more likely to rent than own and, in terms of the overall land-ownership pattern, may have had a negligible effect. However, high demand for a limited resource had a profound effect on land prices, particularly with regard to rent.

Land for rent was in great demand from all quarters. This was a situation that puzzled Bear somewhat, because, with "interest at a little over 4 per cent (on wheat rente mortgages), on even such high prices for the fee-simple of land..., it would not come to as much as the highest of the rents on land let to tenants. Perhaps, this can be partly explained by the existence of burdens upon owners that tenants escape; but apart from that consideration, there is no doubt, a much greater competition for the hiring of land than for its purchase".[30]

Many proprietors may not have been keen to sell such a valuable asset as land. In a situation where demand far outstripped supply, rents were forced up to extravagant prices and the landlord held the advantage. Coleman felt that high rents guaranteed good farming, yet they also stacked the odds against the tenant in times of crisis. Tenant rights were absent from the rural scenario. A prospective farmer lacking collateral could be forced to pay rent up to twelve months in advance, whilst a departing farmer had little claim to compensation for crops growing and labour done.[31] All this was in an economy where if an owner could not find a tenant willing to pay up to £12 an acre, he himself would take up the hard labour required to obtain up to the £90 an acre some were said to get from potato returns.[32] The late nineteenth century was a good time to own land in Jersey.

Rents by the late 1880s, claimed Bear, had become "the margin of profit beyond the cost of the meagre subsistence which satisfies a Brittany peasant".[33] To blame the French or Jersey smallholder, as so many did, for increased rents, monoculture and lack of care for the land, was to miss the Jersey capitalists' rôle in the affair.

In a small Island with a large population, even if tempered by some form of natural regulation, the demand for land had been high for most of the nineteenth century. As Figure 21 shows, during the French Wars, some land, particularly in the west of the Island, Quayle claimed, could obtain as much as £3. 7s .0d. a vergée.[34] Plees, in 1817, said that Grouville land could obtain £5 a vergée rent.[35] By 1859, albeit at a time when agriculture was experiencing a low, up to £3. 12s.0d. a vergée could be obtained. It is, however, after the 1880s and the successes of the early potato that rents increase to a high degree, corresponding with an increase in the number of farmers and French immigrants.

Year	Rents (Vergées)	Source
1815	£3 ~ £3 7s	T. Quayle
1817	£5	W. Plees
1859	£1 16s ~ £3 12s	C.P. Le Cornu
1863	(average) £2 18s	J. Coleman
1883	£2 16s ~ £6	W.E. Bear
1905	£7	H. Rider Haggard
1912	£5 ~ £12	P. Galichet

FIGURE 21. *Rents Available for Agriculture Land 1815 -1912.*

One thing stressed by all who gave figures for rents is the fact that the sum obtainable depended on location and, particularly after 1880, aspect. Le Cornu pointed out how land near St Helier commanded the highest prices. [36] By 1912 the land at L'Étacq, in St Ouen, with its sandy soil and south-facing côtils was commanding by far the highest agricultural prices at up to £12 a vergée. [37]

Comparison between rents and purchase prices is difficult, since the figures available for the latter invariably include the house. Again we must rely on the surprise commentators expressed when hearing figures quoted. Joshua Le Gros sold a 57 vergée farm in 1887 for £6,049. He then bought a 15 vergée farm with a good house and outbuildings, situated a mile and a half from St Helier and including some good terraced land for potatoes, for £2,430. By his reckoning the land itself was worth £126 a vergée. [38] By the 1883 figures he could have obtained well over £6 a vergée in rent. John Gaunt, farming in St Saviour, had bought his own estate several years previous to 1887 at £80 an acre and said that since then he could have made £2,000 profit. He had recently let half the land at £4. 4s.0d. a vergée, but could have easily obtained up to £5. [39] High rents notwithstanding, land purchase prices were high.

The last two decades of the nineteenth century clearly saw important changes in the Jersey countryside. The land now played host to an increased number of cultivators, many of whom were tenants. In a context of great demand over limited supply, rents were forced up throughout the Island and land prices followed suit accordingly. In a vicious circle of capital, agriculturists worked harder to cultivate even smaller pieces of land more intensively. An increasing tonnage of potatoes was produced for a limited market. High profits were necessary to pay off high costs. It was no wonder that people began to show concern at the end of the 1880s.

Yet, how fair was it of the Royal Jersey Agricultural and Horticultural Society to blame the local and French smallholder? And were the long term consequences as dire as predicted, an obsessive monoculture leading to financial ruin?

On a basic level, it must be noted that large and small capitalists were as eager as each other for profit. After all, the potentials of high rents and land prices most benefited the largest landowners. In fact, the eagerness of large capitalists in pursuit of profit surprised some observers. Captain Le Brocq of Broughton Lodge, St Mary, told Rider Haggard that he felt Jersey was the "Isle of White Slavery, since during the potato season men worked from 3 a.m. to 10 p.m... where there is money to be earned capitalists with from £1,400 to £1,600 a year are to be seen toiling in their shirt sleeves". [40] Haggard moved on to visit the 200 vergées farm of Philippe Durell at Augrès, Trinity. "At the farmhouse we were told that its master was engaged in planting potatoes. Walking up a steep lane, we came to a field of about four acres. The scene was busy, about a dozen men being employed in the various operations... [including Durell]". [41]

More illustrative still was the view of the author of an article in the *Quarterly Journal* in 1843, who claimed: "The farmers are generally very independent, yet never above their business". To this effect he recounted a friend's experience who, on his travels in the Jersey countryside, came across the lady of the manor with some surprise, "Here was Miss C., an envied heiress, with a linsey petticoat and all other habiliments corresponding, picking potatoes with her hired workers. This is said to be characteristic of the ordinary farmers of the country". [42]

If there was cause for concern in the late 1880s it was the responsibility of all farmers, large and small. It was also not quite as dire as some suggested. Even Bear, who was concerned with the direction in which Jersey agriculture appeared to be heading, was confident for its future, calling the crisis of the 1880s "but a diminution of the former prosperity". The pioneer prices of the growers of 'earlies' would "remain only as memories; but where one man obtained handsome returns from Covent Garden twenty years ago, there are now ten or more receiving thence much larger sums, and fair, though not extravagant profits". [43]

If, as one can infer from Bear, the increase in farmers and demand for the land in the 1880s deprived a select group of agriculturists of their profits by overproduction, the dissemination of wealth continued well into the next century. Rider Haggard, visiting Jersey twenty years after Bear, verified his conclusions, stating that he was "amazed at the prosperity of the place", and that whilst it was true "that the inquirer hears some grumblings and fears for the future; but when on top of them he sees a little patch of 23 acres of land. and is informed that quite recently it sold at auction for £5,760 to be used, not for building, but for the cultivation of potatoes, he is perhaps justified in drawing his own conclusions. Even on the supposition that these values have touched high-water mark, and that the tide of agricultural wealth may be expected to recede to some extent, the industrious husbandmen of Jersey are, he feels, in no danger of immediate ruin". [44]

Fears of imminent monoculture are not borne out by Galichet's case studies in 1912. If anything, his studies reflect a move away from the basic balance of livestock and potatoes to include outdoor tomatoes and some market gardening, particularly fruit and flowers. Thus François Houillebecq, the son of a French agricultural labourer, farming at St Clement's Farm, in the parish of the same, worked 120 vergées, the main part of which was rented, with some 30 cows, 60 vergées of potatoes, 30 vergées of tomatoes and some fruit trees. James Baudains owned 30 vergées at Gibraltar Farm, St Peter, less suitable for tomatoes and other fruit, and concentrated on the traditional division of pastoral and arable. He managed to retain five cows and three heifers alongside a regular crop of potatoes. [45]

Galichet's case studies reflect a streamlining of agricultural practice in the latter half of the nineteenth century, but in substance are little different from the mid-century studies of Girardin in 1857 and Le Cornu in 1859. [46] Averaging out the studies of these two men reveals 48 per cent of the land in cultivation to have been pasture, 23 per cent roots, 17 per cent corn and 12 per cent potatoes. By 1900, in the breakdown provided by the Board of Agriculture, a concentration on pasture (62 per cent) and potatoes (27 per cent) had occurred. [47] The cattle population showed continuity in the same period, numbering 12,037 in 1866 and 12,272 in 1900. [48]

The figures then do not portray agriculture in a state of monoculture. The mixed farm lived beyond the fears of the 1880s, and even then was continuing to diversify. A specialist article by William Bear on garden farming pointed to the beginnings of tomato and grape cultivation in the 1880s. At this time cultivation took place under glass and was restricted to a few larger growers, particularly the vineries of George Bashford and Langellier's nursery, both in St Saviour. [49] By the time of Rider Haggard's visit in 1900 a few more farmers had diversified and flowers also were now being grown. [50] By the 1920s Jersey farmers were to turn to outdoor tomatoes in a big way, particularly in the east of the Island, though they still maintained a balance of pastoral and arable. [51]

Thus far we have shown that there was a structural change in Jersey agriculture between about 1870 and the turn of the century. The change scaled down an already small scale agriculture, sharing the use of the land, if not its ownership, between a greater number. The implications of a large number of independent units producing for the same market resulted in local concern that was genuinely economic. Middle-class landowners watched as the traditional modes of agriculture changed before their eyes.

Yet the concern expressed by the larger, perhaps gentlemen, farmers represented something more than economics. The new agricultural capitalists were held to be motivated by profit alone and did not care for the traditions of the land, nor the responsibility to society that ownership bestowed upon one. Alongside native culprits were the worst offenders of them all, the Breton immigrants, who were considered to be interlopers and parasites. The rural middle class was faced with a body of smallholders over whom they feared they had but little control. These fears must be understood in the context of the paternalist rôle assumed by the upper-middle class since the foundation of the Royal Jersey Agricultural and Horticultural Society.

Social and Racial Concerns

From the outset of its establishment in 1833, the Royal Jersey Agricultural and Horticultural Society was, as we observed in Chapter 3, cast as a gentlemen's society, representative of the rural upper middle class of established Jersey families. The guiding light of the Society was its rôle as model and educator to the rural community. Its main aim was the raising of standards in agriculture but this meant more than pure economics. Rule number three of its constitution stated an object of the Society as "being to create a spirit of industry and emulation and thereby to promote the public good". Premiums were to be offered for "the improvement of Agriculture, breeding of Cattle, and improved domestic economy, cleanliness, and comfort in Cottagers, and also for the encouragement of industry and good behaviour among servants and labourers in husbandry".[52]

To read the minutes of the Royal Jersey Agricultural and Horticultural Society in the 1830s and 1840s is to observe a body of gentlemen agriculturists genuinely and actively striving to elevate Jersey agriculture to the levels of high farming, that is units of production that were well balanced and scientifically operated. To this end scientific lectures by English academics like Dr. Preshaw's on agricultural chemistry in 1845, crop trials for potatoes and wheat such as those of 1835, annual farm cleanliness competitions and cattle shows, judged upon a model scale of points, were designed to give the Jersey farmer a product that could be exported to a market which demanded quality.[53]

The emphasis on advancement was reflected in a membership made up of individuals like Sir John Le Couteur who spent his time in scientific experiments, striving to find pure crop varieties and fine livestock blood lines. His extensive letters to Thomas Knight, the English potato expert, reflect a keenness of purpose and broad knowledge of his subject.[54]. His expertise on wheat earned him a front page profile in the English periodical *The Farmer's Magazine* in 1846.[55] Like Le Couteur, C.P. Le Cornu was the author of a prize winning essay on agriculture for the Royal Agricultural Society of England in 1859.[56] He too was a large farmer, at La Hague in St Peter. These men represented the leading lights of the Royal Jersey Agricultural and Horticultural Society.

There was a great belief among Society members that, providing the correct example was set, a natural dissemination of good farming practices was possible, even for the labouring class. Cottager prizes were to be awarded to native inhabitants of the countryside, their eligibility determined by how much they paid in rates.[57] The winner of the cottager prize in 1846 was Nicolas Poingdestre, who farmed at d'Hautrée in St Saviour, the report on him claiming that "this able and intelligent person with the assistance of his equally worthy wife, form a pattern to small farmers".[58]

Farm servants too, were in need of training and reward, although a projected register of 'good servants' in 1835 never really caught on.[59] The Annual Report of 1836 noted that "whatever betters the conditions of the labourer tends to elevate his moral character and make him a more useful member of society".[60] Members were urged to encourage neighbouring smallholders and labourers to enter competitions, which would result in the man of the house employing his "leisure hours in cultivating and ornamenting his little Garden, adding much to the comfort of himself and family, instead of wasting his strength, both of mind and body, in the dissipation and abominable vice of the gin shop". [61] In 1852 Lieutenant-General Helier Touzel introduced to the Society his idea for an Industrial School, for the training of girls for the household and boys for agricultural service, an idea that was taken up at a later date for the education of deprived children for this purpose. [62]

In 1858 the Society looked back on what it considered to have been a successful quarter century; "Let us bring to our remembrance the Jersey farm as it stood some thirty years ago, stocked with ill-fed and ill-shaped beasts, that knew not the taste of mangolds, carrots or swedes, nor scarcely of hay, whose winter food consisted chiefly of straw and a few watery turnips, and also the wretched stabling in which they were confined, without ventilation or drainage, where what is now appreciated as a valuable manure was allowed to waste away, or to remain stagnant till it became productive of disease; further the tillage of the soil carried on in the most primitive manner, without the least regard to order, cleanliness or appearance, where the hoe was unknown, and the broad hedgerow, abounding in brambles, served as a nursery for all manners of weeds, the seeds of which in general, being allowed to ripen, fell, and flourished where should have been the clean crop". [63]

However, the proclaimed success belied an organisation which, as we have seen in Chapter 7, had some problems persuading the rural community to accept the rôle destined for it. Within five years of the Royal Jersey Agricultural and Horticultural Society's establishment, membership had decreased to half of the original 250. [64] By the late 1840s, the country parishes had created their own independent agricultural organisations, and whilst the Society chose to interpret the move as an example of its beneficial education, there is no doubt that the move was a separatist one. [65] The withdrawal of the States grant in 1842, on the grounds of misappropriation of funds designated as prizes for the poor, was symbolic of how the rural community viewed the Society's gentlemanly pretensions. [66]

Funds had not actually been misappropriated and it is doubtful whether the rural bloc in the States really thought that they had. The Royal Jersey Agricultural and Horticultural Society was adamant that the services rendered by it "to the community at large, will be justly appreciated by all who approach the subject with unprejudiced minds". [67] But the minds of ordinary farmers had been prejudiced by what they saw as a gentleman's society whose English-like pretensions had little to offer them and which never missed an opportunity of self-congratulation. [68]

The independence of the rural community faced with what it saw as interference was to trouble the Royal Jersey Agricultural and Horticultural Society for much of the nineteenth century. In the Annual Report of 1858 those agriculturists who grew potatoes were singled out for major criticism, having ignored Society suggestions to avoid high yielding inferior qualities.[69] The Annual Report of 1886, in a period of agricultural depression as we have seen, sounded very similar to that of 1858: strong-headed smallholders were ignoring sound advice and aiming for all-out profit.[70]

As the number of smallholders was evidently on the increase by the 1880s, matched by a rise in potato production, it followed that the Royal Jersey Agricultural and Horticultural Society had a much harder task on its hands. The issue of control and education was confounded by the arrival of a large body of French immigrants.

As early as 1861 the increase in Breton farmers had been noted by the Society. It was, stated the Annual Report of that year, "surprising to see what they achieve simply by avoiding any habit tending to luxury, and by devoting their whole attention and movements strictly to their business. It is quite clear that this class is gaining ground in every sense of the phrase".[71]

The majority of the French nationals who came to the Jersey countryside in the latter half of the nineteenth century did so as migrant agricultural labourers. In the 1880s Bear claimed that as many as 3,000 Bretons were coming to the Island regularly for the potato harvest, many without secured work.[72] French labour was essential to the rural economy, particularly at peak harvesting times, since the potato required a quick lift to reach the early market.

Working in gangs, Bretons could often number as many as 25 to 30 on a single holding. On François Houillebecq's farm of 120 vergées in St Clement, for example, at least 25 Bretons were employed for the potato season; this in addition to eight permanent staff.[73] Their life was a hard one. Those staying at Edward Marett's farm, Le Boulivot in Grouville, worked long hours and slept on "paille étalée" in nearby sheds, with a food supply of potatoes and cider provided by the proprietor.[74]

Variable harvest times and the resulting uncertainty as to when exactly French labour was required meant that the treatment of Bretons was often negligent. William Bear noted that during his visit in 1881 "these poor people came over too soon, the crop being very late. Their case was a sad one, as they came over with scarcely any money, and they could not afford to pay for lodgings. Since in the previous year they had herded so thickly in the cheap lodgings of the town as to leave a great deal of disease behind them, the authorities had fitted up the cattle market, to the extent of putting straw in the sheds and pieces of sailcloth in front, for their reception. Over six hundred of them, men, women and children, slept in these comfortless lodgings. As a rule, when they have work in the country, they sleep under hedges, when the weather is fine, or in sheds or in stacks".[75] Galichet commented that he could not imagine an Anglo-Saxon putting up with the sort of living conditions he saw provided for Bretons. [76]

From the very outset a social and racial discrimination against the immigrant Bretons was evident although it ranged from real prejudice to mere irritation at the French presence. The Reverend Voisin's article in the *British Journal of Inebriety* in 1904 illustrated the harsher side to anti-French feelings. The main tenet of his argument was that Bretons were inferior and, among other things, he criticised them for having "little regard for personal cleanliness or the ordinary rules of hygiene, and besides consuming large quantities of cider, indulg[ing] freely in common brandy". [77] On the other hand, Rider Haggard witnessed local sour grapes when he was told by one farmer that the Bretons stayed in Jersey long enough to master local techniques and then returned to France, in the neighbourhood of St Malo, to put them into practice and compete in the export market. [78]

At the root of the bad feeling was the fact that many French labourers saw in Jersey the potential for economic and social advancement, and decided to stay. Those who could save enough money became, as Bear noted, "anxious competitors for small farms, and will pay almost any rent for them". [79] Coleman too, noted the French presence, citing what he called an example of "extraordinary industry and thrift", a Breton tenant farmer leasing 12 vergées, from his former employer, at £4 10s a vergée, plus an extra £16 a year house rent, who still managed, via farming and outside labouring, to save enough to bank £40 a year. [80] Numerically, the permanent French presence in Jersey increased from 2,100 in 1851 to 5,836 in 1901. [81] In 1881, they represented 30 per cent of the permanent labour force. More significantly, French immigrants constituted 7 per cent of the total number of farmers. [82]

It rankled when migrants became immigrants and then took up farming. As keen competitors for the land the French were "looked upon as interlopers, and are not liked by the Jerseymen proper, who are very amiably disposed towards the English who have rarely interfered in this way for though now and again individuals have tried their hands at the occupation, it has not been a success. We have not the frugality or industry of the French people, and we do not so readily take to 'petite culture'". [83]

Debarred by law from purchasing real estate in the Island, foreigners found that various routes around this obstacle were open to them. The more legalistic way was to be naturalised as a British subject, but, said Bear, "The authorities are not pleased at seeing the land more and more occupied by Frenchmen, and they are not at all disposed to facilitate the acquisition of rights of purchase by the foreigner"; permission would be granted only after several years residence and "very charily even then". [84] Marrying locally was another option, although equally successful was having children born in the Island, whose right to purchase land and extend the lifetime usufruct to his/her parents solved the problem. [85]

If Galichet's case-studies are anything to go by, remaining isolated and maintaining a non-Jersey stance was far from the intention of French farmers in the Island. Edouard Luce of Northdale Farm, St Ouen, was farming a rented holding of 110 vergées. In operation, his farm with its 40 head milking herd and potato cultivation resembled any other in the district. Luce was born in Cherbourg and did not come from a rural background. He had arrived in the Island at the age of twelve with his parents, and soon found agricultural work with a local patron, who took a keen interest in him, an interest which led to Luce working his own unit. Marrying a Jersey girl no doubt helped the process of assimilation, and in 1912 one of Luce's daughters had just married a neighbouring farmer's son. In 1897, Luce was naturalised by a vote of the States, something he said was a great honour. By the time of Galichet's visit, Luce's long time benefactor, Philippe Le Feuvre, was Connétable of St Ouen. [86]

François Houillebecq of St Clement's Farm, St Clement, was the son of a French labourer from Villedieu in La Manche. By 1912, François was farming 120 vergées, a small part of which he owned. As an Anglican, François was heavily involved in the running of the parish church. He was also nominated as Deputy for St Clement. To see Houillebecq, said Galichet, you would not know he was of French origin. [87] Like Houillebecq, Philippe Ozouf of Le Tapon Farm, St Saviour, was second generation French, and on the day that Galichet visited, 20 neighbours were occupied with helping him out with threshing and haymaking. By contrast, Ozouf was a Roman Catholic, but was also heavily involved in the running of his church. [88]

Galichet's three case-studies of Frenchmen farming in Jersey may ignore the smaller, more isolated and anonymous French tenant farmers, whose very existence depended on keeping nose to the grindstone. It is also to be noted that his case studies were of farmers of Norman origin and not of Bretons. There is little to suggest, however, that the smaller tenants were that much different in outlook from their more successful peers and, since the ultimate aim of such industrious workers was to own their own land, it is likely that they did not intend to stay separate and distinct from the rural community. Though evidence is scanty for less prosperous cultivators, what we can say is that Breton immigrants would have stood out among the rural community, be it by dress, patois or religion. Whatever their intentions, Bretons were an identifiable target for prejudice.

The Catholic Church followed the French immigrant into the countryside and helped to reinforce an identity distinct from that of the rural community. By 1872 two Catholic churches had been built in the countryside, that of St Matthew in the parish of St Peter, and St Martin in the parish of the same name. At this stage these churches were what one French priest described as "missionary investments". [89] The congregation was nearly all French, although by 1910 the Order of the Oblates recorded that their priests were visiting 270 families around

St Matthew's Church alone, a figure which must have included some locals. [90]

Jersey's country Catholic churches look incongruous in their surroundings even to this day, and the effect must have been all the more striking in the late nineteenth century. It was a presence exacerbated by the fact that Catholicism represented a double threat, as both an alien religion and an alien nationality. This much was recognised by Father Bourde, an Oblate priest, in 1882 and he admitted that "Jersey people do not like the French, and they have good reason for that". [91] Thus by religion alone the French presence possessed the potential to upset native sensibilities.

Whatever the intentions of the mass of French immigrants in the countryside, their presence alone thus constituted some form of threat. The comments of the States Comité d'Immigration in 1906 are understandable in this light: "Tant que l'immigration française trouvera ici des conditions de travail meilleures qu'en France, nous devons aussi nous occuper sérieusement de ses conséquences et de son influence sur l'avenir de notre île". [92] Centuries of animosity between Jersey and France, be it based on political or religious considerations, were not easily forgotten. When the Royal Jersey Agricultural and Horticultural Society expressed its opinion on the presence of non-local small-holders in 1861, it was expressing in economic terms what appears to have been the general country attitude towards the Bretons; they were welcome only as a transient labour force. [93]

The fears expressed about the increasing French presence tell us much about the rural mentality. The French tenant farmers were the first people to come into the Jersey countryside and make use of it to their own gain. The English presence in Jersey had remained essentially an urban phenomenon, few venturing into the countryside and even fewer taking up agriculture. Arduous labour and intensive agriculture did not represent an overwhelming obstacle to immigrant French, the majority of whom had experienced these conditions as labourers. Such an existence was all the more palatable in the knowledge that as a tenant farmer, and possible future proprietor, one's destiny remained very much in one's own hands. French immigrants were merely emulating the industriousness and thrift that observers so willingly praised in the Jersey farmers. The French immigrant was playing the rural game by Jersey rules.

In a revealing publication, undated but published sometime in the early 1900s, C.P. Le Cornu outlined what he claimed was the general view of the larger Jersey farmers, of whom he was one, regarding the recent changes in local agriculture and the implications for rural society. The decline in the dairy industry at the hands of potato cultivation, said Le Cornu, reflected a wider change based on the fact that "a considerable portion of the land under cultivation is not as formerly tilled by the proprietors, but let to a thrifty class of persons, many of French nationality or extraction, who make farming a momentary speculation, and whose interest in the future of the land is nil".[94] 'Cato the Censor', a regular contributor to the local press in the 1860s and 1870s, also linked a decline in standards and prosperity to the 'petit fermier', deaf to agricultural improvements and economical efficiency.[95]

Le Cornu's attitude reflected concern not only for the future of agriculture, but also for a rapidly changing Jersey. Interestingly, he emphasised the belief prevalent in the Royal Jersey Agricultural and Horticultural Society from the outset that livestock breeding represented a superior form of agriculture. The cattle industry was viewed as the cherished backbone of Jersey agriculture and any move away from it could only be detrimental.[96] Tenant farmers, be they local or French, represented a threat to the rural middle class idyll.

A major theme of Le Cornu's article was that the preservers of the land, those interested in its well being, were the owners of it. The new class of tenants was not interested in such traditions and responsibilities: "The pride which the Jersey farmer's wife formerly took in her dairy management is not a feature in the classes to which reference has been made".[97] On a basic level what concerned Le Cornu was, firstly, that increased profits were creating a new breed of small-holder, that, secondly, this new class was providing an introduction to the land for immigrant French and, finally, that the results of these developments were detrimental to economy and society, as evidenced by the exorbitant rents now available even for the smallest of agricultural units.

However, what was really disliked about the new class of tenant smallholder was that it represented capitalist forces which had little time for the traditions of the land. According to Le Quesne, writing in 1848, much store had been placed locally in the "moral influence of the possession of land".[98] Indeed Le Quesne's thesis, in his work *The Channel Islands and Ireland*, was that the problems of poverty, starvation and political disquiet experienced in Ireland could be minimalised by peasant proprietorship, along the lines of the Channel Islands. The result of such proprietorship in the Channel Islands, he claimed, was that "the people are well clad, well fed, well housed, and they have an interest, a proprietorship in the soil they till, and can say with an honest pride, 'this house and this land are mine; I have inherited them from my fathers, or acquired them by industry, and I shall transmit them to my children'. Persons thus circumstanced are attached to their country, to its free institutions, to its laws, which secure to them their inheritance and the power and ability of maintaining their position; which encourage industry and economy; and are productive of general happiness".[99]

Le Quesne was not alone in his interpretation of the value of peasant proprietorship for Jersey society as a whole. A century earlier Philippe Falle had spoken of a "happy class of substantial freeholders".[100] In Guernsey, Henry Tupper, in his *Observations on the Law of Descent of Real Estate in the United Kingdom*, similarly argued the positive gains to be obtained from such a system. [101]

Outside observers, too, marvelled at the virtues of a society of small proprietors. Pierce Mahoney, a large landowner in Ireland, told the British Land Commissioners about the Islands: "if I could see this country [Ireland] as generally prosperous and happy, I should willingly adopt their institutions as the price". [102] William Thornton suggested that if Arthur Young had known about proprietorship in Jersey it would "have induced that candid writer to lay aside his prejudices, and to acknowledge that, tried by his own test, small farms had come off victorious, as best answering what he had himself pronounced to be the main purpose of agriculture". [103] Foster Zincke claimed that in the Jersey small proprietor were combined the three functions of landowner, capitalist and labourer, "a combination which ensures no separation or opposition of interests". [104]

Tenant farmers undermined the very principles upon which such praise was based. If prosperity, happiness and stability depended on peasant proprietorship, any change in this basic structure was interpreted as a threat to the rural community. As a body, tenants could not be considered as responsible in looking after the land when their only motive was profit. When the tenants in question were French the position was naturally worse since they were ignorant of local traditions and responsibility.

In many respects this situation was seen by the Royal Jersey Agricultural and Horticultural Society, by the States (as observed in the Immigration Report), and by the larger landowners (as represented by Le Cornu and Le Quesne) as a threat to the influence they had previously had over Jersey society. The Royal Jersey Agricultural and Horticultural Society responded to the threat in paternalist fashion. Ever since its establishment its self-appointed mission was the education of small-holders as to their responsibilities in land tenure. These responsibilities were bound up with what the Society called 'high farming', which might in the Jersey context fairly be called the scientific discipline of agriculture and the duties of proprietorship. Potato culture had undermined these efforts. The Society resolved in 1900 to make the education of tenant farmers its priority. More particularly, it stated "The youth of the Island", that is the local young prospective agriculturists, "should be stimulated to follow the calling of his ancestors and not abandon the fields for town occupations". Via a modern agricultural education "land will .remain in the occupation of Jerseymen to the common advantage of all classes". [105]

The appeal to young Jerseymen to save their heritage was also mooted by the States Comité d'Immigration. It concluded in 1906 that the major problem was the outward flow of "une large part de sa jeunesse la plus capable et la plus entreprenante. Par contre elle reçoit une immigration étrangère numériquement proportionnelle, mais relativement beaucoup moins avancée". [106] As to why such a number of young Jerseymen were leaving the Island

and showing a lessening taste for agriculture the Immigration Report could only speculate in general terms, citing a new awareness of the world's potential brought by general education and modern communication.

As we have observed in the previous chapter, some young Jerseymen may have been shrinking from the demands of late nineteenth century capitalist agriculture. It was suggested by Bear that the increase in tenantry was a direct result of an over-powering work ethic in the rural community. In practice this ethic meant that to farm in Jersey involved labouring on your own account. Bear noted how "It may be suggested that those [farmers] who own moderately large farms, or what are deemed such in Jersey, might farm the land without working constantly upon it; but the universal testimony in the island is that this would not do, as it is only by working with the few men he employs that the Jersey farmer can thrive". [107]

This work ethic was a fundamental part of small proprietorship. A landowner worked hard for himself and would work for no one else. Rider Haggard was told that "a Jerseyman, as a rule, will only work for himself". [108] A proprietor caught up in the economic expansion of the 1880s had to work doubly hard to keep up. The result of this vicious circle of moral obligation and economic necessity, said Bear, was that "young Jerseymen who inherit land are tempted to let it, and to supplement the income which they thus obtain by engaging in commercial or other pursuits. Many of them shrink from the unremitting and arduous labour in which their parents have spent their lives, and which they have shared during their boyhood". [109]

Viewed in this light, the growth in tenantry in the late nineteenth century reflected, for some at least, a changing perception of the desirability of proprietorship in its historical mould. For the watchdogs of rural tradition, the Royal Jersey Agricultural and Horticultural Society, the larger middle class farmers and the States there was little hope of saving a body of head-strong agriculturists who had shown a strong inclination to go their own way throughout the century. "Everyone must regret," said Bear, echoing the influence of the larger farmers, from which he derived most of his information, "to see the fine race of Jersey farmers men whose ancestors have held land in the island since long before the Norman Conquest diminishing in number as they are". [110]

As Figures 18, 19 and 20 show, the increase in tenantry and decrease in the size of holdings cultivated continued until at least 1914. Economically the effect of these changes, for all the fears of monoculture, was, as we have seen, negligible. Socially, however, as can be observed in the second half of the next chapter, the perceived threat of tenantry had implications for the rural community's view of anglicisation. All who criticised the growth of tenantry did so by identifying this group primarily as French immigrants. In a countryside which was inherently suspicious of immigrants it was felt that a cultural rallying point was required if the influence of the French immigrant was not to overwhelm.[111] The rallying point considered most effective against the social menace of the Breton presence was English culture, particularly the English language. It was ironic that in the defence of the "vieille race Jersiaise" the chosen force was one against which the rural community had spent much of the century fighting.[112]

Conclusion

Jersey agriculture underwent a transformation in the nineteenth century, yet it was a transformation which had remarkably little effect on the rural landscape. In many ways this was a reflection of just how solid a landscape had been created during Enclosure, a patchwork pattern of small fields and lanes which would have required massive upheaval to change. The fields, although reflecting a streamlining of agriculture towards pure capitalist production, bore few crops that had not been present in 1815. The landscape appeared to present an impregnable defence against change.

Similarly, despite some contemporary claims to the contrary, the size of land holdings showed only a slight tendency to decrease over the century. By 1914 a slight increase in holdings under ten vergées was registered but, generally, an earlier pattern from at least 1851 which showed the majority of holdings to be under 45 vergées, was retained. The absence of a large number of newly built rural dwellings and a stable country population throughout the period, the root cause of both of which was to be found in the strongly defined landscape, further support such a conclusion.

In human terms a successful agricultural industry resulted in an increase in farmers, a growing number of whom were tenants, a group which included French immigrants willing to work hard and pay the high rents asked by capitalist Jerseymen. Demographic stability in the countryside hid this internal structural change.

Middle-class prejudice against the small-holder, particularly in tenant mould, and even more so if of French nationality or extraction, accounts for much invective and, to be fair, misinterpretation, from the large landowners. C.P. Le Cornu and others, broadly represented by the Royal Jersey Agricultural and Horticultural Society, targeted this group of small farmers for much economic and social criticism. The charge of monoculture is not borne out by either case studies nor export figures and, if anything, there is evidence to suggest that the basic capitalist balance of livestock and potatoes was being supplemented by diversification into market gardening crops such as the tomato.

The main concern of these gentlemen farmers was that the control of the most sacred of rural concerns, the land, was gradually shifting to a class whose only concern was profit.

Rural society viewed small proprietorship as sacrosanct, as a practice responsible for local well-being and stability. Tenant farmers under constant economic pressure were felt to be unable or unwilling to pay respect to the cherished rules of proprietorship, a balanced agriculture and a pride in the land.

The tenant question was further exacerbated by the advent of the French tenant farmer. As a foreigner to the rural community in nationality as well as agricultural practice the French tenant was seen as a threat in both social and economic spheres. At the root of the prejudice lay the French tenant's ability to strike at rural consciousness where it was most vulnerable, at the grass roots. Previous to the influx of a substantial body of French labourers into the countryside from the 1850s onwards, the rural community had remained immune to local immigration.

By the end of the nineteenth century, the tenant farmer, furnishing high rents to Jersey capitalists and filling a vacuum that many local men had chosen to create by emigration, was an important, but not generally transforming, part of the rural economy. Regardless of local predictions to the contrary, French tenant farmers showed themselves desirous of becoming Jerseymen and accepting the values and traditions of its society as their own.

In the final analysis, the fears of the middle-class members of the Royal Jersey Agricultural and Horticultural Society were more social than economic. The 'high farmers' had experienced great difficulty in their efforts to educate and control small proprietors since at least the 1830s. Now they faced an increasing number of tenant farmers whose interests in the land were seen as less long term than those of peasant proprietors and aimed primarily at profit. This tenant body had developed from the very successes in Jersey agriculture that middle-class farmers had done so much to promote. The Royal Jersey Agricultural and Horticultural Society had little taste for the 'monster' it appeared to have created.

Chapter 10

Cultural Compromise

We have observed in this section how a strongly integrated society could well defend itself institutionally, be it by family practice, parish intransigence or the power of the rural bloc in the States. However, some challenges to traditional practices and identity were not so easily recognised, assessed and responded to. Nonconformism and the English language were two such forces; very different in themselves yet, as religion and medium of communication, touching in their own way on crucial definitions of the rural community.

Nonconformism was at once more directly threatening and more readily responded to. It challenged rural society from within, appeared to reject the framework of old and created an alternative focus for a significant section of the population. Faced with an exodus of its congregation, the Established Church was forced to reassess itself and, to a point, to reform. Parishioners, too, reviewed the rôle of the parish in their community life and finding it lacking in certain spheres realigned it onto a more civil footing, a move which allowed its members religious freedom within an otherwise traditional framework. Nonconformism forced compromise because, in the final analysis, Nonconformists were simply everyday members of rural society and were accepted by the generality as such.

The English language and its associate Victorian culture was, by contrast, a far more complex force both in the challenge it presented and the response it engendered. It came to the Island backed by a large body of speakers and represented for many of the local middle class a chance to escape from an intellectual and cultural backwater and enter the world of Victorian values, a world of commercial, social and moral wealth. For the majority of Jerseymen, the large English presence and the English language presented a challenge to their way of life only when agitators like A.J. Le Cras made it an obvious one. Even once a threat had been identified, a combination of a linguistically weak dialect, the bourgeois desires of a section of the population and educational problems, namely Privy Council pressure to conform, left the local community ineffective in response. Compromise as far as the English language and culture were concerned, was forced upon Jersey society.

The Response to Nonconformism

The rapid success of Methodism in Jersey after its introduction in 1774 and the popularity of Nonconformism generally, which by the 1850s had attracted, at a conservative estimate, 10 per cent of the rural community, is an interesting reflection on the state of the Established Church in the same period. By the conscious decision to worship elsewhere a section of the Jersey population was showing its discontent with the existing situation.

As we observed in Chapter 4, with the exception of the French Wars period, the general response to Nonconformism, and Methodism more particularly, was toleration. The Established Church took up no official position on the issue. Some clergymen were a little more vociferous. The Reverend Philippe Filleul stood out from his fellow rectors with his intolerant attitude. After successively tolerant deans, Filleul's appointment as Rector of St Helier in 1850 marked a sudden change. His wrath was directed at the curate of St Jude's, who had displayed friendliness towards local Methodists - indeed, he had participated in their prayer meetings. Filleul suspended him from duty. [1] This was no isolated outburst. Whilst Rector at St Peter (1829-1848), Filleul had been so concerned by the Methodist threat that he had published a plea to his parishioners in the *Magasin de l'Église Anglicane* in 1843, in which he suggested that they come to his church on Sundays for enlightenment. [2] Yet Filleul's behaviour was exceptional and his article a rare example of inter-denominational polemic, which found no equivalent in the *Magasin Methodiste.*

Quite why the Reverend Filleul was so intolerant of Nonconformism is unclear. Others, like the Reverend François Jeune, Rector of St Helier (Dean of Jersey, 1838-1844), had more obvious reason to be openly sympathetic in their attitude. Jeune was the son of a Methodist family, who had been instrumental in the early successes of Nonconformism in the Island. His Methodist background was reflected in his liberal attitude towards Nonconformist burial in the parish churchyard. [3] Nonetheless, he joined Filleul as one of the rare few to express an opinion on the issue.

If ministers showed no particularly hostile attitude to a development which directly affected their rôle in the community, then it was hardly likely that the rest of the community would do so either. After all, as Francois Godfray, a man not generally tolerant of challenges to the existing order, pointed out, most country people had at least one Nonconformist in their family and this tended to temper anti-dissenter feelings.[4] In a society where leading conservative politicians like Godfray, and leading Anglican churchmen like Jeune, had brothers or fathers who were Nonconformists, it was hard to distinguish Methodists as an body separate from the rural community

However, whilst Jersey society's reaction to Nonconformism stressed its non-contentiousness, Methodists were, nonetheless, rejecting a central element in the late eighteenth-century definition of the rural community. And such was the overlap between civil and ecclesiastical spheres in the parish that the result of this was a measure of isolation from the community life they had hitherto shared. Nonconformists were no longer present in the church to receive important court and parish communications via the communal mouthpiece; they had to compromise their moral and religious position to vote and they missed out, to some degree at least, on their social life in the parish. Yet the degree of isolation from communal activities was diminished, almost from the outset, by the response of the rural community which moved to put an end to the Church's secular rôle in the parish.

The Triumph of the Body Civil

During the course of the nineteenth century the Established Church found its secular rôle in the parish increasingly regulated and restricted in favour of the body civil. From holding a near monopoly in communal self-expression the Church found itself, with the exception of the rectors' position in the legislature, confined to religious and spiritual matters and, even then, in the service of a congregation diminished by those who sought God elsewhere.

To a large extent the decline of the Church's rôle in the secular world, as we have observed in Chapter 7, was a result of a move to clarify and define power in the parish, paralleled to a certain extent in the legal sphere by an attempt from 1771 onward to codify and regulate the laws of the Island. [5] In this respect, the *Loi (1804) sur les Assemblées Paroissiales* was the first real attempt to distinguish between civil and ecclesiastical power.[6] Yet in the wake of this initial definition, the popularity of Nonconformism and a willingness on the part of the rural community at large to accept this religious pluralism ensured a continued reappraisal of the distribution of power between the Church and the body civil.

But the redistribution of parish power could go only so far. The move to Nonconformism did deprive some individuals of the chance to serve in high parish office. Amongst the lower to lower-middle classes, from which most rural Methodists came, some individuals, mainly farmers, were high enough up the social scale to be principaux of the parish. For instance, of the eleven trustees at Sion Chapel, in the parish of St John, at least nine were principaux in their respective parishes, Trinity or St John and as such eligible for parish office. [7] This situation was probably quite common since trustees, as guarantors, were of necessity men of property and some wealth. Yet in contrast to near-Methodist oligarchies in some rural parishes in the twentieth century, nineteenth century Nonconformists are conspicuous by their absence from honorary service. Only two Connétables in the nineteenth century were dissenters: Pierre Perrot, brother of the Minister at St John's Independent Church, predecessor to Pierre Le Sueur as leader of the Rose party and reforming Connétable of St Helier 1834-1839; and Philippe Le Vesconte, Methodist and Connétable of Trinity 1868-1877. The other high offices of Jurat and Deputy (established 1857) show a similar dearth of dissenters, there being only two for certain of the former: Jurat Philippe Picot, a member of St John's Independent Church; and Jurat Elie Neel, a Methodist elected to the bench in 1863.

The reasons for this absence were probably traditional. The ambit of and exercise of parish offices were linked closely to the Established Church: police officers even had their own pews in church. This interrelationship continued throughout the nineteenth century, despite the increased differentiation between civil and ecclesiastic spheres. Philippe Gruchy, for instance, in a situation which was not uncommon, combined the office of churchwarden with that of Centenier in St John in 1851.[8] Such an overlap would have made it difficult for a Nonconformist to carry out his office.

Nonetheless, moves were afoot to separate civil and ecclesiastical spheres and this could only be of benefit to Nonconformists. The process commenced with the law of 1804 which made a distinction between the parish civil and ecclesiastic, one which had previously been somewhat blurred.[9] This earlier overlap is reflected in parish records. In the parish of St Ouen the Acts of the Ecclesiastical Assembly do not exist as a separate category until 1804. Previous to this, entries of matters pertaining to the Ecclesiastical Assembly could be found in the Civil Assembly books.[10] In the parish of St Saviour the Civil Assembly books as a separate entity date only from 1808 and the first Ecclesiastical Assembly book with regular entries from 1783; this included the Acts of the Civil Assembly.[11] Generally after 1804 a distinction was made throughout the Island's parishes, though in the parish of St John civil and ecclesiastical minutes run occasionally alongside each other in rather confusing fashion.[12]

Prior to 1804 most Parish Assemblies, civil and ecclesiastical, held their meetings in the parish church, usually in the consistory. This is not surprising since the church was the only official parish building and a Calvinist morality may have precluded the local tavern as an alternative. Nonetheless, after 1804 Parish Assemblies in their civil capacity moved increasingly away from the church, usually to a nearby tavern, occasionally to a private house. In the parish of St Ouen the use of the church as a meeting place for civil affairs ceased in 1806 when parish officers began to meet at the house of Philippe Le Brun. By 1829 they were meeting at a local tavern.[13] Through the course of the century the church as a public meeting place generally retained only the Ecclesiastical Assembly, and was progressively undermined by a move to alternative venues, ranging from St Brelade's use of its hospital, St Helier's use of several major meeting halls and rural parish use of inns, parish schools and, ultimately, purpose built halls.[14]

In itself these early civil moves away from the Church amount to little more than a deliberate attempt to distinguish between civil and ecclesiastical. The 1804 law had defined the separate rôles of the two and reaffirmed the Parish Assembly as the source of power in the parish. More importantly it determined who presided over the Assembly in its different capacities. The rector's rôle was clearly restricted to specific church affairs, such as the election of its officers, choice of gravedigger and repair of the church. There were no funds at the disposal of the Ecclesiastical Assembly; these had to be obtained from the Civil Assembly. By contrast the powers and competence of the Parish Assembly in its civil capacity were not defined.[15]

The year 1804 is too early to suggest a pronounced Methodist influence, but whatever the motives behind the legislation, the law of 1804 restricted the rôle of the parish rector and, by extension, the rôle of the Church in parish affairs.

If the legislation of 1804 had ensured clarification, that which followed involved restriction, namely the undermining of the traditional rôle of the parish church as the communal meeting place. In the *Loi (1831) sur les Élections Publiques,* it was declared that parish elections were no longer to be held in the church porch after Divine service. As the Reverend Edouard Durell explained, "the profanation and the riots which often occurred at contested elections had become a serious grievance, which occasioned frequent complaints and at length alerted the attention of the States".[16] Elections were now to be held on Tuesdays in the newly built Militia sheds, located near to the parish church, or in the case of St Helier and St Brelade, in their respective market-places.[17]

It appears that certain external pressures may have been brought to bear on the States to end Sunday elections. The juxtaposition of virulent party politics and the sanctity of Sunday service was clearly not to everyone's taste. When Bishop Charles Sumner visited the Island in 1830 he witnessed a Sunday election at St Clement and had the scene explained to him by a local clergyman: "le peuplesse rendait aux élections contestées en grand nombre, qu'on buvait une grande quantité de 'grog' aux auberges, et qu'il en résultait les plus grands désordres".[18] Aware of the Bishop's concern, John Le Couteur, whilst Connétable of St Brelade in 1830, followed the matter up and canvassed the support of both the Bishop and Robert Peel, the British Home Secretary (1828-1830), for a reform. "The transferring of an election from the Lord's day to a week day," wrote Le Couteur, "is of itself an act so proper and natural to any Christian mind, that one is at a loss to discover why it should be opposed. But it is so. Strong and influential parties are hostile to the change".[19] Within a year, elections were removed from both Sundays and the parish church.

The final blow in the undermining of the Church's rôle as official medium to the community came in 1842 with the *Loi sur les Publications dans les Églises* which forbade the announcement of parish assemblies or elections, or civil or criminal matters in the parish church or cemetery on a Sunday.[20] The parish reference point was now officially moved from the church itself to a "boîte grillé" which was to be placed "proche la principale barriére du cimitiére" as the official mouthpiece of the community.[21] The move symbolised the eclipse of the churchyard's centrality in parochial life.

Within forty years the communal rôle of the parish church had been successively undermined and whittled down to its religious base. The parish organisation was now primarily a civil affair. The shift from Church to the body civil received its physical embodiment after 1877 in the form of Parish Halls, the majority of which were built close to the parish church.[22] The Parish Hall now replaced the Church as the focal point of the parish.

In the absence of any obvious lobbying by Nonconformists their rôle in the de-secularisation of the Church remains unclear. However, the fact that at least ten per cent of the rural community were effectively precluded from fulfilling their communal functions cannot but have had an influence. The preamble to the *Loi (1831) sur les Élections Publiques* explained how changed circumstances "empêche plusieurs électeurs de donner leur suffrages", and that this had necessitated a change in the "ancienne coûtume.". [23] The Reverend Durell interpreted "électeurs" to mean Christians in the broader sense, many of whom were perturbed by the mixture of Church and party politics. He added, though, that whilst Nonconformists were probably not a direct influence on the legislation, a wrong other than the unseemly behaviour at elections had also been undone; "At the same time many pious Christians were indirectly deprived of their elective franchise, on account of their religious scruples, which prevented them from voting on Sundays". [24]

Furthermore, the legislation passed through the States with ease. The newspapers paid no particular attention to the transition. Placed against the background of the Church's public image (see Chapter 4), this can only suggest a tacit agreement by all sides that the use of the church for secular purposes involved activities and behaviour upsetting to the sensibilities of a section of the population and incompatible with the rôle of the Church in society. This would explain the lack of opposition to the legislation by the clergy and the attitude of a section of Anglican worshippers as expressed by the Bishop of Winchester. In fact the *Loi (1842) sur les Publications dans les Églises* made specific reference to the fact that it was paralleling parliamentary legislation of 1837 on the de-secularisation of the Church, which was itself activated by a general concern as to the Church's secular rôle.[25] The popularity of dissent had brought these concerns to the fore of the political agenda. In the absence of a more direct involvement in these reforms, this is evidence enough to show the influence of Nonconformism in this sphere.

The parish of 1877 was a much fairer reflection of its constituents and their desires than it was in the earlier part of the century. A diminution of the Established Church's rôle in secular affairs was the price that had to be paid for a communal unit that represented all its members. But the Church did not stand idly by as its sphere of influence was curtailed and it is to the Church's response that we now turn.

Church Reform and Renovation

The Church's reaction to its unpopularity and the threat of dissent was an attempt to clean out its own house. This was manifested in various ways. Most contentious were the attempts to reduce the hold which concerns of status and privilege had over parish churches, particularly with regard to pew ownership. Less divisive, but equally important, were the efforts to repair and recondition the church fabric.

The internal reform of the Church in Jersey was not a united effort, rather it relied on the disposition of individual rectors to change. This makes the process of reform difficult to date. Caesariensis, writing under a pseudonym in 1917, dated the period of change to the 1860s when the characteristic tone of the Island Church was set by Evangelicalism. He claimed "there was not wanting a large minority of the Island clergy, and of members of insular families, who would have welcomed an approximation of Jersey Church life to the Church life of the Mother Country, but who were content to take things as they found them for fear of running counter to local feeling. One of the Island's incumbents, holding a large country parish, however, went beyond this stage of passive or restrained goodwill. A parish church, beautifully and correctly restored, elementary schools on Church lines, a district church, and an additional curate to minister therein, testify to the width of his views in planning, and his success in achievement. This example was catching". [26]

The minister he referred to was the Reverend Abraham Le Sueur, Rector of Grouville from 1851 to 1885, who during his incumbency attempted to break the mould of privilege and hierarchy in a Church which, he felt, had done much to alienate its congregation. It is clear that Church reform commenced before Le Sueur's crusade but he is a useful starting point since he provides one of the few insights into the background to these changes.

In a pamphlet entitled "Aux Paroissiens de Grouville", published in 1874, Le Sueur outlined his vision for a reformed Church. In his view the Church had done much to exclude parishioners from Sunday service. In terms of structure and fabric alone, churches with exteriors and interiors in poor repair discouraged regular attendance. But more importantly, the Church had become a bastion of privilege, where status counted more than religion. Le Sueur was convinced that this left many individuals feeling excluded or subject to prejudice. His aim was thus to make the Church more appealing and accessible. As a first step in this direction, Le Sueur targeted a crucial component in the existing set-up, the privilege of pew ownership. [27]

The hierarchical system of pew ownership was a major part of worship in the parish church (see Chapter 4). It was a system which went to the heart of the Church's position in the community, as well as to the rights individuals possessed within its domain. Pews were a source of status, personal rivalry and conflict. Individuals, like C.P. Le Cornu in St Peter in 1872, were prepared to pay out large sums to ensure that their position in church reflected their status. [28] Furthermore, pew owners, like Jean Arthur in St Ouen in 1833, were more than willing to go to the Royal Court to uphold the rights which derived from ownership. [29]

In many parishes, including Grouville, pew ownership was reflected in church interiors which showed no symmetry of plan, with pews arranged in odd fashion. [30] A prime example of this was the parish church of St Lawrence. There, rich pew owners had raised pews from the ordinary level, thus ensuring that only they could view the Sunday service. The owners of Le Colombier and Le Patrimoine pews had gone a step further, each pew being furnished with its own stove and a private entrance to the church. [31]

Already by the early nineteenth century the situation regarding pews became ridiculous and the issue was brought to the fore of Church concern. In 1827 in the parish of St Martin the state of the church was such that the Ecclesiastical Assembly attempted to force pew owners to repair their pews. The opposition this provoked roused the Dean of Jersey, the Reverend Corbet Hue, to dispatch a strongly worded letter to the Island's rectors. In it he claimed that parishes had allowed seats destined for public use and the poor to be sold, a practice he considered "contraire aux règles établies, ce qui seroit dans le cas de porter un préjudice considérable aux intérêts de l'Église, s'il n'y étoit pourvu et remédié". [32] Ecclesiastical law supported the Dean's position. It was implicit in Canon 33 of the Ecclesiastical Canons that pews were for the benefit of the congregation as a whole. [33] Hue demanded some form of restriction on the further alienation of this public property and a clarification of the practice of renting and selling pews, which varied from parish to parish. [34]

Not surprisingly, Dean Hue's declaration sparked off a long running debate throughout parish assemblies and encountered much opposition from vested interests. It also resulted in problems for his fellow rectors. As Dean William Le Breton later told the 1861 Commission, the pew problem related to the extent of secular control inside the church. Did the Surveillants have the right to allow others to sit in unoccupied pews? Did the owner have the right to lock his pew? [35] These were precisely the problems the Reverend Philippe Filleul faced in St Helier when, on a given Sunday, a large mass of people might be forced to stand at the back of the church, whilst rows of pews remained unoccupied. [36] Filleul, a staunch anti-Methodist, like Le Sueur, was keen to reform a state of affairs he considered damaging to the church's public image. [37]

The majority of parishes attempted to clarify the pew situation. In St Clement in 1833 it was decided that the only way to ensure repair was to force it upon the owners. Rights of ownership were temporarily suspended whilst all the pews received a uniform treatment. [38] Likewise in St Brelade in 1839, where the Ecclesiastical Assembly not only decided on uniform repair, but also to charge the proprietors for the work. Furthermore, it was decided that in future there was to be increased strictness over pew sales. [39] The parish of St Peter, however, went a step further. Under the guidance of the Reverend Clement Le Hardy, the parish obtained a Royal Court ruling which upheld the parish's right to control its pews. [40]

This, in turn, was interpreted to mean that occupancy did not imply ownership and that the property of the pew was vested in the parish not in select and privileged individuals. [41]

The response of pew owners to this incursion was mixed. In the parish of St John there was little opposition to a pew reform which restricted each family to one pew, regardless of the number or size of properties owned in the parish. [42] In the parish of Trinity in 1855, on the other hand, the response of intransigent pew owners to proposed structural alterations to the church left the Ecclesiastical Assembly in a complicated wrangle. [43] In Grouville, the Reverend Le Sueur found his reforms consistently blocked by secular opposition, though his intransigent character and tendency to brook no opposition, most obvious in his manipulation of the ecclesiastical records, which he appears to have written and augmented himself, complicated the issue. [44] What is clear is that the debate over pews raged on. In 1863 the Parish Assembly of St Helier spent some considerable time discussing what it felt to be the continuing saga of "propriété des bancs". [45]

In fact the broader desire of local clergymen to renovate their churches perpetuated the pew question. Jersey's churches were in poor repair. The disorganised arrangement of pews meant much valuable space was wasted. The Reverend Le Sueur calculated that in 1866 out of his parish of 2,700 souls, represented by 594 heads of families, 551 heads were totally excluded from having a pew. [46] The answer to the problem was the reorganisation of the church interior: space was to be maximised and the number of public pews increased.

The implications for secular rights again aroused much opposition. In Grouville, after long debate, votes of no confidence and accusations of illegal procedure, the church was finally reorganised by November 1880: 28 out of 71 pews now belonged to the parish. [47] In St Helier, the Reverend Philippe Filleul was forced to settle for a uniform system of private pews sited in orderly fashion, despite his desire to see them abolished altogether. [48] In St Mary the Reverend Balleine's new pews of Gottenburg pine in 1865, installed primarily at his own expense, resulted in outrage from major pewholders. [49] In St Saviour, Charles Starck was so angered at the temporary loss of his pew whilst the church was undergoing repair that he instituted legal proceedings, a move which resulted in a Royal Court decision upholding the Ecclesiastical Assembly's right over the disposition of pews. [50]

In certain instances, internal reorganisation necessitated the enlargement of existing parish churches. This occurred, for instance, at St Saviour's Church in 1841, where an extension added one hundred new seats, and at St Peter in 1886, which found its capacity of 870 inadequate to house both an increased population and the garrison stationed nearby. [51] The large parish of St Ouen went a step further. In 1880 St George's was established as the parish's second church, sited at Portinfer Farm, some three miles north of the parish church. [52]

It was not only the interiors of the churches that required attention, though structural restoration proved less contentious an issue than had pew reform. All of the parish churches attempted restoration of buildings which had remained virtually untouched since the Reformation. The parish church of St Helier had a tree growing out of its steeple prior to the 1860s renovation. [53] Trinity Church prior to its renovation after 1855, under the Reverend William du Heaume, was a building dissected into competing galleries and high pews. [54] In all cases, the repairs undertaken reveal churches in poor condition requiring major attention to structure, such as roofs (Grouville 1838), supports (St. John 1839) floors (St. Lawrence 1888), and fabric, such as windows (St. Mary 1861), and organs (St. Peter 1829). [55]

Renovation in the countryside was matched by church building and the creation of new ecclesiastical districts in the urban parts of the Island to meet the demands of an expanding population. In the Town, an area embracing St Helier, St Saviour and St Lawrence, the churches of St James (1829), All Saints (1834), St Matthew (1839), St Mark (1843), St Luke (1851) and St Andrew on the Esplanade (1870) were established. The new ecclesiastical districts of St Luke (1846), St Andrew (1870) and St Simon (1872) further dissected the parishes and provided more evidence of a changing Church.

All this Church reform and renewal was undertaken without reference to the Nonconformist challenge. Yet, the appearance of new and impressive Nonconformist chapels throughout the Island and their continued rejuvenation as congregations increased cannot but have had an impact on the Established Church's thinking. The potential for such is illustrated by the concern shown by the trustees at St John's Independent Church at the appearance of what they called "une vaste et superbe Chapelle à l'usage des Wesleyens", within view of their own place of worship. The new Sion Chapel was held responsible for drawing away members of the Independent congregation. [56]

Methodists brought to the rural landscape large, grey temple-like structures. These were at their most magnificent at St Ouen (1871) and at Sion (1880), testament to the popularity of dissent in these areas. In certain instances, Methodist chapels utilised the siting of the parish church at the centre of the community by building nearby, such as Bethlehem Chapel in St Mary and St Martin's Chapel in the parish of the same. Other chapels utilised more contemporary settlement growth, such as Sion, on a busy meeting point between parishes, and Six Rues at the already expanding Carrefour Selous in St Lawrence. Even more illustrative of an expanding popularity was the extension of earlier chapels or the building of new and larger structures in close proximity to the old. At St Aubin, in St Brelade, a new larger chapel was built in 1868, only fifty years after the original one was established. At Six Rues the new 1861 chapel was likewise sited close to the smaller one of 1811, which now became a subsidiary hall and school.

Furthermore, the Established Church's reform programme ran alongside a vigorous and self-financed Methodist building campaign. As we observed in Chapter 4, Methodism was financed by its followers, even to the extent of having its own local bank, the Joint Stock Bank. The Established Church, by contrast and in spite of its official link with the parish, experienced great difficulties in raising capital. Parish funds were generally low and principaux not keen to pay more rates than absolutely necessary. In at least three country parishes, bank notes were issued to finance repairs to the church. [57] As the Reverend Abraham Le Sueur discovered, congregation members were not keen to finance restoration programmes aimed at undermining their precious pew privileges. [58]

Where parish funds were not forthcoming the onus was on the clergyman. It was not unusual for the parish rector to have to dip into his own pocket to finance repair. As we saw in Chapter 4, this form of financing could involve significant sums. Lack of money could easily thwart efforts to reform. The Reverend William du Heaume's attempts to extend the availability of services by introducing evensong in 1850 floundered temporarily when no funds were forthcoming to pay for candles, since the new service was not altogether a popular idea among regular churchgoers. [59] The most absurd example of a solution to financial problems was the Reverend Philippe Filleul's scheme in St Helier in 1858, whereby he persuaded parishioners to invest in sheep in New Zealand for a modest return, with additional profits devoted to the church restoration fund. [60] Such initiative notwithstanding, the Church's financing of reform paled somewhat when compared with that of the Methodist's building programme.

The repair and renovation of parish churches were clearly necessary from a purely structural point of view, regardless of Methodist successes. But if the experiences of England and Wales can be fairly extended to Jersey, such programmes can be interpreted as an attempt to reconstitute the Established Church on a more popular footing. [61] This was reflected in the evangelicalism of the Reverends Abraham Le Sueur and Philippe Filleul, whose clear intention was to broaden the appeal of the Church to as wide a congregation as possible. The generality of restoration and reorganisation in the Island's Anglican Churches would suggest these motives were paralleled by other ministers.

Clearly, the result of the Methodist challenge was a number of major problems for the Church and the civil parish . However, it must be stressed that there was a crucial difference between the perceived threat of Methodism and that actually intended. Methodism in Jersey was not outwardly aggressive nor political, and it is doubtful that its adherents intended to challenge the community as such. They left the Established Church for spiritual and social reasons, in a quest for something they believed to have been lost and forsaken by that body. In this respect, Methodism must be seen as a striving for the traditional roots of the community. This is most evident in their attitudes to burial, an event which brought to the fore questions of allegiance and identity.

The Burial Question

The parish cemetery represented the communal resting place of an individual's ancestors, a most important link of continuity with the past. Many families owned a burial plot, sometimes more than one. The social significance of a plot in the parish churchyard is illustrated by the phraseology used by increasingly strict parish assemblies in the nineteenth century which, due, among other things, to pressure of space, decided that if a family moved away from the parish and retained no property therein, its rights to pews and burial plots were to be forfeited; when this occurred a family was said to have disposed "de ses heritages". [62]

Burial presented something of a problem for Nonconformists. Like other Jersey folk, Methodists cherished the social and spiritual significance of the parish churchyard. But control of the cemetery was the prerogative of the rector of the parish and it was he who conducted the services of the Church within his own domain. An individual who had consciously left the Established Church for another denomination was faced with little choice but to be buried in the parish cemetery by the parish rector, using the Anglican service.

To a certain extent this situation was avoided by those rectors, such as the Reverends François Jeune and Jacques Hemery of St Helier (see Chapter 4), who allowed Nonconformists to be buried in the parish churchyard according to their chosen rites. The extent of this toleration is all the more appreciated when it is realised that such a policy was in direct contravention of Church rules. Whilst Canon 19 of the Ecclesiastical Canons gave parish ministers control of all burials, it also stipulated that the Book of Common Prayer should be followed at all times.

Some Parish Assemblies, too, showed themselves sympathetic to the plight of Nonconformists. In the parish of St John, for instance, the regulations for the new cemetery in 1867 stipulated that "Toute personne n'étant pas en Communion avec l'Église et désirant réquerer les services d'un ministre Nonconformiste pour officer à l'inhumation d'un mort dans le Cimetiére, aura la faculte de la faire pourvu qu'elle en previenne le recteur ou son vicaire, et acquitte les honoraires dudit Recteur ainsi que ceux du Lecteur". [63]

Not all were as tolerant. At St Saviour's cemetery in 1844 the Rector, the Reverend Samuel Wright, refused entry to a Methodist minister leading a burial party for the Anthoine family into the churchyard. [64] This was an isolated incident, but in the same parish, only a few years later, a division among parishioners as to the regulations governing the new cemetery showed how some individuals were not willing to accommodate Nonconformist demands. Article 16 of the new cemetery regulations enabled all denominations to be buried in the cemetery by the relevant officiating minister, provided that the stipend remained with the rector. Those opposed to the article saw it is an attack against the common law and attempt to turn the parish cemetery into some sort of "company", no doubt a reference to the attempts of dissenters to establish independent cemeteries. [65] In St Ouen, on the other hand, the regulations for the new cemetery in 1830 simply made no mention of provision for Nonconformists; those requiring a burial plot were to apply through the usual channel of the Ecclesiastical Assembly. [66]

Only one weak attempt was made at legislative level to clarify the position. Such had been the rancour surrounding St Saviour's new cemetery in 1848 that the Bishop of Winchester had refused to confirm its establishment. The Connétable of St Saviour, Francois Godfray, no doubt influenced by the fact that his family included some Methodists, responded with a Projet de Loi in the States which, he claimed, would respect both the rectors' rights and religious liberty. The Projet, which in many respects resembled the aforementioned St John's solution of 1867, was deferred and no more was heard of it. [67]

Given that no uniform attitude to Nonconformist burial in Church of England churchyards existed, local dissenters responded to their predicament with the creation of alternative resting places. In the 1850s at least five independent cemeteries were established throughout the Island, set-up behind trusts similar to those holding legal title to Nonconformist chapels in order to avoid the problems of inheritance and bankruptcy. [68] The new cemeteries were strategically located at points central to groups of parishes. This was most evident at Sion, where Macpela Cemetery (1851) was established on the boundaries of St John, Trinity and St Helier, and Philadelphie Cemetery (no date available, though the tombstones would suggest the 1850s) at St Peter, which could serve the western parishes of St Ouen, St Mary and St Peter. [69] Here again the Nonconformists had brought a change to the rural landscape and diverted social patterns away from the traditional communal centre.

Macpela Cemetery stands testament to this day to the early success of the Island's independent cemeteries. It allowed all individuals to be buried there, with no restriction as to the service used. As a result it proved immediately popular with the French 'proscrits' exiled in the Island. 'Proscrit' burials had been banned in the parish of St Helier in 1853 because they were considered too political and blasphemous. Macpela now became the destination for long funeral processions from St Helier and the location for even longer burial speeches by the likes of Victor Hugo. [70]

In the absence of burial books, none of which have been located, the number of tombstones in independent cemeteries show that many Nonconformists turned away from their traditional burial sites. It is equally clear, however, that some dissenters preferred to retain their traditional links with the community of the dead and bury family in the parish churchyard, albeit at the risk of burial by Anglican service. This can be gauged by the fact that the Island's independent cemeteries were simply not big enough to cater for the number of local Nonconformists. Furthermore, as the experience of Grouville's dissenters shows, when given the option between independent or traditional cemeteries, provided there was a choice of service, the latter quite clearly prevailed.

As early as 1848 the demand for space in Grouville cemetery, augmented by the burial of foreigners and members of the British armed services, became most pressing. [71] The problem was exacerbated by the siting of the church and cemetery which effectively left the area surrounded on all sides either by road or meadowland. The Ecclesiastical Assembly's solution was an alternative resting place at Les Mielles, near the seashore and nearly a mile away from the church. The site was established as a parish cemetery in 1849. Yet within only two years, it became clear that parishioners disliked a resting place so far away from the traditional churchyard and it remained unused. [72]

Nonconformists in the parish established their own burial ground in 1852. This was no doubt a response to the lack of space in the parish churchyard and perhaps even to the new Rector, Abraham Le Sueur (1851-1885), a known anti-dissenter. The independent Cimetière de la Croix was located across the road from Grouville church, on a site no doubt viewed with jealous eyes by parish officials who had been forced to locate the new churchyard at Les Mielles. Judging by the tombstones the independent cemetery was put to immediate use. But this was not to last. In 1881 the burial question was turned on its head. The *Parliamentary Burials Act 1880,* which allowed parishioners to be buried in the parish churchyard with the rites of their choice, was extended to the Island. [73] Many Nonconformists returned to their former burial grounds. In 1884 a previously thriving Cimetière de la Croix was offered to the parish, and purchased in 1888, its continued existence as an independent cemetery jeopardised due to lack of funds from burials. [74] Given the option, many Nonconformists showed themselves keen to return to their "heritages".

The burial question provides a most interesting reflection on the communal attitudes of local Methodists, and of Jersey rural society generally. It appears that it was not difficult for the individual to separate and keep distinct in his mind the Church in its secular and religious rôles. To be buried in the parish churchyard, even if your spiritual needs had taken you away from the Established Church, was a reinforcement of your communal and social existence. It was never the intention of Methodists to reject the communal values of Jersey society.

Looking at it another way, we may ask to what extent the Methodists attempted to construct a separate identity? In spiritual terms this was an ambition realised by the creation of a separate infrastructure of buildings, churchyards, finance, internal government and worship. But whilst inside the Jersey country chapel, to judge by better documented English and Welsh experiences, worship was doubtless a less formal and more egalitarian affair than might be found in a parish church, in social composition its hierarchy and deference structure was not all that different from that outside.

In the final analysis this idea that the Methodist and Anglican congregations were not all that far apart can be illustrated by observing a leading member from each. P.J. Brée, of La Sente, Grouville, and C.P. Le Cornu, of La Hague Manor, St Peter, were both leading men in the latter part of the nineteenth century. Both of them were renowned agriculturists and conservatively minded politicians. They were men of some wealth. Two parallel Jerseymen differing only in religion; Brée, a Methodist lay-preacher and leading member of La Rocque Chapel; Le Cornu, a traditional churchman, considering pews important enough to fight over in 1872, and a member of St Peter's Church significant enough to have a plaque to his memory inside the church.[75]

All this is not to say that Methodism was simply a reproduction of the community at large, but that in essence it was very similar. Thus any challenge that resulted from the popularity of Methodism in the country was kept within recognisable bounds. It was a threat to the Established Church, to its pride if nothing else, and we can gauge this by the Anglican attempts to broaden its appeal to the population from the mid-nineteenth century onward. But it was not a real threat to the community. A simple shift of the parish to a civil footing enabled the parish organisation to encompass the changes brought about by the successes of Nonconformism. In other words the community responded with a compromise acceptable to its members.

The Language Question

In stark contrast to the challenges brought about by the popularity of Nonconformism and the response it engendered from both Church and community, the challenge of the English language revealed the inadequacy of the rural bloc in dealing with a force that operated outside its framework of understanding and control. The whole language question was complex, difficult to identify, difficult to comprehend and, hence, difficult to respond to.

Much of the rural community's power to defend its privileges and traditions from external influence relied on the ability to localise the challenge and force any confrontation on its own terms and within its own structures. In all cases it was dependent on its leading members identifying the threat and mobilising community resources. The threat of the English language was that it operated on many levels simultaneously. It was supported internally by a large body of speakers and a Jersey middle class desirous of acquiring it, externally by the Crown's insistence on conformity in education and more generally still by the official view that British possessions should reflect British nationality. No effective defence was mounted against the incursions of the English language, partly because of this complexity of the challenge and, even more so, because of the apparently ambivalent attitude of Jersey's upper middle-class leaders.

The Cultural Response

As early as the 1840s, in the wake of the Carus Wilson case (see Chapter 5), a section of the population showed itself aware of the threat to Jèrriais from English and the implications of such a challenge. Carus Wilson's defiance of the Royal Court and his attempt to ridicule the local language represented the attitude of but a few political agitators; the response to his outrage, however, reflected a growing concern among some members of the Jersey middle class. [76] The identification of a threat was most evident in the newspapers, particularly the *Chronique* and the *Nouvelle Chronique*, and, to a lesser extent, the *Constitutionnel.* That the awareness should come from the press reflects the absence of any other intellectual medium and the fact that the leading members of the Jersey intelligentsia saw this as the only forum for their ideas.

This awareness was enhanced and broadened by the 1850s, but more obviously in the 1870s, by a cultural response, again through the medium of the press, which sought to give Jèrriais both an intellectual base and a defensive rôle. Through the work of a small group of populist poets, no more than a dozen throughout the century, the attitudes of the native population to a changing Jersey society were made apparent.

The first individual to turn to dialect writing in the nineteenth century, the first such recorded since the twelfth-century poet Wace, was Matthieu Le Geyt in the 1830s. Le Geyt's subject matter was local incidents brought to a more lofty plane. Surprisingly, in view of ethnic stirrings elsewhere, his work bore no nationalist trait, rather it tended to criticise the anti-modernist and backward-looking traits of the local community. Thus, in his poem "Adraisse es chains de la Vingtaine du Mont au Pretre par un Vingtgny naguerre d'une' aoûte pâraisse" the refusal of the country to accept new roads, even when financed by the States, was portrayed as: "Comme des bêtes saie, rester dans vot' puté, Comme ces animàouts là, y vos faout varvoté". [77] Similarly, in his 'Le Dialogue entre Jeanneton de Saouvoeux et Nénai de St Ouen' the latter parish, already cast as the bastion of tradition and the past, was represented as introverted and anti-urban, a restraint on a modernising Jersey. [78]

Le Geyt's work established a mould which would determine much of the dialect work for the rest of the century. He was essentially a cultural poet not a nationalist writer and those that followed, whilst maybe joining the two elements in sentiment, rarely fused them in their work. Lebarbenchon, in his study of Norman language poetry, makes the point that Le Geyt's work was more a response to the cultural diffusion that resulted from the influx of a large number of immigrants, mainly the English, than a linguistic reaction against any perceived threat. [79] This is supported by the fact that at Le Geyt's time of writing the 1830s there was no obvious awareness of a threat. After Le Geyt, dialect writers became far more aware of their rôle in a society under seige linguistically and of the need to create some form of intellectual basis for Jersiais.

The important distinction implicit above between an overtly nationalist literature and a more academic response is most evident in the work of Robert Pipon Marett. As an advocate, Connétable of St Helier (1856-1858) and finally Bailiff in 1880, Marett was a reformist in the mould of Pierre le Sueur, involved in the Jersey Reform League and in the running of the French language reformist paper *La Patrie* (1849-1855). [80] He was, too, an ardent Jersey nationalist and on the hustings in 1856 proclaimed "First and foremost I am a Jerseyman, jealous to preserve our nationality: I am proud of the title of being a British subject to have descended from these glorious Normans who left their country to avoid persecution, but I will not allow our nationality to be swallowed up into that of England". [81]

In his poetry, by contrast, Marett went a step further than this raw nationalism, preferring instead to utilise a deep understanding of the Island to bring Jèrriais to its highest level of both grammar and expression. [82] His nationalism and his staunch defence of Jersey institutions in the political arena were not represented in his work which, instead, concentrated on providing the language with a literature and, hence, a credibility that had been found wanting since the challenge of the English language.

Marett's intentions, though not his style, were paralleled by others, notably by the endeavours of A.A. Le Gros, a St Peter's farmer and Connétable of the same parish. [83] It was ironic, considering his lifetime devotion to Jèrriais, that he received his education at Victoria College, the establishment of which represented the triumph of those who wished to anglicise. His main academic work was the publication of pieces in local dialect, and between 1868 and 1875 published annually *La Nouvelle Annaie, Piéches Originalles en Normand Jersiais*. [84] His other main literary preoccupation, the compilation of a dialect dictionary, bore fruit with the publication of the *Glossaire du Patois Jersiais* in 1924. [85]

On a more populist level, although in similar vein, was the appearance in the local French language press of a host of dialect characters, like 'Mon Anmin Flippe', 'Me Jean et mon couesin Ph'lip', and 'Bram Bilo'. The characters represented simple but observant rustics, lamenting the challenges to their society, decrying the changes to the Island and reasserting local values. The question of language featured prominently, as L'Ami Flippe showed in his criticism of the election manifesto of one Jean Cabot:

"Chès gens-là veulent la loi angliache.
Et y save' bain qu' dans les États,
Maĉt' Jean lus dit tout haut commèche
Que nous, Jèrriais, n'en voulons pas". [86],
Me Jean' too, could tell his cousin 'Ph'lip',
"Qu'est qui perdra Gerry ?, chest bain la langue angliaise,
A chinquante ans d'ichin' non n' paslla pus un mot,
De man bouan patois". [87]

The major distinction between these rustic soothsayers and the more academic works was the formers' direct political content, often a means for those involved in newspapers to further their views in the guise of an appealing character. With the likes of 'L'Ami Flippe' came a sense of identity, brought on by an anecdotal and semi-humourous style. Such characters were portrayed as if they represented a host of like-minded people out in the country who were concerned about the undermining of the treasured 'temps passés'. [88]

What then were the effects of these two movements, which shared origins and intentions, but not means? There are several factors which suggest that readership of dialect poetry was broad. Firstly, the fact that Jersey supported a large number of newspapers, four major ones in the 1850s - *La Chronique*, *Le Constitutionnel*, the *Jersey Times* and the *British Press* - is suggestive of a fairly wide readership in itself. This might be extended to the anthologies of local poetry by Abraham Mourant and A.A. Le Gros who, after all, published for commercial as well as cultural reasons. Secondly, whilst newspapers did not publish circulation figures, it is clear that they reached the extremities of country parishes. Many is the Jersey farm building which to this day has scraps of nineteenth-century newspapers tacked to its walls and doors, though quite why this is so is unclear. As Victor Hugo noted, with some surprise, in the 1850s, the Jersey people were well informed, both about local politics and world affairs. [89] Even earlier than this, in 1798, W.T. Money had noted how as he passed through the parish of St Lawrence, the parish elders were busy discussing "the subjects of Irish Treason, and the conjectured expedition of Bonaparte into Egypt". [90]

What the influence of the local cultural awakening was, however, is not so easy to discern. This is not to say it had no influence. Parish Assemblies, as we have seen elsewhere (Chapters 5 & 6), viewed the threats to the local way of life as any other challenge to country power and responded accordingly. But there is no sign that country folk made any concerted efforts to champion their own culture. This is not surprising. The local tongue and culture remained paramount in the countryside throughout the nineteenth century. Dissemination of dialect works in the rural community, albeit in a written form of Jèrriais which was new to the Island, was preaching to the converted.

The local intelligentsia, on the other hand, was stirred to act by the need to champion a local culture and identity. This was made manifest in the Channel Islands' Exhibition of 1871. Held at Victoria College and no doubt inspired by the Great Exhibition of 1851, the Exhibition drew together the multifarious elements that could be said to represent the local identity, be they historical, artistic or economic. [91] Here was the first concerted effort to assert an image of the Islands as something distinct from the various anglicising influences at work.

The importance of an identity was made even more evident by the attempts to place Jersey culture within an institutional framework. The intelligentsia chose to defend their language and heritage by means of a Société Jersiaise. As in other spheres, the Island's tendency to utilise structural means of defence was made apparent.

Actually, the Société Jersiaise had a precursor, albeit one which was shorter lived and of more modest aspirations. As early as the 1840s, in true salon style, a Société d'Émulation had been established, its aim, local literary pursuits. We know little about it other than the fact that the dialect poet Henri Luce Manuel was involved in it and that Tréhounais won a prize essay competition in 1843 initiated by the society, for his work on Jersey history. [92]

It was, however, the Société Jersiaise, established in 1873, which brought together the various local intellectual currents and encouraged the increasing penchant for the past. Its founding aim was "L'étude de l'Histoire et de la Langue du Pays, la conservation des Antiquités de l'Ile et la publication de Documents Historiques". [93] Its founders, A.A. Le Gros (Connétable and poet) and Philippe Langlois (poet), and its first committee, including R. Pipon Marett (advocate, reformist and poet), W.L. de Gruchy (academic and Jurat), James Boeille (local educationalist) and C.P. Le Cornu (agriculturalist and seigneur), represented the leading intellectuals and members of Jersey society. [94]

The *Chronique* felt the founding of this intellectual organisation to be crucial. "Depuis longtemps," it claimed in 1873, "les idées Jersiaises semblent se perdre et se fondre insensiblement dans les idées anglaises....", but, "heureusement que le sentiment patriotique n'est pas encore éteint et que les personnes les plus influentes de la société de l'Île, celles qui sont à la téte des affaires du pays fondent une société entièrement Jersiaise, dont l'effet principal sera de conserver au pays son autonomie et de faire aimer cette Île en la faisant mieux connître, non seulement des étrangers, mais même de ses habitants". [95]

The stated aims of the Société Jersiaise reflected neither the overtly political nor populist educator themes that the *Chronique* wishfully suggested. It nonetheless reflected the views of its founders in claiming that "Les traits les plus caractéristiques d'un pays sont sa langue, ses institutions, son histoire; et c'est dans une connaissance intime de cette dernière, qu'un peuple puise ces sentiments de dévouement et de patriotisme qui font sa force et sa vie, et qui empêchent sa décadence".[96]

The Société Jersiaise was not a political lobby group. This is an important point, particularly if we consider that the majority of its eighty members in 1873 were local politicians, Connétables, Jurats and Rectors. Its bulletins contained no contemporary analysis of language, politics or economics. In fact, if anything, the early work appears to have concentrated on archaeology, very much in vogue at the time, and ironically, since the man involved in much of the work was English his articles were in that language.[97] The Société's response to any perceived changes or threats to its society was very much in the mould of the academic dialect poets: high learning without an obvious partisan or nationalist intention. The local press interpreted this policy as a sell-out, a foresaking of all that the Jersey past meant to its people for commercial gain.[98] On the other hand, it might be interpreted as a measured reaction to what was rapidly becoming a *fait accompli*. Ultimately, it was a response hindered by those very factors which ensured the success of English culture in the Island: the anglophile desires of a section of the Jersey middle-class, including Société members, and, more significantly in terms of a defence, the failure to mount an effective institutional barrier via the States.

The Failure of the Institutional Response

Jersey's institutional response to the English cultural threat was weak from the outset. Whilst a public awareness of the threat to the local language had been forming since the early 1840s, stimulated by a cultural response in the form of dialect poetry and prose, the subject received no serious attention at legislative level until 1860. In that year a debate took place on the teaching of French in the Island. It was stimulated by the newly-built Victoria College, although broadened to the language question generally. The debate did little other than air conflicting opinions and reflected a general inability to present a united front in defence of the local tongue.[99]

The ability of the local population to utilise its institutions in self-defence was, as we have seen, something much in evidence in nineteenth-century Jersey. On the Victoria College issue alone (see Chapter 5), the Island's institutional strength had given much cause for concern to supporters of the English-style public school. "I cannot disguise from myself that great mischief will issue," wrote the Lieutenant-Governor, Frederick Love, in 1853, "should the mixed committee [which included some States members] be permitted to persevere in legislating for the College, as it is the opinion of all those interested in the welfare of the College, as well as myself, that from what has already taken place, private interest will predominate to the injury, if not destruction of the institution, which, at present, promises such benefit to the Island by the introduction of the English language and instruction in preference to those of France".[100]

The Lieutenant-Governor's fears were to an extent justified. In 1852, François Godfray had shown the full power of the rural bloc when he led a successful opposition in the States against the appointment of the Reverend W.G. Henderson as mathematics master, on the grounds that he could not speak French.[101] It proved, however, to be a minor victory, for in 1860 the Privy Council ruled that the Crown, which financed the College, should hold a controlling majority on the Mixed Committee.[102] Structural defences were ineffective against external financial pressure and the internal complicity of those who wished to see the English language triumph.

In the 1860 States debate, it was again François Godfray (now a Deputy for St Saviour) who led the attack. He expressed his deep concern for the fact that French was being taught in Island schools primarily as a foreign language. An anecdote attributed to the late Lieutenant-Governor, Godfrey Mundy, was repeated to effect: "Preserve your language if you wish to preserve your independence". Nonetheless, despite exchanges, the renewed debate of 1861 did little else than appoint a committee to look into the matter.[103] In both sessions, two rectors, the Reverends Philippe Guille of St Martin and Abraham Le Sueur of Grouville, showed themselves to be very much in favour of the advance of the English language.

The answer of the States to the language question finally came in 1873, when it was decided to link local financial aid to schools to the compulsory teaching of French.[104] It was an attempt to reassert the pre-eminence of the French language, but was weakened from the outset by the fact that the teaching of English was assured an equal place throughout the Island's education system by the continued and financially necessary link with the Privy Council.

The teaching of English in Jersey was not an option. In 1871 the Privy Council had temporarily withdrawn its educational funding in a successful attempt to coerce the States into adopting Parliament's 1870 *Elementary Education Act*. The apparent reluctance of Parliament and the Privy Council to avoid direct interference in Island affairs, as observed in the wake of the Royal Commission of 1861 (see Chapter 6), clearly did not extend to areas where it controlled the purse strings. The point was not missed by the *Nouvelle Chronique*, which appreciated that the compulsory visits of English School Inspectors meant pupil assessment in the English language. The withdrawal of funds as a lever of conformity left only one option, if the local identity was to be preserved: the creation of an independent 'national' education policy.[105]

Any hope of such an education policy ended with the bank crashes of 1873 and, more particularly, 1886 (see Chapter 3). The crash of what was known locally as the States Bank in 1886 and the imprisonment of the Treasurer of the States for fraud revealed an Island as yet unprepared or unable to take full control of its financial affairs. [106] If the States' solution of 1873 was *de minimis* it was one forced upon the legislature by both circumstance and external pressure.

The weak attempt at solving the linguistic dilemma was also beleaguered in other respects. Several of the country clergy had pointed out to the 1861 Commission that the choice of English as the language of instruction had been determined by the superiority of English 'rudimentary books'; all instruction naturally followed in that tongue. [107] Similarly, if the compulsory teaching of French was a basis to protect the national identity, then what exactly was that identity? The cultural movement could as yet offer little more than a broad, linguistic identity, the representative characters of which were rustic soothsayers.

The States' School Inspectors showed themselves aware of the problem. Monsieur Bouchet's French Report for 1882 warned how "le jour ou Jersey verrait disparaître sa langue nationale, serait marqué par la grande calamité publique". [108] This concern was behind a move in 1871 to create a text book style history of Jersey for use in primary schools, which though receiving financial backing from the Assembly of Governor, Bailiff and Jurats, never reached fruition. [109]

Thus the official local solution to the language question, as voiced by the States in 1873, remained the teaching of the French language. Yet it was a tongue almost as foreign to rural Jèrriais speakers as it was to urban English speakers. More significantly, English was given equal status in education. French was to be taught alongside the very language that was threatening the Jersey identity.

By the 1880s a new concern appeared to confound the issue and further undermine the local tongue. The introduction of a large body of Breton labourers to the Island and the decision of many of them to stay on, saw a local reaction tantamount to a social and economic racism. The threat of a French cultural takeover in the countryside brought down certain leading members in Jersey society, unsure of their own cultural foundations, on the side of the English language as a necessary means of effective opposition.

The bias against the French was one of historical standing. This much was noted by Victor Hugo when he said "Jerseymen and Guernseymen are certainly not English without wanting to be, but they are French without knowing it". [110] As we have observed in Chapter 9, French immigrants were primarily agricultural labourers, willing to pay the high rents demanded by Jersey landlords in the hope that this might lead to some measure of economic independence. The majority of them were in a position of social and economic inferiority.

However, their presence was numerically significant, and much of it was in the countryside. This presence was accentuated by their religion and the building of Catholic churches in the Island. Some concern was not unnatural. In other words, Bretons stood out amidst the rural community and as such presented an obvious threat.

The Breton challenge had to be curbed. The question occupied the States' attention far more than had the threat of the English language. Frenchmen, claimed the Reverend Edouard Le Feuvre of Grouville, in debate in 1891, were driving out locals from the countryside, the result of which was the introduction of a culture which bid fair to overwhelm local institutions. The point was repeated by the specially appointed States' Comité de l'Immigration of 1906. It is clear from both sources that the concern stemmed from the fact that the French presence was in the countryside, the bastion of Jersey power and identity. The English presence, by contrast, was in the Town. Hence the solution proposed by both the Reverend Le Feuvre and the Comité de l'Immigration: the assurance that the English language would be thoroughly applied in local education. [111] It was curious how the English language could be utilised as a weapon by both sides of the linguistic camp.

The anti-French feeling engendered by the Breton presence had far more to do with the prejudices of an increasingly anglicised Jersey middle-class than it did any real cultural threat from that quarter. Given the social composition of the Bretons and their objectives, it was an irrational response. But it was one which showed how much a section of the Jersey middle-class had changed in half a century.

By the turn of the nineteenth century many of the individualist traits recognised as an historical characteristic among the rural community had taken on the appearance of bourgeois pretension. To enter the farmhouse of a middle-class Jerseyman in the late nineteenth century could prove an experience far different from that of earlier in the century. Gone was the simplicity, bordering on parsimony, and instead the picture portrayed by Bear in 1888: "There is nothing suggestive of penury in the style of living that the larger Jersey farmers adopt. After finding [him] at work in the field with his men, it is somewhat surprising to a stranger to be conducted by him into a drawing room fitted with all the modern decorations found in a middle-class suburban residence". [112] Galichet, too, pointed out the taste for comforts and bourgeois ease: James Baudains' taste for Longfellow, his daughters' involvement in amateur dramatics, and the importance of the piano to the parlour. [113]

Individualism and bourgeois pretension were not necessarily odd bedfellows. Many of the characteristics one points to as evidence of an embourgeoisement process were naturally present in the Jerseyman's make-up. Individualism and the importance of the household as opposed to the communal, often expressed in England and France as a move away from village life, were traits of the Jerseyman from the feudal period. On the other hand, the desires for the trappings of bourgeois life were intertwined and in many ways inseparable from the desires to adopt English gentlemanly values and lifestyles, most evident in the adoption of the English language. French immigrants drew attention away from the conscious efforts of sections of the Jersey middle class to anglicise both their own lifestyles and those of their society.

Any institutional response to the advance of the English language was thus hampered by several major and, as it turned out, insurmountable obstacles. In February 1900 this state of affairs was officially recognised by the legislature when the States of Jersey decided that the English language could be used in their debates. [114] The decision was the most poignant and official statement as to the advance of the English language in the Island. A similar measure had failed to pass the vote, albeit narrowly, in 1893. [115] The English language was now considered sufficiently representative to be used in the political decision making of the States, the bastion for so long of rural power. It was a move which represented a *de facto* realisation of the advance of the English language in the Island. It was a reality recognised elsewhere too and one succinctly represented at grass-root level by the decision of the trustees of La Rocque Methodist Chapel in 1901 to purchase English hymnals instead of the traditional French ones. [116] The 1900 decision must have surprised few people.

The Decline of Jèrriais and the Implications for the Jersey Identity

The success of the English language had certain implications for the Jersey identity. Jèrriais, the language of the hearth, as expressed in traditions, customs and institutions, was viewed as an important component of that identity. The *Chronique* stated the case most lyrically in 1844. The local tongue, it claimed, was the touchstone of the rural identity and of the peasantry "l'ancre de salut des nationalités, ...qui, lui, aime son pays sans le crier sur les touts et met la langue de ses pères et son coeur dans le même panier". [117]

By 1900 the state of the local language was such as to place the local identity in question. At its most basic, the linguistic divide was that of Town and country. English was the language dominant in the Town. All points of contact with people of English origin, the majority of whom showed no tendency to learn either French or the less accessible Jèrriais, were of necessity in English. The large number of English speakers, concentrated predominantly in the urban areas of St Helier, St Saviour and St Clement, enabled the English language to continue and, ultimately, to dominate. Friedrich Engels, on his second visit to Jersey in 1874, commented on the urban spread of the language: "There are two small railways here now, (running east and west from St Helier, along the south coast) on which you never hear a word of French". [118] The spread was to continue.

In the countryside there can be little doubt that Jèrriais still dominated in 1900. An analysis of the younger generation provides the best indicator of the advance of the English language and the log books of Trinity School, geographically far more accessible than the still distant parishes of St Mary and St Ouen, show that in the 1890s country children were still struggling with the English language. [119] Among the older generation English may have formed the language of commerce but in the parish assemblies the French language was retained as the medium of discussion and record until at least the 1930s. It survived as long as it served a communicative need.

The States decision of 1900 was thus a reflection of the popular use of English but not of its dominance. Jersey society retained a linguistic division of separate but overlapping spheres. A tripartite division of language between French, Jèrriais and English remained until well into the twentieth century.

A Jèrriais increasingly restricted to the countryside was, however, a weakened language. In 1866 the *Chronique* charted its decline as representative of the weakening Jersey identity. The period 1830 to 1850 it labelled the "Génération de bâtarde", that of 1850 to the time of writing the "Génération de renégats n'ayant plus de 'Jèrriais' que le nom, et qu'on verra bientôt à l'oeuvre". [120] The paper gave no comparable analysis at the turn of the century, but it is doubtful that it would have seen cause to be hopeful.

Newspaper editorialists and correspondents on the subject searched for a scapegoat to blame for the decline of the local tongue. All were united in their indictment of the middle class, of which they were a part, for its ambition and pretension. Here was the class that had abandoned its heritage in the belief that "succès et anglicanisation ont tout un". [121] All contributors showed themselves willing to be associated with traditional values and to represent the voice of the championed countryside in moralistic tone, yet offered no constructive advice and no alternative perspective from which to defend the native tongue and, hence, the local nationality.

The local bourgeoisie, be they Town-based or from the country, could not fairly escape charges of complicity in the local cultural decline. As one French author, assessing the change brought about by commercial success as early as 1849, pointed out: "Plus d'un Jersyais, par ambition, se consolerait d'être Anglais". By comparing the experiences of Jersey and Guernsey he felt much could be understood, the latter being "Moins considérable et moins importante que sa voisine, cette dernière île est à la fois plus normande et plus anglaise. D'une part, le fond de la population a mieux conservé qu' à Jersey sa naïveté primitive, ses moeurs un peu rudes, son patois du XIIe siécle; de l'autre, l'influence brittanique s'est fait plus fortement sentir dans les hautes classes. De l à deux races distinctes:

l'une, celle des villes et des maisons de plaisance, riche et visant au luxe; l'autre, celle des campagnes et des champs, simple et satisfaite de peu". [122]

Implicit in this argument was the assertion that some degree of anglicisation was the price to pay for commercial success; language was a part of that price. It is clear that a section of the anglophile local middle class was willing to pay that price. But it is equally clear that certain members of the local intelligentsia were not willing to allow the cost to be the suppression of local culture. Their problem after the mid-nineteenth century was to construct some form of unifying identity from component parts weakened by the challenge from the English language and culture.The attempts of the poets and lexicographers to establish an academic and artistic base for Jèrriais were a response to the threat of anglicisation. But the local tongue, its use undermined, as we have seen in this chapter and Chapter 5, by a variety of factors, was not a powerful enough platform upon which to build an identity.

The local intelligentsia turned to a broader base. In the establishment of the Société Jersiaise there was an attempt to redefine the substance of nationality away from language to something more solid and all-embracing: the Island's historic rights or as one commentator put it, "Nos Privileges". [123] The Jersey nationality was to be founded on something which an already well-defined society, geographically and historically at least, shared, its historic privileges.

In fact the Société Jersiaise represented a rejuvenation of traditional notions of identity rather than any new cultural nationalism. Plees had made the point in 1817 that nationality was not something that the Islanders had ever been forced to think about particularly. He did not deny Jersey's loyalty to the Crown but suggested it sprang from "hereditary impression", not any genuine identification of spirit or cause. [124] The point was well taken. Laying aside all loyalties and views of Crown overlordship, Jersey was in many respects an entity distinct from the English mainland, expressed at a most potent level in its law, political structures and language. One only need study one of the many petitions from the Island demanding verification and vindication of its many historical rights and privileges to observe this distinction.

Such a definition differentiated between the Island of Jersey and England, and the question of a nationality or a separate identity was required in this context only. In no way was Jersey suggesting that it was desirous of independence, rather it required a definition of its identity in a relationship which was in many ways tantamount to dependence.

The breadth of historical rights as a basis of nationality was important because it allowed for dissent within the camp. The success of the English language, particularly via a uniform education system, could be taken aboard and utilised as a catalyst to the Jersey identity.

Indeed, as the *British Press and Jersey Times* pointed out in 1868, there was but little option other than to include English as part of that identity.[125] Similarly, whilst the decline of the local language as a means of communication could not be reversed, its existence as a part of the unique Jersey experience would live on in the Island's historically-based identity.

As a form of long term defence the concept of Jersey nationality, though perhaps ethnicity is the more appropriate term, cleverly utilised the bonds of the community, its mentality and its institutions. Likewise, by placing that concept of shared values and privileges in the context of the past it allowed for such an identity to be born through the triumph of the English language. Ultimately, however, the absence of Jèrriais from the construct weakened the Island's separate and distinct identity. The success of the English language made the introduction and acceptance of its associated culture all the more effective in the following century.

Already by 1900 there were signs that Jersey society had moved beyond its traditional affiliations of loyalty to the Crown towards something approaching an acceptance of English culture. The local manifestations of mourning that followed the death of Queen Victoria in 1901 were extensive: newspapers were bordered in black; bells tolled in the parish churches and memorial services were filled to capacity; society meetings, banquets and balls were cancelled; the Island forwarded a telegram of its deepest sympathy.[126] But all this was to be expected in an Island which had for centuries sworn allegiance to the Crown. More significant, were the reactions to the incidents and issues of life in Britain and the Empire. A prime example of this was the reaction to the raising of the seige of Mafeking in 1900. Here was a story that the local press covered in detail for the full 217 days of the Boers' seige. When victory came the celebrations were extensive: shops and schools were closed; thanksgiving services were held; festivities rang in the streets of St Helier.[127] The integration of English culture into Jersey society was already well under way.

The Parish Compromised

Elsewhere too there were ominous signs that Jersey society had not weathered the storm of nineteenth-century change as well as might have appeared at first sight. Culturally, the Island always looked prone to an effective challenge but, institutionally, the rural bloc had shown itself in full command. However, both challenge and response had weakened the parish, the unit so central to its power and way of life. By the end of the nineteenth century that most fundamental of Jersey institutions was a parish compromised.

In Chapter 7, we concluded by showing the Jersey parish in a powerful position. And certainly, if restrictive legislation alone was the criterion by which to analyse the influence and progress of modernisation and reform on the parish structure, then the historian might fairly say that the rural power bloc in the States had ensured no harm came to its treasured parish organisation. However, by the 1880s and 1890s there is evidence to suggest that in the defence of its institutions the rural bloc was not as astute as it thought, at least not when it came to less obvious and direct threats. It was possible for communal values and concerns to become confused and the outcome, as in the case of primary education, could be a curtailment of parish power.

No parish appears to have been opposed to the idea of compulsory primary education, but the commitment there to contained in the *Loi (1899) sur Écoles Élémentaires et l'Instruction Obligatoire* held the seeds of increased government involvement in the affairs of the individual and of a centralisation which ultimately served to undermine the power of the parish. Parish schools were to be controlled by a centralised States' committee and finance in part determined by English Education Inspectors. [128] In time-honoured fashion parishes set about establishing committees to deal with the overview of parish education, but parish dissatisfaction with the unprecedented scale of States' involvement was expressed throughout the Island. In St John, the Parish Assembly criticised the undermining of individual liberties. [129] In St Helier, the Parish Assembly showed concern for the incursions on the private sector which would result from the Law. [130]

Much appeared to have changed in the course of the century. In 1814 a long tradition of independence had been reflected in the refusal of many of the country States members to accede to the Bailiff's proposal to thank General Don for his contribution to the Island's modernisation (on Don's road system see Introductory section), there being a general feeling that the price of his advances, infringement of local privileges and individual liberties, was too high. [131] Now in the 1890s the parishes themselves were acceding to a curtailment of those very ideals, in their agreement to allow the English Education Department to interfere in local education. [132]

The Jersey Militia, too, was experiencing organisational changes which showed how the parish was ceasing to be the focal point of all Island activity. The regimental structure of 1771 had drawn battalions from groups of three parishes. The North-West Battalion, for example, was recruited from the parishes of St Ouen, St Mary and St John. Parish integrity had been retained by ensuring that Militiamen performed compulsory guard duty only along the coastline of their own parish. But general dissatisfaction with both the principle and organisation of the Militia finally roused the British Government, which funded the force, to compel a reform which reduced it from five regiments to three. More importantly, the reform paid no heed to the parish system. [133] Back in 1842, when these changes had first been mooted, the Parish Assembly of St Ouen had expressed its concern for the effect of such a plan, which could only serve to undermine traditional structures. Parishioners now faced the possibility of guard duty in St Brelade, contrary to "comme d'ancienneté". [134] But the 1877 reform reflected popular attitudes to military service which had steadily worsened as the century progressed. In 1816, 3,384 Islanders had signed a petition against the establishment of paid Militia officers and sergeants, claiming this to be a threat to the very core and traditions of the defence force. [135] By the 1880's growing disaffection with Militia drill, the exemptions bestowed upon moneyed individuals and the social pretensions of those with military titles had resulted in an urban based Anti-Compulsory Militia Law League. [136] Clearly, not all parish-based institutions retained popular support.

In other spheres, too, parish-based institutions were under attack and Parish Assemblies voiced their concern. In the parish of St John the seemingly innocent idea that the judge appointed to the Petty Debts Court, established in 1852, be paid for his service was seen as a threat "de nos institutions honorifiques". [137] Mention of challenges to "d'usage", "de ses heritages" and "nos privileges" become more numerous as the century progresses. [138] In 1863, that most communal of practices, the Indictment or first trial, consisting of the defendant's Connétable and twelve of his sworn officers, was abolished, the needs of a reformed penal code being felt to override parochial traditions. [139]

Ironically, little heed was paid to what would prove the most effective challenge to the parish, the widespread popularity of Nonconformism. The divorce of the parish civil from the parish ecclesiastic, in large part the result of the Methodist challenge, resulted in the reconstitution of the municipal body in more powerful and consolidated form. Yet ultimately a parish devoid of its earlier ability to represent its community in every sphere of social, political and religious life, was a parish weakened. No longer in the nineteenth century was the spiritual home of all Jerseymen to be found within the parish framework. The ability to survive socially and religiously outside the parish sphere, save for political representation and law enforcement, left the door open for a further move away from the communal past.

The parish had not escaped compromise. As a crucial indicator of how Jersey society fared against the challenges of the nineteenth century, it did not emerge totally victorious. Nonetheless, political power at Island level and a general faith in the parish as a communal framework, left the parish, and by extension the rural community, in a still powerful position. The parish remained, for the main part, guided "comme d'ancienneté" and relatively unrestricted by statutory guidelines. If Centenier Duparcq's burning of a forged five-pound note in front of the culprit perturbed the Commission of 1861, communal justice did not appear to concern the majority of the Jersey country folk. [140] Similarly, cynical Commissioners might not have believed one witness before them when he claimed his devotion to honorary duty was founded on his love for his Island, but there were plenty of countrymen who would have done so. [141]

The parish continued to function as the primary communal framework in Jersey society because the majority of Jersey society wished it so. It was a parish compromised, just as Jersey society had been forced to give ground to the various forces ranged against it. However, in the face of the pressures of modernisation, both from within and without, the parish remained the bastion of Jersey's independent historical development.

Chapter 11

The Conclusion

In 1875 John de la Haye wrote a long letter to the *British Press and Jersey Times* entitled 'An Expedition Across the Island of Jersey'. It recounted a walk from Millbrook, on the outskirts of the parish of St Helier, in the south of the Island, to the northernmost parish of St John. It was a journey retracing a walk he had completed some forty years earlier and reflected many of the changes in the outward appearance of the Island during that period.[1] It provides a most useful starting point for a broad overview of the major themes of this work.

Arriving at Millbrook from the Town by train, John de la Haye then climbed the short sharp incline to the top of the southern hills at Mont Félard, from which he surveyed the scene. "The elevated position of the locality from whence a splendid view of St Aubin's is obtained, has led to the building of mansions occupied by English residents; and here the taste, or want of taste, exhibited by our architects or builders, is conspicious. A stereotyped style of architecture is adopted, all being an adoption of the fashionable plain Italian villa, a style admirable, suitable when marble is the material used, but very different in stucco, But could anything cause the visitor to forget the monotonous character of the prevailing architecture it would be the shrubs and flowers which are seen in profusion...."

"The fields on each side of the road to St Lawrence's Church exhibit a rare degree of luxuriance, the result of high cultivation; and that the farmer does not lose his labour is evident from the aspect of their dwellings. Everything around denotes prosperity, if not wealth. One of the farmhouses, with a southern aspect, the gable being near the road, I remember visiting some forty to fifty years ago, but bewildered by the change effected, it was with some difficulty that I identified the spot. In my early days it appeared as when built in the seventeenth century, with thatched roof, small windows, and enormously thick rough built walls and chimneys. In the garden plot in front were seen, in admirable confusion, cabbages and cabbage roses, gooseberries and currants,.. the wall flower, the sweet william, and the inevitable rosemary...."

"In those days the door was left open as if to invite the visitor. On entering the passage, the farmer's daughter soon appeared still holding her needlework in her hand to welcome the visitor. Then there was her attire, which was no triumph of her dressmaking, for it was home-made, and her neat though strongly made shoes which were made to do duty on Sundays by being brightly polished and furnished with sandals. ...Nothing now remains of the old farmhouse, except the walls and these are not visible, as they are concealed beneath their new drapery. A few years ago they were delivered over to the tender mercies of the plasterer, and the once venerable building is made to consist of imaginary blocks of white marble. The owners are evidently wealthy and passably educated, but here is evidence that what is termed education does not always include the study of aesthetics. When a pure taste prevails we shall see farmhouses built in a style approximating to the Tudor, with granite left visible; the porch consisting of massive oak; while the lawn in front, instead of being closely shaved by means of a mower, will exhibit a crop of waving grass. The simple, the beautiful and the sublime will replace the pretty, the pigmy and the namby pamby. It is a curious fact that our farmers give English names to their small estates, while the English residents prefer French names".

"But I am digressing. Near the window sits an old lady.... she is the once merry maiden of 1825, now grandmother to a bevy of young ladies. They are as rosy as she was herself; but in dress they present a wide contrast, and the sandal shoes of the earlier part of the century have been replaced by a more masculine footwear, invented probably as indicative of women's rights...."

"St. Lawrence's Church has similarly changed. Another mile and I reach a cosy village [the newly developed Carrefour Selous] in which, strangely enough, no two buildings are alike in architecture... Time presses and I reach the five-mile stone. Here traces of white cement become small by degree and beautifully less. The farmhouses appear in their ancient glory and the ancient dialect of the Island is still spoken. The spire of St John gleams in the distance...."

The letter meanders gently along a south to north route, a path from a modern and much changed Jersey to the backwood preserves of the northern country parishes, reassuring in their retention of a familiar past. It is in effect a romantic dressing-up of a much more complex picture, one where the bounds of old and new, between what de la Haye represents as sanctioned by time and as imposed by whimsical fashions, are not as obvious as he makes out.

Yet this expedition provides one of the clearer understandings of the many forces at work in Jersey society in the nineteenth century, something paralleled perhaps only by some of the poets discussed in the previous chapter. One can reasonably doubt whether John de la Haye actually makes the physical journey, for much of what he reflects upon is far more in the line of a literary walk through various contemporary issues pertinent to a changing Jersey.

It is highly relevant that de la Haye writes in English and addresses his piece to the leading English newspaper. The linguistic point is extended in the article and when he reaches the boundaries of St John he is literally crossing the border into the land of his native tongue, all that behind him is, by implication, a foreign land. Yet one cannot but interpret the changes he refers to as, if not superficial, at least minor in scale. De la Haye's criticisms are seemingly about architectural and aesthetic values, about a society whose wealth has led to the ornamental trappings and surface beautifying of bourgeois society.

It is all too easy to view what happened to Jersey and its rural community in the nineteenth century on this level, to examine the various external and internal forces at work in the Island and to conclude in the final analysis that what occurred there was of no earth-shattering importance. And, certainly, the view of Jersey as an insignificant backwater becomes plausible when its experience is compared, for example, with the blood-shedding struggles of European nationalism or the conflicts and struggles of industrialisation in England in the same period. Such an interpretation has been aided by the major argument of this work, reflected, perhaps unwittingly, in de la Haye's tale, namely, that the potential forces for challenge and change in Jersey society appear by the end of the nineteenth century to have been fairly comfortably assimilated or contained. One is left with the seemingly petty observations of fashionable tastes and bourgeois aspirations, surface representations of a seemingly successful containment job on Jersey's version of the nineteenth-century modernisation process. Yet a qualification must be made. The modernisation process in Jersey was subtler than this suggests. If at mid-century its challenge to Jersey society seemed stronger than it was, its containment by the end of the century was also more apparent than real

This study has tried to convey something of this subtlety. Care has been taken in the terminology used to suggest its nature. The importance in making a distinction between the forces faced by Jersey society as either change or challenge and the response to them as either continuity or defence must be emphasised. Essentially we are distinguishing between developmental change in a framework of acquiescence and the positive or active forces of challenge which provoked a defensive reaction. The value of this distinction lies in the fact that, as we have seen, the forces working upon Jersey did so at different levels and derived from alternative external and internal sources. To the obvious positive political challenge from the Le Cras reformist group the rural bloc responded with resolution and cunning to defend local institutions. To the less obvious linguistic and cultural challenge, compounded by external British pressure and internal collaboration by a section of the middle class, any response was undermined by a failure to recognise an attack and rested on a more passive level of traditional usage and practice. On the one hand we have the defensive mobilisation of the local native power base, on the other, at its most extreme a non-response, a reliance on a continuity of the older ways.

The distinction is important because, whilst one emphasis gives the rural community an active rôle in recognising and responding to the challenges it faced, the other shows a society reliant in its response on the Island's isolated existence and peculiar political position. In the long term effect of these forces the distinction becomes a crucial one, because where a challenge could be identified and responded to, most notably on the issue of political reform, the local community was most successful in defending itself. However, where no challenge was immediately recognised or was not positively met by a defence, as in the language question, a reliance on society's natural barriers proved fatal to the traditional Jersey way of life.

Thus, on the one hand, for all the considerable change in Jersey by 1900 the basic local structures and institutions remained relatively unscathed and the power base firmly vested in the rural bloc. Jersey society was still firmly in the grip of the rural oligarchy and a parish organisation which had demonstrated its ability to remain as the fundamental communal unit of Island life. Nonetheless, a security at the core masked a vulnerability in key areas. Linguistically, English had invaded most aspects of Jersey life and, allied with a favourable education system, was placed on an unstoppable path to dominance. In the countryside an internal demographic self-regulation resulted in an increasing French presence and in changing landholding patterns. In the urban areas a voice distinct from tradition had been raised and an urban consciousness evolved, albeit unwilling in the final reckoning to sacrifice its shared past with the countryside for political and economic gains, but quite willing to agitate for concessions and representation. The bones of Jersey's past remained intact but in the course of the nineteenth century the foundations for a greater onslaught were effectively laid.

The Napoleonic Wars advertised Jersey's existence to the world and provided a catalyst to an already active local entrepreneurial spirit to reach out and expand the local economy. Jersey, previously hindered in its development by an insubstantial resource basis and relatively small population, now provided itself with the extra dimension required to launch its economy and turned to the marketplaces of the world. It was a move aided by geographical location and a political advantage derived from its association with the English Crown, factors which attracted an immigrant population to the Island, willing to inject both funds and people into capitalist expansion. By 1820 a population of 28,600 peaked even the wartime total and, with its labour, skills and capital, provided the backbone for what was to prove nearly a half century of merchant success.

External expansion into the cod and carrying trades was matched by backward linkage and hinterland development. Shipbuilding, re-exporting, minor manufacturing and a rapidly increasing local consumer market reflected the financial and commercial powers of the merchant houses. The urban population of St Helier, augmented by English immigrants and local migrants from the countryside, spilled over into neighbouring parishes. By 1851 the Jersey urban population made up over two-thirds of the census total. A pre-French Wars urban development consisting of a small triangle alongside the Town rock was by 1850 an urban sprawl that had filled the St Helier basin, reached the Town hills and extended in linear form along the east and west coast.

In the countryside, where a previous capitalist expertise was similarly developed, advantage was taken both of Jersey's peculiar trading privileges vis-à-vis the English mainland, which allowed it to export local produce tariff free, and of the marketing and transport structures created by the merchant economy. Utilising traditional landowning patterns and the diplomatic and scientific skills of the Royal Jersey Agricultural and Horticultural Society, Jerseymen identified the Jersey cow and the potato as their most marketable commodities. Championed by a rural power bloc which ensured country interests received priority treatment, agriculture, particularly by the 1870s, was proving itself a most remunerative industry.

The relationship between the urban industries of the merchant houses and shipbuilders and the traditional agricultural interests was from the very outset problematic, governed as much by power as economics. Both sectors were essentially distinct, there being little need for an interchange of capital or labour. Agriculture did, however, use the trading infrastructure established by the urban-based economy and its refusal to acknowledge this fact and to make any concessions to urban capitalist wealth or power resulted in much conflict and proved a source of agitation for political reform. After centuries of landed rule, rapid economic expansion and demographic growth threw up a bloc capable of challenging rural might.

The decline of the merchant economy reflected the differences between the urban and rural economic sectors and provided in some senses a victory for the rural bloc. Whilst both sectors relied on their ability to exploit Jersey's trading privileges, the merchant sector, spread out world-wide in a complex trading framework, was far more vulnerable to shifting economic forces and the changing political and economic strategies of the great powers. Agriculture, by contrast, had a secure local base and provided products that were in ever increasing demand from England's expanding industrial population. When the fall of the great merchant houses came in the 1880s, in a crisis immediately precipitated by local financial collapse though more a result of a longer term decline in markets, the rapprochement between Britain and France and the rise of the steamship, it took much of the urban trades with it and much of the workforce too. Agriculture was seemingly immune.

Yet whilst agriculture was left at the economic helm, the effects of economic and demographic growth had taken their toll on the countryside too. Ostensibly, the countryside continued unchanged, the landscape remaining a network of small fields and lanes, interspersed with a relatively small number of farmhouses and a stable population. Few English immigrants ventured into a rural domain which remained an economically and socially hostile environment to non-locals. Agriculture, however, required a labour force, particularly at the peak times of planting and harvesting, and from at least the mid-century increasing numbers of French migrant labourers were brought to the Island. Many decided to stay on in what must have seemed like a land of plenty and attempted to farm for themselves. Behind seemingly stable country populations was in reality an inflow of French workers and outflow of locals, who emigrated to the new world.

By the 1880s leading representatives of the rural bloc were expressing concern at the French presence in the countryside, fearful of their social and economic effect. The immigrants, many of whom were willing to pay the high rents demanded in a high-profit and high-cost industry, became tenant farmers. They were targeted by the States and the Royal Jersey Agricultural and Horticultural Society as the cause of unfavourable tendencies in land-use and the decline in standards of agriculture. The fears expressed reflected concerns over social control of a growing body of tenant farmers, who were accused of rejecting sound practices in pursuit of quick profit. The concern was in many respects unfounded and clouded by racial considerations based on the influence of perceived French inferiors on the country folk. By the end of the century it was apparent that despite a short term depression in the 1880s agriculture had stabilised again. On a cultural level the rural community was well on the way to assimilating a willing French immigrant population.

Compared with the crises faced by the urban-based industries in the latter half of the nineteenth century agricultural problems paled somewhat. Both the potato blight in the 1840s and the depression of the 1880s were overcome relatively unscathed. Much of this had to do with the nature of Jersey agriculture and its enterprising attitude. Despite fears to the contrary a balanced agriculture of crops and livestock was generally retained up to at least the early twentieth century. Similarly, rural Jersey had little need to involve itself in the urban industries, requiring neither their capital nor their labour. Ultimately, the power of the rural bloc at Island level ensured the agricultural interest remained paramount.

Jersey society was shaped around an agricultural population. Its social structures, its laws and its government reflected the interests of the land. The growth of a significant urban population, a major part of which was non-local in origin, added a new dimension to a previously rural community. The urban bloc, not surprisingly, wished society to reflect its interests and rights more closely. These demands ranged from a proportionate share of local power to a reform of certain of the laws and institutions along lines more conducive to business and justice. By implication such demands required a weakening of the rural bloc's domination of state and society. Economic change became political challenge.

Already by the 1820s a divergence of interests and priorities separated the rural and urban communities. Country intransigence as to the concerns of the Town ensured an economic and political divide, one which resulted in clashes in the legislature where the commercial sector found itself effectively outvoted. But the demand for reform revealed a complex web of allegiances and loyalties. Urban reformers were divided between the desire to reform and the need to uphold the Island's ability to govern itself without overpowering interference from the Crown in Council. The urban group split into two: the larger body composed of locals dedicated to reform from within and a smaller group of English agitators, led by A.J. Le Cras, committed to root and branch reform of local institutions and willing to invoke even the power of Parliament.

All Jersey reformers were joined by their aims but any further unity was weakened by the degrees to which separate groups were willing to go towards achieving them. The local judiciary and the major administrative and political unit of the Island, the parish, provided the focus for most criticism. At the centre of a much despised judicial/legislative overlap lay the office of Jurat, a reflection of political bias and rural prerogative, which left the administration of justice problematic and without continuity. Parish power, too, was perceived as a source of inequity, an oligarchic power retained throughout the Island by manipulation of the rating system, which determined the electorate, and by the discretionary powers of the parish police.

The largest body of reformers, centred around the Connétable of St Helier, Pierre Le Sueur, and decidedly local in composition, found themselves torn between competing concerns. The desire to realign society to suit their economic and social needs was undermined by the unwillingness to mobilise the powers of external pressure - the Crown and, ultimately, Parliament - because of the implications of such a move for Island independence. Thus, a body which at times even found itself augmented by rural reformers, was left to reform from within. Successes, however, were minimal and more a result of external lobbying by the Le Cras group.

The small group of reformers led by Le Cras were most successful mobilisers of outside opinion. In the Island the group was despised because of its methods and willingness to transgress local independence by appealing directly to Parliament. As agent provocateur Le Cras remained outside Jersey society and failed even to mobilise a large body of English residents who appeared to appreciate the need to remain within bounds acceptable to the society they had chosen to live in. Le Cras' motives for reform were personal and less coherent than the mainstream reformers. His ultimate intention was to prove that Jersey's claim to independence was based on fraud and usurpation and to uncloak its parasitic nature; he believed such motives justified direct agitation.

Lack of wide based support notwithstanding, Le Cras' reformers proved most successful at agitating. Whilst the two investigative Royal Commissions of 1847 and 1861 were appointed by the Crown in response to a perceived widespread demand for reform, they were in a more direct sense a result of Le Cras' persistent lobbying. Yet a quasi-victory in 1852, when the Island was forced into some degree of reform - such as the establishment of a town police force and a petty debts court - was seen by Le Cras as purely cosmetic. He continued his campaign and concentrated all efforts on eliciting the support of individual M.Ps, a course which finally bore fruit in 1864 when a Parliament, previously reluctant to intervene, gave the Island an ultimatum to reform its judiciary.

Yet the rural oligarchy was let off the hook by what amounted to a sham referendum which enabled the local authorities to prove the popular nature of local institutions. Parliament, not unlike the mainstream reformers, showed itself unwilling to cross the bounds of constitutional precedence and in reward for over six centuries of loyalty to the Crown Jerseymen were allowed to continue on their course ever closer to near-independence. What had amounted to the major onslaught of the period on the rural bloc was pushed aside with ease.

Ultimately, Jersey was spared major political and legal reform by the rural bloc's strength in depth and the unwillingness of reformers to go beyond the bounds of loyalty to local independence and local institutions. If anything, the rural community strengthened its rôle in society, ensuring that any reform was quickly assimilated into a framework of control and understanding. Thus, when the urban bloc finally achieved an increase in political representation in 1854 with the introduction of the office of Deputy, the rural bloc saw to it that the office remained dependent on parish cliques and that the country's voting power in the legislature was undiminished.

Crucial to the rural community's defence of its power and privilege was the parish, presented throughout this book as the institutional linchpin in Jersey society. The power of the parish was historically ill-defined and unrestricted. Its ability to invoke impassioned interest and rivalry among the majority of rural folk can be witnessed through the vehemence of party politics in the first half of the nineteenth century. The introduction and widespread appeal of Nonconformism, particularly Methodism, in the Jersey countryside threatened to undermine the previous rôle of the parish, which had for so long depended on a unity of communal life combining secular and religious interests within the same framework. Yet what occurred was a tacit acceptance of individualism in religion and the Established Church's demise in power terms proved the body civil's gain.

If the parish as body religious was weakened as a result of the success of Nonconformism, it was simultaneously recast as an all-powerful body civil, broadened to encompass religious diversity with the powers of its officers multiplied. The rural community defended itself against challenge via an institution whose durability was evidenced by time. Nonconformism enhanced the power of the parish.

Clearly, in the face of direct challenge the rural community proved adept and adroit in defending itself institutionally. Judging the power of the parish, as a manifestation of the rural bloc, by its perceived rôle in Jersey society or by the limited degree of restrictive legislation imposed on it during the course of the nineteenth century, the historian could fairly conclude that the forces of modernisation and major change had been successfully contained within the traditional parish structure.

Yet the Jersey parish was no longer representative of its community on every level of life. Nonconformism, albeit itself accommodated, had breached the parish's historic comprehensiveness. The breach was like that of an iceberg, of which only the tip shows. But already before the end of the nineteenth century the rural community had proved susceptible to challenge in other spheres too, notably in the threat of the English language and culture and even in the advance of education.

One of the most obvious manifestations of change in Jersey by 1900 was the progress of the English language. Jèrriais proved no match for a tongue that was structured and standardised and supported by a body of local and immigrant residents who were convinced of its intellectual and moral superiority. The challenge of the English language became a cultural challenge that operated on many levels and the complications which ensued from middle-class approval of its advance and overtones of desirable conformity with England left the rural community powerless in its advance.

Intellectually and culturally Jersey society was weak. It was a small, previously isolated community, ill-prepared for a cultural onslaught. Jèrriais was a spoken tongue without a developed written form. There was no local literary tradition and the intelligentsia was confined to a handful of advocates and seigneurs. No serious attention was paid to the issue at legislative level until 186, and no counter attempted to the advance of English until 1873 when the teaching of French was linked to financial aid for schools. The issue had come to the fore at least as early as the 1840s with the Carus Wilson affair.

The establishment of Victoria College in 1854 represented the apex of anglophile desire among the local middle class. It also reflected the close link between the development of local education and the plight of the local tongue. A secularised education system, following the undermining of religious control in the late eighteenth century, received no effective supervision or modicum of centralisation until at least the 1870s and in the meantime the English language had taken root in the syllabus. The advance of the language was settled beyond doubt when, tied up as the question was with questions of loyalty and anglo-uniformity, the Privy Council enforced stringent regulations by means of its finance for local education.

The language and education question revealed the inadequacy of the rural community in dealing with a force that refused to operate within its framework of understanding and control. An institutional response did not suffice. Language and education were tied in with so many other considerations that a single line of defence, as in the political sphere, could not operate.

In the final analysis the seeming contradictions in the Jersey experience are to be viewed in the context of institutional strength and cultural and linguistic weakness. This peculiar dichotomy was bridged somewhat by the taking aboard of the English language and culture as a catalyst for a Jersey identity. Such moves were strengthened by an ongoing process towards a greater degree of independence, a process completed, or at least suspended at a point determined by the United Kingdom, by the end of the Second World War. Yet the Jersey society which remained after the challenges of the nineteenth century was to all intents English in its cultural and linguistic spheres.

This work began with the image of Jersey as an Island, able after 1204, due to its geographical and peculiar historical position, to utilise the sea as a defensive barrier against the outside world. After the various changes and challenges of the nineteenth century that barrier's effectiveness was much reduced. With the forces of change effectively planted within Jersey society itself it was to prove increasingly difficult to minimise external influence.

Sources

Chapter 1

Institutuions and settlement

1 G. Dury, *The Channel Islands: The Report of the Land Utilisation Survey of Britain* (London 1950), pp. 7-18; J. Le Patourel 'Guernsey, Jersey and their Environment in the Middle Ages', *Rep. and Trans. of Société Guernesiaise* (TSG) XIX (1975), 435-437.

2 Joshua Le Bailli, Jersey Chamber of Commerce, 1860 quoted in R. Ommer, 'A Peculiar and Immediate Dependence of the Crown': The Basis of the Jersey Merchant Triangle', *Business History XXV* (1983), 107.

3 See R.G. Le Herissier, *The Development of the Government of Jersey 1771-1972* (Jersey 1973); F. de L. Bois, *A Constitutional History of Jersey* (Jersey 1972).

4 Blackstone, *Commentaries* (London 1765), Vol. 1.,104, quoted in W.J. Heyting, *The Constitutional Relationship between Jersey and the United Kingdom* (Jersey 1977), 2.

5 J. Le Patourel, The Political Development of the Channel Islands', *Nos Îles: A Symposium on the Channel Islands* (London 1944), 13.

6 J. Le Patourel, *The Medieval Administration of the Channel Islands 1199-1399* (London 1937), 31.

7 On Privateering see W.R. Meyer, "The Channel Island Privateers 1793-1815,' in A.G. Jamieson (Ed.), *A People of the Sea: The Maritime History of the Channel Islands* (London 1986),173-195; on the spy network in revolutionary France, A. Cobban, 'The Beginning of the Channel Isles Correspondence, 1789-1794', *English Historical Review LXXVII* (1962), 39-52.

8 A.G. Jamieson, "The Islands and British Maritime Strategy 1689-1945', in A.G. Jamieson, *A People of the Sea* op. cit., 220-244.

9 J.R. McCulloch, *A Statistical Account of the British Empire* (London 1837), Vol I, 232-234.

10 R. Montgomery Martin, *A History of the British Colonies* (London 1835), Vol. V., 459-517.

11 Duke of Wellington, *Memorandum on the Defence of the United Kingdom, 19/10/1845* British Library Add. Ms. 40461; for local reaction to this boost see, *Chronique de Jersey* (*CJ*) 8.1 and 12.1. 1848.

12 R.G. Le Herissier, op. cit., 35.

13 G.F.B. de Gruchy, *Medieval Land Tenures in Jersey* (Jersey 1957), 39.

14 J. Le Patourel, 'Guernsey, Jersey and their Environment in the Middle Ages', op. cit., 8-9.

15 G.F.B. de Gruchy, op. cit., 93.

16 Ibid., 141, 176-177.

17 Ibid., 177.

18 A. Cobban, *A Social Interpretation of the French Revolution* (Cambridge 1988), Chapter 4.

19 Le Fief de la Fosse, Document dated 1868 in La Hague Documents, Société Jersiaise. The Documents include court records and assorted papers from the Fiefs of La Fosse, de Nobretez and des Niémes.

20 Le Fief de Nobretez, Book of Aveux 1792-1851, in Ibid.

21 Le Fief de Nobretez, Court Sessions 1748-1851, in Ibid.

22 'Petition de Jean Le Hardy', *Bull. Ann. Société*

Jersiaise (BASJ) III (1895), 309-331.

23 *Code of Laws for the Island of Jersey 1771* (Jersey 1968).

24 M. Syvret and J. Stevens, *Balleine's History of Jersey* (Chichester 1981), 189-194.

25 Ibid. It is unclear who the petioners were.

26 Ibid. R. Mayne, *The Battle of Jersey* (London 1981).

27 Parish of St Ouen, Acts of the Civil Assembly ACA, 1785.

28 St. John meeting referred to in, *Gazette de L'Ile de Jersey* 31/12/1791; St Helier meeting in ACA St Helier 22/3/1855.

29 *Gazette de L'Ile de Jersey* 31/12/1791.

30 *CJ* 26/3/1855.

31 J. N. L. Myres, 'The Origin of the Jersey Parishes: Some Suggestions', *Ann. Bull. Société Jersiaise* XXII (1978), 163.

32 G.F.B. de Gruchy, op. cit., 148-149; J. Le Patourel, op. cit., 99.

33 G.F.B. de Gruchy, op. cit., 120.

34 J.N.L. Myres, op. cit.,168.

35 Ibid., 170.

36 Ibid.

37 G.F.B. de Gruchy, op. cit., 148-149.

38 J. Le Patourel, op. cit., 99.

39 Ibid.

40 Ibid.

41 R. Mollet, 'Ouye de Paroisse 1463', *ABSJ* XVII (1959), 255-257; R. Mollet, 'Contrats and the Ouye de Paroisse', *BASJ* XVI (1954), 195-199.

42 F. de L. Bois, *The Parish Church of St Saviour* (London 1976), 105.

43 P. Falle, *An Account of the Island of Jersey* (Jersey 1694)., 207; and F. de L. Bois, op. cit., 109.

44 G.F.B. de Gruchy, op. cit., 156.

45 Ibid, 159-161.

46 Ibid.,153-155.

47 *Jersey Times* (*JT*), 24 & 31/1/1854, 17/2/1854, 17/3/1854; Parish of Trinity ACA 15/9/1853 & 14/3/1854. The parish was ruled by the Royal Court to be in default of a loan payment and ordered to pay interest. The Parish Assembly disagreed and refused, leaving the Connétable, bound by oath to obey the Assembly, in contempt of court, for which he was gaoled. The duties of the chief officer of the parish are set out in the 'Serment des Connétables', *Code of Laws for the Island of Jersey 1771* (Jersey 1968), 176-177.

48 T. Dicey, *An Historical Account of Guernsey* (London 1751), 36-37.

49 J. Le Couteur, Diary Ms. Société Jersiaise, 17/10/1826, Diary Book 2/72.

50 See for instance, his dealings with an apple thief in St Aubin whose penitence resulted in a let-off with a stern warning. Ibid., 23/10/1826 Diary Book 2/75.

51 G.F.B. de Gruchy, op. cit., p. 153.

52 F. Victor Hugo, *La Normandie Inconnue* (Paris 1857), 138.

53 G.F.B. de Gruchy op. cit., 152-158.

54 Ibid.

55 Ibid.

56 J. Le Patourel, 'The Political Development of the Channel Islands', op. cit. 31

57 A.J. Eagleston, *The Channel Islands Under Tudor Government 1485-1642* (Cambridge 1949), 49, 55-57. The Channel Islands spent three years within the diocese of Salisbury until their transfer to that of Winchester in 1499.

58 J. Le Patourel, op. cit., 31.

59 A.J. Eagleston, op. cit., 62-64.

60 J. Le Patourel, op. cit., 31. For a copy of the Church Constitution see P. Falle, *An Account of the Island of Jersey*. 4th Edition (Jersey 1835), Appendix XII, 245-262.

61 A.J. Eagleston, op. cit., 128-145.

62 Ibid.

63 R.G. Le Herissier, op. cit. 18-19.

64 See generally M. Syvret & J. Stevens, op. cit., pp. 189-194.

65 An Accurate Survey and Measurement of the Island of Jersey, Surveyed by Order of his Grace the Duke of Richmond 1795.

66 W.T. Money, 'Diary of a Visit to Jersey, September 1798', *BASJ* XII (1932), 40.

67 Anon, 'Les Iles de la Manche', *Revue des Deux Mondes* (1849), 945.

68 A Map of the Island of Jersey, surveyed by H. Godfray, 1849.

69 G. Shaw-Lefevre, 'The Channel Islands', *Fortnightly Review* XXVI (1879), 487.

70 Census of Jersey 1788. Ms. Société Jersiaise Library.

71 L'Estourbillon, Les Familles Françaises à Jersey pendant La Révolution (Nantes 1886); Census of Jersey 1806 Ms. Carried out for General Don, Société Jersiaise Library.

72 Census of Jersey 1841.

73 G.F.B. de Gruchy, 'The Town of St Aubin in the Past', *St Aubin's Magazine* (October 1917).

74 For instance see, W.R. Meyer, op. cit., and R.E. Ommer, 'The Cod Trade in the New World', in A.G. Jamieson op. cit, 245-269.

75 A.G. Jamieson, 'Harbours, Lighthouses, Charts and Lifeboats of the Channel Islands', 409, in Ibid.

76 G.F.B. de Gruchy, *Medieval Land Tenures in Jersey* , op. cit., 170-171.

77 Ibid., 169-170.

78 *BASJ* III (1894), 289, quoted in Ibid. 170; see also, S. Harris, 'The Village Community of Alderney', *Sociological Review XVIII* (1926), 265-278.

79 G.F.B. de Gruchy, op. cit.

80 C.E.B. Brett, *Buildings in the Town and Parish of St Helier* , (Belfast 1977), 14.

81 Ibid.

82 Ibid 13.

83 Rev. J. Skinner, Journal of 1827. Ms. British Library No. 33699, 229.

84 W.E. Bear, 'Glimpses of Farming in the Channel Islands', *Journal of the Royal Agricultural Society of England XXIV*, (1888), 371.

85 See for instance: W.E. Bear, Ibid., 365-397; H. Rider-Haggard, *Rural England: Being an Account of Agricultural and Social Researches Carried out in the Years 1901 and 1902 ., Vol. 1* (London 1906); F. Zincke, 'The Channel Islands and Land Tenure', *Fortnightly Review XIX* (1876), 1-8.

86 The Parish of Trinity, Census of Jersey 1851.

87 The Richmond Map, 1795 op. cit.

88 T. Quayle, *A General View of the Agriculture and Present State of the Islands on the Coast of Normandy*. Board of Agriculture (London 1815), 48.

89 See J. Stevens, *Old Jersey Houses , Vols. 1 & II* (Chichester 1965 & 1977).

90 Information collated from the Census of Jersey, 1851.

91 J. Stevens, Vol. II., op. cit., 56 & 62.

92 C.P. Le Cornu, op. cit., 38.

93 T. Lyte, *A Sketch of the Island of Jersey* (London 1808), 281

94 T. Quayle, op. cit., 193-4.

95 M. Syvret and J. Stevens, op. cit., 219.

96 Parish of St Helier, ACA 27/6/1810.

97 See N.R.P. Bonsor, *The Jersey Railway* (Oxford 1962), and *The Jersey Eastern Railway* (Oxford 1965); W.J. Carman, *Channel Island Transport* (Guernsey 1987).

98 P. Falle, op. cit., 97.

99 T. Quayle, op. cit., 67.

100 *Loi (1891) sur le Partage d'Héritages*, Recueil de Lois, Tome IV (R de L., T.) (1908), p. 214; *Loi (1926) sur les Héritages Propres*, R. de L., T. VI (1939), 403.

101 *Loi (1851) sur les Testaments d'Immeubles*, R de L., T. II (1879), p. 5.

102 Ordre du Conseil 24/9/1635, *Ordres du Conseil*, Vol. 1.

103 P. Falle, op. cit., 100.

104 T. Quayle, op. cit., 52.

105 P. Galichet, *Le Fermier de L'Ile de Jersey* (Paris 1912), 15.

Chapter 2

Economic and Social Life

1 R.E. Ommer, 'A Peculiar and Immediate Dependence of the Crown: The Basis of the Jersey Merchant Triangle', *Business History XXV* (1983), 107.

2 Anon, 'Jersey as Regards its Husbandry and Agricultural Classes', *Quarterly Journal of Agriculture XIII* (1843), 374-375.

3 P. Heylin, *Full Relation of Two Journeys to France and the Adjacent Islands, Book VI* (London 1656), 293.

4 G.F.B. de Gruchy, *Medieval Land Tenures in Jersey* (Jersey 1957), 172-173.

5 P. Heylin, op. cit., 301.

6 E. Cotes, *The Second Journey: Containing a Survey of the Estates of the Islands Guernsey and Jersey*. Book VI (London 1656), 301.

7 J. Poingdestre, *Caesarea, Island of Jersey* (Ms. 1682), p. 3. Société Jersiaise.

8 P. Falle, *An Account of the Island of Jersey* (Jersey 1694), 100-102.

9 G.F.B. de Gruchy, op. cit., pp. 165-166.

10 P. Falle, op. cit., 101.

11 G.H. Dury, 'Some Land Use Statistics for Jersey in the Late Eighteenth Century', *Bull. Ann. Société Jersiaise (BASJ)* XV (1952), 442.

12 P. Falle, op. cit., 106.

13 F. Le Couteur, 'A Treatise on the Cultivation of Apple Trees and the Preparation of Cider', in W. Pitt, *A General View of the Agriculture of the County of Worcester* (London 1810), 340.

14 B.J.R. Blench, 'Some Notes on the Agriculture of Jersey in the Seventeenth Century', *Tijdschrift Voor Econ. En Soc. Geografie* (1962), 51-52.

15 J.G. Speer, 'Pommage' *Ann. Bull. Société Jersiaise (ABSJ)* XX (1970), 164-173.

16 Camden, *Britannica* (London 1586), 2.

17 Acte des États 12/4/1608 in P. Falle, op. cit., 362-363.

18 Quoted in M. Syvret and J. Stevens, *Balleine's History of Jersey* (Chichester 1981), 91-92.

19 J. Poingdestre, op. cit., 4-5.

20 P. Dumaresq, *A Survey of the Island of Jersey* (London 1685), 16.

21 A.G. Jamieson, 'Introduction', in A.G. Jamieson (Ed.), *A People of the Sea: The Maritime History of the Channel Islands* (London 1986), xxxiv.

22 W.J. Heyting, *The Constitutional Relationship between Jersey and the United Kingdom* (Jersey 1971), 115.

23 Act of Parliament 1716, in Ibid., 116.

24 G.H. Dury, *The Channel Islands*, op. cit., 39.

25 *Jersey Times (JT)* 4/4/1851.

26 Letter written by James Playfair 1781, Ms. Société Jersiaise.

27 Acte des États 12/8/1786, *Actes des États 1780-1785* (Jersey 1911), 26, E. Parmalee Prentice, 'American Dairy Cattle', *Rep. and Trans. of Société Guernsiaise (R and TSG)* XIV (1946), 65.3

28 R.N. Salaman, *The History and Social Influence of the Potato* (Cambridge 1949), 167.

29 G.H. Dury, 'Some Land-Use Statistics', op. cit., 440-441.

30 J. Le Couteur, Diary Ms. 1840 Letter Book No. 8., 118, Société Jersiaise.

31 G.H. Dury, op. cit., 441.

32 For a discussion of the 1801 Returns see: W.G. Hoskins, 'The Leicestershire Crop Returns of 1801' in W.G. Hoskins (Ed.), *Studies in Leicestershire Agrarian History* (Leicester 1949), 127-145.

33 'Replies to the Request of Lord Pelham, Secretary of State to the Dioceses, to Give Acreage Returns, 1801', Public Record Office (P.R.O.) HO 67/24.

34 Ibid.

35 T. Quayle, *A General View of the Agriculture and Present State of the Islands on the Coast of Normandy. Board of Agriculture* (London 1815).

36 P. Heylin, op. cit., 303. N

37 Anon, *The Groans of the Inhabitants of Jersey* (Jersey 1709).

38 M. Syvret and J. Stevens, *Balleine's History of Jersey* (Chichester 1981), 190.

39 Ms. 1800, La Hague Documents, Société Jersiaise.

40 M. Syvret and J. Stevens, op. cit., 190-197.

41 T. Quayle, op. cit., 77.

42 'Replies to the Request of Lord Pelham', op. cit.

43 T. Quayle, op. cit., 100-107.

44 Ibid. Appendix V, 323.

45 Rev, F. Le Couteur, op. cit., 339; T. Quayle, Ibid. According to Le Couteur one hogshead was equal to 60 gallons.

46 T. Quayle, Ibid.

47 Acte des États, 12/8/1786, op. cit.

48 E. Parmalee Prentice, op. cit. 65.

49 'Replies to the Request of Lord Pelham', op. cit.

50 W. Plees, *An Account of the Island of Jersey* (Southampton 1817), 124-126.

51 J. Stead, *A Picture of Jersey* (London 1809), 209-210.

52 T. Quayle, op. cit., 207.

53 J. Stead, op. cit., 212.

54 W. Plees, op. cit., 84-86.

55 A.G. Jamieson, 'Voyage Patterns and Trades' in A.G. Jamieson (Ed.), op. cit., 377-378.

56 Ibid.

57 P. Falle, op. cit., XII

58 See for instance, F. Zincke, 'The Channel Islands and Land Tenure', *Fortnightly Review* XIX (1876), 2-5.

59 Census of Jersey, 1851.

60 The Land Registry provides the most detailed index to ownership, but it is more helpful for the size of individual fields as opposed to holdings and excludes those not involved in land transactions.

61 Trinity Parish Rate Book, 1823.

62 St. Clement Parish Rate Book, 19/11/1805.

63 St. Mary Parish Rate Book, 1858, Bound Island Rate Book (Jersey 1858).

64 St. Helier Parish Rate Book, 1858, in Ibid.

65 H.D. Inglis, *The Channel Islands* (London 1834), 71.

66 Registre Publique 29/3/1909, Livre 351. 275-281.

67 P. de Carteret, Trinity Manor Farm Diary 1820/21 Ms. Société Jersiaise, 7-16/11/1820.

68 *Chronique de Jersey* (*CJ*) 20/5/1868.

69 R. Ommer, "From Outpost to Outport': The Jersey Merchant Triangle in the Nineteenth Century" (McGill University, Ph.D., 1979), 291-293.

70 Ibid.

71 St. Clement Parish Rate Book, 26/1/1890.

72 St. Martin Parish Rate Book, 25/9/1811.

73 St. Brelade Parish Rate Book, 15/3/1811.

74 Census of Jersey, 1851.

75 St. John Parish Rate Book, 1858, Island Rate Book (Jersey 1858).

76 Census of Jersey, 1851; Island Rate Book, Ibid.

77 Poor Law Report, 1834, British Sessional Papers XXX (1834), 663.

78 Census of Jersey, 1851.

79 C.P. Le Cornu, 'The Agriculture of the Islands of Jersey, Guernsey, Alderney and Sark', *Journal of the Royal Agricultural Society of England* XX (1859), 36.

80 Annual Report 1843, Horticulture Section, Royal Jersey Agricultural and Horticultural Society (RJAHS).

81 Census of Jersey, 1851.

82 G.S. Hooper, *History and Statistics of Asiatic Cholera in Jersey*. Pamphlet (Jersey 1833), 10.

83 *JT* 18/3/1851.

84 Parish of St Saviour, Acts of the Ecclesiastical Assembly (AEA), Book II 1821, in F. de L. Bois, *The Parish Church of St Saviour, Jersey* (London 1976), 4.

85 *CJ* 27 & 30/1/1847, 3/2/1847.

86 Ibid, 3/4/1847.

87 Parish of St John, Acts of the Civil Assembly (ACA) 23/8/1817.

88 Parish of St John, AEA 17/1/1811.

89 T. Quayle, op. cit., 189-191

90 Parish of St John, ACA 2/10/1819.

91 Census of Jersey, 1851.

92 Parish of St John, ACA 6/11/1793.

93 *CJ* 10/10/1846.

94 Parish of St John, ACA, Elizabeth Buck to America 6/6/1871, anonymous family to Canada 5/4/1889.

95 W. Plees, *An Account of the Island of Jersey* (Southampton 1817), 127.

96 Report of the Commissioners Appointed to Inquire into the Civil, Municipal and Ecclesiastical Laws of the Island of Jersey (London 1861), 583-584.

97 W. Berry, *The History of the Island of Guernsey* (London 1815), 300.

98 Ibid; T. Quayle, op. cit., 225-226.

99 H.D. Inglis, op. cit., 57-59.

100 Ibid.

101 W. Plees, op. cit., 80.

102 P. Dalido, *Jersey: Ile Agricole Anglo Normande* (Vannes 1951), 154

103 J.B. Murdoch, *Notes and Remarks Made in Jersey, France, Italy and the Mediterranean in 1843 and 1844* (London 1846), 36-37.

104 'An Old Jersey Farmer' in *British Press/ Jersey Times* (*BP/JT*), 2/3/1880.

105 P. Galichet, op. cit., 27-28.

106 P. Kropotkin, *Fields, Factories and Workshops* (London 1918),167-168.

107 T. Quayle, op. cit., 64; F.F. Dally, *An Essay on the Agriculture of the Channel Islands* (Guernsey 1860).

108 On social life in Jersey in the post-Reformation period see A.J. Eagleston, *The Channel Islands under Tudor Government 1485-1642* (Cambridge 1949).

109 *Code of Laws for the Island of Jersey 1771* (Jersey 1968), 56-57.

110 Rôles Ecclesiastiques (R.E.) 2/6/1788.

111 See for instance the sentence imposed on Guillaume Langlois for scandalous behaviour, R.E. 16/6/1788.

112 Census of Jersey, 1851.

113 H.D. Inglis, op. cit., 58.

114 E.O.B. Voisin, 'Inebriety in Jersey', *British Journal of Inebriety*, (1904), 168-169.

115 Anon, *Letters From Jersey* (Cambridge 1830), 58-59; P.E. Brée, *A Short Sketch of the Origin and Development of Methodism in La Rocque*. Pamphlet (Jersey 1932), 14.

116 H.D. Inglis, op. cit., 87.

117 Anon, *Quarterly Journal of Agriculture*, op. cit., 378.

118 Rev. J. Skinner, Journal of 1827. British Library Ms. 33699, 251.

119 J.H. L'Amy, *Jersey Folklore* (Jersey 1927), 59-66.

120 Ibid., 85-100.

121 *St. Martin's Parish Magazine*, January, 1896.

122 Ibid.

123 H.D. Inglis, op. cit., 61.

124 It appears that St Peter was the first parish to create a separate association. *JT* 14/1/1848.

125 For prosecutions see, for instance, *BP/JT* 21/7/1874.

126 On the grievances of the Militia soldier see: J. Sullivan, *The Channel Islands Militia* (London 1871).

127 N. Le Cornu, 'The Royal Jersey Artillery and the Jersey Militia System 1771-1877', *Bulletin of Jersey Society in London* III (1988), 111.

128 R. Lemprière, *Customs, Ceremonies and Traditions of the Channel Islands* (London 1976), 128-130, 175-176.

129 H.D. Inglis, op. cit., 64-65.

130 Ibid.

131 Ibid., 60.

132 R. Lempriere, op. cit., 131.

133 Ibid., 127.

134 J. Stead, op. cit., 33-34; W. Plees, op. cit., 85.

135 On folklore generally, and the link between specific Jersey customs and their Norman counterparts, see R. Lemprière, op. cit.

136 W. Berry, op. cit., 300.

137 W. Plees, op. cit., 80.

138 Ibid., 85.

139 D.T. Ansted & R.G. Latham, *The Channel Islands* (London 1862), 549.

140 P. de Carteret, Diary, op. cit., 7-16/11/1820.

141 J. Le Couteur, Diary, op. cit., 22/5/1800, Letter Book M5. Société Jersiaise.

142 For example, *JT* 7/1/1848 when attendance was said to be, "nearly one hundred of the élite of our Island society".

143 On the role of the community in rural society see, P.M. Jones, 'Parish, Seigneurie and the Community of Inhabitants in Southern Central France' *Past and Present* 1981, 74-108, and *Politics and Rural Society The Southern Massif Central* (Cambridge, 1985).

144 C.P. Le Cornu, Diary, Ms., 16/6/1872, La Hague Documents.

145 Parish of St John, ACA 21/1/1818, 17/1/1811.

146 F. de L. Bois, op. cit., 96.

147 T.F. Priaulx, 'Les Chemins-de-L'Église', *Bulletin Guernsey Society* XVII (1961), 3.

148 Parish of St Clement, ACA 10/6/1785.

149 Ibid., 19/6/1785.

150 For instance, see, Parish of St John, ACA 25/3/1883.

151 R.G. Le Herissier, op. cit., 89.

152 J. Le Couteur, Diary, op. cit., 6/8/1826, Diary Book 2/60.

153 *Loi (1856) sur l'Augmentation du Nombre des Membres des États,* Lois et Reglemens, Tome II (1879), 89.

Chapter 3

The Economic Development of Nineteenth-century Jersey

1 L. De Lavergne, *Essai sur l'Economie Rurale de l'Angleterre* (Paris 1882), 307-309; P. Kropotkin, 'The Possibilities of Agriculture', *Forum* (1890), 615-626.

2 Anon, 'Jersey as Regards its Husbandry and Agricultural Classes' *Quarterly Journal of Agriculture* XVIII (1843), 374-375.

3 R.E. Ommer, 'From Outpost to Outport: The Jersey Merchant Triangle in the Nineteenth Century' (McGill University, Ph.D. thesis, 1979), 321-324.

4 *Chronique de Jersey (CJ)* 9/11/1816, 7/12/1816.

5 *CJ* 21/11/1816.

6 *CJ* 8/5/1819.

7 Ibid. See also Parish of St Helier, Acts of the Civil Assembly (ACA) 29/9/1813 and 3/1/1814 for the attitude of the urban population to protectionist policies.

8 R.E. Ommer, 'The Cod Trade in the New World' in A.G. Jamieson (Ed.), *A People of the Sea: the Maritime History of the Channel Islands* (London 1986), 256.

9 A.G. Jamieson, 'The Channel Islands and Smuggling, 1680-1850', in Ibid., 195-219.

10 R. Mudie, *The Channel Islands* (London 1839), 63-64.

11 Census of Jersey 1821, 1831, and 1851.

12 R. Mudie, op. cit., 114-115.

13 Census of Jersey, 1851. Five distinct and separate sample census districts are the basis for these figures.

14 H.D. Inglis, *The Channel Islands* (London 1834), 129-30.

15 Ibid., pp. 120, 126-7, 129-130.)

16 Anon, *Queen of the Isles* (London 1841), 62-63.

17 A.G. Jamieson, 'Shipbuilding in the Channel Islands', in A.G. Jamieson, op. cit., 295-296.

18 H.D. Inglis, op. cit., 129.

19 R.E. Ommer, 'From Outpost to Outport', op. cit., 44-48.

20 *Almanack du Chronique 1815*, 60-63.

21 A.G. Jamieson, 'Shipbuilding in the Channel Islands', op. cit. 297.

22 A.G. Jamieson, 'Island Shipowners and Seamen 1700-1900', in A.G. Jamieson, *A People of the Sea,* op. cit., 325-327.

23 Anon, 'The Commerce of Jersey', *Guernsey and Jersey Magazine V* (1837), 137-138, 180-181.

24 A.G. Jamieson, 'Island Shipowners and Seamen 1700-1900', op. cit.,354.

25 *The Times* 20/5/1822; Translation of the Report of the Committee of the Piers and Harbours on the Oyster Fishery presented to the States of Jersey on 28/1/1834 and Other Documents Relating to Said Fishery (Jersey 1837), in A.G. Jamieson, 'The Local Fisheries of the Channel Islands', in A.G. Jamieson, *A People of the Sea*, op. cit., 436.

26 Statistics calculated from the Census of Jersey, 1851.

27 R.E. Ommer, 'From Outpost to Outport', op. cit, 262.

28 Ibid.

29 Anon, 'The Commerce of Jersey', op. cit., 137.

30 Ibid.,312.

31 R.E. Ommer, op. cit, 277-285.

32 Ibid., 46.

33 Ibid., 36-41.

34 Ibid., 242.

35 Ibid.

36 Ibid, 243.

37 London Customs Bills of Entry 1840, Colindale Library. These particular figures were tabulated by A.G., Jamieson, 'Voyage Patterns and Trades', in A.G. Jamieson (Ed.), op. cit., 385.

38 Ibid., 'Shipbuilding in the Channel Islands', 290-291.

39 A.G. Jamieson, 'Shipbuilding in the Channel Islands in the Nineteenth Century', *Journal of Transport History* III (1982), 65-66.

40 Ibid., 73.

41 R.E. Ommer, op. cit., 292.

42 Ibid., 283.

43 Philippe de Quetteville, President Jersey Chamber of Commerce, to President of the Board of Trade, Minute Books, Chamber of Commerce December, 1841, in R.E. Ommer, 'The Cod Trade in the New World', in A.G. Jamieson (Ed.), op. cit., 263.

44 W. Plees, op. cit., 124-126; H.D. Inglis, op. cit., 129-130; D. Ansted and R.G. Latham, *The Channel Islands* (London 1862), 407-408, 561.

45 T. Quayle, *A General View of the Agriculture and Present State of the Islands on the Coast of Normandy*. Board of Agriculture (London 1815), 213. The survey was one of many commissioned by the Board of Agriculture at this time to determine the effect of the French Wars on British agriculture.

46 P.C. Dubost, 'Les Fêtes Agricoles de Jersey', *Journal De L'Agriculture* (1879), 289.

47 P. Kropotkin, 'The Possibilities of Agriculture', op. cit., 623.

48 W.E. Bear, 'Garden Farming', *Quarterly Review* CLXVI (1888), 435-436.

49 On high farming in nineteenth-century England see, J.D. Chambers and J.E. Mingay, *The Agricultural Revolution 1750-1880* (London 1966).

50 C.P. Le Cornu, 'The Agriculture of the Islands of Jersey, Guernsey, Alderney and Sark', *Journal of Royal Agricultural Society of England* XX (1859), 37.

51 J. Girardin and E.J. Morière, 'Excursion Agricole à Jersey', *Société Centrale D'Agriculture du Département de la Seine-Inférieure* (Rouen 1857), 31-37.

52 T. Quayle, op. cit., 80-81.

53 Trinity Manor Farm Diary, Ms. Société Jersiaise, 4/10/1820-28/10/1821.

54 C.P. Le Cornu, 'The Potato in Jersey', *Journal of the Royal Agricultural Society of England* VI (1870), 133.

55 Abstract of Parish Returns of Acreage of Crops and Livestock, 1900, Public Record Office HO 14/325.

56 C.P. Le Cornu, op. cit., 54.

57 W.E. Bear, 'Glimpses of Garden Farming in the Channel Islands', *Journal of the Royal Agricultural Society of England* XXIV (1888), 382.

58 J. Girardin and E.J. Morière, op. cit., 24-28.

59 W.E. Bear, 'Garden Farming', op. cit., 416.

60 C.P. Le Cornu, 'The Agriculture of the Islands', op. cit., 53.

61 These statistics are drawn from the *Almanack du Chronique*.

62 Acte des États 12/8/1786, *Actes des États 1780-1785* (Jersey 1911), 26.

63 See for instance, Acte des États 19/9/1822, 18/3/1826 (Unpublished), States Greffe.

64 Preamble to Acte des États 12/8/1786, op. cit.

65 *Gazette de Jersey* 13/8/1791.

66 *CJ* 14/7/1827.

67 E. Parmalee Prentice, 'American Dairy Cattle', *Rep. and Trans. Société Guernesiaise* (TSG) XIV (1946), 54.

68 *JT* 29/5/1853.

69 J. Thornton, 'Jersey Cattle and Their Management', *Journal of the Royal Agricultural Society of England* XVII (1881), 220-221.

70 *British Press & Jersey Times* (*BP/JT*) 21/11/1879.

71 E. Parmalee Prentice, op. cit., 54, 58.

72 R. Bradley, *The Gentleman and Farmer's Guide for the Increase of Cattle* (London 1729) in G.E. Fussell, 'Channel Island Cattle: The Making of the Breeds', *Bulletin Veterinary History* 1 (1973),1.

73 G. Culley, *Observations on Livestock* (London 1786),51-2, in Ibid, 1.

74 Ibid.

75 T. Quayle, op. cit., 171.

76 Ibid., 281.

77 Ibid., 280.

78 Ibid., 177.

79 Ibid., 180.

80 Rule No. 3, Inaugural Meeting of the Royal Jersey Agricultural and Horticultural Society (RJAHS), 26/8/1833.

81 J. Stevens, *Victorian Voices* (Jersey 1969), 112.

82 T. Quayle, op. cit., 219.

83 G.R. Mingay, *Rural Life in Victorian England* (London 1977), 62-63. See also, J.A. Scott Watson, *The History of the Royal Agricultural Society of England 1839-1939*(London 1939).

84 See for example, *CJ* 18/5/1816, 27/8/1845: *BP/JT* 12/6/1862.

85 Members' Meeting, RJAHS 9/4/1834.

86 Annual Report, RJAHS 2/9/1834.

87 Annual Report, RJAHS 8/1/1842.

88 J. Le Couteur, 'On the Jersey, Misnamed Alderney, Cow', *Journal of the Royal Agricultural Society of England* V (1844), 45-46.

89 C.P. Le Cornu, 'The Agriculture of the Islands', op. cit., 52.

90 *JT* 17/11/1848.

91 Cited in *BP/JT* 3/8/1878.

92 Cited in *BP/JT* 15/8/1872.

93 Annual Report, RJAHS 27/1/1866.

94 E. Whetham, 'The Trade in Pedigree Livestock 1850-1910', *Agricultural History Review* XXVII (1979), 47-50.

95 *BP/JT* 5/10/1866.

96 *BP/JT* 22/5/1883.

97 J. Le Couteur, Diary Ms. op. cit, 5/4/1851, Diary Book 12/17.

98 *The Cultivator* in *BP/JT* 29/3/1880 and 1/4/1880.

99 J. Burn Murdoch, *Notes and Remarks Made in Jersey, France, Italy and the Mediterranean in 1843 and 1844* (Edinburgh/London 1846), 31-32.

100 C.P. Le Cornu, 'The Agriculture of the Islands', op. cit., 51.

101 W. Bear, 'Glimpses of Farming in the Channel Islands', *Journal of the Royal Agricultural Society of England* XXIV (1888), 385.

102 Members' Meeting, RJAHS 26/1/1887.

103 Agricultural Returns, 1866, Public Record Office, op. cit.

104 Agricultural Returns 1900, Ibid.

105 H. Rider Haggard, *Rural England: Being an Account of Agricultural and Social Researches Carried Out in the Years 1901 and 1902*. Vol. 1. (London 1906), 88-89.

106 M.F. Escard, 'Jersey et ses Institutions', *Société D'Économie Sociale* 10/2/1896, 14.

107 C.P. Le Cornu, op. cit., 48.

108 T. Quayle, op. cit., 106.

109 C.P. Le Cornu, 'The Potato in Jersey', op. cit., 130.

110 *London Customs Bills of Entry* 1829/1830

(including Liverpool, Bristol and Hull) Colindale Library.

111 Annual Report, RJAHS 5/9/1838.

112 Ibid.

113 See Figure 4. earlier in this chapter.

114 Retours Faisons Août 1848 des Vingtaines, Paroisse de St Martin. Ms. Société Jersiaise.

115 T. Quayle, op. cit., 106.

116 C.P. Le Cornu, 'The Potato in Jersey', op. cit., 133.

117 Ibid., 133.

118Members' Meeting, RJAHS 14/1/1846.

119 Statistics from the *Almanack du Chronique.*

120 Ibid.

121 *JT* 5/10/1858.

122 C.P. Le Cornu, 'The Potato in Jersey', op. cit., 133.

123 Statistics from the *Almanack du Chronique.*

124 Annual Report, RJAHS 9/1/1858

125 Annual Report, RJAHS 29/1/1859.

126 Statistics from the *Almanack du Chronique.*

127 Annual Report, RJAHS 12/1/1861.

128 Ibid.

129 C.P. Le Cornu, 'The Potato in Jersey', op. cit., 138-139. The profitability of Jersey agriculture is discussed in Chapter 8.

130 M. Syvret and J. Stevens, *Balleine's History of Jersey* (Chichester 1981), 246.

131 Statistics from the *Almanack du Chronique.*

132 J. Stuart Blackie, 'Jersey', *Macmillan's Magazine* (1883/4), 28-29.

133 P.C. Dubost, 'Les Fêtes Agricoles de Jersey', *Journal de l'Agriculture 1879,* 239.

134 Census of Jersey, 1881. This estimate derives from an analysis of six country parishes.

135 R.E. Ommer, 'From Outpost to Outport', op. cit., 257.

136 A.G. Jamieson, 'Voyage Patterns and Trades', op. cit., 385.

137 R.E. Ommer, op. cit., 38-39.

138 Chamber of Commerce, Minute Book 20/4/1805, in Ibid., 41.

139 Ibid.

140 R.E. Ommer, op. cit., 59.

141 Ibid.

142 Inaugural Meeting of the RJAHS, 26/8/1833.

143 Ibid.

144 Members' Meeting, RJAHS 7/11/1838, *CJ* 9/5/1846; Members Meeting, RJAHS 8/1/1842. The relationship between the R.J.A.H.S. and the rural community will be looked at in more detail in Chapters 7 and 8.

145 Parish of St Helier, ACA 7/5/1819, *CJ* 8/5/ and 5/6/1819.

146 *CJ* 20/5/1820, 18/8/ & 16/10/1821; Report from the Select Committee on the Present State of the Trade in Corn between the Channel Islands and the United Kingdom, Parliamentary Papers (1835), XIII.

147 Ordre du Conseil 22/5/1866, a copy of which accompanies the Annual Report, RJAHS 25/1/1867.

148 See the *BP/JT* 1/10/1866.

149 *CJ* 11/9/1819, 5/12/1835.

150 R.E. Ommer, op. cit., 56.

151 Ibid.

152 See, William. Davies, *The Harbour that Failed* (Alderney 1983).

153 R.E. Ommer, 'The Cod Trade in the New World', op. cit., 263.

154 A.G. Jamieson, 'Shipbuilding in the Channel Islands', op. cit., 77-78.

155 *CJ* 14/5/1873.

156 *CJ* 5/11/1873.

157 R.E. Ommer, 'From Outpost to Outport', op. cit., 309.

158 Ibid., 312.

159 Ibid.

160 *Nouvelle Chronique* 13/1/1880.

161 Chamber of Commerce, AGM 1880, in Ibid., 311.

162 Chamber of Commerce, AGM 1881, Ibid.

163 Annual Report, RJAHS 3/12/1873.

164 Annual Report, RJAHS 27/1/1886.

165 W.E. Bear, 'Garden Farming', op. cit., 433.

166 Annual Report, RJAHS 29/1/1859. See also P.J. Perry, 'The Development of Cross-Channel Trade at Weymouth, 1794-1914: Geographical and operational Factors', *Transport History* II (1969), 244-257.

167 *BP/JT* 25/5/1880.

168 See for instance, *BP/JT* 12/6/1874, 6/8/1878, 3/6 and 8/4/1879.

169 M. Syvret and J. Stevens, op. cit., 245.

170 *British Press Almanack* 1849.

171 Petition, RJAHS 28/3/1835 in RJAHS papers for 1835.

172 W. Bear, 'Garden Farming', op. cit., 413.

173 39 & 40 Vict. (36), in W.J. Heyting, op. cit., 117.

Chapter 4
Religion and the Church

1 M. Syvret and J. Stevens, *Balleine's History of Jersey* (Chichester 1981), 211.

2 Census of Jersey, 1851.

3 Information on the Rectors comes from various sources, particularly church lists and census material. I am grateful to the genealogical section of the Société Jersiaise for the information on the family connections of the local clergy.

4 J. Stevens and J. Arthur, *The Parish Church of St Mary, Jersey* Pamphlet (Jersey). No figure is given as to the size of Balleine's contribution. Parish of Trinity, Acts of the Ecclesiastical Assembly (AEA) 11/12/1842.

5 G.R. Balleine, *A Biographical Dictionary of Jersey* (London 1948), 281.

6 H.D. Inglis, *The Channel Islands* (London 1834), 159.

7 G.F.B. de Gruchy, *Medieval Land Tenures in Jersey* (Jersey 1957), p. 94.

8 Evidence of General Helier Touzel, Queen's Receiver, *Report of the Commissioners Appointed to Inquire into the Civil, Municipal and Ecclesiastical, Laws of the Island of Jersey* (London 1861), 460-468.

9 G.F.B. de Gruchy, op. cit.,94.

10 Anon, *Letters From Jersey* (Cambridge 1830), 58.

11 H.D. Inglis, op. cit., 159.

12 P. Falle, *An Account of the Island of Jersey* (Jersey 1837 Edition), p. 208. Falle believed the provision made for the clergy to be, "no way adequate to their labours", 207.

13 Parish of St Ouen, Act of the Civil Assembly (ACA) 29/7/1763.

14 This guarantee was given statutory basis in 1771 with the, *Réglemens pour l'Administration des Biens des Trésors de l'Eglise, et des Pauvres,* Code of Laws for the Island of Jersey 1771 (Jersey 1968), 205-206.

15 Parish of St Ouen, AEA 15/2 & 15/5/1816.

16 Census of Jersey, 1851.

17 Parish of St Ouen, AEA 31/5/1838; F. de L. Bois, *The Parish Church of St Saviour* (London 1976), 138.

18 Evidence of Rev. George Poingdestre, Commission of 1861, op. cit., 655-660.

19 En Convocation Ecclesiastique (the regular meeting of the Island's clergy), 27/5/1833 and 4/4/1834.

20 For instance, see the 1888 attempt in the States of Jersey to abolish feudal rights ,

where the rectors stood together against the measure, *British Press* and *Jersey Times* (*BP/JT*) 9/2/1888.

21 Canon 14. A copy of the Canons can be found in P. Falle, op. cit., 250.

22 Information on the Rectors and their movements is drawn from various sources, particularly the earlier mentioned church lists.

23 J.N.L. Myres, 'The Origin of Some Jersey Parishes: Some Suggestions', *Ann. Bull. Société Jersiaise* (*ABST*) XXII (1978), 170.

24 Parish of St Ouen, AEA 25/1/1859; Letter from Connétable Jean Pipon to the Governor of Jersey, in English, recommending that the Reverend Ricard be considered for the additional post of barracks chaplain, 2/12/1813. La Hague Documents Ms. No. 42, Société Jersiaise.

25 *Chronique de Jersey* (*CJ*) 1/12/1838.

26 On the Durell case see A. Mourant, *Biographie de Pierre Le Sueur* (Jersey 1861) and Anon, *Recueil des Pièces Authentiques relatives aux Poursuites vers le Réverend Edouard Le Vavasseur dit Durell* (Jersey c. 1841-1850).

27 On Durell's past arguments with the parish see *Edouard Nicolle, Connétable -v- Reverend Durell, Rôles Ecclesiastiques* (*R.E.*) 30/5/1825; on the Ecclesiastical Court in legal dispute, Ibid. 16/10/ and 23/10/1837.

28 Private Manuscript quoted in G.R. Balleine, op. cit., 575. see also, J. Dorey, *Notice Biographique sur la Reverend Thomas Sivret* (Jersey 1870).

29 Rev. J. Lemprière, *Sermon Prêché dans le Temple de St Helier 1789* (Guernsey 1789) Pamphlet (incomplete).

30 H.D. Inglis, op. cit.,161.

31 *R.E.* 8/12/1794.

32 For details of disputes see, G.R. Balleine, op. cit., 255.

33 *Ex Parte Bailhache et autres* 31/10/1817, *Ordres du Conseil* (*O du C*) V (Jersey 1901), 146-150.

34 *CJ* 13/12/1817.

35 *CJ* 20/11/1819; *Ex Parte Frossard* 31/3/1821, *O du C.*, op. cit., 181-198.

36 For instance see *BP/JT* 2/1/1864, 27/2/1870 and 18/3/1880.

37 Parish of St Ouen, AEA 30/5/1833, 19/9/1834 and 10/5/1836.

38 *R.E.* 8/6/ and 9/11/1782, 29/11/1802.

39 Parish of Trinity, ACA 10/6/1869 and 2/7/1879.

40 *R.E.* 28/10/1792.

41 For instance, Reverend Michael Dupré, Rector of St John 1809-1818, was simultaneously chaplain to a Foot Regiment in England, leaving a curate in his place on the Island. G.R. Balleine, op. cit., 260.

42 Parish of St Ouen ACA 27/4/ and 13/6/1789.

43 *R.E.* 30/6/1794.

44 *R.E.* 21/10/ and 18/11/1799. Also, in the Royal Court, Causes Remises (C.R.), Livre 3, 22/10/1801, 175-177.

45 *R.E.* 28/6/1813 and 21/11/1814.

46 *R.E.* 18/5/1818 and 12/6/1820.

47 *R.E.* 8/11/1813.

48 Most parish churches and ecclesiastical records list their rectors and the dates of their incumbency.

49 See for example, *BP/JT* 2/1/1864, Parish of Trinity, AEA 27/6/1850.

50 On the reaction of the Reverend Durell to the accusations against him see, A. Mourant, op. cit., 22-35.

51 *R.E.* 5/6/1837. See also a case in St John in 1810, where the Rector refused to swear in elected officers. *C.R.* Livre 4 c.1/6/1810, folio 42.

folio 42.

52 See, for instance, the pew plan for Holy Trinity, Parish of Trinity AEA 19/7/1850, and that of St Martin le Vieux, Parish of Grouville, AEA 24/2/1880.

53 J. Le Couteur, Diary Ms. Société Jersiaise, 9/7/1826, Book 2/51.

54 Anon, op. cit., 58-59.

55 Anon, *Queen of the Isles* (London 1841),. 40.

56 Anon, Letters from Jersey, op. cit., 58-59.

57 *BP/JT* 1/7/1873.

58 F. Guiton, *Histoire du Methodisme Wesleyen dans les Iles de la Manche* (London 1846), 33-39.

59 Ibid., 44.

60 M. Lelièvre, *Histoire du Methodisme dans les Iles de la Manche* (Paris & London 1885), 319.

61 F. Guiton, op. cit., 37.

62 Ibid.,148-152.

63 Ibid., 148-220.

64 Ibid., 60. Reference is made in both Guiton and Lelièvre to, H. de Jersey, *Vie du Jean de Quetteville,* but no copy of the work has been discovered.

65 Ibid.,62, 67.

66 M. Lelièvre, op. cit., 297.

67 Ibid., 295.

68 P.E. Brée, *A Short Sketch of the Origin and Development of Methodism in La Rocque* (Jersey 1932). Pamphlet.

69 G.R. Balleine, op. cit., 216.

70 Ibid., 43-44.

71 Livre du Samedi 3/6/1794 No. 130 Folio 149.

72 Ibid., 7/5/1795 No. 131 Folio 97, 177; 8/6/1795 No. 132, Folio 231.

73 Methodist Petition 21/6/1794 in, M. Lelièvre, op. cit., 357-358.

74 Livre de Poursuite Criminelles 27/6/1796 No. 1, Folio 137.

75 See, for instance, the judgements on Philippe Perchard, Thomas Baudains, Jean Sinel and Clement Guillaume, in Ibid., No 1, Folio 108 and 109.

76 Acte des États 18/10/1798, *Actes des Etats 1795-1798* (Jersey 1916),142.

77 M. Lelièvre, op. cit., 380.

78 General Gordon, in, N. Le Cornu, 'The Jersey Militia 1719-1819', Undergraduate Long Essay, University of Warwick 1981, 9.

79 Ibid.

80 Ibid., Footnote 47. Acte des Etats 23/10/1795, op. cit., 18-19. The suppression of civil disorder had previously been the responsibility of the English garrison based in the Island. It is unclear why the States decided to change.

81 Ordre du Conseil 28/1/1799, *Ordres du Conseil* IV (1771-1812) 382-385. F. Guiton, op. cit., 82-103.

82 Ordre du Conseil 28/4/1810, Ibid., 540-542. See also, Anon, *The Remarkable Trial of Philippe Arthur*. Pamphlet (London 1808).

83 Livre de Poursuites Criminelles 15/6/1819, No. 6, Folio 257; F. Guiton, op. cit., p. 31.

84 G.R. Balleine, op. cit., 254. Similarly without obvious explanation is the tolerant attitude of the Reverend Jacques Hemery, Dean 1844-1849. CJ 1/4/1848.

85 D.M. Thompson, *Nonconformity in the Nineteenth Century* (London 1972).

86 D.A. Bellenger, *The French Exiled Clergy* (Bath 1986), 4.

87 H. Hettier, *Relations de la Normandie avec les Iles pendant l'Emmigration* (Caen 1885), 89.

88 G.R. Balleine, op. cit., 201-204.

89 F. Guiton, op. cit., 99.

90 Livre de Poursuites Criminelles 26/9/1797 No. 1, folio 137.

91 M. Lelièvre, op. cit.,297. Lelièvre does not give a date for Valpy's action, but the latter was Rector of St Mary, 1777-1804.

92 Rev. E. Durell, Introduction and Notes, in P. Falle, op. cit., 413.

93 M. Lelièvre, op. cit., 433-444.

94 F. Guiton, op. cit., 134.

95 Ibid, 168-173, 207-211.

96 The number is based on well authenticated chapels, but there were certainly more, both in St Helier and the countryside, although there is little known about them. A good example of a chapel whose history is unrecorded is still the standing place of worship at Maufant, St Saviour, built in 1811, according to the tablet above the entrance.

97 F. Guiton, op. cit., 148-152.

98 Ibid., 152-157.

99 J.P. Le Quesne, *A Short History of St John's Independent Church*. Pamphlet (Jersey), 1.

100 P.E. Brée, op. cit.

101 The local Methodist archive lists records for all the chapels in the Jersey/French circuit. The Sion records are the only group not missing. There is a similar problem for English circuit material.

102 Sion Trust Minutes 12/8/1826: first entry (includes a brief history of the chapel).

103 Ibid. On the troubles of problems arising from the creation of public trusts of nonconformist chapels in the nineteenth century see, W.E. de Faye 'Trusts in Jersey', a paper read before the Jersey Society in London on 8th December 1950.

104 Ibid. 9/12/1840; on the crash of the joint stock bank, see *CJ* 10/1 and 17/1/1874.

105 P.E. Brée, op. cit. 6-7

106 Ibid., 8-13.

107 Sion Trust Minutes, op. cit., 25/11/1835.

108 Ibid., 22/7/1844.

109 P.E. Brée, op. cit., 21.

110 Sion Trust Minutes, op. cit., 11/12/1876.

111 Ibid., 22/8/1876.

112 Ibid., 19/12/1877.

113 J.P. Le Quesne, op. cit.

114 H.D. Inglis, op. cit., 112.

115 Methodist Baptisms (Jersey/French Circuit) 1831-1852. Bound Volume, Methodist Archive.

116 Census of Jersey, 1851.

117 Sion Trust Minutes 22/8/1876.

118 M. Lelièvre, op. cit., 430.

119 Returns of Accommodation 1911 Wesleyan Chapel Committee (Jersey/French Circuit) Ms. Methodist Archive.

120 M. Lelièvre, op. cit., 121.

121 See generally, O. Chadwick, *The Victorian Church. Vol. I* (London 1966); D. Bowen, *The Idea of the Victorian Church* (Montreal 1968), 376-387; R. Currie, *Methodism Divided* (London 1968)

122 J. Obelkevich, *Religion and Rural Society: South Lindsey 1825-1875* (Oxford 1976).

123 R. Currie, 'A Micro Theory of Methodist Growth', *Proceedings of the Wesleyan Historical Society* XXXVI (1967), 63-73.

124 D. Hempton, *Methodism and Politics in British Society, 1750-1850* (London 1984), 75.

125 Sion Chapel Trust Minutes 12/8/1826.

126 Ibid., 9/7/1856 Pew Accounts.

127 Timetable for Wesleyan Preachers, 1858, Ms. Société Jersiaise.

128 Census of Jersey, 1851.

129 J. de Quetteville, *Nouveau Recueil de Cantiques Spirituels* (Jersey 1795).

130 J. de Quetteville, *Recueil de Cantiques à l'Usage de la Société Appelée Methodiste* (Guernsey 1818).

131 P. Galichet, *Le Fermier de l'Ile de Jersey* (Paris 1912), 64-67.

132 Ibid.; I am also grateful to the Brée family of La Sente, Grouville.

133 Caesariensis, *Reminiscences of Church Life in Jersey* (London 1917), 16.

134 *Jersey Times* 10/12/1850, 20/2/1852; *BP/JT* 19/2/1881 and 22/9/1882.

Chapter 5

Language and Anglicisation

1 F. Le Maistre, *Dictionnaire Jersiais-Français* (Jersey 1966).

2 See, for example, *Chronique de Jersey (CJ)* 5/6/1861.

3 W. Berry, *The History of the Island of Guernsey* (London 1815), 300.

4 P. Falle, *An Account of the Island of Jersey* (London 1837), Introduction by Rev. E. Durell, 392.

5 W. Plees, *An Account of the Island of Jersey* (Southampton 1817), 51.

6 The dictionary of F. Le Maistre, op. cit., is the standard work on Jèrriais, but sadly says nothing about the historical development of the language.

7 Reverend. J. Skinner, Journal of 1827 Ms, British Library No. 33699, 222.

8 T. Quayle, *A General View of the Agriculture and Present State of the Islands on the Coast of Normandy* (London 1815), 225-226.

9 T. Quayle, ibid.

10 H.D. Inglis, *The Channel Islands* (London 1834), 111.

11 J. Poingdestre, *Caesarea or a Discourse on the Island of Jersey* (Jersey 1682); P. Dumaresq, *Survey of Ye Island of Jersey* (London 1685); P. Falle, *An Account of the Isle of Jersey* (London 1694).

12 P. Falle, op. cit., (1734 Edition), 125-126.

13 T. Quayle, op. cit., 223

14 W. Plees, op. cit., 51.

15 T. Quayle, op. cit., 224;

16 W. Berry, op. cit., 300.

17 H.D. Inglis, op. cit., 111-112.

18 W. Plees, op. cit., 50.

19 J.R. McCulloch, *A Statistical Account of the British Empire* (London 1837), I, 232-4.

20 Duke of Wellington, *Memorandum on the Defence of the United Kingdom*, 10/9/1845, British Library, Add. Ms. 40461.

21 Lieutenant-Governor of Guernsey to Sir George Grey, 1846, Public Record Office, Kew, HO 45 1339.

22 W. Plees, op. cit., 53.

23 H.D. Inglis, op. cit., 162, 164-165.

24 First Report of the Commissioners Appointed to Inquire into the State of the Criminal Law in the Channel Islands (London 1847); Report of the Commissioners Appointed to Inquire into the Civil, Municipal and Ecclesiastical Laws of the Island of Jersey (London 1861).

25 Lieutenant-Governor of Guernsey, 1846, op. cit.

26 T. Quayle, op. cit., 223-224.

27 See, for instance, articles entitled, 'Chair ou Poisson' *CJ* 27/5/1865, 'Qui Vive Normandie ' *CJ* 21/4/1866.

28 *St. Martin's Parish Magazine, 1890*; *CJ* 5/6/1866.

29 J. Stevens, *Victorian Voices: An Introduction to the Papers of Sir John Le Couteur* (Jersey 1969).

30 J. Le Couteur, Diary Ms., 27/8/1859. Letter

Book 10, 100.

30 Parish of St Brelade, ACA, 30/11/1794

32 H.D. Inglis, op. cit., 29-34.

33 Members Meeting, Royal Jersey Agricultural and Horticultural Society (RJAHS) 15/11/1834.

34 *Jersey Times (JT)* 7/11/1856.

35 *CJ* 18/9/, 21/9 and 25/9/1844.

36 *CJ* 1/2/1845.

37 *Jersey and Guernsey News* 4/1/1845 et seq.

38 *CJ* 26/4/1844.

39 *CJ* 25/9/1844.

40 *CJ* 25/8/1844.

41 *JT* 7/11/1856.

42 *British Press/Jersey Times (BP/JT)* Almagamated 1860, 28/8/1868.

43 J. Likeman, 'Education in Jersey in the Nineteenth Century with Particular Reference to the Teaching of French', MA (University of London 1987), 75.

44 Ibid., 38; P. Ahier, The History of Primary Education in Jersey from Early Times to 1872 Ms. Société Jersiaise, 194.

45 Report of the Commissioners 1861, op. cit., xlviii.

46 *BP/JT* 25/5/1880.

47 Report of the Commissioners, 1861, op. cit., xlviii.

48 *JT* 14/1/1848.

49 *CJ* 21/1/1857.

50 Parish of St John, Act of the Civil Assembly, (ACA), 11/4/1895.

51 Report of the Commissioners, 1861, op. cit., xlviii.

52 Ibid., xlix.

53 Trinity School Log Book 31/12/1897, J. Likeman, op. cit., 94.

54 Ibid., 19/5/1886, 90-91.

55 Report of the Commissioners 1861, op. cit., xlviii. The document mentioned was supplied by A.J. Le Cras.

56 The most concentrated effort to do so came in 1966 with, F. Le Maistre, *Dictionnaire Jersiais Francais,* op. cit.

57 Select Committee Report on the Education of the Poor 1816-1818, Ms. Société Jersiaise. The information was supplied by the Rectors.

58 Canon 40 & 41. A copy of the Ecclesiastical Canons may be found in, P. Falle, *An Account of the Island of Jersey* (Jersey 1837), 250-262.

59 Ibid., Canon 41.

60 Rôlesles Ecclesiastiques 25/5/1789.

61 Select Committee on the Education of the Poor, op. cit.

62 M. Syvret and J. Stevens, op. cit., 69.

63 *CJ* 1/4/1848.

64 Evidence to the Commission, 1861, op. cit., 655-660.

65 Ibid., 660-668.

66 Ibid., an intervention by Reverend Philippe Filleul, Rector of St Helier.

67 Evidence, Ibid.

68 P. Ahier, The History of Primary Education in Jersey From Early Times to 1872, Ms., Société Jersiaise, 90.

69 Acte des États 25/2/1794, *Actes des États* 1780-1800 (Jersey 1911), 64-65.

70 Acte Des États 29/8/1836.

71 Report of the Commissioners 1861, 652.

72 Ibid., 660-668.

73 Ibid., lxviii. In 1787 the Crown gave the Assembly of the Governor, Bailiff and Jurats "the right of managing and disposing of revenues arising from the Duties upon Wines and other foreign liquors imported into the Island", Ordre du Conseil 12/9/1789, *Ordres*

du Conseil Vol. V(1771-1812)(Jersey 1900), 211-215.

74 Evidence of the Reverend Le Couteur Balleine, Rector of St Mary, in Ibid., 652.

75 Evidence of the Reverend Abraham Le Sueur, Rector of Grouville, in Ibid., 650-655.

76 *BP/JT*11/7/1864. By 1870, a petition signed by 224 Grouville parishioners was handed to the States, asking for moves to facilitate the opening of the school. *CJ*2/2/ and 28/5/1870.

77 Parish of St John, ACA 13/1/1893.

78 Select Committee on Education, op. cit.

79 P. Ahier, op. cit., 90. Act.

80 'Règlement sur les Écoles Élémentaires', *Lois et Reglemens, Tome* II (1879), 55.

81 General James Reynett, Lieutenant-Governor of Jersey, to Sir William Somerville, 2/4/1847, Ms. Société Jersiaise.

82 Le Reverend Docteur Jeune à Monsieur le Bailli: Correspondence Relatif à l'Etablissement d'un College à Jersey, 1/6/1847 Ms. Société Jersiaise.

83 P. Ahier, A Short History of Secondary Grammar Education in Jersey, as Exemplified in the Story of Victoria College Jersey. Ms. Société Jersiaise 1964; D.J. Cottrill, *Victoria College Jersey 1852-1972* (London 1977).

84 *CJ* 15/12/1860.

85 D. Corkery, *The Fortunes of the Irish Language* (Cork 1968); G. Morgan, *The Dragon's Tongue* (Narberth 1966).

86 F. Victor Hugo, quoted in P. Stevens, *Victor Hugo in Jersey* (Chichester 1985), 28.

87 *JT*8/6/1849, 2/11/1852; Lieutenant-Governor of Guernsey to Sir George Grey 1843, op. cit. It appears it was the officers' limited knowledge of French and Guernesiais that was restrictive.

88 *CJ* 27/5/1865.

89 J. Le Couteur, Diary op. cit., 3/9/1846 Book 8, 80.

90 *CJ*9/6/1855.

Chapter 6
The Political Challenge

1 R.G. Le Herissier, *The Development of the Government of Jersey 1771-1972* (Jersey 1974), 37-38.

2 Ibid., 108-110.

3 *Révocation des Trois Ordres du Conseil; et confirmation de Six Actes des États, Lois et Règlemens, Tome II*(1879), 40-46. '(Hereafter, L. et R., T.). Report of the Commissioners Appointed to Inquire into the State of the Criminal Law in the Channel Islands (London 1847). Report of the Commissioners Appointed to Inquire into the Civil, Municipal and Ecclesiastical Laws of Jersey (London 1861).

4 J. Stuart Blackie, 'Jersey', *Macmillan's Magazine* (1883/4), 36.

5 Census of Jersey, 1851. The figures for St Helier are drawn from five separate sample districts. Those of independent means are those individuals who classed themselves as such in the Census returns. The term is taken to mean those who were either retired or wealthy enough to live off unearned income.

6 H.D. Inglis, *The Channel Islands* (London 1834), 114-115.

7 Ibid., 29-30. Of the life on an English gentleman in early nineteenth century-Jersey see, A. Este, Journal 1814. Ms. Société Jersiaise.

8 See for instance, the Greffier's notice on the increase in vagrancy cases in 1848 and his recommendation that parishes bring paupers to Court, from where they would be returned to the place of their birth. *Jersey Times* (*JT*) 19/5/1848.

9 *Chronique de Jersey* (CJ) 6/4/1844.

10 C. Le Quesne, *A Constitutional History of Jersey* (London 1856), 455.

11 *British Press and Jersey Times* (*BP/JT*) 1/2/1886.

12 Commission 1847, op. cit., xxviii.

13 R.G. Le Herissier, op. cit., 57.

14 For a criticism of the Privy Council's role, see Ibid., xviii.

15 M. Syvret and J. Stevens, *Balleine's History of Jersey* (Chichester 1981), 199-205.

16 *CJ* 19/6/1819.

17 *Ex Parte Marett* 14/10/1817, *Ordres du Conseil* (*O du C.*) V, p. 6.

18 M. Syvret and J. Stevens, op. cit., 240.

19 *BP/JT* 20/10/1870.

20 The Report of the Royal Commission Deputed to the Island of Jersey in 1811 (Guernsey 1813), 25.

21 Ibid.

22 Commission 1847, op. cit., xvi.

23 Ibid., xliii.

24 Jersey Court Bill 26/6/1861 (Second Reading: postponed until 1864), *Hansard's Parliamentary Debates*, CLXII., column 1712.

25 Commission 1847, op. cit., xl. The *Loi (1804) au Sujet des Assemblées Paroissiales,* had given the Connétables and Centeniers the right to vote in the Assembly outside their period of office, L. et R., T. 1 (1878), Article 2, 48.

26 Commission 1847, op. cit., xl.

27 Ibid.

28 Ibid., 161-162.

29 Ibid., xxxix.

30 Evidence of Philippe Godfray, Ibid., 157.

31 Evidence of Abraham Aubin, Ibid., 186.

32 Commission of 1847, op. cit., 460-468.

33 Parish of St Ouen, Acts of the Civil Assembly (ACA) 1/16/1840.

34 Ibid., 10/6/1840.

35 Ibid., 10/5/1843.

36 Parish of St Helier, ACA 29/9/1813; 8/1/1814.

37 *CJ* 11/9/1819.

38 *CJ* 5/12/1835.

39 Parish of St John, ACA 15/12/1835; Parish of St Clement ACA, 9/12/1835.

40 Parish of St Helier, ACA 14/1/1836.

41 *JT* 16/1/1836.

42 Report from the Select Committee on the Present State of the Trade in Corn between the Channel Islands and the United Kingdom, Parliamentary Papers (1835), XIII. The appendix includes the various petitions.

43 R.E. Ommer, 'From Outpost to Outport: The Jersey Merchant Triangle in the Nineteenth Century' (McGill University, Ph.D. thesis 1979), 277-285.

44 *CJ* 9/11 & 7/12/1816.

45 *CJ* 15 & 18/5/1847.

46 *CJ* 30/3/1836.

47 *CJ* 9/12/1816, 11/10/1828.

48 *CJ* 22/12/1838, 5/1/1839.

49 *CJ* 30/3/1836.

50 Jersey Court Bill, 1861 (First Reading), *Hansard* CLXII., cols. 1626-1627.

51 Ibid. See also *Jersey and Guernsey News* (*JG/N*), 1/1/1857, 17/3/1859.

52 Anon, *English Writs versus Jersey Privileges: The Proceedings in the Case of Dodd and Merrifield.* Pamphlet (Jersey 1858), 6.

53 Ibid., 8.

54 The analysis of the law here relies on the conclusions of the Commissioners of 1861, op. cit., lxxx-lxxxi.

55 See for instance, *The Jurist IX*, 1845, 393-

401; *Law Magazine II*, 329-335; J. Bowditch, *A Series of Letters on the State of the Laws of the Channel Islands.* Pamphlet (London 1844); E. Fowler, *Habeas Corpus in the Channel Islands.* Pamphlet (Jersey 1858).

56 *JG/N* 21/3/1840. Petition on Behalf of Rigby Collins 1/8/1842, to the Privy Council, in Sundry Papers Relating to the Three Orders in Council of 1852, Bound Volume, Société Jersiaise.

57 *JG/N* 2/7/1842. J. Bowditch, op. cit.,2-3.

58 *BP/JT* 8/1/1850 and 2/2/1858.

59 Commission 1861, op. cit., x.

60 Ibid.

61 See, for example, the Court Book, Fief de la Fosse, III, La Hague Documents, Société Jersiaise.

62 P. Stevens, 'Marx and Engels in Jersey', *Ann. Bull. Société Jersiaise (ABSJ)* XXIV (1987), 356.

63 *BP/JT* 4/6/1860.

64 Petition to the States, Lieutenant-Governor and Privy Council on the Laws of Wills and Inheritance, July 1846, PRO HO 45/926 106390.

65 L. et R., T. (1878),195. Chapters 8 and 9 take a more detailed look at the Island's property laws.

66 L. et R., T. III (1882), 260-263.

67 Rente Book of T. Blampied, 1877-1923. Ms. Société Jersiaise.

68 Evidence of John Le Couteur, to the Commission of 1861, op. cit., 693.

69 Evidence of Charles Trebeck, Ibid., 247.

70 Petition 1846, op. cit.

71 G.F.B. de Gruchy, *Medieval Land Tenures in Jersey* (Jersey 1957), 137.

72 L. et R., T. II (1879), 5.

73 Evidence of Philippe Godfray, Merchant, to the Commission of 1861, op. cit., 161.

74 Evidence of Philippe Aubin, Connétable of St Helier, in Ibid., 548-550.

75 *BP/JT* 3/12/1869 & 24/4/1871. Unusually, Centenier Slater was fined £10 for the unlawful arrest.

76 Cited in *BP/JT* 10/9/1860.

77 Petition for the Augmentation of States Members, to Governor, Sir J.H. Reynett, circa October 1848. PRO 45/926 2838.

78 Evidence of Pierre Le Sueur, Connétable of St Helier, Commission 1847, op. cit., 194.

79 Calculated from the Island Rate List (Jersey 1858).û

80 Parish of St Helier ACA 15/3/1838, 20/3/1854.

81 *JT.* 13/6/1848. This is the first year a local English newspaper is available to the historian in its entirety.

82 A. Mourant, *Biographie de Pierre Le Sueur* (Jersey 1861). Ms. Société Jersiaise, 121-122. The work was never completed and deals with Le Sueur's life only up to 1840.

83 *CJ* 3/3/1839.

84 Parish of St Helier, ACA 11/6/1839.

85 Commission 1847, op. cit., xxxix.

86 Parish of St Helier, ACA 24/12/1839.

87 Petition for a Paid Police Force, *circa* 1850, Public Record Office HO 45/926 2838.

88 Major General, Sir Edward Gibbs, Lieutenant-Governor of Jersey, to Sir William Somerville, Bart, 26/8/1846, PRO HO 45/2838 926; Commission 1847, op. cit., xxxviii.

89 Commission 1861, op. cit., 51.

90 A. Mourant, op. cit., 125.

91 Memorial of the Jersey Reform Committee to the Commissioners (Jersey 1859).

92 Commission 1861, op. cit., 51.

93 Ibid.

94 See for instance, *The Origin and Power of*

the States (1855), *Jersey, its Constitution and Laws* (1858), *The Laws of Jersey and Some Existing Abuses* (1858), Pamphlets, Société Jersiaise.

95 A.J. Le Cras to Viscount Palmerston 10/2/1853, Pamphlet of an original letter, Société Jersiaise.

96 A.J. Le Cras, *The Laws, Customs and Privileges in the Island of Jersey* (London 1839).

97 A.J. Le Cras, *On the Philosophy of Divine Revelation* (London 1847).

98 Ordre du Conseil 30/8/1841, *O du C.*, VI, pp. 137-141.

99 Correspondence from the *English and Foreign News*, on the "defects of the laws of succession" and "the political police", forwarded to the Home Office by A.J. Le Cras 14/10/1845, HO 45/926. It is not known how successful the boycott was.

100 *Hansard*, 7/5/1846, Col. 176.

101 *CJ* 10/10/1846.

102 1847 Commission, op. cit. List of Witnesses, 3.

103 J. Le Patourel, *The Medieval Administration of the Channel Islands 1199-1399*(London 1937), 114, 116-117.

104 A Petition on Behalf of Captain Rigby Collins, 1/8/1842, op. cit.; A Petition to the Governor, Bailiff and States, 11/6/1839, op. cit.; A.J. Le Cras to Viscount Palmerston, 10/2/1853, op. cit.

105 On the Chartist experiences of George Julian Harney and his exile in Jersey see, G.J. Harney, *The Harney Papers* (Assen 1969), Edited by F. & R. Black.

106 1847 Commission, op. cit., l-li.

107 Ibid., vii.

108 Ibid., zliii.

109 Ibid., xli.

110 Ibid., xliv-xlix.

111 Ibid., xxvii.

112 Ibid., li. Quoted from Robert Pipon Marett's publication of the seventeenth-century works of Philippe Le Geyt, Jersey's most authoritative constitutional historian.

113 Deputation from the Petitioners to Sir George Grey, Secretary of State for Home Affairs, 15/8/1848, Public Record Office, HO45 926.

114 Parish of St Helier, ACA 14/9/1848.

115 *JT* 2/4/1849.

116 *JT* 12/11 & 13/12/1850. See also, Sundry Papers Relating to the Three Orders in Council, op. cit.

117 G.R. Balleine, op. cit., 388.

118 *Révocation des Trois Ordres du Conseil; et confirmation de Six Actes des États,* op. cit., 40-46.

119 Petition of the States of Jersey 5/5/1852, Petition of the Ratepayers and Householders of Jersey 11/2/1852, in Sundry Papers Relating to the Three Orders in Council, op. cit.

120 The Joint Appendix to the Cases of the States of the Island of Jersey and of Certain of the Ratepayers and Householders of the said Island 5/5/1852, in Ibid. Report from the Select Committee on the Present State of the Trade in Corn between the Channel Islands and the United Kingdom, Parliamentary Papers (1835), XIII, 290.

121 Petition 1852, Ibid.

122 *Loi ordonnant l'organisation d'une police salariée à St Hélier, Loi réglant le nombre des Centeniers de St Hélier et de St Martin, et augmentant les pouvoirs des Officiers de Police, Loi modifiant la practique dans la Rédaction des Dépositions en Matiéres Criminelles, Loi établissant une Cour pour le Recouvrement de Menues Dettes; Loi modifiant la Procédure de la Cour Royale; Loi établissent une Cour pour la Répression de Moindres Délits; Loi établissant une cour pour le recouvrement de menues dettes,* 61, *Revocation des Trois Ordres du Conseil,* op.

cit, 47-75.

123 Ibid. See also R.G. Le Herissier, op. cit., 43-45, 58-60.

124 *Loi* (1856) *sur l'Augmentation du Nombre des Membres des Etats*, R. et L., T. II (1879), 81.

125 G.R. Balleine, op. cit., 454 and A. Mourant, op. cit., 124-128.

126 Petition to Privy Council, quoted in G.R. Balleine, Ibid., 388.

127 Le Cras to Palmerston 17/11/1853; to Walpole 20/7/1858, in Sundry Papers, op. cit. See also his pamphlets, *The Origin and Power of the States* (1855), *The Laws of Jersey and Some Existing Abuses* (1858), op. cit.

128 Petitions 21/5/1858 and 15/2/1859, in Sundry Papers, op. cit.

129 *Hansard* May 1858 and Feb 1859.

130 Petitions 21/5/1858 and 15/2/1859 in Sundry Papers, op. cit.

131 Commission 1861, op. cit., Analysis of the Evidence, xxxix-cxxv.

132 Memorial of the Jersey Reform Committee to the Commissioners (Jersey 1859).

133 1861 Commission, op. cit., lxxvii.

134 Ibid., lxxxi.

135 Ibid., lxxix-lxxx.

136 See the concerns of Joseph Hume, M.P., *Hansard* 113 (1850), col 643-645; Richard Cobden and John Bright, Ibid., 117 (1851), col 816-819. The subject receives a full treatment in A.G. Jamieson, 'The Channel Islands and British Maritime Strategy, 1689-1945', in A.G. Jamieson (Ed.), *A People of the Sea: The Maritime History of the Channel Islands* (London 1986), 229-243.

137 *Règlement sur les Écoles Elementaires*, L. et R., T. II (1879), 55.

138 R.G. Le Herissier suggests this attempt to involve Parliament directly in Channel Island affairs was unprecedented, op. cit., 59.

139 This belief can be found in most of Le Cras's publications and correspondence, for instance see, Letter to Palmerston 10/2/1853, in Sundry Papers, op. cit.

140 Jersey Court Bill (First Reading), op. cit., col. 1712.

141 Ibid., col. 1716.

142 Jersey Court Bill (Second Reading), op. cit., col. 1624-1633

143 Jersey Court Bill (Second Reading resumed), *Hansard* CLXXIV 6/4/1864, cols. 516-530, 3/5/1864, cols. 2052-2053.

144 'The Humble and Dutiful Address and Petition of Landed Proprietors, Merchants and other Inhabitants', February 1864, presented by John Le Couteur and William Lempriere; 'Petition of the Committee for the Reform of the Royal Court of Jersey', October 1864, in *O du C.* 5/3/1866, VI (1835-1867), 279 & 378.

145 'In the Matter of the Jersey Jurats', *English Law Reports* XVI (1866), 173-174.

146 Ibid., 174. The bill was actually withdrawn 21/5/1865.

147 Ordre du Conseil, op. cit., 364.

148 Ordre du Conseil, op. cit., 385. Le Cras died in May 1869, G.R. Balleine, op. cit., 391.

149 Jersey Court Bill (First Reading), op. cit., cols. 1715-1716.

150 Representation of the States of Jersey, 7/4/1864, In the Matter of the Jersey Jurats, op. cit., 174.

151 Ibid., 182.

152 Jersey Court Bill (First Reading), op. cit., col. 1716.

153 Jersey Court Bill (Second Reading), op. cit., col. 1629.

154 E. Flower, op. cit.

Chapter 7
The Parish: Politics and the question of Reform

1 C. Le Quesne, *A Constitutional History of Jersey* (London 1856), 7.

2 Communication from J. Carré, First Report of the Commissioners Appointed to Inquire into the State of the Criminal Law in the Channel Islands (London 1847), 271-277; Evidence of Thomas Le Cornu, Report of the Commissioners Appointed to Inquire into the Civil, Municipal and Ecclesiastical Laws of the Island of Jersey (London 1861), 593-595; *British Press/Jersey Times* (BP/JT), 24/4/1871.

3 Communications from J. Carré, op. cit.

4 G.R. Balleine, *A Biographical Dictionary of Jersey* (London 1948), 388.

5 *Chronique de Jersey* (*CJ*), 27/6/1818.

6 Rev. E. Durell, Introduction to, P. Falle, *An Account of the Island of Jersey*(Jersey 1837), viii.

7 J. Le Couteur, Diary. Ms., 11/10/1832, Letter Book 4/34. Société Jersiaise

8 H.D. Inglis, *The Channel Islands* (London 1834), 36

9 R.G. Le Herissier, *The Development of the Government of Jersey 1771-1972* (Jersey 1974), 30, 84-86. The Code of 1771 was a compilation of the existing laws, excluding the Coûtume de Normandy, and its significance is explained in the Introductory Section.

10 J. Sullivan, Biographie de François Godfray. Ms. (Jersey c. 1870).

11 A. Mourant, Biographie de Pierre Le Sueur. Ms. (Jersey 1861), Société Jersiaise.

12 *Le Constitutionnel* (*CT*) 1/1/1820; *CJ* 1/1/1825. The paper actually began in 1814, but became obviously partisan in 1825.

13 G.R. Balleine, op. cit., 291-293.

14 See Godfray's arguments for a tariff barrier to protect agriculturists in 1835, *CJ* 5/12/1835.

15 See A. Mourant, op. cit., and J. Sullivan, op. cit. This is a picture drawn from many sources, particularly local newspapers.

16 Parish of St Helier, Act of the Civil Assembly (ACA), 11/6/1839.

17 Letter from Jean Pipon, Connétable of St Peter, to the Governor of Jersey, 2/12/1813. La Hague Documents Ms. No. 42, Société Jersiaise; see also *CJ* 1/12/1838.

18 A. Mourant, op. cit.; J. Sullivan, op. cit.

19 Lieutenant-Governor of Jersey to Sir W.E. Bart Somerville, 26/8/1846, Home Office Papers PRO HO 45/926 2838.

20 J. Le Couteur, Diary, op. cit., 17/10/1826, Diary Book 2/72.

21 W.L. de Gruchy, *Jersey: My Reminiscences*, Jersey Society in London. Occasional Publications V (1923), 7-8.

22 I am grateful to Henry Coutanche for this information.

23 Commission of 1847, op. cit.,190-200.

24 Rev. G. Whitley, *Memories of Youth on a Jersey Farm*, Jersey Society in London. Occassional Publications X (1949), 10.

25 *CJ* 22/10/1825, *CT* 29/10/1825.

26 J. Le Couteur, Diary, op. cit., 13/5/1826, Diary Book 2/40-41.

27 Ibid., 2/51.

28 *CJ* 11/8/1841.

29 Information on the Connétables in this chapter, unless otherwise indicated, has been collected by the author from various sources, including the records of the Royal Court and the parishes of Jersey.

30 Parish of St Ouen, ACA 20/11/1839; *CJ* 13/3/1841.

31 *Loi (1835) sur le Rât Paroissial et les Elec-*

tions Publiques, Lois et Règlements, Tome. (L. et R., T.) 1 (1878),199-200.

32 Commission of 1847, op. cit., xl.

33 L. et R.,T. I (1878), 48-50.

34 Furnished by J. Gardner to the Commission of 1847, op. cit., 264-265. It is quite likely that the right to vote was bestowed as some form of reward for honorary service.

35 Commission of 1861, op. cit., 596.

36 The Report of the Royal Commission Deputed to the Island of Jersey in 1811 (Guernsey 1813), 22.

37 John Le Couteur, Diary, op. cit., 17/10/1826, Diary Book 2/72.

38 Ibid., 19/2/1826, 2/21.

39 Commission of 1847, op. cit.,129-130.

40 Parish of St Ouen, ACA 11/9/1787.

41 Commission of 1847, op. cit., 161-162.

42 Commission of 1861, op. cit.,596.

43 Commission of 1847, op. cit., 458-459.

44 Parish of Trinity, ACA 25/7/1835.

45 Du Heaume et autres v Le Rossigno, Ordre du Conseil 8/10/1831, Ordres du Conseil (*O du C*) V (Jersey 1901), 227.

46 Commission of 1847, op. cit., 162. Commission of 1861, op. cit.,584-586. Article 1 of the *Loi (1835) sur la Rât Paroissial et les Elections Publiques* , was supposed to enable parishioners to seek early redress, for both rate surcharge and exclusion from the electoral register. R. de L., T. I (1878), 200-201.

47 Commission of 1861, op. cit., lxii.

48 *Jersey and Guernsey News* 14/10/1845.

49 *BP/JT* 24/4/1871.

50 *CJ* 20/12/1856; as an example of negative complaints see the evidence of A.J. Le Cras, Philippe Duheaume and Charles Romeril, Commission of 1847, op. cit., 127-128, 129-130 and 130-132 respectively.

51 Royal Court, Causes Remises 19/1/1805 Vol. III, fol. 228.

52 P. Falle, *Caesarea; Or an Account of the Island of Jersey* (Jersey 1837 Edition), p. 7.

53 Commission of 1847, op. cit., 190-200.

54 A. Mourant, op. cit., 79-83.

55 *Loi (1839) sur le Quorum des États* R. de L.T. II (1879), 79.

56 Members' Meeting, Royal Jersey Agricultural and Horticultural Society (*RJAHS*), 28/3/1835.

57 *CT* 27/10/1838.

58 J. Le Couteur, Diary, op. cit., 16/1/1837, Letter Book L4/195.

59 Members' Meeting RJAHS 8/1/1842.

60 Members' Meeting RJAHS 15/9/1838.

61 Annual Report RJAHS 6/12/1843.

62 *CJ* 9/5/1846.

63 Ibid., and *JT* 9/5/1846.

64 Annual Report, RJAHS 1/12/1883.

65 Parish of St John, ACA 3/12/1846; Parish of St Clement ACA 26/9/1848; Parish of St Ouen, ACA 10/6/1840.

66 *CJ* 29/8/1840. See also, Parish of St Brelade, ACA 21/11 and 12/12/1838.

67 *CJ* 17/1/1853.

68 On François Godfray's reform period see, *CJ* 12/1/1854, 26/11/1856 and 15/8/1857.

69 *Le Magasin de L'Ile,* October 1784. The writer suggested that St Helier should have eight representatives, St Saviour four, St Brelade three, down to the smaller St Mary and St Clement, who would have only two.

70 *JT* 16/1/1836.

71 *CJ* 30/3/1836; Parish of St Helier, ACA 30/3/1836.

72 A. Mourant, op. cit., 82-83. Parish of St Helier, ACA 28/2/1839.

73 *JT* 25/2/1848.

74 R. de L., T. II (1879), 81-85.

75 Commission of 1846, op. cit., xxvii, xliii.

76 A. Mourant, op. cit., 90-91.

77 Loi (1854), op. cit., 85.

78 *JT* 23/1/1857.

79 Parish of St John, ACA 28/4/1885.

80 Parish of Trinity, ACA 6/4/1864.

81 W.L. de Gruchy, *My Reminiscences, Jersey Society in London*, Occasional Publications, V (1923), 8-10. Josué Falle, who served alongside Clement Hemery in office as Deputy, was likewise Connétable of St Helier in 1864.

82 L. et R., T. II (1879), 55-57.

83 Parish of St Ouen, ACA 28/12/1846. See also, Parish of St John, ACA 3/12/1846, and, Parish of St Clement, ACA 15/12/1846.

84 Commission of 1847, op. cit., xlix.

85 *Loi (1840) sur les Centeniers et Officiers de Police*, L. et R., T. I (1878), 254-255.

86 Parish of St Helier, ACA 31/12/1839.

87 *Loi ordonnant l'organisation d'une police salariée à St Helier*, Revocation des Trois Ordres du Conseil et confirmation de Six Actes des Etats, L. et R., T. II (1879), 55.

88 Article 4, *Loi sur les Police Salariée*, op.xcit., 255. On the Six Actes des États see Chapter 6.

89 *Rât pour subvenir aux frais de la Police Salariée*, L. et R., T. II (1879), 309-310. For Touzel's comments see Chapter 6, Commission of 1847, op. cit., 460-468.

90 This suggestion is backed up by W.L. de Gruchy's *Reminiscences*, he himself a Connétable of St Helier (1876-1878) and a Jurat (1878-1886), op. cit., 10-14.

91 *CJ* 16/9/1848.

92 Compare the reaction of the Parish of St Helier, ACA 14/9/1848, to that of the Parish of St John, ACA 28/9/1848.

93 See, for instance, Nicolas Arthur (of La Falaise) against M. La Gerche for the post of Connétable in St Mary, *CJ* 20/11/1852. See also, St Helier 19/1/1856, St John 20/12/1856 and St Ouen 1/5/1869.

94 *CJ* 20/2/1846 & 3/2/1849.

95 *CJ* 10/1/1857. See also election of 1863 *CJ* 27/12/1862.

96 W.L. de Gruchy, op. cit., 55-58.

97 *BP/JT* 10/1/1880. Their wish was not granted until the *Loi (1907) augmentant le nombre des Députés de la Paroisse de St Helier Let.* R., T. V (1935), pp. 139-141. See also, Parish of St Helier ACA 24/2/1886.

98 L. et. R., T. III (1882), 234-256. *The Loi (1835) sur le Rât Paroissial et les Elections Publiques* 55, was an earlier and weaker precedent, which enforced an annual setting of the rate in the month of January and introduced a process whereby those dissatisfied could seek redress at a parish meeting, L. et. R., T. I (1878), 199-205.

99 *BP/JT* 10/1/1880.

100 *Loi (1815) sur les Assemblées Paroissiales*: Ordre du Procédure, L et. R., T. I (1878), 81-82. This followed a Royal Court decision against Gedeon Dallain, Connétable of St Lawrence, who at a parish meeting had refused to produce the "billet de convocation".

101 L. et R., T I (1878), 202-203; *Loi (1835) sur les Élections Contestées*, L. et. R., T. I (1878), 206-208.

102 *Réglement (1859) modifiant la Loi du 1852*, L. et. R., T. II (1879), 91-92.

103 Loi (1897) sur les Élections Publiques, L. et. R., T. IV (1908), 347-380.

104 L. et R., T. I (1878), 48-50.

105 *Acte des Etats autorisant la suppression des*

Appentis Militaires et la construction de Salles Paroissiales 1877 L. et R., T. III (1882), 163-169.

106 The desecularisation of the Established Church and its implications for the parish in its civil mould is dealt with in Chapter 10.

Chapter 8

Demographic Patterns: Urban change and Rural stability

1 All statistical data of a demographic nature is drawn directly or calculated from the Census of Jersey 1821 to 1891.

2 Such an attitude reflects a natural bias against outsiders and the absence of English farmers in the Island. See, for instance, P. Galichet's case study of James Baudains of Gibraltar Farm, St Peter, in, *Le Fermier de L'Ile* (Paris 1912), 55; see also, J. Coleman, 'Jersey Farming', *The Field* (October 1866), 505.

3 B.J.R. Blench, 'The Jersey Cholera Epidemic of 1832', *Ann. Bull. Société Jersiaise (ABSJ)* XXIX (1966), 149-151. See also, G.S. Hooper, *History and Statistics of Asiatic Cholera in Jersey* (Jersey 1833).

4 Letters in the local press, often from Jerseymen in the colonies, suggest that emigration was becoming popular. For a good example see the article entitled, 'Temptations to Emigrate', *Jersey Times (JT)*, 19/1/1849.

5 *Chronique de Jersey (CJ)* 1/2/, 15/5 and 17/5/1837.

6 B.J.R. Blench, op. cit.

7 William. Davies, *The Harbour That Failed* (Alderney 1983), Chapter 10. The St Catherine's Harbour project employed over 350 labourers. On the oyster fishery see, A.G. Jamieson, 'The Local Fisheries of the Channel Islands', in A.G. Jamieson (Ed.), *A People of the Sea: A Maritime History of the Channel Islands* (London 1986), 436.

8 R.E. Ommer, 'The Cod Trade in the New World', in A.G. Jamieson (Ed.), Ibid., 263-266; A.G. Jamieson, 'Shipbuilding in the Channel Islands', in Ibid., particularly 310-312.

9 The sample study of St Helier was carried out on five electoral districts in 1851 and 1881 chosen throughout the parish to give a uniform picture. Due to census changes in the delineation of districts there is not a total overlap, but in both 1851 and 1881 roughly 3,000 people were analysed. All census forms include information on origins and occupations.

10 Annual Report, Royal Jersey Agricultural and Horticultural Society (RJAHS), 26/1/1873.

11 *British Press/Jersey Times (BP/JT)*, 24/4/1889.

12 *JT* 25/3/1853.

13 In 1853 the shipwrights organised an Island-wide strike for higher pay and successfully gained a compromise 3d extra per day. *CJ* 2/7 and 15/10/1853.

14 *JT* 19/1/1849. See also *JT* 20/6/1851 and a letter from a group of six locals who emigrated to New Zealand, one reporting back, "I myself have done very well", *JT* 13/7/1852.

15 *CJ* 4/2/1852.

16 *CJ* 19/6/1852.

17 A.G. Jamieson, 'The Channel Islands and Australia: Maritime Links in the 1850s', *Great Circle* (1983), 42. This estimate applies to emigration direct from the Channel Islands only.

18 *CJ* 19/6/1852.

19 *CJ* 4/12/1852, 5/2 and 23/3/1853.

20 *JT* 1/6/1852.

21 Parish of St John, Acts of the Civil Assembly (ACA) 26/12/1832.

22 *JT* 7/4/1854.

23 Crew list of the Schooner *Freedom*, *CJ* 4/9/1852.

24 A.G. Jamieson, op. cit., 42.

25 *JT* 4/10/1866, 21/1/1869; *CJ* 15/1 & 19/2/1853.

26 See for instance, the more general survey of J. Le Garignon, 'La Présence Jersiaise en Gaspésie', *Revue d'Histoire et Traditions Populaires de la Gaspésie 62/62* (1978).

27 A.G. Jamieson, 'Overseas Settlement of Islanders', in A.G. Jamieson (Ed.), op. cit., 277-278,

28 Ibid.,283-284

29 See for instance, *CJ* 9/9/1871, 10/4/1872 and 19/2/1876.

30 W.E. Bear, 'Glimpses of Farming in the Channel Islands', *Journal of the Royal Agricultural Society of England* XXIV (1888), 372-373.

31 *Code of Laws for the Island of Jersey 1771* (Jersey 1968), 129-132.

32 Rev. E. Durell, Preface to, P. Falle, *Caesarea or An Account of the Island of Jersey* (Jersey 1837), 390-391.

33 W.E. Bear, op. cit., 366.

34 *J. Stuart Blackie, 'Jersey', Macmillans Magazine* 1883/4, 33-35.

35 J.J. de Carteret, Diary Ms. Late Nineteenth Century, Private, Collection.

36 J. Arthur, 'Le Seelleur du Villot', *Ann. Bull. Société Jersiaise* XXV (1990), pp. 338-339.

37 *BP/JT* 2/3/1880.

38 P. Galichet, op. cit., 23-32.

39 *BP/JT* 11/1/1862.

40 *JT* 28/3/1851.

41 P. Jeremie, *An Essay on the Laws of Real Property in Guernsey* (Guernsey 1851), 3. The essay formed part of a petition.

42 *JT* 25/7/1848.

43 *CJ* 8/10/1864.

44 *BP/JT* 9/2/1888.

45 On the 1848 attempt to abolish seigneurial rights see *JT* 1851.

46 L. et R., T. II (1879), 5.

47 L. et R., T. I (1878), 507-508.

48 L. et R., T. II (1879), 3.

49 *L. et R., T* IV (1908), 214-227.

50 Article 9, ibid.

51 *Loi (1891) sur les Testaments d'Immeubles*, L. et R., T. IV (1908), 181-183.

52 *JT* 25/7/1848; L. et R., T. II, 101-105.

53 Commission of 1861, op. cit., Recommendations 2, 3 & 4, lxxvii-lxviii.

54 Ibid., Recommendation 3, lxxvii.

55 L. et R., T. III (1882), 260-363.

56 J. Stuart Blackie, op. cit., . 34.

57 F. Zincke, 'The Channel Islands and Land Tenure', *Fortnightly Review* XIX (1876).

Chapter 9

The Maintenance of Small-scale Agriculture

1 Annual Report, Royal Jersey Agricultural and Horticultural Society (RJAHS), 9/1/1858.

2 Annual Report RJAHS 22/11/1886.

3 Ibid.

4 All statistics are drawn from the almanacks of the *Chronique* and the *British Press/Jersey Times.*

5 F. Zincke, 'The Channel Islands and Land Tenure', *Fortnightly Review* XIX (1876), 5.

6 W.E. Bear, 'Glimpses of Farming in the Channel Islands', *Journal of the Royal Agricultural Society of England* XXIV (1888), 376.

7 *BP/JT* 20/10/1892.

8 W.E. Bear, op. cit., 385; for 1850s prices see, C.P. Le Cornu, 'The Agriculture of the Islands of Jersey, Guernsey, Alderney and

Sark', *Journal of the Royal Agricultural Society of England,* XX (1859), 51.

9 J. Burns Murdoch, *Notes and Remarks Made in Jersey, France, Italy and the Mediterranean in 1843 and 1844* (Edinburgh/London 1846), 31-32.

10 W.E. Bear, op. cit., 387.

11 J. Coleman, 'Jersey Farming', *The Field* (October 1886), p. 541.

12 W.E. Bear, 'Glimpses', op. cit., 376.

13 Ibid.

14 Ibid.

15 H. Rider Haggard, *Rural England: Being an Account of Agricultural and Social Researches carried out in the Years 1901 and 1902 Vol. I* (London 1906), 102.

16 *BP/JT* Almanack, 1887.

17 *BP/JT* Almanack, 1888.

18 H. Rider Haggard, op. cit., 87.

19 W. E. Bear, 'Garden Farming', *Quarterly Review* CLXVI (1888), 413-415.

20 J. Coleman, op. cit., 506.

21 *BP/JT* 23/11/1886.

22 J. Coleman, op. cit., 541.

23 RJAHS, Annual Report 12/1/1861.

24 The figures for 1851 and 1881 are drawn from six sample parishes in the Censuses of these two years. A small percentage of farmers did not give details as to their size of holding. The 1914 figure, the first source with this information available after 1881, comes from the Abstract of Parish Returns 1914, Public Record Office HO 14/325.

25 T. Quayle, *A General View of the Agriculture and Present State of the Islands on the Coast of Normandy. Board of Agriculture* (London 1815), 52.

26 C.P. Le Cornu, op. cit., 36.

27 Poor Law Report 1834, British Sessional Papers XXX, 663.

28 J. Coleman, op. cit., 506.

29 T. Quayle, op. cit., 54; W. Plees, *An Account of the Island of Jersey* (Southampton 1817), 84.

30 W.E. Bear, Glimpses, op. cit., 372.

31 J. Coleman, op. cit., 506.

32 H. Rider Haggard, op. cit., 91.

33 W.E. Bear, op. cit., 387.

34 T. Quayle, op. cit., 54.

35 W. Plees, op. cit., 84.

36 C.P. Le Cornu, op. cit., 36.

37 P. Galichet, *Le Fermier de L'Ile de Jersey* (Paris 1912), 6.

38 W.E. Bear, op. cit., 371

39 Ibid.

40 H. Rider Haggard, op. cit.,102.

41 Ibid., 91.

42 Anon, 'Jersey as Regards its Husbandry and Agricultural Classes' *The Quarterly Journal of Agriculture* XIII (1842/3), 376.

43 W.E. Bear, op. cit., 387.

44 H. Rider Haggard, op. cit., 103.

45 P. Galichet, op. cit., 89-93, 54-59.

46 J. Girardin and E. Morière, 'Excursion Agricole à Jersey', *Societe Centrale D'Agriculture du Departement de la Seine-Inferieure* (Rouen 1857), 36-40; C.P. Le Cornu, op. cit., 37. For a discussion of these studies see Chapter 3.

47 Abstract of Parish Returns of Crops and Livestock, 1900, PRO HO 14/325.

48 Ibid., 1866 and 1900.

49 W.E. Bear, 'Garden Farming', op. cit., 435. See Chapter 3.

50 H. Rider Haggard, op. cit., 85 and 102.

51 A.M. Barbier and F. Schmitt, 'Voyage d'Etudes de l'Union des Syndicats Agricoles Vosgiens', Août/Sept 1931. Pamphlet, 67-82.

52 Rule 3, Rules and Regulations, Members' Meeting RJAHS 29/8/1833.

53 Members' Meetings, RJAHS 18/1/1845, 7/11/1835, 14/6/1834, 9/4/1834.

54 M. Mylechreest, 'Questions and Answers: the Correspondence between Sir John Le Couteur and Thomas Andrew Knight', *Ann. Bull. Société Jersiaise* XXIV (1986), pp. X237-244.

55 'Colonel Le Couteur', *The Farmer's Magazine*, March 1846.

56 C.P. Le Cornu, op. cit.; J. Le Couteur, 'On the Jersey Misnamed Alderney Cow', *Journal of the Royal Agricultural Society of England*, V (1844), 43-50.

57 Members' Meeting, RJAHS 6/9/1834.

58 Annual Report, RJAHS 18/1/1845.

59 Members' Meeting, RJAHS 7/3 and 19/8/1835.

60 Members' Meeting, RJAHS 7/9/1836.

61 Annual Report RJAHS (Horticultural Section), 9/2/1843.

62 H.G. Shepherd, *One Hundred Years of the Royal Jersey Agricultural and Horticultural Society 1833-1933* (Jersey 1934), 22.

63 Annual Report RJAHS 9/1/1858.

64 Members' Meeting RJAHS 7/11/1838.

65 Members' Meeting RJAHS 15/9/1838 and 1/2/1843; *CJ* 9/5/1846.

66 Annual Report, RJAHS 6/12/1843.

67 Annual Report, RJAHS 15/9/1838.

68 See François Godfray's letter of accusation in *Le Constitutionnel* 27/10/1838 and J. Le Couteur, Diary Ms., 16/1/1837, Letter Book L4/195, Société Jersiaise.

69 Annual Report, RJAHS 9/1/1858.

70 Annual Report, RJAHS 22/11/1886.

71 Annual Report, RJAHS 12/1/1861.

72 W.E. Bear, 'Glimpses', op. cit., 381-382.

73 P. Galichet, op. cit., 90.

74 Ibid., 146.

75 W.E. Bear, 'Glimpses', op. cit., 381-382.

76 P. Galichet, op. cit., 45.

77 E.O.B. Voisin, 'Inebriety in Jersey', *British Journal of Inebriety* (1904), 168.

78 H. Rider Haggard, op. cit., 89.

79 W.E. Bear, 'Glimpses', op. cit., 372-373.

80 J. Coleman, op. cit., 506.

81 Census of Jersey 1851 and 1881.

82 Figure calculated from analysis of six country parishes, Census of Jersey 1881.

83 J. Coleman, op. cit.,506.

84 W.E. Bear, 'Glimpses', op. cit., 372-373. No record of the number of French immigrants naturalised in the nineteenth century has been located. For an example of a naturalisation, see, J. F. Arthur, 'Patchwork from Crabbe', *Ann. Bull. Société Jersiaise* xxv (1992) 647-48.

85 Rapport de l'Immigration d'Etrangers en cette Ile (Jersey 1906), 8.

86 P. Galichet, op. cit., 94-98.

87 Ibid., 68-72.

88 Ibid., 89-93.

89 V. Igoa, *A Hundred Years of Life in Jersey 1880-1980.* Pamphlet. (Jersey 1980), 8-10. This provides one of the few sources on Catholicism in nineteenth-century Jersey.

90 Ibid.,18.

91 Ibid., 9.

92 Rapport de l'Immigration d'Etrangers en cette Ile (Jersey 1906), p. 16

93 Annual Report, RJAHS 12/1/1861.

94 C.P. Le Cornu, 'The Jersey Dairy Industry', Pamphlet. RJAHS (*c.* 1900), 6.

95 BP/JT 12/2/1867 'Is Agriculture Improving in Jersey'.

96 C.P. Le Cornu, 'Agriculture of the Islands', op. cit., 37; Members' Meetings RJAHS 2/9/1834 and 8/1/1842.

97 C.P. Le Cornu, 'The Jersey Dairy Industry', op. cit., 6.

98 C. Le Quesne, *Ireland and the Channel Islands or A Remedy from Ireland* (London 1848), iii-iv, 137-138.

99 Book Review, *The Economist* 10/6/1848.

100 P. Falle, *Caesarea: Or an Account of the Island of Jersey* (Jersey 1837), xiii.

101 H. Tupper, *Observations on the Law of Descent of Real Estate in the United Kingdom; its Origin and Bearing on the Social Condition of the People* (London 1868).

102 C. Le Quesne, op. cit., 111.

103 W.T. Thornton, *A Plea For Peasant Proprietors* (London 1874), 41.

104 F. Zincke, op. cit., 490.

105 Annual Report, RJAHS 2/3/1900.

106 Rapport de l'Immigration, op. cit., 6.

107 W.E. Bear, 'Glimpses', op. cit., 373.

108 H. Rider Haggard, op. cit., p. 96.

109 W.E. Bear, 'Glimpses', op. cit.

110 Ibid.

111 Comité d'Immigration, op. cit., 16-24.

112 Ibid., 20.

Chapter 10
Cultural Compromise

1 G.R. Balleine, *A Biographical Dictionary of Jersey* (London 1948), 282-283.

2 *Le Magasin de l'Eglise Anglicane* April 1843, 247-248.

3 G.R. Balleine, op. cit., 335.

4 *Chronique de Jersey*, 1/4/1848.

5 *Code of Laws for the Island of Jersey 1771* (Jersey 1968).

6 *Lois et Reglemens Passés par les États de Jersey*, Tome 1 (1878), 47. (hereafter L. et R., T.)

7 The nine could be identified from both the rate lists of St John and Trinity in the 1830s and the Census of Jersey, 1841. Shared names made the other two trustees uncertain.

8 Census of Jersey, 1851.

9 L. et R., T 1 (1878), 47.

10 Parish of St Ouen, Acts of the Ecclesiastical Assembly (AEA) Book 1, 24/10/1804. For an Ecclesiastical Assembly entry in the Civil Assembly records see, Acts of the Civil Assembly (ACA), 29/7/1763.

11 Parish of St Saviour, ACA Book 1 5/1/1808, AEA 10/7/1783.

12 See for instance, Parish of St John, ACA 21/1/1818, which is an ecclesiastical entry.

13 Parish of St Ouen, ACA 10/9/1806, ACA 10/6/1829.

14 The parish of St Brelade used the hospital from at least ACA, 12/8/1770. This is partially explained by the distance of the parish church from the centre of settlement at St Aubin. St John's Civil Assembly used local taverns from at least ACA, 8/8/1827 and the parish school intermittently from ACA, 21/11/1865.

15 Loi (1804), op. cit.

16 Rev. E.Durell, Introduction and Notes to, P. Falle, *An Account of the Island of Jersey* (Jersey 1837), 413.

17 L. et R., T. 1 (1878), 165-166.

18 *CJ* 17/7/1830. It is worth noting that Reverend Philippe Filleul, at St Peter's church at this time, was also involved in the fight to abolish Sunday elections, see G.R. Balleine, *A Biographical Dictionary of Jersey* (London 1948), 282.

19 J. Le Couteur, Diary Ms., Société Jersiase 1830, Letter Book L3/53. It has proved impossible to substantiate further the external link with the reform of 1831.

20 L. et R., T. II (1879),321-324.

21 Ibid.

22 *Acte des Etats autorisant la suppression des Appentis Militaires et la construction de Salles Paroissiales 1877, L. et R., T.* III (1882), 166-170.

23 L. et R., T. 1 (1878), 165.

24 Rev. E. Durell, op. cit., 413.

25 L. et R., T. II (1879), 321. See also, F.W. Cornish, *History of the English Church in the Nineteenth Century* (London 1910).

26 Caesariensis, *Reminiscences of Church Life in Jersey* (Jersey 1917), 20. Sources have failed to reveal a local link with the Oxford Movement, popular among some clergy in mid-nineteenth-century England and aimed at countering the liberalising and rationalising tendencies of the Church.

27 Parish of Grouville, AEA 1874.

28 C.P. Le Cornu, Diary MS., 16/6/1872, La Hague Documents.

29 Parish of St Ouen, AEA 30/5/33. See Chapter 4.

30 Pew plan, Parish of Grouville, AEA 28/1/1873.

31 P. Harrison, *Jersey's Parish Churches.* Pamphlet (Jersey 1965), 7.

32 En Convocation Ecclesiastique, the meeting of local clergy, 20/5/1827.

33 Canon 33, a copy of which can be found in P. Falle, op. cit., 252.

34 En Convocation Ecclesiastique, op. cit.

35 Report of the Commissioners Appointed to Inquire into the Civil, Municipal and Ecclesiastical Laws of the Island of Jersey (London 1861), 543-558.

36 *British Press/Jersey Times*(*BP/JT*), 28/3/1860.

37

G.R. Balleine, op. cit., 282-283.

38 Parish of St Clement, AEA 6/1/1829 and 8/1/1833.

39 Parish of St Brelade, AEA 10/7/1839 and 6/5/1841.

40 Parish of St Helier, ACA 18/12/1863, a discussion on the 'proprieté des bancs'.

41 Ibid. This view is supported by the fact that pews, unique among an individual's possessions, did not pass on to creditors in bankruptcy.

42 Parish of St John, ACA 13/12/1867.

43 Parish of Trinity, AEA 30/3/1855. See also Parish of St Ouen, AEA 5/7/1855 and the Parish of St Clement, AEA 6/5/1899.

44 See his writings for the year 1859 in the Parish of Grouville, AEA where he compiles a complicated argument, using English ecclesiastical sources, to show that pew sales are illegal and that usage only is permitted.

45 Parish of St Helier, ACA 18/12/1863.

46 Parish of Grouville, AEA 6/3/1866.

47 Parish of Grouville, AEA 4/11/1880.

48 G.R. Balleine, op. cit., 284.

49 J. Stevens & J. Arthur, *The Parish Church of St Mary, Jersey.* Pamphlet (Jersey), 7.

50 F. de L. Bois, *The Parish Church of St Saviour* (London & Frome 1976), 101-102.

51 F. de L. Bois, op. cit., 98-100; P. Harrison, op. cit., 27.

52 St. George's Church, St Ouen. Pamphlet (Jersey 1980).

53 Photograph of the parish church of St Helier (circa 1860), Société Jersiaise.

54 Parish of Trinity, AEA 30/3/1855.

55 Architectural information in J. McCormack, *Channel Island Churches.* (Chichester 1986), 190-262; P. Harrison, op. cit., 7, 24, 27.

56 J.P. Le Quesne, *A Short History of St John's Independent Church*. Pamphlet (Jersey), 3.

57 Parish of St Brelade, ACA 27/1/1829; Parish of St Clement, AEA 4/9/1833; Parish of St Ouen, AEA 24/1/1851.

58 Parish of Grouville, AEA 2/2 and 8/3/1870.

59 Parish of Trinity, AEA 27/6/1850; a similar problem was encountered in Grouville, see the *Jersey Times* (*JT*), 4/11/1851.

60 Reverend. P. Filleul, An Earnest Appeal to the Stewards of the Lord's Goods, Inviting their Aid. Pamphlet (Jersey 1858).

61 For instance see, J. Obelkvich, *Religion and Rural Society: South Lindsey 1825-1875* (Oxford 1976).

62 See for instance, Parish of St Ouen, AEA 7/8/1849 and 5/7/1855 and Parish of St Clement, AEA 6/5/1849.

63 Parish of St John, ACA 13/12/1867.

64 *CJ* 14 and 18/9/1844.

65 *CJ* 1/4/1848.

66 Parish of St Ouen, AEA 26/5/1830.

67 *CJ* 1/4/1848.

68 Almorah Cemetery, 1855. Ms Société Jersiaise.

69 Four were genuinely independent, the fifth, Philadelphie, and perhaps others, was denominational, adjoined to the Methodist Chapel, yet, "À l'usage de toutes les cults" (inscription on cemetery gates).

70 P. Stevens, *Victor Hugo in Jersey* (Chichester 1986), 57-59.

71 Parish of Grouville, AEA 31/8/1848 and 18/5/1852.

72 Ibid., 21/2/1849 and 28/8/1849. Les Mielles dates from 1809.

73 Acte de Parlement (43 & 44 Vict. c. 16, 4/12/1880), registered "in Jersey 10/1/1881, L. et R., T III (1882), 366-369.

74 Parish of Grouville, AEA 5/2/1884, 2/12/1888.

75 The main source on the life and character of P.J. Brée is, P. Galichet, *Le Fermier de L'Ile de Jersey* (Paris 1912),20-22, and the Brée family papers. On C.P. Le Cornu, papers at the Société Jersiaise and, among other alternatives, a description in, G.R. Balleine, op. cit., 368-369.

76 *CJ* 25/9/1844.

77 A. Mourant, *Rimes et Poésies Jersiaises de Divers Auteurs*. (Jersey 1865), 1-2.

78 Ibid., 5-11.

79 R.J. Lebarbenchon, *La Grève de Lecq: Littératures et Cultures Populaires de Normandie* (Cherbourg 1988), 105.

80 G.R. Balleine, op. cit., 481-483.

81 *JT* 2/2/1856.

82 See for instance his, 'La Buonne Femme et ses Cotillons', 'La Fille Malade' in *CJ* 18/1 and 8/2/1851; also printed in A. Mourant, op. cit. 81-84, 94-99.

83 Perhaps the exception to this qualification is the rather elegiac style of H.L. Manuel, see, for instance, 'Une Malédiction', in A. Mourant, op. cit.,157-158.

84 G.R. Balleine, op. cit., 394-395.

85 *Glossaire du Patois Jersiaise* (Jersey 1924). Published by the Société Jersiaise.

86 'Adraisse és vrais Trin'tais' and 'Election de la Trin'tais', in A. Mourant, op. cit., 226-231.

87 *CJ* 6/7/1864.

88 See for instance, *CJ* 6/7/1864, 29/9/1873, 19/6/1875.

89 P. Stevens, op. cit., 31.

90 W.T. Money, 'Diary of a Visit to Jersey', *Bull. Ann. Société Jersiaise* (BASJ) (1932), p. 41.

91 Official Catalogue of the Channel Islands' Exhibition (Jersey 1871), Pamphlet, Société Jersiaise; *CJ* 29/6/1871.

92 G.R. Balleine, op. cit., 474-475. On H.L. Manuel see, M. Tréhounais, *L'Histoire, la Topographie, la Constitution, les Moeurs, et la Langage de Jersey* (Jersey 1844).

93 *Bull. Ann. Société Jersiaise* Volume I (1873) No I.

94 Ibid.

95 *CJ* 1/2/1873.

96 Aim 2, *BASJ*, , op. cit,. p. 2.

97 See for instance, M. Bull, 'Report of the Excavation of the Cromlech 'Les Cinq Pierres', Jersey', *BASJ,I* (1875), pp. 6-10.

98 See for instance, *CJ* 16/2/1893.

99 *BP/JT* 7/12/1860.

100 P. Ahier, A Short History of Secondary Grammar Education in Jersey. Ms. Société Jersiaise, 98-99.

101 Ibid.

102 *Ordre du Conseil* 26/10/1860, Société Jersiaise.

103 *BP/JT* 6/5/1861.

104 J. Likeman, 'Education in Jersey in the Nineteenth Century, With Particular Reference to the Teaching of French', M.A. (University of London 1987), 107-108.

105 *Nouvelle Chronique* 16/9/1871.

106 *CJ* 14/5/1873; *Nouvelle Chronique* 13/1/1886.

107 Report of the Commissioners Appointed to Inquire into the Civil, Municipal and Ecclesiastical Laws of the Island of Jersey (London 1861), xlix.

108 P. Bouchet, Report to the States of Jersey Elementary Education Committee 1882, in J. Likeman, op. cit., 102.

109 P. Ahier, op. cit., 215.

110 P. Stevens, op. cit., 28.

111 *BP/JT* 16/2/1891; Rapport du Comité de l'Immigration d'Étrangers (Jersey 1906).

112 W.E. Bear, 'Glimpses of Farming in the Channel Islands', *Journal of the Royal Agricultural Society of England* XXIV (1888), 373-374.

113 P. Galichet, op. cit., 54-59.

114 Projet d'Actes sur l'Emploi de la Langue Anglaise 4/12/1899.

115 *BP/JT* 16/2/1893.

116 P.E. Brée, *A Short Sketch of the Origin and Development of Methodism in La Rocque*. Pamphlet (Jersey 1932), p. 19.

117 *CJ* 6/9/1844.

118 P. Stevens, 'Marx and Engels in Jersey', *ABSJ* XXIV (1987), 57.

119 J. Likeman, op. cit., 91-94.

120 *CJ* 21/4/1866.

121 Ibid.

122 Anon, 'Les Iles de la Manche', *Revue des Deux Mondes* (1849), 964-965.

123 *CJ* 21/4/1866.

124 W. Plees, *An Account of the Island of Jersey* (Southampton 1817), 53.

125 *BP/JT* 28/8/1868.

126 *BP/JT* 22, 23, 24 and 27/1/1901; *CJ* 23 and 26/1/1901.

127 *BP/JT* 19, 21 & 22/5/1900; *CJ* 23 & 30/5/1900, 2/6/1900.

128 L. et R., T. IV (1908), 467.

129 Parish of St John, ACA 11/4/1895. See also Parishes of St Ouen, ACA 9/4/1895 and St Clement, ACA 8/6/1900.

130 Parish of St Helier, ACA 25/1/1893.

131 *CJ* 6/8/1814.

132 *Loi* (1872) *sur les Écoles Élémentaires*, L. et R., T.III (1882), 65-70; *Loi (1879) sur les Écoles Élémentaires*, Ibid., 228-342; *Loi (1897) sur l'Etablissement d'Écoles Élémentaires*, L. et R., T. IV (1908), 343-346.

133 N. Le Cornu, 'The Royal Jersey Artillery and the Jersey Militia System 1771-1877', *Bulletin of the Jersey Society in London* III (1980), pp. 36-39.

134 Parish of St Ouen, ACA 3/5/1842.

135 *CJ* 19/10/1816.

136 *BP/JT* 17/5/1883.

137 Parish of St John, ACA 17/1/1851.

138 For instance see, Parish of St Ouen, ACA 28/12/1846, Parish of St Clement, ACA 26/9/1848, and Parish of Trinity, ACA 6/4/1864.

139 *Loi (1864) Réglant la Procedure Criminelle*, L. et R., T. II (1879), 201-228.

140 Commission of 1861, op. cit., 157-160.

141 Ibid., xlii.

Chapter 11
The Conclusion

1 *British Press/Jersey Times* 8/10/1875.

Bibliography

Unpublished Sources

London

British Library, London:

Skinner, J., Journal of 1827 Add. 33699.

Wellington, Duke of, Memorandum on the defence of the United Kingdom 19/10/1845 Add. 40461.

Public Record Office, London:

Home Office Papers. London Customs bills of entry (Colindale) HO45, Privy Council Papers.

Abstract of Parish Returns 1877-1920 HO 14/325.

Replies to the Request of Lord Pelham, Secretary of State to the Dioceses, to give Acreage Returns, HO 67/24.

Jersey

Ecclesiastical Court Records, Deanery Archive:

En Convocation Ecclesiastiques (Committee of Local Clergy) 1750-1900.

Rôles Ecclesiastiques, 1750-1900.

Le Couteur Papers, Société Jersiaise Library:

Le Couteur, J, Diary. 1820-1831, 1839-1875

Le Couteur, J, Letter Books 1820-1875

La Hague Papers, Société Jersiaise Library:

Le Cornu, C.P., Diary. Ms.

Fief de la Fosse Papers 1750-1900.

Fief de la Hague Papers 1750-1900.

Fief de la Nobretez Papers 1750-1900.

Fief des Nièmes Papers 1750-1900.

Methodist Archives, Wesley Grove, Jersey:

Methodist Baptisms (Jersey/French Circuit) 1831-1852.

Returns of Accommodation 1911, Wesleyan Chapel Committee.

Sion Trust Minutes 1826-1900.

Timetable for Wesleyan Preachers, 1858.

Parish Records, Jersey

Civil:

(Held at individual Parish Halls).

Grouville, St Brelade, St Clement, St Helier , St John , St Ouen, Trinity, 1750-1900

Ecclesiastical:

(Generally held by the Parish Rectors).

Grouville, St Brelade, St Clement, St John, St Ouen, Trinity, 1750-1900.

Royal Court Records 1750-1900:

Livre du Causes Remises.

Livre d'Heritages.

Livre de Poursuite Criminelles.

Livre du Samedi.

Registre Publique.

Royal Jersey Agricultural and Horticultural Society:

Minute Books, 1833-1900.

Société Jersiaise Library, Jersey

Miscellaneous:

Almorah Cemetery 1855.

Census of Jersey' 1806.

Census of Jersey Militia, 1815.

Census of Jersey 1821 1881.

De Carteret, P., Trinity Manor Farm Diary 1820/1.

De Carteret, J.J., Journal Late Nineteenth Century. Privately Owned. 'Este, D., Journal 1814.

Rente Book of T. Blampied, 1877-1923.

Retours Faisons 1848 des Vingtaines, Paroisse de St Martin.

Reverend Docteur to Jeune Monsieur le Bailli: Correspondence Relatif Etablissement d'un College Jersey 1/6/1847. A Select Committee Report on the Education of the Poor, *c.* 1816-1818.

Trinity Manor Farm Diary, 1820/21.

Published Sources

Parliamentry Papers:

Hansard's Parliamentry debates, 1800-1900.

The Report of the Royal Commission Deputed to the Island of Jersey in 1811 (Guernsey 1813). *Poor Law Report*, 1834. British Sessional Papers XXX (1834).

Report from the Select Committee on the Present State of the Trade in Corn between the Channel Islands and the United Kingdom. Parliamentry Papers XIII (1835).

First Report of the Commissioners Appointed to Inquire into the State of the Criminal Law in the Channel Islands (London, 1847).

Report of the Commissioners appointed to Inquire into the Civil, Municiple and Ecclesiastical Law of Jersey (London, 1861)

Privy Council Papers:

Ordres du Conseil IV, 1771-1812 (Jersey 1900)

Odres du Conseil V, 1813-1834 (Jersey 1901)

Ordes du Council VI, 1835-1867 (Jersey 1906)

States of Jersey Papers:

Actes des États, 1779-1800 (Jersey 1910-1916)

Lois et Règlemens Passés par les États de Jersey Tome I 1771-1850 (Jersey 1978)

Lois et Règlements Passés par les États de Jersey Tome II 1851-1871 (Jersey 1879)

Lois et Règlements Passés par les États de Jersey Tome III 1872-1881 (Jersey 1882)

Lois et Règlements Passés par les États de Jersey Tome IV 1882-1899 (Jersey 1908)

Maps

An Accurate Survey and Measurement of the island of Jersey. Surveyed by Order of the Duke of Richmond, 1795. Société.

A Map of the Island of Jersey, Surveyed by H. Godfrey, 1849. Société Jersiaise.

A Map of the Island of Jersey, Surveyed by H. Godfray 1849.

Newspapers

British Press 1832-1848

Jersey Times 1832-1848

British Press and Jersey Times (amalgamate) 1848-1900

La Chronique de Jersey 1814-1900

Le Constitutionnel 1820-1876

Books and Articles

Ahier, P., *A Short History of Secondary Grammar Education in Jersey, As Exemplified in the Story of Victoria College Jersey*. Ms.

Ahier, P., *The History of Primary Education in Jersey From Early Times to 1872*, MA (University of London) 1965.

Anderson, A., *Trade Between the Channel Islands and Southampton in the Mid Eighteenth Century, Ann. Bull. Société Jersiaise (ABSJ)* XVIII (1964), pp. 445-451.

Anon, English Writs versus Jersey Privileges: The Proceedings in the Case of Dodd and Merrifield. Pamphlet (Jersey 1858).

Anon, Jersey as Regards its Husbandry and Agricultural Classes, *Quarterly Review* XII (1842/3), 369- 378.

Anon, Les Iles de la Manche, *Revue des Deux Mondes* (1849), 937-967.

Anon, *Letters from Jersey* (Cambridge 1830).

Anon, *Queen of the Isles* (London 1841).

Anon, Recueil des Pièces Authentiques Relatives aux Poursuites vers le Reverend Edouard Le Vavasseur dit Durell. Pamphlet (Jersey *c.* 1841-1850).

Anon, The Agricultural Problem in Jersey. Pamphlet (Jersey 1907).

Anon, The Commerce of Jersey, *Guernsey and Jersey Magazine* V (1837)

Anon, *The Groans of the Inhabitants of Jersey* (Jersey 1709).

Anon, The Remarkable Trial of Philippe Arthur. Pamphlet (London 1808).

Ansted, D. and Latham, R.G., *The Channel Islands* (London 1862).

Arnold, A., Free Land and Peasant Proprietorshi', *Nineteenth Century* VII (1880), 297-317.

Balleine, G.R., *A Biographical Dictionary of Jersey* (London 1948).

Barbier, A.M. and Schmitt, F., 'Voyages d'Etudes de l'Union des Syndicats Agricoles Vosgiens', (Août/ Septembre 1931), 67-82.

Bear, W.E., Garden Farming, *Quarterly Review* CLXVI (1888), 407-438.

Bear, W.E.,Glimpses of Farming in the Channel Islands, *Journal of the Royal Agricultural Society of England* (*JRASE*) XXIV (1888), 365-397.

Becker, H., *An Agric-Horticultural College for Jersey* (Jersey *c.*1900).

Berry, W., *The History of the Island of Guernsey* (London 1815).

Blackie, John S., Jersey, *Macmillan's Magazine* XLIX (1883/4),27-39.

Blench, B.J.R., Some Notes on the Agriculture of Jersey in the Seventeenth Century, *Tijdschrift Voor Econ En Soc Geografie* (1962), 51-52.

Blench, B.J.R., Seaweed and its Use in Jersey Agriculture, *Agricultural History Review* (1966), 122- 128.

Blench, B.J.R., Trinity Manor Farm in the Early Nineteenth Century, *Ann. Bull. Société Jersiaise* XVII (1964), 437-444.

Blench, B.J.R., The Jersey Cholera Epidemic of 1832', *ABSJ* XIX (1966), 146-151.

Blench, B.J.R., A Note on the Jersey Trench Plough, *ABSJ* XIX (1968), 315-318.

Blench, B.J.R., La Population et le Peuplement de Jersey Avant 1806, *Norois* LIV (1967), 227-239.

Boase, J.J., Travels of J.J. Boase Ms. (British Library 1865).

Bois, F. de L. , *A Constitutional History of Jersey* (Jersey 1972).

Bois, F. de L. , *The Parish Church of St Saviour* (London 1976).

Bonamy, Samuel, A Short Account of the Island of Guernsey Ms (British Library 1749).

Bonsor, N.R.P., *The Jersey Railway* (Oxford 1962).

Bonsor, N.R.P., *The Jersey Eastern Railway and the German Occupation Lines in Jersey* (Oxford 1965).

Bowditch, J., A Series of Letters on the State of the Laws of the Channel Islands. Pamphlet (Jersey 1858).

Brett, C.E.B., *Buidings in the Town and Parish of St Helier* (Belfast 1977).

Caesaria, Of the Landing Places about the Island of Jersey (Ms Late 17th Century).

Caesariensis, *Reminiscences of Church Life in Jersey* (London 1917) For Private Circulation.

Carman, W.J., *Channel Island Transport* (Guernsey 1987).

Cliffe Leslie, T.E., *Land Systems and Industrial Economy* (London 1870).

Clowes, W., The Strategical Value of the Channel Islands, *Nineteenth Century* CCLXXXVI (December 1900).

Cobban, A., The Beginning of the Channel Isles Correspondence, 1789-1794, *English Historical Review* LXXVII (1962), 39-52.

Coleman, J., Jersey Farming, *The Field* (October 1886).

Corkery, D., *The Fortunes of the Irish Language* (Cork 1968).

Cotes, E., *The Second Journey: Containing a Survey of the Two Estates of the Two Islands of Guernsey and Jersey*. Book. VI (London 1656).

Cottrill, D.J., *Victoria College Jersey 1852-1972* (London 1977).

Cox, Reverend Thomas, *Magna Britannia (A Survey of Britain)*. Vol II (London 1720).

Craig, R., The African Guano Trade, *Mariner's Mirror* L (1964), 25-55.

Cruickshank, C., *The German Occupation of the Channel Islands* (Channel Islands 1975)

Culley, G., *Observations on Livestock* (London 1786).

Dalido, P., *Jersey: Ile Agricole Anglo Normande* (Vannes 1951).

Dally, F.F., *An Essay on the Agriculture of the Channel Islands* (Guernsey 1860). Davies, W., *Fort Regent: A History* (Jersey 1972).

Davies, W., *The Harbour That Failed* (Alderney 1983).

Dendy, W.C., *The Islets of the Channel* (London 1858).

Denison, Edward, *Letters and Other Writings* (London 1872).

Dicey, T., *An Historical Account of Guernsey* (London 1751).

Dickinson, A.S.H., 'The Story of the Jersey Public Library', *ABSJ* (1937), pp. 259 275.

Dorey, J., Notice Biographique sur le Reverend Thomas Sivret. Pamphlet (Jersey 1870).

Douglas, D., The Rise of Normandy, Raleigh Lecture on History, May 28 1947.

Dubost, P.C., Les Fêtes Agricoles De Jersey, *Journal De L'Agriculture* Juillet Septembre 1879), 239-330.

Dumaresq, P., *A Survey of the Island of Jersey* (London 1685).

Duncan, J., *The History of Guernsey with Occasional Notices of Jersey, Alderney and Sark* (London 1841).

Dunlop, A., On Influenza in Jersey, *Glasgow Medical Journal* (June 1890), 1-4.

Dury, G.H., The Climatic Problem: Discussion of a Century of Records, *Rep. and Trans. Soc. Guernesiais* (1948), 279-297.

Dury, G.H., Notes on Jersey Agriculture in 1801 as Compared with 1949, *BASJ* XV (1951), 332-340.

Dury, G.H., *The Channel Islands: The Land of Britain: Land Utilization Survey* (London 1950).

Dury, G.H., Some Land Use Statistics for Jersey in the Late Eighteenth Century' *BASJ* XV (1952) 440-441

De Gruchy, G.F.B., The Town of St Aubin in the Past, *St Aubin's Magazine* (October 1917).

De Gruchy, G.F.B., *Medieval Land Tenures in Jersey* (Jersey 1957).

De Gruchy, W.L., Jersey: My Reminiscences, *Jersey Society in London Occasional Publications* (1923).

De La Morvonnais, A., 'Compte Rendu D'Un Concours Agricole à Jersey', *Bulletin De La Societe Agriculteurs De France'* (1877).

De Lavergne, M.L., *Essai sur L'Èconomie Rurale de L'Angleterre* (Paris 1858).

De Quetteville, J., *Nouveau Recueil de Cantiques Spirituels* (Jersey 1795).

De Quetteville, J., *Recueil de Cantiques l'Usage de la Société Appelée Methodiste* (Guernsey 1818).

Eagleston, A.J., *The Channel Islands under Tudor Government 1485-1642* (Cambridge 1949).

Edwards, G.B., *The Book of Ebenezer Le Page* (Sussex 1981).

Ellis, M.F.H., The Channel Islands and the Great Rebellion, *BASJ* (1937),191-247.

English Law Reports,In the Matter of the Jersey Jurats', XVI 1866), 173-183.

Escard, M.F.,Jersey et ses Institutions, *Société D'conomie Sociale* (February 1896). L'Estourbillon, R., *Les Familles Francaises Jersey pendant la Revolution* (Nantes 1886).

Falle, P., *An Account of the Island of Jersey* (Jersey 1694), (Revised 1734), to which notes are added by Durell, E., (Jersey 1837).

Farmer's Magazine, Colonel Le Couteur, III (March 1846), 196-200.

Filleul, P., An Earnest Appeal to Stewards of the Lord's Goods, Inviting their Aid. Pamphlet (Jersey 1858).

Flower, E. *Habeas Corpus* in the Channel Islands. Pamphlet (Jersey 1858).

Ford, G.W.,The British Channel Island Shipping Company Ltd., *Sea Breezes* (September 1953), 180- 201.

Fowler, Edward Parsons, *The Alderney and Guernsey Cow* (London 1855).

Franklyn, W.N., *The Laws and Customs of the Channel Islands and Their Abuses* (Jersey 1857).

Fussell, G.E., Channel Island Cattle: The Making of the Breeds, *Bulletin of Veterinary History* I (1973),

Galichet, P., *Le Fermier de L'Ile de Jersey* (Paris 1912).

Gastineau, E.T., *A Hobble Through the Channel Islands in 1858* (London 1860).

Girardin, J. and Moriére, E.J., Excursion Agricole à Jersey, *Societe Centrale D'Agriculture Du Department De La Seine Inferieure* (1857), 70.

Glossaire du Patois Jersiaise, Société Jersiaise, (Jersey 1924).

Gow, R.M., *The Jersey: An Outline of Her History During Two Centuries 1734-1935* (New York 1936).

Guernsey Society, *The Guernsey Farmhouse* (Guernsey 1978).

Guiton, F., *Histoire du Methodisme Wesleyan dans les Iles de la Manche* (London 1846).

Habitant de Jersey, *Les Droits de Seigneur ou Un Drame à Jersey* (Jersey 1859).

Haggard, H. Rider, *Rural England: Being an Account of Agricultural and Social Researches Carried Out in the Years 1901 and 1902*. Vol I. (London 1906).

Harney, G.J., *The Harney Papers*, (Eds) Black, F.G. and R.M., (Assen 1969).

Harris, S., The Village Community of Alderney, *Sociological Review* XVIII (1926), 265-278.

Harrison, P., Jersey's Parish Churches. Pamphlet (Jersey 1965).

Hatton, C. Lord. The State of Guernsey (Ms. Late 18th Century).

Haynes, R., *A Brief Description of Jersey* (London 1826).

Heylin, P., *The Second Journey: Containing a Survey of the Estates of the Two Islands*

Guernsey and Jersey. Book VI (London 1656).

Hettier, H., *Relations de la Normandie avec les Iles pendant 'Emmigration* (Caen 1885).

Heyting, W.J., *The Constitutional Relationship Between Jersey and the United Kingdom* (Jersey 1977).

Hill, C.L., *The Guernsey Breed* (Iowa 1917).

Hooper, G.S., *History and Statistics of Asiatic Cholera in Jersey.* Pamphlet (Jersey 1833).

Hugo, F. Victor., *La Normandie Inconnue* (Paris 1857).

Igoa, V., *One Hundred Years Life in Jersey* (Jersey 1981).

Inglis, H.D., *The Channel Islands* (London 1834).

Jamieson, A.G., Shipbuilding in the Channel Islands in the Nineteenth Century, *Journal of Transport History* III (1982), 63-79.

Jamieson, A.G., The C.I. and Australia: Maritime Links in the 1850s, *Great Circle* V (1983), 40-47.

Jamieson, A.G., (Ed.) *A People of the Sea: The Maritime History of the Channel Islands* (London 1986).

Jeremie, P., *An Essay on the Laws of Real Property in Guernsey* (Guernsey 1851).

Johanet, H., *L'Ile de Jersey* (Jersey 1883).

Johnson, C.W., *The Farmer's Encyclopaedia* (London 1842).

Keene, H.G., The Channel Islands, *English Historical Review* II (1887), 21-40.

Kellett-Smith, S.K., 'The Guernsey Cholera Epidemic of 1832' *Rep. and Trans. Soc. Guernesaise* (1980), 643-655.

Knocker, G.S., *Freemasonry in Jersey* (Lowestoft 1930).

Kropotkin, P., *Fields, Factories and Workshops* (London 1898).

Kropotkin, P.,The Possibilities of Agriculture, *Forum* (New York 1890), 615-626.

Lavergne, L., *Essai sur l'Economie Rurale de l'Angleterre* (Paris 1882).

Lebarbenchon, R.J., *La Grève de Lecq: Littératures et Cultures Populaires de Normandie* (Cherbourg 1988).

Le Cornu, C.P., The Agriculture of the Islands of Jersey, Guernsey, Alderney and Sark, *J.R.A.S.E.* XX (1859), 32-67.

Le Cornu, C.P., The Potato in Jersey, *J.R.A.S.E.* VI (1870), 127-140.

Le Cornu, C.P., The Jersey Dairy Industry, Pamphlet (Undated).

Le Cornu, N., The Jersey Militia 1791-1819: The Impact of the Revolutionary and French Wars', Undergraduate Long Essay, (Warwick University 1981).

Le Cornu, N., The Royal Jersey Artillery and the Jersey Militia System 1771-1877, *Bulletin of the Jersey Society in London* III (1980).

Le Couteur, F., A Treatise on the Cultivation of Apple Trees and the Preparation of Cider, in Pitt, W., *A General View of the Agriculture of Worcester* (London 1810).

Le Couteur, J., On the Use of the Great or Jersey Trench Ploug, *J.R.A.S.E.* III (1842), 40-48.

Le Couteur, J., On the Jersey Misnamed Alderney Cow, *J.R.A.S.E.* V (1844), 43-50.

Le Cras, A.J., *The Laws, Customs and Privileges and the Administration in the Island of Jersey* (London 1839).

Le Cras, A.J., *On the Philosophy of Divine Revelation* (London 1847).

Le Cras, A.J., Letter to Viscount Palmerston 10/2/1853. Pamphlet (Jersey 1853).

Le Cras, A.J., The Origin and Power of the States. Pamphlet (Jersey 1855).

Le Cras, A.J., Jersey, its Constitution and Laws. Pamphlet (Jersey 1858).

Le Cras, A.J., The Laws of Jersey and Some Existing Abuses. Pamphlet (Jersey 1858).

Le Cras, A.J., *Memorial of the Jersey Reform Committee to the Commissioners* (Jersey 1859).

Le Garignon, J., La Présence Jersiaise en Gaspésie, *Revue d'Histoire et Traditions Populaires de la Gaspesié* 62/63 (1978).

Le Herissier, R.G., *The Development of the Government of Jersey 1771-1972* (Jersey 1974).

Le Maistre, F., *Dictionnaire Jersiais-Français* (Jersey 1966).

Le Maistre, F., An Nineteenth-Century Inventory, *ABSJ* XX (1972), 379-384.

Le Maistre, F., La Bergerie at St Ouen, *ABSJ* XXI (1975),m359-62.

Lemprière, J., Sermon Prêché dans le Temple de St Helier 1789. Pamphlet (Guernsey 1789).

Le Patourel, J., *The Medieval Administration of the Channel Islands 1199-1399* (London 1937).

Le Patourel, J., The Political Development of the Channel Islands, *Rep. and Trans. Soc. Guernesiaise* (1946), 27-34. Originally in, *Nos Îles: A Symposium on the Channel Islands* (London 1944).

Le Patourel, J., 'Guernsey, Jersey and their Environment in the Middle Ages' *Rep. and Trans. Soc. Guenesiaise* XIX (1975), 435-461.

Le Quesne, C., *A Constitutional History of Jersey* (London 1856).

Le Quesne, C., *Ireland and the Channel Islands* (London 1848).

Le Quesne, J.P., A Short History of St John's Independent Church. Pamphlet (Jersey).

Lelièvre, M., *Histoire du Methodisme dans Les Iles de la Manche* (London/Paris 1885).

Lewis, S., *A Topographical Dictionary of England* (London 1849).

Likeman, J.H., Education in Jersey in the Nineteenth Century with particular reference to the teaching of French M.A. (University of London 1987).

Lyte, T., *A Sketch of the Island of Jersey* (London 1808).

Macculloch, J.R., *A Statistical Account of the British Empire* (London 1837).

Macculloch, J.R., *A Treatise on the Sucession to Property* (London 1848).

Martin, R. Montgomery, *A History of the British Colonies* (London 1835), Vol. V.

Mayne, R., *The Battle of Jersey* (London 1981).

McCormack, J., *Channel Island Churches* (Sussex 1986).

Meyer, W.R., The Channel Island Privateers, 1793-1815, in Jamieson, A.G., (Ed.), *A People of the Sea*, op. cit.

M'Mahon, T., *Letters in Answer to Charges Against the Political Conduct and Religious Tenets of the British and Irish Catholics* (Jersey 1827).

Mollet, R., Contrats and the Ouye de Paroisse, *BASJ* XVI (1954), 195-199.

Mollet, R., Ouye de Paroisse 1463, *BASJ* XVII (1959), 255-257.

Money, W.T., Diary of a Visit to Jersey, September 1798, *BASJ* (1932), 36-48.

Morden, R., *The New Description and State of England* (London 1695).

Morgan, G., *The Dragon's Tongue* (Narbeth 1966).

Morton, J.C., *A Cyclopaedia of Agriculture* (London 1855). 2 Vols.

Mourant, A., Biographie de Pierre Le Sueur (Jersey 1861). Pamphlet Unfinished.

Mourant, A., *Rimes et Poésies Jersiaises de Divers Auteurs* (Jersey 1865).

Mudie, R., *The Channel Islands* (London 1839).

Murdoch, J. Burn., *Notes and Remarks Made in Jersey, France, Italy and the Mediterranean in 1843 and 1844* (Edinburgh/London 1846).

Mylechreest, M., Questions and Answers: the Correspondence Between Sir John Le Couteur and Thomas Andrew Knight, *ABSJ* XXIV (1986), 237-245.

Myres, J.N.L., The Origin of the Jersey Parishes: Some Suggestions, *BSJ* XXII (1978), pp. 163 176.

Obelkevich, J., *Religion and Rural Society: South Lindsey 1825-1875* (Oxford 1976).

Ommer, R.E., From Outpost to Outport: The Jersey Merchant Triangle in the Nineteenth Century (McGill University, Ph.D. thesis, 1979).

Ommer, R.E., All the Fish of the Post, *Acadiensis* X (1981), 107-123.

Ommer, R.E., A Peculiar and Immediate Dependance of the Crown: The Basis of the Jersey Merchant Triangle, *Business History* XXV (1983), 107-124.

Perry, P.J., The Development of Cross Channel Trade at Weymouth, 1794 -1914: Geographical and Operational Factors, *Transport History* II (1969), 244-257.

Plees, W., *An Account of the Island of Jersey* (Southampton 1817).

Poingdestre, J., *Caesarea or a Discourse on the Island of Jersey* (Seventeenth Century Ms., published Jersey 1889).

Powell, G.C., *Economic Survey of Jersey* (Jersey 1971).

Prentice, E. Parmalee, 'American Dairy Cattle', *R. and TSG* XIV (1946), 48-103.

Quayle, T., *A General View of the Agriculture and Present State of the Islands on the Coast of Normandy.* Board of Agriculture. (London 1815).

Ragg, A.E., *A Popular History of Jersey* (Jersey 1896).

Rosse, Earl of., *A Few Words on the Relation of Landlord and Tenant* (London 1867).

Ruskin, John., The Works of John Ruskin 1903-1912. *Fors Claviera* Vol. III.

Scribner's Magazine, A Farmer's Vacation, V and VI (1875), 401-427, 574-591.

Shaw Lefevre, G., The Channel Island', *Fortnightly Review* XXVI (1879), 482-491.

Shepard, H.G., *One Hundred Years of the Royal Jersey Agricultural and Horticultural Society* (Jersey 1934).

Siccardo, F., Survivance de la Langue Française aux Iles Anglo Normandes, *Annali della Facolta di Scienze Politiche* III (1975), 405-452.

Simpson, D. and Small, T., The Potato Industry in Jersey, *Empire Journal of Export Agriculture* VI (1938), 95-103.

Stevens, J., *Old Jersey Houses* I and II (Sussex 1965 and 1977).

Stevens, J., *Victorian Voices* (Jersey 1969).

Stevens, J. and Arthur, J.F., 'Inventories of Household Effects', *ABSJ* XX (1972), 361-378.

Stevens, J. and Arthur, J.F., The Parish Church of St Mary, Jersey. Pamphlet (Undated).

Stevens, P., Jersey's Abundant Agriculture, *ABSJ* XXIII (1982), 209-223.

Stevens, P., The Godfray Names, *Channel Island Family History Journal* XVII (1982/3), 10-20.

Stevens, P., *Victor Hugo in Jersey* (Chichester 1985).

Stevens, P., Marx and Engels in Jersey, *ABSJ* XXIV (1987), 356.

Sullivan, C., *A Black Case for the Military Annals of Jersey* (1852).

Sullivan, J., *The Channel Island Militia* (London 1871).

Sullivan, J., Biographie de Francois Godfray. Pamphlet (Jersey c. 1875).

Syvret, G.S., *Abrege Historique* (London 1832).

Syvret, M. and J. *Stevens, Balleine's History of Jersey* (Chichester 1981).

Thompson, D.M., *Nonconformity in the Nineteenth Century* (London 1972).

Thornton, J., Jersey Cattle and Their Management, *J.R.A.S.E.* XVII (1881),220-240.

Thornton, W., *A Plea for Peasant Proprietors* (London 1874).

Town and Country Magazine, The, Account of England: Hampshire (April 1774),171-174.

Tréhounais, *L'Histoire, la Topographie, la Constitution, les Moeurs, et Langage de Jersey* (Jersey 1844).

Tupper, F. Brock, *The History of Guernsey* (Guernsey 1854).

Tupper, H., *Observations on the Law of Descent of Real Estate in the United Kingdom; its Origin and Bearing on the Social Condition of the People* (London 1868).

Valpy, Richard., *Selection of Letters in Annals of Agriculture* (Ed. Arthur Young) (1785), Vol. IV, V, IX and XIV.

Voisin, E.O.B., Inebriety in Jersey, *British Journal of Inebriety*, (1904),168-185.

Whetham, E., The Trade in Pedigree Livestock 1850-1910, *Agricultural History Review* XXVII (1979), 47-50.

Whitley, G.,*Memories of Youth on a Jersey Farm*, Jersey Society in London Occasional Publications (1949).

Zincke, F., The Channel Islands and Land Tenure, *Fortnightly Review* (1876),18.

Index